*The Dominion Partnership
in Imperial Defense,
1870–1914*

The
Dominion Partnership
in Imperial Defense,
1870–1914

BY
DONALD C. GORDON
Department of History
University of Maryland

THE JOHNS HOPKINS PRESS, BALTIMORE, MARYLAND

© 1965 by The Johns Hopkins Press, Baltimore, Maryland 21218
Printed in the United States of America
Library of Congress Catalog Card Number 65–11661

This book has been brought to publication with the assistance
of a grant from The Ford Foundation.

TO

NORMA, ELLEN, AND VICKI

PREFACE

During the nineteenth century, the British Empire changed from an association between a ruling power and its subordinates, to a band of freely collaborating nation-states. Such a transformation naturally brought in its train the need for an adjustment in defense arrangements. To survey and chronicle the problems of imperial defense as they were affected by the changing character of empire is the purpose of this work. It takes up the story at the point where Professor R. L. Schuyler in his *Fall of the Old Colonial System* ended his account: with the recall of the legions.

The author has received much generous assistance during the course of his work. The United States Educational Commission in Australia, administering the Fulbright program in that country, made study and residence there possible. The Australian National University in Canberra gave kindly hospitality. Further support was granted by the American Philosophical Society (the Penrose Fund), and by the General Research Board of the University of Maryland.

The author's indebtedness to archivists and librarians is great. Thanks are due to the staffs of the Australian National Library, the National Archives, and the Australian National War Memorial Library in Canberra, the Public Archives of Canada in Ottawa, the Library of Congress, especially the Government Publications Room, the Public Record Office (London) and the Manuscript Department of the British Museum, and the McKeldin Library of the University of Maryland. While these institutions furnished much aid from the wealth of their holdings, assistance of a more specialized type was graciously given on occasion by the Library of the Institute of Historical Research, the Institute of Commonwealth Studies, the Library of Australia House, and the Navy League, all in London, and by the librarians and information officers of the Canadian, Australian, and New Zealand embassies in Washington, D.C.

Professor Gerald Graham, Rhodes Professor of History at the University of London, kindly lent me the unfinished manuscript of the late Admiral Sir Herbert Richmond cited in Chapter III. Through the agency of Mr. Ian MacLean, Archivist of the Commonwealth of Australia, Professor J. La Nauze of the University of Melbourne was good enough to make available some material from the Deakin papers in his custody. Professor J. W. Davidson, Professor of Pacific History in the Australian National University at Canberra, gave assistance and counsel during the early period of work in Australia. The interest and assistance extended by Lady Baddeley and the late Sir Vincent Baddeley is acknowledged with thanks, as is the intelligent and painstaking work of Mrs. Margaret Hesketh-Williams of London. The author is grateful to the Controller of Her Majesty's Stationery Office for permission to use manuscripts of Crown copyright records in the Public Record Office, London. He further acknowledges the courtesy of the *Political Science Quarterly*, which permitted use of material first appearing in an article by the author in Vol. LXXVII, No. 4 (Dec., 1962), pp. 526–45, of that quarterly, and also the *Journal of Modern History* (published by the University of Chicago Press) for similar permission with regard to material from "The Admiralty and Dominion Navies, 1902–1914," Vol. XXXIII, No. 4 (Dec., 1961), pp. 407–22 (© by the University of Chicago). And finally, the author's indebtedness to his wife for aid and encouragement is immeasurable.

CONTENTS

INTRODUCTION

British colonial policy in the nineteenth century was greatly influenced by a desire to emancipate the United Kingdom from the burdens of empire. The adoption of free trade ended the restrictions on British commerce. The increasing extension of responsible government to many colonies relieved British officials of the harassments of their internal administration. And the early reaction of many British political leaders to the establishment of responsible government in the colonies was that Britain could now logically further free herself from imperial burdens by vesting in the colonies greater responsibility for their own defense. Self-defense seemed the logical corollary of self-government.

In the military sphere it was comparatively easy to put this policy into effect, though it was not done without some controversy. But this was action in many ways peripheral in its effects on imperial defense arrangements, for the main burden of that defense was borne not by the military forces of the Crown, but rather by the Royal Navy.

Adjusting the naval arrangements of the Empire to the facts of responsible government, to the growth of the colonies in wealth and maturity, and to their insistence that they have a voice in the making of such defense arrangements was not easy. Military defense had a naturally fragmented character, with garrisons scattered throughout the apparent danger spots of the nineteenth-century Empire. This fragmentation was of course emphasized when Canadians, Australians, and other peoples of the Empire became responsible for their own military arrangements. But no such division or fragmentation seemed either possible or desirable in naval defense. The sea was one; the fleet that patrolled it should be one; and the command over that fleet should be one. There was no room in this for a division of authority which reflected the political polycentrism of the Empire. Despite the fact that the Board of Admiralty, in the days of *Pax Britannica* and the "gunboat" navy, displayed an occasionally uncertain grasp of strategy, this was a principle generally adhered to.

It was a principle reinforced by the long and proud tradition of the Royal Navy, with its aura of complete professionalism. Though time and testing events were to disclose that the professionalism was not as complete as it might have been, against it any colonial pretension smacked of the rankest amateurism. This was a view held not only in British circles, but also in many segments of colonial society. And the naval defense of empire, or any part of it, was too serious to be entrusted to amateurs. Colonials might play at soldier without serious harm to anyone, but naval defense was a different matter.

And indeed, there was justice in this. A fully professional service demanded sufficient opportunity for promotion to attract men of ability to it, and there was little likelihood of this when any colonial naval force would have only one or two vessels, and thus little opportunity for promotion to positions of command.

The principle of complete unity in naval arrangements was reinforced by the fact that colonial governments lacked the power to bind by law their people outside their own territory. This might be no serious disadvantage for coast-hugging small craft or revenue cutters, but for seagoing vessels it would mean that there was no legal sanction for either control of the vessel or discipline of the crew. There was the further complicating circumstance that any such sea-going vessel might create an international incident, for which the imperial government would be legally responsible. A sea-going naval craft was too serious a weapon to allow in the hands of a legally irresponsible agent such as a colonial government.

Yet another factor assuming increasing importance was the reception of the doctrines of Mahan and Admiral Philip Colomb by the Royal Navy. The ascendancy of the "Blue Water" school of naval strategists in the Royal Navy deprived colonial governments of any role they might have had before such ascendancy became complete. In the pre-Mahan navy, there were the gunboats, which policed the outer reaches of empire along the coasts of Africa and among the islands of the Pacific. But the passing of the gunboat era, the development of the dreadnought, and the concentration of naval thought on the day when the great new behemoths of the sea would meet in combat left no room for the comparatively meager contributions that colonial governments might be able to make on their own. The best they could do was to reinforce the line of battle by contributions to the Royal Navy, either in ships or in money, but in any case unencumbered by any colonial aspirations for control over the gifts they gave.

Strategic truth was not the whole truth in imperial defense, however, and it was necessary to come to terms with other elements as well. One was the desire for self-respect and dignity among the colonial leaders, a respect and dignity which they did not find in simply turning over either money or ships to the Royal Navy. Another was the assertive nationalism, sometimes coupled with a distrust of imperialism, held by certain colonial groups, especially in Canada and Australia. A measure of political accommodation to pressures from these elements had to be made, even though it might have to be in ways beyond the bounds of accepted strategy.

Adding to the weight of such factors as these was the increasing fear in some colonial minds that the concentration of British naval might in the home waters left the outer fringes of empire exposed and undefended. This was felt particularly in Australia and New Zealand. Efforts of these governments to create naval forces of their own were certainly unsupported by any aspect of naval theory of the time, but they were based on political considerations, plus the thought that aid might be more freely forthcoming to them in an emergency if they had made an honest effort for themselves. The Lord, and the Admiralty, it was hoped, would help those who first helped themselves.

Complicating these issues was the notable tendency of British officialdom to lecture and admonish colonial leaders *du haut en bas*. While such leaders, and the peoples whom they represented, were not quite regarded as those "lesser breeds without the law" of whom the poet sang, that certain condescension toward foreigners which had frequently been observed in British life was not lacking in relations with colonial societies. Undoubtedly there was much that was provincial and gangling in colonial life, much that seemed to justify the Disraelian comment that colonists were those who had left England "to fleece a flock and find a nugget." But it was not always appreciated in Whitehall that this might not be entirely so, that these same colonists were the founders of societies and eventually the leaders of political communities which, however adolescent and gangling, had aspirations and assertions of their own.

The problem, then, was to establish a basis for collaboration in defense between self-governing communities, one of which had traditions of leadership and authority behind it, the others seeking in defense affairs a role they thought commensurate with their developing status and stature. Though the defense of India was a major preoccupation—indeed, the major concern—of British officials for many of the years covered in this study, India does not enter prominently into the account of events given here. There were doubtless elements of a truly collaborative character in the Anglo-Indian defense arrangements, but it was not collaboration of the type required between the governments of the United Kingdom and the leading dominions; it was not collaboration between governments that drew their power from different political constituencies.

The books were not entirely closed on the clash of views between the Admiralty and at least some of the dominions when the coming of war relegated the dispute into obscurity. But in the development of dominion nationalism, in the emergence of some of the dominions from the shadow of imperial tutelage, the arguments and dissensions over the sharing of naval defense honed and sharpened dominion self-consciousness. And the most effective imperial policy came from the recognition of that self-consciousness, and the acceptance of it as a basis of imperial collaboration. It would be too much to say that in disunity there was strength, for the fundamental unity of the Empire existed, regardless of the forms of defense organization. But the additions to the fighting strength of empire that came from the peoples and governments of the dominions were the products of freedom; the collaboration that was achieved came about through those basic processes of freedom: bargaining and politics. And it is difficult to believe that it could have been achieved in any other way.

The Dominion Partnership
in Imperial Defense,
1870–1914

CHAPTER I

THE LABORS OF
THE MILLS COMMITTEE

The idea that empire was a burden, returning few advantages to compensate for the demands it made upon the British taxpayer, was widely accepted among the ruling circles of mid-nineteenth-century Britain. Few political leaders advocated the cutting of the imperial connection and the abandoning of the colonies to a doubtful independence. But many believed and urged that every step should be taken to lessen the costs of empire for Britons at home.

In so far as these alleged costs of empire could be measured, the charge for the maintenance of military garrisons in the colonies was greatest, since the British army in the post-Napoleonic War period was largely an Indian and colonial force. Most of the troops were stationed not in the British Isles, but overseas—on every rock in the ocean where a cormorant can perch, as Sydney Smith said. Sir William Molesworth both described and indicted the whole policy in a speech in the Commons in the late eighteen-forties: "Thus, activated by an insane desire of worthless empire, into every nook of our colonial universe we thrust an officer with a few soldiers; in every hole and corner we erect a fortification, build a barrack, or cram a storehouse full of perishable stores. . . ."[1]

While the expenses of the British troops in India were carried on the Indian budget, the costs of the forces stationed in other parts of the Empire amounted to approximately one-third of the military budget of the British government. And these costs seemed to be steadily mounting.[2]

To some of the nation's military leaders, fearful of the intentions of governments and legislators toward the army, and suspicious of the politician's concern for the taxpayer's interests, there was perhaps some

[1] H. E. Egerton (ed.), *Selected Speeches of Sir William Molesworth* (London, 1903), p. 247.
[2] C. P. Stacey, *Canada and the British Army, 1846–1871* (London, 1936), pp. 38–43.

advantage in having the bulk of the army tucked away in the obscure recesses of empire. Out of sight, perhaps out of mind. For in a political society both jealous for the taxpayer's welfare and traditionally fearful of military power as a threat to the prevailing liberties, the best things to be said for a peacetime military establishment were that it was small, cheap —and unobserved.[3]

But the imperial garrisons did not escape the vigilant eye of the free trade liberals or the colonial reformers of the period. The costliness of the garrisons drew heavy fire, as did the strategic weakness of scattering British forces about the Empire. Certainly it was unlikely that the small garrisons gave any real security to the colonies in which they were stationed. They were not sufficient to deter a powerful enemy from mounting an attack. Indeed, their only deterrent effect was to check the colonists from taking any effective measures in their own behalf, for why should they assume the burdens of defense when the British taxpayer was apparently still willing to bear the cost?

Nor could it be argued that the garrisons added to the security of the British Isles. In order to guard the extremities, the heart of empire was stripped of forces. The view of the Duke of Wellington in 1847 that England could be invaded within a week after the outbreak of war with a major power added substance to this argument. If the government were reluctant to increase the size of the military establishment, the imperial forces abroad might at least be brought home to give the British subject some of the security for which he was paying.

The political arguments were not less telling. The extension of self-government to the major colonies seemed to demand in all justice that those colonies pay for at least part of their defense arrangements. New duties and responsibilities should surely accompany the new powers which had been conferred upon the colonial governments of Canada and Australia. Of Canada specifically, but with all the other self-governing colonies in mind, Lord Grey, Secretary of State for War and Colonies in the first Russell Government, wrote in 1851: ". . . the time is now come when the people of Canada must be called upon to take upon themselves a larger share than they have hitherto done, of expenses which are incurred on this account, and for their advantage. Of these expenses, by far the heaviest charge which falls upon this country is that incurred for the military protection of the province."[4]

There was a dark suspicion in the minds of some of the reformers that the colonists were far too frequently making a good thing out of the

[3] R. C. K. Ensor, *England: 1870–1914* (Oxford, 1936), p. 9.
[4] Grey to Elgin, March 14, 1851, quoted in Stacey, *Canada and the British Army, 1846–1871*, pp. 79–80.

presence of the British garrisons in their midst. It was charged that the availability of such forces to bail them out of trouble encouraged them in reckless, adventurous policies of aggression and land grabbing against native tribes, where otherwise fear of the retaliatory action of such tribes would have induced in colonial minds a more circumspect—and moral—policy. The white settlers in New Zealand were especially regarded as guilty of fomenting trouble with the Maori tribes and then calling on the imperial forces to defeat them. Often such defeats were used to justify even larger land confiscations than those which had been the original cause of trouble. Any such suspicions, at a time when British humanitarianism and the Exeter Hall influence were at their height, were bound to arouse criticism of a policy that put British forces in New Zealand and continued to maintain them there, apparently to be accomplices in the land thefts of the settlers. And on a lesser scale of crime, there was the belief that in many instances colonial pressure for the maintenance of garrisons overseas was largely due to the agitation of colonial merchants who hoped to profit by selling goods to the military commissariat. To Molesworth, these were "sinister interests" who saw a chance for profit in every increase in imperial expenditure and in every skirmish or frontier war with Kaffir or Maori.

It was Lord Grey who finally inaugurated the policy of troop withdrawal. Despite the fact that he was a dedicated free trader, Grey was not among those who felt that the adoption of free trade would inevitably mean the cutting of the imperial ties and the transformation of the colonies into independent states. His was rather the conception of shared burdens, of a new pattern of shared power and responsibility, as the practice of responsible government deepened and widened. The encouragement of a more self-reliant attitude in the colonies, however, implied no lessening of Great Britain's duty to stand as the final guarantor of the security of the colonies.

It was not Grey's policy to withdraw garrisons regardless of imperial responsibilities or of the consequences. But the imperial government was not going to haggle with colonial governments over the size of the garrisons. It would station troops abroad as it deemed necessary for imperial purposes. Any larger forces that colonial governments might want they could have, if they paid for them. Or, if colonial governments preferred to raise their own police or militia forces, they could rely on the imperial government for the necessary advice and assistance. The diminution of the garrisons was to be accompanied by a policy of encouraging the colonies to take steps for their own security.

It was quite reasonable that the new policy should be applied in the Australian colonies. Menaced neither by a great neighbor bent on "manifest destiny" expansion, nor by native tribes with any formidable war-making capacity, these colonies enjoyed a greater security than Canada, New Zealand, or the Cape. The small British garrisons stationed there performed only routine garrison duties or were diverted to duties that would have been more suitably carried out by a police force. Lord Grey pointed all this out in a dispatch to Governor Charles Fitzroy of New South Wales[5] when he ordered the transfer of all but a handful of the garrison to New Zealand. Her Majesty's Government still had the duty of assuring the safety of the colony from any attack by a foreign power, but the colonists were expected to assume the duties of internal order and security by the formation of local police forces and militia units.

Lord Grey eventually had his way, but not without local protest and opposition. Governor Fitzroy argued that British troops were needed for the maintenance of order in the colony. In view of the high level of wages prevailing in the colony, it simply was not feasible to seek to establish a local police force; no man of necessary character would join for the wages which the colonial government could afford to pay. Further, the problems of law and order existing in New South Wales were aggravated, if not created, by the manner in which the colony had been settled and peopled.[6] Convict transportation to New South Wales, a course followed largely to suit British interests, imposed upon Britain the obligation to protect the colonists from the lawlessness created by that policy. This argument had perhaps the greater pertinence in view of Grey's belief in the desirability of continuing convict transportation despite a mounting volume of Australian objections. But Grey prevailed, and some of the troops were transferred to New Zealand.

Grey was also able to apply his policy in Canada, where its success could be attributed largely to prevailing political conditions. Canadian garrisons might be reduced because of the diminution of political unrest with the granting of responsible government, and because of the settlement of boundary disputes with the United States in 1842 and 1846. Other parts of the Empire were not so peaceful. New Zealand had just passed through the first of the Maori wars, and in the Cape and Natal the constant threat of trouble with the Kaffirs clearly made any reduction in the size of imperial garrisons impossible. The Grey policy had been

[5] Robert L. Schuyler, *The Fall of the Old Colonial System* (New York, 1945), p. 217. The *Sydney Morning Herald* growled about Grey's "despoiling our garrison of one-half of its military force." John M. Ward, *Earl Grey and the Australian Colonies, 1846–57* (Melbourne, 1958), p. 61.

[6] For example, the Legislative Council of New South Wales, with the convict origin of many of its citizens in mind, urged that the character of the population of Sydney was not such as to make the formation of police or militia groups expedient.

initiated, but far from carried into effect, when the Russell Government resigned from office in February of 1852.[7]

Grey's successors in the Colonial Office continued the policy initiated by Grey, and with the same varying degrees of success. Some reductions in the size of forces were achieved in the Cape, but efforts in the West Indies to remove forces from the outer islands and concentrate them at Barbados were mired down in difficulties created by lack of available barrack space.

The outbreak of the Crimean War in 1854 brought no sweeping changes in the disposition of imperial forces in colonial areas, nor in imperial military policy. The military needs of the war led to an acceleration of the existing plans for the withdrawal or reduction of the imperial garrisons, but the needs of the colonial areas were apparently such as to allow few great changes. Various colonies continued to make their demands on imperial military resources, and these demands were met despite the pressures of war. Conditions in South Africa did not permit any reductions in military strength, and the outbreak of violence in the gold fields of Victoria (the affair of the Eureka stockade) led to the reinforcement of the local forces rather than their decrease. It was only in Canada that any substantial reduction in the size of the imperial garrisons seemed feasible. Improvement in relations with the United States seemed to permit considerable further withdrawals from the garrison there, and by the end of the Crimean War, British forces in the Canadian and maritime areas were down to less than 3,000 men.[8]

If the innovations of war did not then include any new policy toward the imperial garrisons, things were not entirely unchanged. The war brought vigorous efforts in several of the colonies to create effective militia forces; there was no apparent lack of that spirit of self-reliance so much sought by the advocates of the reduction of the overseas garrisons. Militia and volunteer forces were raised in Canada and Australia, and though some of the enthusiasm created by the war soon languished, a beginning had been made in the assumption by colonial governments of at least some degree of responsibility for their own defense.

Other aspects of British policy, however, were not always consistent with the doctrine of colonial self-reliance. Efforts to transform the colonies even in small measure into recruiting grounds ran directly counter to this idea. Yet the drain of the war on the limited resources of trained man-

---

[7] Many aspects of Grey's policy in both South Africa and New Zealand had come under increasing attack, and fear of a vote of censure against Grey may have prompted the resignation of the government. (John M. Ward, "The Colonial Policy of Lord John Russell's Administration," *Historical Studies, Australia and New Zealand,* IX [Nov., 1960].)

[8] Stacey, *Canada and The British Army, 1846–1871,* p. 90.

power did lead to occasional suggestions and efforts to secure recruits from the colonial areas of the Empire. In view of the relative security of Canada, the idea of raising troops there was attractive. Tentative suggestions along this line, however, met with a chilly response from a Canadian provincial government concerned with the formation of a militia force, and anxious to reserve what military manpower the colony had for that force. There was the further difficulty that even with the heightened patriotism of war, it would be hard to find many eager to take the Queen's shilling per day instead of the dollar per day which even unskilled labor earned in Canada. The ten-year enlistment period was still another obstacle to such recruitment. Aside from the questionable wisdom of seeking such manpower in a colony taking its first tentative steps in the formation of its own military forces, there was the larger issue of whether the self-reliance sought could ever be reconciled with an imperial military policy that subordinated the needs of the colony to the demands of the imperial war establishment. But the recruiting suggestions were not pushed to the degree that its inconsistency with the objective of self-reliance was glaringly apparent.

If the suggestion for recruitment in the colonial areas argues that encouragement of colonial self-reliance was not the established policy of the imperial government, the hasty return of British regiments to Canada at the conclusion of the Crimean War supports this. Over the objections of a man with such ripe experience of the North American area as Lord Elgin, a former governor of Canada, the imperial garrisons in Canada were enlarged again when relations with the United States took a turn for the worse.[9] Despite all of the wavering course of imperial policy, the war had furnished ample testimony of the existence of a fund of imperial loyalty in the colonies. The formation of the colonial forces was one attestation of this, and the large sums contributed to funds for the relief of the suffering of the troops in Crimea was another. But the swift return to the "things as they were before the war" policy suggests that the display of colonial self-reliance and of imperial loyalty made little impression on those who shaped British policy.

Yet for the governors of the two colonies that had been most active in defense preparations, the recent events had had their lesson. In Canada, the able Sir Edmund Head had learned a good deal about Canadian military weaknesses as the province took its first steps in the organization of its own defense. Despite the discouragements and difficulties, however, he apparently felt that in the future Canada should not only maintain an effective military force for her own defense, but should, as the wealth and

[9] In some measure this was due to the irritation in the United States over the ill-advised efforts of British officials to find recruits for the British army in the United States.

the military proficiency of the provinces increased, take a share in the defense of the Empire beyond her borders. Indeed, he envisaged a day when the defense of the Empire might be a joint responsibility.[10]

More specific suggestions for collaboration came from Sir William Denison, Governor of the Australian colony of New South Wales. Sir William, an army engineer, had passed a good deal of his life in the colonial empire. He had served in Canada in the digging of the Rideau Canal and had been Lieutenant Governor in Tasmania before he became Governor of New South Wales in 1854. During the war years, he had worked energetically at the task of improving the defenses of Sydney. It is easy to see how such a task might be likely to encourage a consideration of the problems of imperial defense.

Some of Sir William's ideas were not likely to endear him to imperial authorities. Sir William, it would seem, had become too colonial-minded. It was his contention that any of the risks of war which threatened the colonies arose from their connection with Great Britain. Actually, the security that Britain offered to her colonies would not have been needed but for their link with her. Despite this, he still believed that the imperial tie was profitable for both parties, and that the colonies had a duty to assist in the external defense of empire as well as to care for their own internal peace.

He saw little but confusion and attendant injustice in the existing arrangements of imperial defense. There was no general principle on which the costs of the imperial garrisons were shared. Some colonies were required to pay for most of the imperial troops they had within their borders, as in Australia. Other colonies got the garrisons entirely at the charge of the British taxpayer, with no colonial contribution assessed. Victoria, where the principal threat came from the turbulent mobs in the gold fields rather than from external invasion, paid a subsidy for the British forces stationed there. New South Wales, where the threat could come only from abroad and as a result of the imperial connection, also paid a subsidy. Assessment of subsidies, apparently, was not based on whether the threat to a colony was internal or external, or on whether the colony was valuable or valueless in imperial trade or finance. The only ascertainable principle seemed to be an appraisal of local needs by the imperial authorities, balanced against the same officials' conception of the colonial capacity and willingness to pay. Colonies willing to pay for their garrisons were forced to pay; those unwilling were not forced but got the garrisons just the same.

In place of this confusion, Denison suggested that the colonial and imperial governments should share equally the costs of the imperial

[10] D. G. G. Kerr, *Sir Edmund Head* (Toronto, 1954), pp. 138–42.

garrisons in the colonies. But since, in many instances, the colonies would then be making a substantial contribution to the system of imperial defense, these governments should also have the responsibility of determining the size of the force to be stationed within their borders. Denison even extended the idea to naval defense and suggested that any vessels of the Royal Navy specifically allocated for the defense of a colony should be maintained jointly by an equal sharing of the charges.

Denison's suggestion had a chilly reception from officialdom. Herman Merivale of the Colonial Office expressed surprise that so clear-headed a man should have become so thoroughly colonial in his viewpoint.[11] But the basic objection to the plan formulated by the Governor of New South Wales was that it would deprive the imperial government of control over a portion of its armed forces. Admittedly, said Merivale, the proposal had the virtue of simplicity, but it seemed to him very doubtful whether "in such a military system as ours we could part with the right to reduce the garrison if troops were suddenly wanted elsewhere."[12] Such a scheme really could not be adopted without undermining the central authority of the Empire. The Grey policy of requiring the colonies to pay for any troops that they wanted above the imperial quota was adhered to.

Denison's proposal, which included a reference to naval matters, provoked from the Admiralty a statement of naval policy in colonial defense. This statement laid down principles to guide the United Kingdom and the various colonies in the assessment of their responsibilities in naval defense. It pointed out that naval defense differed greatly from military, and that it was quite impossible to deal with the naval defense of each colony separately. Land defense could be local, real naval defense could not. There could be localized naval forces such as floating batteries, small gunboats and the like, manned by a marine militia. Any such force should be created and maintained by a colony, not by the Royal Navy. But general naval defense was another matter. "It is perfectly impossible," said the Admiralty statement, "to localize naval defence."[13] The same vessels that could easily fall prey to enemy sea power when stationed separately in colonial waters would form an adequate defense when united. These considerations prohibited any sea-going colonial marine force. It would be impossible to imagine that each colony would not want to keep any vessel which it helped to maintain in its own waters. And yet it would be imperative that any such vessels should act in conjunction with others under the command of the Senior Naval Officer of the station.

---

[11] Great Britain, Public Record Office, Colonial Office (henceforth cited as C.O.) 201/486, Denison to C.O., Sept. 8, 1856, Minute by Merivale.
[12] C.O. 201/494, pp. 426–27.
[13] C.O. 201/590, Admiralty Memorandum, Jan. 24, 1857.

Such basic strategic considerations aside, the Admiralty put forward other arguments against colonial naval forces. No doubt, they said, the naval forces maintained by the East India Company were generally efficient, but different systems of control and discipline had made some of the joint operations carried on with the Royal Navy dangerous. The same difficulties might well arise with colonial naval forces. Also, such forces would be confined to one area and climate for long periods, and this might be dangerous to the health of the crews. The Admiralty did suggest that a colonial contribution toward the maintenance of an augmented naval force might be advantageously agreed upon.

The general reaction of both naval and military authorities to Denison's suggestion was a strong opposition to the idea of allowing colonial authorities any share in the command of British forces maintained in their areas. Colonial payments or contributions not dependent upon participation in command, however, would be generally welcomed. Colonial opinion on Denison's suggestion was never tested.

The outbreak of the Mutiny in India in 1857 again saw the stirrings of an imperial patriotism in the colonial areas. Although offers of service came from militia units in Canada, the military authorities had little regard for these volunteers and turned a cold shoulder to their offers. But the fighting in India and the consequent strain on the military resources of the Crown rendered the possibility of recruitment for the regular forces in the colonies attractive again. The provincial government of Canada was approached and its assent secured to the project of raising a regiment there. The recruiting goal was speedily reached, and command was given to the Adjutant General of the Canadian Militia. Although the regiment formed, the 100th Royal Canadians, was not the first military unit ever recruited in a colony, it was the first regiment so raised for service with British arms anywhere on the globe. The project was not, of course, Canadian. Canada merely furnished the manpower for a regiment which was British officered, British equipped, and British financed. The 100th Royal Canadians were part of the British regular forces and had nothing to do with Canadian military activity. While the general business recession in Canada in 1857 may have been a factor, the relative ease with which recruits were obtained was evidence again that the colonial empire held military assets which, if wisely handled, could be of inestimable value to the imperial cause.

In 1859 another sounding of official opinion was taken on the question of the colonial garrisons. The Colonial Office, which had been an adjunct of the War Office, in 1854 was made a separate department of state. This left the military officers without any effective guide as to policy and size for the colonial forces. In the spring of 1859, the Secretary of State for

War, Major General Jonathan Peel, sought the creation of an interdepartmental committee to formulate a definition of the respective
liabilities of the War Office and the separate colonies regarding military
expenditure. In seeking the establishment of this committee, Major
General Peel stated his own belief that the British had the obligation to
defend the colonies against any foreign foe, and to a lesser degree against
the incursions or attacks of any formidable native tribes. But Britain should
not assume the whole burden, nor should there be any military expenditure for purposes of internal policing.[14]

The requested committee was created, with representatives of the War
Office, the Treasury, and the Colonial Office forming its membership. It
found that expenditure on colonial military garrisons had not appreciably
diminished despite the efforts which had been made in that direction.
In the year ending March 31, 1858, British expenditure on such garrisons
was nearly £4,000,000; the military expenditure of colonial governments
was approximately £380,000. There were still almost 50,000 British
troops scattered about in the colonies. There was no consistency in the
ratio between colonial and imperial contributions toward defense charges.
Canada spent annually about £40,000 largely on the maintenance of the
militia, while the imperial charges for Canadian garrisons amounted to
£261,000. In the then separate colonies of New Brunswick and Nova
Scotia, regions in which the British expenditures amounted to about
£190,000, the two colonial governments together spent less than £500.
At the other end of the scale was the Australian colony of Victoria. There
the imperial government maintained forces which cost £44,000 per year,
while the colony paid almost £95,000 per year in order to have the
services of extra troops at her disposal. Perhaps the most glaring of all the
imbalances existed in the Cape. In 1857–58 the imperial government
kept there a garrison of over 10,000 troops at a cost of £796,000; the Cape
government spent about £35,000 a year toward the maintenance of a
small police force.[15]

The members of the interdepartmental committee were not able to
reach agreement on their report. George A. Hamilton for the Treasury
and John Robert Godley for the War Office formed the majority and were
in agreement that the existing system placed far too great a burden on the
British taxpayer and did not give sufficient encouragement or scope for
the colonial spirit of self-reliance to assert itself. But they were in doubt
whether the existing chaotic arrangements would be better ended by
gradual application of the "take it or leave it" principle of Lord Grey, or

[14] Schuyler, *The Fall of the Old Colonial System*, p. 222; Great Britain, Parliamentary
Papers (henceforth cited as Parl. Pap.), 1860, Vol. XLI (282), p. 3.
[15] *Ibid.*, p. 4.

whether something of the equal sharing of costs proposed by Governor Sir William Denison could be successfully adopted. The two men tended to support a form of the latter idea, and their majority report suggested that while Britain should bear the whole cost of the maintenance of garrisons in such imperial fortresses as Gibraltar and Malta, there should be a sharing of costs in the self-governing colonies. They felt that the colonies should be allowed to decide the nature of their own defenses, and that Britain could reasonably offer to pay a portion, possibly one-half, of the costs involved. This grant-in-aid system would encourage self-reliance and initiative on the part of the colonies and relieve the British taxpayer of some of the burden he was currently carrying.

To Sir Frederick Elliot, the Undersecretary of the Colonial Office and the representative of that office on the committee, the approach of the majority of the committee was too doctrinaire and schematic. There was far too much diversity among the colonies in resources of wealth and manpower, and in their degree of exposure to the risks of attack, both from foreign states and from native tribes, to permit the application of any simple or formalistic approach. There could be no escaping the need to weigh the circumstances of each colony separately and to apportion military charges on the basis of such appraisals. There was, he felt, not one problem but many, and in such a situation no rule could take the place of the judgment of Her Majesty's Government.[16] Elliot also stressed that Britain's obligation toward her colonies did not rest simply on the fact that in their dependent condition they were bound by decisions of foreign policy and of peace and war made by the imperial government alone. Some of the colonies, at least, were important to Britain in war for the furnishing of essential supplies. In point of pride, prestige, or honor, Britain might be equally obligated to defend all of her colonies; in point of military necessity, there were some she had to defend for her own interest and success in making war. Elliot believed that the policy inaugurated by Lord Grey still had more to commend it than any of the suggestions made by his associates on the committee.

To Elliot's argument that the differences between colonies rendered any uniform policy impractical and unfair, the majority rejoined that it was not the duty of Britain to equalize the natural advantages and disadvantages existing among her colonies in either military or civil matters. Poor states must be content to be less well off. Further, if a colony was so poor as to be unable to take a share in its own defense, it was most unlikely that it would whet the appetite of any possible aggressor; its poverty would be its safeguard.[17]

[16] *Ibid.*, p. 19.
[17] Cf. Parl. Pap. 1861, Vol. XIII (423), pp. 319–23.

And so, despite such reservations as those expressed by Elliot, the prevalent attitude of the Colonial Office was that the assumption of responsible government by the colonies carried with it the duty of taking steps for the creation of some police and security forces. Sir Edward Bulwer-Lytton, Colonial Secretary in 1859, wrote to Sir George Bowen, first Governor of the new Colony of Queensland, that one of his first duties would be to see that the colonists looked to their own internal security. "Try to establish a good police; if you can then get the superior class of colonists to assist in forming a militia or volunteer corps, spare no pains to do so. . . . A colony that is once accustomed to depend on Imperial soldiers for aid against riots, etc., never grows up into vigorous manhood."[18]

There was certain to be interest in the recommendations of any committee dealing with such a contentious issue as colonial garrisons, even though the committee was created mainly for the guidance of the War Office alone. In the Commons, Charles Adderley, a leading member of the colonial reform group, emerged as the foremost spokesman of those who wished to bring about the reduction of the imperial forces. When a government spokesman referred to the work of the interdepartmental committee, Adderley demanded the publication of the report. The report, when published, certainly shed little new light, but it furnished Adderley and others with further material with which to attack the status quo, and it led to demands for the formation of a Select Committee of the House, which might once more probe into the existing military system of the Empire. Among those pressing for such a committee was Arthur Mills, M.P. for Taunton, who had long been interested in the colonial empire, had written a book on colonial constitutions, and was a leading member of the colonial reform group of the Commons. Under the pressure of the insistant demand, Prime Minister Palmerston gave a somewhat grudging assent to the formation of the committee. Arthur Mills became its chairman.

The Select Committee of the Commons on Colonial Military Expenditure was the most important and distinguished body to consider the political problems associated with imperial defense during the nineteenth century. Its report has been called "the most important single document in the long series of events which was to lead at last to the evacuation of the self-governing colonies by the imperial army."[19] Certainly the significance of the report cannot be belittled; it was constantly cited during the remaining decades of the century as a statement of policy which later generations should not lightly discard. But it did not initiate that policy,

[18] Sir George Bowen, *Thirty Years of Colonial Government* (London, 1889), I, 82.
[19] Stacey, *Canada and the British Army, 1846–1871*, pp. 123–24.

nor did it contain any ideas that were not at the time of its writing the veriest commonplace of imperial statesmanship, at least for most of those in Britain who were in any way concerned with colonial matters. It crystallized prevailing attitudes, stated them in moderate terms, and then won the support of a vote in the Commons after a languid debate.

The membership of the committee was a distinguished one. The majority of its members were either past or future Cabinet members; among them were two future Prime Ministers, and several who had been or would be Colonial Secretary. One of the members whose political careers did not include the rewards of office was the forceful Radical J. A. Roebuck, who had chaired the committee that had brought in the blistering report of military maladministration during the Crimean War. The bias of the group was overwhelmingly Whiggish and Liberal. Critics of the existing system of imperial garrisons were considerably more prominent than its defenders, if indeed any at all could be so classified.

The terms of the resolution creating the committee were broad and comprehensive. In other hands, an inquiry so defined might easily have probed deeply into the entire system and strategy of imperial defense. But if such an inquiry were possible, this was not the committee to make it, for this matter did not lie within the range of its members' interests. In the main, it considered that its task was to seek ways in which the disadvantages of empire might be diminished and the Briton freed from some of the burdens of his imperial power. Its attention was focused on the imperial forces in the self-governing colonies, with most of the members of the committee set on bringing about the withdrawal or the substantial diminution of those forces. Any larger aspects of imperial defense were peripheral to this main concern. So also was any aspect of naval defense, for the navy was little involved in the political problems and the intricate financial arrangements arising from the stationing of troops in the colonies. To determine the extent of Britain's military obligations to the self-governing colonies, and to ascertain how those obligations might best be met, was the nub of the inquiry.

The proceedings of the committee reflected the belief of most of its members that Britain gained little if any practical advantage from the existence of its overseas empire. Honor and duty, a sense of responsibility toward the colonies, might compel the maintenance of the existing arrangements; that there was anything positive to gain from the situation was a suggestion rarely heard. The possibilities of collaboration in the early intimations of a developing imperial patriotism in the colonies, such as the offers of support during the Crimean War and the emergence of volunteer groups, were largely ignored. Committee members and witnesses alike seemed to regard the Empire, if not with positive distaste, at least as a burden which the British would have to bear with resignation and fortitude until its onerous responsibilities might be relinquished with honor and dignity.

This attitude was simply a reflection of the anti-imperialist sentiment of the time. But those committee members and witnesses who might be called Colonial Reformers, and who did not subscribe to anti-imperialist views, were equally intent upon ending the system of colonial garrisons. They felt that such forces were a barrier to the growth of a true imperial loyalty based on the development of healthy self-reliance among the colonial peoples. The extent of agreement among many committee members—including men like Adderley, Mills, and John Robert Godley, a leading witness—was reinforced by years of personal friendship. At times the tone of the proceedings appeared to be that of a happy little clique, all strengthening each other's faith in the one true doctrine of colonial administration.[20]

The array of some twenty witnesses who appeared before the committee during the three months it heard testimony included past and present Colonial Secretaries, several prominent political figures, and spokesmen for the defense services. Official colonial opinion, on the other hand, was largely unrepresented. One or two who could be regarded as representatives of the colonial viewpoint were heard from, chiefly because they happened to be visiting in London and were available to give their testimony. On the whole, however, the record shows little interest in sounding out colonial leaders. No one was heard, for instance, who could speak for Canada. The colonial interest as such was represented mainly by spokesmen for the Colonial Office. Hugh Childers, who had lived in Victoria and been prominent in the political life of the colony, made a point of seeing that acknowledgment was made of the military efforts of that colony; he also expressed concern that under the War Office's system of accounting the contributions of Victoria were lumped in with those of New South Wales. Aside from such occasional interventions, however, colonial opinion counted for little in the committee's activities.[21]

The testimony presented to the committee made clear the diversity and confusion of the existing garrison arrangements. There were more than 44,000 troops stationed overseas in colonial garrisons, and slightly more than half of these were in imperial fortresses: in the Mediterranean, Bermuda, Halifax, St. Helena, and Mauritius. The rest of the forces were in colonies proper, with a heavy concentration in New Zealand and South Africa. The imperial government paid approximately £1,715,000 per annum toward the maintenance of these forces, and the various

[20] William S. Childe-Pemberton, *Life of Lord Norton* (London, 1909), pp. 68, 163.
[21] Parl. Pap, 1861, XIII, 52.

colonial governments contributed £370,000, the largest amounts coming from Ceylon and Victoria in Australia.[22]

The imperial forces were stationed in the colonies for various reasons. It was intended that they should provide those colonies needing it with protection from external aggression, and that they should protect European settlers against native tribes, as in New Zealand and the Cape. But they were also to furnish the local militia with an example of effective military discipline and organization, and to quell any internal unrest or domestic violence, as in Jamaica from a population largely composed of freed slaves, and in Tasmania from the convict groups.[23] Those in British Columbia were used chiefly to construct roads.[24]

If a variety of factors governed the distribution of the forces, an equal variety of financial arrangements had been entered upon for their maintenance. Of the thirty-three dependencies to which Britain furnished military assistance, eleven made some contribution to the imperial costs; some five or six furnished some local forces for their own defense.[25] In some cases, the contribution to the imperial costs took the form of the provision of barracks and supplies for the troops; in others the costs of certain of the fortifications of the colony were borne by the colonial government.[26] Several of the Australian colonies, because of the high level of wages and generally high costs of living, paid the officers and men of the garrisons a colonial allowance to supplement their regular imperial pay. The imperial government had been forced to match this for units in colonies that paid no such stipends,[27] and in view of this the value of the total contribution made by the colonies was perhaps exaggerated. The figure of £370,000 included these colonial allowances, which Britain would not ordinarily have made and which therefore provided no relief for the British treasury but, on the contrary, placed an added burden upon it.

Despite the lopsided nature of the "sharing" of the costs of defense, and the confusions arising from the carrying arrangements under which British troops were stationed in the colonies, there was general agreement that Britain retained the responsibility for the defense and security of the colonies. Some disagreement existed about the extent of the obligation. John Robert Godley felt that when the people of an old land "swarmed" off to a new one, "there is neither justice nor policy in permitting the emigrants to throw on those whom they leave behind the responsibility and charge of keeping the new society together. . . ."[28] Gladstone in his testimony was not so outspoken, but wished, for the better development of colonial self-reliance and pride in themselves, that the colonies might

---

[22] *Ibid.*, p. 275.   [23] *Ibid.*, pp. 132–33.   [24] *Ibid.*, p. 4.   [25] *Ibid.*, p. 1.
[26] *Ibid.*, pp. v, 9, 11.   [27] *Ibid.*, p. 10.   [28] *Ibid.*, p. 323.

assume the primary responsibility for their own defense,[29] and might come
to resent the presence of imperial forces in their midst. This, however,
was not intended to mean the abandonment of imperial duties of defense.
On the contrary, Gladstone felt that a large part of military defense would
have to be borne in Great Britain, and that this was a burden which
could be gladly and proudly borne and which would strengthen the bonds
of empire.[30]

None of the testimony indicated any desire to abandon the colonies to a
precarious independence. But there was substantial evidence of the belief
that the military arrangements of empire had been much better handled
in the eighteenth century. To men like Adderley and Godley, that seemed
the golden era of self-reliance and manly initiative on the part of the
colonies. Both were in solemn agreement that in the struggles with France
in North America, the colonial militia had borne their arms with great
distinction. Godley said he knew of "no history more fruitful in the record
of heroic deeds"[31] than the colonial achievements of British North America
against France in Nova Scotia in 1710 and against the fortress of Louisburg
in 1745. He soberly agreed with Adderley's flight of historical fancy that
the Virginia militia alone had been sufficient to repulse attacks of the
French regular forces on their borders during the Seven Years' War.[32]

If the consensus among members of the committee and witnesses alike
was that Britain remained responsible for the safety of the colonies, this
responsibility was felt more keenly where the colonies might be endangered
by external attack, since such danger was likely to arise from a foreign
policy controlled solely by the imperial government. But there was feeling
that the colonies failed to appreciate the major contribution made to
their defense by the power of the Royal Navy. The Colonial Secretary,
the Duke of Newcastle, commented that he had frequently had to point
out to some of the Australasian colonies that the Channel Fleet, operating
in waters near the British Isles,[33] constituted a defense of Australia. Rear
Admiral James Elphinstone Erskine, recently in command of Royal Navy
forces in Australian waters, maintained that the defense of Australia was
assured by the existence of predominant sea-power, and that this was a
cheaper and more efficient method of defense than the proliferation of
military stations on the land mass of the continent.[34] And Rear Admiral
Sir Charles Elliott, who had been Governor of Bermuda and Trinidad,
said he never had been able to understand the purpose of maintaining
military forces in Canada.[35]

While there was general agreement about the duty of defending the
colonies, whether by naval or military means, there was much difference

[29] *Ibid.*, p. 122.   [30] *Ibid.*, p. 258.   [31] *Ibid.*, p. 320.   [32] *Ibid.*, p. 123.
[33] *Ibid.*, p. 199.   [34] *Ibid.*, pp. 213–14.   [35] *Ibid.*, p. 67.

of opinion on the question of whether troops should be held in colonies for purposes other than that of defense against external aggression. In addition to the costs paid by the British taxpayer for the maintenance of such forces, many other arguments were raised against the practice. For one thing, the effect of the colonial garrison was to vitiate any colonial efforts toward their own defense. Robert Lowe, a former member of the New South Wales Legislative Assembly, put it most succinctly: the presence of one imperial soldier prevented one hundred colonials from arming and drilling.[36] Gladstone, too, felt that the imperial garrisons had an enervating effect on colonial efforts.[37] And Godley argued that the military achievements of the eighteenth-century colonists clearly demonstrated the needlessness of imperial forces.[38]

There was the fear, too, that the presence of colonial garrisons led to military adventures and land grabbing policies which provoked native wars, wars that meant the use of the British forces and made the British soldier and taxpayer responsible for snatching the colonial chestnuts out of the fire. The Duke of Newcastle put forward this view in his statement that the presence of imperial forces seemed to make the colonial governments less restrained in their handling of native problems.[39] He felt that the more a local government assumed control of native policy, the stronger was the case of the imperial government in requesting local contributions to defense, so as to diminish the chestnut-snatching burdens of the imperial forces.[40] Robert Lowe, soured on colonial governments generally by his clashes with emergent democracy in New South Wales, agreed with this point of view and said that leaving British garrisons in the colonies amounted "to placing a thunderbolt in the hands of a child."[41] The existing government of New South Wales was, he felt, unfit to be entrusted in any way with the disposition of Her Majesty's forces for any purpose whatever.[42] Their presence in the colony might be a formidable obstacle to the amicable separation of the colony from Britain when the time came, for they might become, like Fort Sumter, isolated outposts surrounded by hostile populations.[43]

War Office spokesmen urged the desirability of bringing troops home from the colonies for the sake of the general strength of the Empire. Lord Herbert of Lea (Sir Sidney Herbert), Secretary of State for War, spoke of the anxiety to accumulate as many troops in the British Isles as possible, and to have correspondingly few in the colonies. And the Undersecretary, Godley, said that the farflung distribution of the forces was a weakness.[44] But such arguments did not gain universal assent. Many of the witnesses

[36] *Ibid.*, p. 229.   [37] *Ibid.*, p. 259.   [38] *Ibid.*, p. 123.   [39] *Ibid.*, p. 205.
[40] *Ibid.*, p. 204.   [41] *Ibid.*, p. 223.   [42] *Ibid.*, p. 220.   [43] *Ibid.*, p. 221.
[44] *Ibid.*, p. 122.

felt that the obligations of empire extended to providing some degree of protection against the dangers of native wars, however provoked, and against domestic violence. The situation was put in its simplest form by Lord Herbert of Lea, who, despite his wish to keep a preponderance of troops at home, said, "You cannot let your people have their throats cut, when a battalion of troops, if sent out, would prevent it."[45] Nor did this practical statement exhaust the Secretary of State's view on the matter. He could see no harm in maintaining small forces in the colonies. Even in colonies unthreatened by any possible outbreak of native war, the presence of the redcoats was a symbol of the unity and power of empire. And if such forces were kept to reasonable size, they might not be a vitiating influence on the establishing of colonial forces; rather the reverse, for they would set a standard of military proficiency that any militia would almost be bound to emulate.[46]

Sir John Burgoyne, Inspector General of Fortifications, shared this opinion, affirming the need to keep at least some of the imperial forces in Canada to help in shaping the Canadian militia. Left to their own devices in matters of training and efficiency, the militia would, Burgoyne was unhappily convinced, be imperfectly led and badly handled.[47] He felt constrained to say this despite the fact that the maintenance of imperial forces in Canada was no easy task, especially for engineering units. High wages in the United States were a constant temptation,[48] and desertion, frequently with the connivance of local authorities, had been such a commonplace in the small units sent to Prince Edward Island that the War Office no longer felt it either desirable or feasible to try to keep forces there.[49]

But most of the testimony against any policy of precipitate withdrawal of the garrisons came from the then Secretary of State for Colonies, the Duke of Newcastle, and from Lord Grey, who had wrestled with the problem of military garrisons in the past. Both raised their voices against some of the cherished ideas of members of the committee. Grey did not share Adderley's unbounded admiration for the military arrangements of the old Empire. Colonial militia forces, he said, had never been really subject to the test of conflict with European armies, and as for the American example, the Maoris of New Zealand were a more formidable foe than had been the Indian foes of the eighteenth-century colonists.[50] Grey doubted the wisdom of shifting too great a burden of defense to the young

---

[45] *Ibid.*, p. 247.   [46] *Ibid.*, p. 246.

[47] *Ibid.*, p. 81. This view was shared by Lord Monck while Governor General of Canada. He felt that the withdrawal of imperial forces would lead to the collapse of the military instruction system in Upper Canada. Stacey, *Canada and the British Army, 1846–1871*, p. 157.

[48] *Ibid.*, p. 85.   [49] *Ibid.*, p. 196.   [50] *Ibid.*, p. 159.

colonial economies. Such a change, he felt, might serve the short-term interests of the British taxpayer at the expense of the long-term interests of the growing colonial areas. It would be bad policy to check the latter's economic growth for the sake of a few thousands of pounds per year.[51] And with the authentic accents of Exeter Hall, Grey questioned the advisability of allowing to certain colonial governments the greater voice in native and land policies, which would follow their assumption of greater burdens of defense.[52]

The Duke of Newcastle rejected the idea that any rigid rule or principle could be laid down to govern the maintenance of imperial garrisons; the case of each colony, he felt, stood on a different footing. No doubt colonies ought to contribute in some form or other to their defense, but a local force might be desirable in some colonies and far from good in others.[53] As for the obligations which Britain had toward its colonies, he believed that the duty of defense fell on Britain. He could see no reason why a colony would wish to remain within the Empire unless the mother country gave it security.[54] And the obligation of defense did extend, he felt, to the protection of colonists against the dangers of native wars.[55] The alternative to the presence and use of British troops would be the establishment of commando units: "If you give liberty to every man to carry his rifle and to shoot every native he sees carrying off, however small, a portion of his property, that might perhaps obviate the necessity for sending regiments."[56] But the result would be lawlessness, under whatever name such a military system might operate. Nor did he feel that the granting of responsible government really affected the nature of this problem.[57]

If Newcastle was willing to see Britain continue much of the existing arrangement, the Undersecretary of the Colonial Office, Herman Merivale, was largely noncommittal about troop withdrawal other than from Australia. Since the forces there were largely for "sentiment and parade," there should be no practical difficulty about their withdrawal.[58]

The testimony of the three colonists who appeared before the committee varied according to the colony they represented. The two from New Zealand[59] were both of the opinion that the solution of the problem lay in turning over to colonial authorities control of native policy and land sales. They reasoned that if the colonists had to pay the bills arising from the policies they adopted, the colonists would not go to war. The imperial garrisons, they felt, simply encouraged costly wars. If these forces were reduced to one or two companies, New Zealand would undertake to

[51] *Ibid.*, p. 156.   [52] *Ibid.*   [53] *Ibid.*, p. 185.   [54] *Ibid.*, p. 192.
[55] *Ibid.*, p. 203.   [56] *Ibid.*, p. 202.   [57] *Ibid.*, p. 203.   [58] *Ibid.*, p. 132.
[59] Sir Charles Clifford, eighteen years a settler, and for six years Speaker of the New Zealand House of Representatives, and Mr. Walter Brodie, a member of the same body in the 1850's.

furnish its own defense against the Maoris, provided that control of land policy was in colonial hands.[60]

Sir Stuart Donaldson, a member of the Legislature of New South Wales for several years and the holder of various cabinet posts in the colonial government, was more concerned about naval than military defense. While it was desirable that a small force of British troops be retained in Australia as a nucleus in the shaping of Australian units, he felt that New South Wales and other Australian colonies would benefit more from additions to local naval rather than military strength. He said that French naval forces in Australian waters were larger than those of Britain. There was, he maintained, considerable feeling that the French were establishing a cordon of power in islands around eastern Australia, and that it was incumbent upon Britain to reinforce her naval power in the region. This feeling was the stronger since the taxpayers of Sydney might be involved in war arising from the quarrels and attitudes of the taxpayers of Bristol, and "we have no voice in the complications which may bring us under the influence of the quarrel."[61] This emphasis upon the naval defense of Australia prompted consideration of the matter of colonial subsidy for such increased naval forces. Sir Stuart said that such subsidies would in all likelihood be so small that it would be beneath the dignity of the imperial government to solicit them; and yet, he pointed out, if they were given, the colonial governments would surely wish to have some voice in determining the movements of the vessels to which they were contributing.[62]

If the report of the committee had been based on the testimony furnished by the majority of the witnesses, it is at least arguable that no great change in the existing arrangements would have been recommended. Much was said in favor of the withdrawal of the British forces from the self-governing colonies. With the exception of the Australian areas, however, it was equally argued that there were many practical difficulties that would impede any speedy reduction of troops. Withdrawal might be immediately effected in Australia, but not in Canada, New Zealand, or the Cape. Indeed, if there was truth in the Duke of Newcastle's assertion that the maintenance of troops in Canada was in support of an imperial rather than colonial interest, then withdrawal of forces from that colony would certainly seem remote. Past and present officials of the Colonial Office did speak of the possibility of improvements in the military arrangements, but on the basis of the policy laid down by Grey, with consideration to be given to the varying conditions in individual colonies. Looking at the testimony of the whole array of witnesses, great and near-great alike,

---

[60] Parl. Pap., 1861, Vol. XIII, pp. 183–84, 234.
[61] Ibid., p. 176.   [62] Ibid., p. 177–78.

it is difficult to discern any overwhelming demand for the cessation of the existing military system.[63]

But aside from the spokesmen for the Colonial Office, more of the great were critics of the existing state of affairs. For the War Office, Lord Herbert sought a greater concentration of military manpower in the British Isles. Gladstone, Chancellor of the Exchequer, putting the question in the larger context of imperial relations, saw in military withdrawal a step toward greater colonial stature and increased colonial self-reliance and manliness, and felt that it would bring closer the time when the Empire would be essentially an association of free peoples. And a future Chancellor, Robert Lowe, urged withdrawal because of his basic anti-imperialism and dislike of much of colonial life in general.

If there was a considerable divergence in the views of the witnesses, a consensus of the committee members was apparently more easily developed. The chairman, Arthur Mills, submitted a set of draft resolutions as a working basis of the report, as did Lord Stanley, a former Colonial Secretary and member of the group. Mills's draft urged the desirability of concentrating the military forces of the Empire, and of reliance on the naval power of Britain for the security of the outlying portions of the Empire. He felt that the best way of securing the reduction of the military garrisons was to carry further the policy laid down by Lord Grey.[64] Garrisons should be stationed in the Empire for imperial purposes and according to the judgment of Her Majesty's Government. Lord Stanley's draft roughly paralleled the one submitted by Mills. He was, however, more outspoken in his condemnation of anything that smacked of a doctrinaire approach to the problem, and led off with a statement to the effect that the varying circumstances of each colony made the adoption of any uniform rule concerning colonial military problems impractical.[65]

Adderley was not content with either of the suggested drafts and sought to plug up the loopholes. He sought the deletion of any references to "local resources" as a factor that imperial authorities ought to consider when they came to assess their responsibilities for the defense of any colony. On this he was defeated by a vote of 11 to 1. Another suggestion made by Adderley, that the colonies should also be held responsible for a share in the defense against external attack, was defeated by 10 to 2, Adderley being joined in the minority by W. E. Baxter. His effort to limit the area of imperial responsibility more sharply than in the draft resolutions was also rejected. Yet despite the natural havering over the terms of the report to the House, the resolution presented by Mills to the Commons on March 4, 1862, reflected with reasonable accuracy the thoughts of the committee members.

[63] *Ibid.*, pp. 265–66.   [64] *Ibid.*, p. xiii.   [65] *Ibid.*

The resolution was studiously moderate in tone, as was the speech of Mills urging its adoption. It accepted the responsibility of the imperial government for furnishing aid to all portions of the Empire in any war arising from the consequences of imperial policy. As for difficulties arising within the colonies themselves, the resolution said that the "main responsibility" for caring for their own internal order ought to be undertaken by colonies having self-government. Mills said that all of the witnesses had agreed upon this principle. The argument that without the restraining influence of British troops, colonial governments and peoples would resort to barbarous depredations against native peoples, Mills dismissed as an "insult" to the colonial peoples. In this he was supported by the seconder of the resolution, Charles Buxton, whose name was a guarantee that the welfare of native peoples had not been forgotten by the framers of the resolution. Buxton argued that if the maintenance of imperial forces was designed to check wars with native tribes, then the bloody war being waged in New Zealand, the numerous campaigns against the Kaffir tribes in Africa, and the plight of the Indian tribes in Canada were all proof that such a policy had failed. The real consequences of the policy had been to instill in the minds of the colonists the knowledge that if war occurred the costs would not fall on them. "So far, indeed, from war being considered an evil, it had been hailed as a positive advantage, causing, as it did, a vast outlay of money in the colony; and the colonists consequently had been much more ready to trespass on the rights of the natives than cautious in avoiding offence."[66]

Only one member of the House of Commons, other than the members of the Mills Committee, spoke on the resolution. This was T. C. Haliburton, the Nova Scotian humorist known as "Sam Slick." He commented that the time did not seem appropriate for the passage of any such resolution, a reference to the *Trent* affair. With this minor caveat, the resolution passed the House after a short and lackluster debate. But not without change. Committee member Baxter succeeded in getting the acceptance of an amendment that he had failed to have adopted by the committee in its deliberative sessions, an amendment to the effect that colonies ought to assist in their external defense as well as caring for their own internal security.[67] The temper of the House, or of those few members who were there for the debate, is suggested by the adoption of an amendment that would add to the defense responsibilities to be shared by the self-governing colonies.

[66] Great Britain, *Hansard's Parliamentary Debates* (henceforth cited as *Hansard*), 3d Series, CLXV, 1039, March 4, 1862.
[67] *Ibid.*, pp. 1048, 1060.

There was little if anything new in the terms of the Mills Committee resolution. For more than a decade, imperial authorities had been trying to reduce the garrisons and arouse the colonial governments to more vigorous action for internal security, with varying degrees of success. Nor did the Baxter amendment really modify or change the picture, for it threw no greater potential burden on the colonial governments. Any force organized for internal security would in all likelihood be available for service against any foreign aggression.

The adoption of the resolution did, however, endow the existing policy with a new measure of authority. The system of military garrisons still had some years to live; the exigencies of the *Trent* affair had recently led to strong reinforcements being moved to strengthen the British Canadian position in North America. But as evidence of the existence of a prevailing dissatisfaction with the garrison system, the work of the committee and the subsequent resolution adopted by the House of Commons were overwhelming.

Most significant of all, the adoption of the resolution, which was in a sense a declaration of national policy, helped clear the air for the formulation of a strategy of imperial defense. Until the obsessive question of the colonial garrisons had been dealt with, the weak and ineffectual arrangements ended, and the irritations arising from them abated, any clarification of thought about defense was unlikely. The resolution did not clear the troops from every cormorant's rock throughout the Empire, but it did, for the first time, point the way toward a more rational and collaborative organization of the Empire's defense responsibilities.

CHAPTER II

THE WITHDRAWAL
OF THE LEGIONS

The adoption of the Mills resolution in March, 1862, may have heralded the day when the imperial forces would be withdrawn from the self-governing colonies, and when those colonies would assume the responsibility for their own defense. But that day came only with what many felt was painful slowness; ten years elapsed between the hearings of the Mills Committee and the final withdrawal of the legions.

The delay was caused by the impact of irresistible events. On the North American continent, the mighty antagonists of the American Civil War threatened to involve Canada one way or the other in the struggle. And after the war, there remained the threat of the Fenian raids on Canada, and the talk of powerful men in Washington, such as Charles Sumner, about the desirability of securing Canada as compensation for the damages inflicted on American interests by the British-built commerce raiders. In addition, the machinations of various American interests and officials in the Red River country aroused Canada's fears for her western lands.

Nor were affairs working out much better in New Zealand. There, two thousand Maoris were able to pin down a considerable force of imperial and colonial troops. In the mid-sixties, some 10,000 imperial troops were committed to the struggle, and until that menace could be abated, prospects for their recall were slim indeed.[1]

It was only the Australian colonies which seemed to enjoy sufficient peace and security to allow the withdrawal of the forces, and even here no forthright or decisive action was taken. On June 26, 1863, the Secretary of State for the Colonies, the Duke of Newcastle, sent a round robin letter to the Governors of the Australian colonies. He laid down the principle

---

[1] *Cambridge History of the British Empire* (henceforth cited as *C.H.B.E.*), VII, Part 2, 138.

that in colonies possessing responsible government, the imperial government had only a limited obligation to contribute to their defense, save in exceptional circumstances arising from their situation or the character of their population. In general, imperial aid would be available only in war or at times when war seemed likely. Newcastle felt that in the Australian case, the imperial obligation was met by the existence and power of the Royal Navy. Australia was confronted with no threat from a neighboring state, nor did it have the problems arising from warlike native tribes. Despite this general principle, however, the imperial government was still willing to continue to allot British troops for garrison duty in Australia, but only under certain conditions. Fifteen companies, plus the headquarters wing of another regiment, would be assigned there as a nucleus on which colonial troops might be modelled, in return for a fair contribution towards their cost from the various colonial governments. The offer did not apply to Western Australia, for the United Kingdom did not intend to dispatch any forces there. Nor did the offer apply to Tasmania, where the vestiges of the former convict system were still apparent; if troops were needed there, their maintenance would be a proper charge against the imperial treasury.

Instead of the colonial allowances some of the colonies had paid in the past to meet the costs of the garrisons, the Colonial Office suggested that troops be paid for at the rate of £40 per year for each infantryman, with a higher rate for forces with special training. The men to be assigned to various Australian colonies would number about 1350, and the costs to the colonies for their services would be about £54,000 a year.[2]

Thus the exigencies of empire and the lack of a determined application of the policy of withdrawal prolonged the stay of the garrisons in the self-governing colonies. In the late sixties, of the approximately 140 battalions in the British Army, some forty were based in the United Kingdom; one hundred other battalions were either stationed in the Empire, including the self-governing colonies, or were in passage to or from stations abroad. There were about 15,000 imperial troops still in Canada and the Maritime areas, and between five and six thousand still in Australia and New Zealand.

Yet the doom of the system was already apparent. Both Conservative and Liberal governments were moving towards its destruction. One of the last acts of the Duke of Buckingham, Colonial Secretary in the Derby-Disraeli Ministry, was to inform the Canadian authorities that it had been decided to reduce further the forces in North America. The garrisons in Ontario and Quebec would be pruned to 5,000 men, and those in the

[2] Victoria, Legislative Assembly, *Votes and Proceedings*, III, 1875–76, "Report of the Royal Commission on the Volunteer Forces," 218–19.

Maritimes to some 3,600 men, including the garrison of the imperial fortress of Halifax.[3]

It remained for the first Gladstone Government to bring about the recall of the legions, and to end the domiciling of imperial forces in the self-governing states of the Empire. The Gladstone Government went about the task vigorously, impelled both by ideological zeal and the practical requirements of British defense. The fervor of Gladstone and his associates for the ending of this use of British troops had not abated since the time of the Mills Committee. Gladstone believed as ever that responsibility in defense must accompany responsibility in government. In debate on the Canadian Railway Loan Bill in 1867, he repeated his belief that what he called the system of vicarious defense, in addition to keeping a heavy burden on the British taxpayer, depressed the tone of political life in the country in which it existed. An end of such arrangements was needed to bring the country to the full possession and enjoyment of freedom. Also, in the case of Canada, the defense allegedly secured by the presence of British troops there actually constituted a danger to the Canadian community, for the colony was attacked by Fenian raiders only as a means of wounding Britain through hitting the troops Britain had there. This ran parallel with the opinion recorded in a memorandum he had drawn up in 1864, in which he stated the belief that "the more Canada and the British colonies are detached, as to their defensive not less than their administrative responsibilities, from England, the more likely the Union will be to study friendly relations with them: but, on the other hand, the more we make ourselves the prominent personages in defending British North America, the more the Americans will feel that through the Colonies they wound us in honour and in power. . . ."[4]

While Gladstone's urging of the recall of the garrisons arose from his conception of effective and enduring imperial relations, the possible economies in such withdrawal appealed to a government that had come to power on the electioneering cry of retrenchment. Others of the Gladstone Government, more doctrinaire in their thought on the problem, less comprehensive and generous in their ideas, brought up additional arguments for the recall. In a debate on appropriations for additions to the fortifications of Quebec and Montreal, Robert Lowe, the Chancellor of the Exchequer, said with a characteristic sneer that the proposed fortifications seemed intended as a kind of nucleus around which could gather "a sort of vapoury mass—the Canadian militia—whose existence

[3] Stacey, *Canada and the British Army, 1846–1871*, p. 201.
[4] Quoted in Paul Knaplund, *Gladstone and Britain's Imperial Policy* (New York, 1927), p. 238.

has been that of a nebulous order, through which you can see a star of the sixteenth magnitude."[5] Lord Granville, the Colonial Secretary, was notoriously pessimistic about Canada. He shared the opinion of the majority of the Cabinet that Canada would not be successfully defended against the United States, and that any ill-will which the latter had toward Canada was due to its relationship with Britain. The best solution of the problem of the North Atlantic triangle was that Canada might eventually be of the mood and strength to proclaim its independence.[6]

But it was Edward Cardwell, the Secretary of State for War, who was responsible for the practical considerations of military efficiency. Cardwell sought at the same time to obtain a reduction in military costs and an increase in fighting strength. With these two considerations in mind he shared the distaste for the scattering of military power in the colonies. As Colonial Secretary in the previous Whig-Liberal Government, he had ordered substantial reductions in the forces in New Zealand as soon as affairs there seemed to allow; and he was the sponsor of the Colonial Naval Defence Act, clearly designed to encourage a greater measure of participation by colonial governments in defense duties. Cardwell proposed early in 1869 to reduce the forces in all the colonial Empire, dependent as well as self-governing areas, from 50,000 to about 26,000. Reductions in costs would accrue from a reduction in the size of some of the regiments when they were brought home to the United Kingdom.[7]

The end of imperial garrisons on their soil was not universally accompanied by cries of anguish and recrimination from the self-governing colonies. In Victoria, for instance, there had been increasing questioning of the value of the subsidy system, and the occasion for the final withdrawal came when the colony asked for assurance that the troops it paid for would be available in war as well as in peace. The imperial authorities refused to give any such assurance, and the withdrawal of the forces was accomplished there in an atmosphere of regret over the ending of a long association between the colony and the British army, but with no emotional trauma.

A major factor in the formation of the attitude prevalent in Victoria was annoyance that the contribution which the colony made towards the maintenance of the imperial forces there gave Victoria no voice in the composition of the forces. Sir James McCulloch, the Colonial Premier, told the Legislative Assembly that as long as the colony paid for any part

[5] Great Britain, *Hansard*, 3d series, CLXXVII, 1580, March 13, 1865.
[6] *C.H.B.E.*, III, 22.
[7] Stacey, *Canada and the British Army, 1846–1871*, p. 209. An interesting consideration of the background of the Colonial Naval Defence Act is B. A. Knox, "Colonial Influence on Imperial Policy, 1858–1866: Victoria and the Colonial Naval Defence Act, 1865," *Historical Studies, Australia and New Zealand*, XI (Nov. 1963).

of the troop costs, it felt entitled to get the service of the class of troops which in the view of the local authorities were of the greatest use in local defense. The colonial government wished for the services of artillerymen rather than infantry, but the imperial authorities were not agreeable to the tying up of such highly trained forces in parts of the Empire where they were not likely to be of any real use.

No such demands for guarantees of the retention of the troops or for a voice in the nature of the forces stationed within their boundaries were made by New South Wales or South Australia, the other two colonies which contributed towards imperial garrisons. Despite this, the chief of the Victoria government said that the proposed withdrawal of the garrisons was the only course consistent with responsible government, and with the policy generally outlined and followed by the imperial government.[8]

There was a tone of general irritation in the debate in Victoria over the issue of control; the Premier was not the only participant in the discussion to whom the issue was important. One member alleged that even though the colony voted the funds for the troops, it could get no account of how the money was spent. The position of the Governor was unsatisfactory, for he was in this matter not the head of the Victoria government, but the agent of the imperial authority.[9]

Things were different in Canada and New Zealand. There the air was full of accusations and recrimination, coming in part from the feeling of the colonists that they were being left naked to their enemies. Sir John Macdonald of Canada put a stiff-upper-lip quality into a letter to Lord Carnavon: "We must however beat it as best we may, and we intend, with God's blessing, to keep our country, if we can, for the Queen against all comers."[10] But in New Zealand the reaction to the withdrawal of the troops was somewhat more violent and lacking in the Macdonald tone of imperial responsibility. With the latest of the Maori wars (1868) a recent memory, the withdrawal of the troops heightened the atmosphere of insecurity in the two islands. Some spoke of seeking a form of political association with the United States, and the government broached the possibility of the colony's neutrality in any future conflict that involved Britain.[11]

The bitterness arising from the announced intention of troop withdrawal was compounded in New Zealand by the refusal of the Colonial Office to have the imperial government stand as guarantor of a loan that the colonial government wished to place on the London money market.

[8] Victoria, Parliamentary Debates, 1879, X, 878.
[9] Ibid., p. 884.
[10] Donald Creighton, John A. Macdonald, the Old Chieftain (Boston, 1956), p. 61.
[11] C.H.B.E., VII, Part 2, 217.

The brusque and lecturing language used by the Colonial Office in its response added to the offense of the refusal.

In the Commons, New Zealand found a defender in Viscount Bury, who charged British policy with having sown the wind that the colony had reaped in the whirlwind of native wars. Now imperial protection was being withdrawn at a time when the colonists were still in deep distress. Bury did not think the House of Commons would resist "the cry of a nation in its direst peril." He feared, however, that unless New Zealanders were able to rely on Britain for aid they would seek it from Australian volunteers, "whose wild spirits would seek in the confiscation of native lands the reward of any assistance they might render."[12]

The whole issue of colonial policy, and particularly the controversy aroused by the announced intention of the troop withdrawal from New Zealand, was ventilated in the Lords. Lord Carnarvon attacked the withdrawal, maintaining that economy could be purchased too dearly, and that the costs of the garrisons were the only real charges paid for the advantages of empire. He felt that there would be no real economy in simply bringing the forces home; since the troops were as much a charge on the Treasury at home as in the Antipodes, it would be necessary to reduce the size of the over-all forces. Carnarvon urged that the existence of empire entailed responsibility, adding, "I know that it is sometimes said that if the Colonies go trade will remain exactly the same. But depend upon it trade flows greatly in the channels of political influence. . . ." British troops in the colonies were an outward and visible sign of the unity of empire which was greatly prized by the colonists. Further, such forces were of great use in furnishing training cadres for colonial militia and volunteers. Through such training and association the military strength of the empire would grow. Carnarvon deplored the harsh tone and severe logic of some of the Colonial Office dispatches to New Zealand, couched as if there were "debtor and creditor account between them and us. . . ." Lord Granville's customary courtesy, he suggested, had departed from him in his dealing with New Zealand.[13]

Yet, while Carnarvon attacked the policy of the Gladstone Government in the withdrawal of troops from New Zealand, there was very little substantive difference between the two positions. Gladstone felt that contributions by the colonies to the Empire's military strength were the more likely if based on a covenant of freedom, and if the principle of voluntarism were adhered to. In his testimony to the Select Committee in 1861, he had expressed this belief. And two decades later, in a speech in Leeds in October of 1881, he had returned to this theme: that from the affection

<hr />

[12] *Hansard*, 3d series, CXCVIII, 466–67, July 22, 1869.
[13] *Ibid.*, CXCIX, 199–204, Feb. 14, 1870.

of the colonies for Britain "we may obtain assistance and advantage that compulsion would never have wrung from them, and may find that all portions of the British Empire have one common heart, beating with one common pulsation, and equally devoted to the honour and interests of their common country."[14] Carnarvon regarded the small forces that he felt should be maintained in the colonies as symbols which might evoke the voluntary action sought by Gladstone. But whether the garrisons should be withdrawn *in toto*, or whether token units should be kept in the colonies as symbols of the unity of empire, was a minor disagreement compared to their shared opinion that some form of military co-operation between Britain and the self-governing colonies would continue even if the imperial forces were withdrawn.

However hopefully Gladstone might talk in vague phrases about a sharing of the responsibilities of freedom with the colonies, and however optimistically Carnarvon might look forward to the "military organization of the Empire," such expectations of co-operation were largely limited to the idea that the colonies might co-operate with Britain in defense of their own frontiers. More than that was not hoped for. Sufficient of the strain of pessimism about empire, engendered by the free trade economists and reflected in the writings of men like Goldwin Smith, survived to make any other prospect seem most improbable. Sir Charles Dilke voiced the prevailing mood when he wrote in *Greater Britain* in 1868: "It is not likely however, nowadays, that our colonists would, for any long stretch of time, engage to aid us in our purely European wars. Australia would scarcely find herself deeply interested in the guarantee of Luxembourg, nor Canada in the affairs of Servia. The fact that we in Britain paid our share —or rather nearly the whole cost—of the Maori wars would be no argument to an Australian, but only an additional proof to him of our extraordinary folly. We have been educated into a habit of paying with complacency other people's bills—not so the Australian settler."[15] Nor was Dilke alone in this belief. Thus it was felt that if, with the ending of the garrisons, there were trouble again in the Canadian West, it was Canada's business; if there were future Maori wars, New Zealand must handle them. And equally, if there were trouble in India, or Egypt, or the Mediterranean, it was the responsibility of Britain to deal with it. It was to be each colony for itself in internal defense and the keeping of order, and Britain for them all in defense against external attack. No other distribution of responsibility was anticipated.

With the immediate complaint of the garrison removed, the Empire did not seem to be quite the burden it had been. Resentment over the costs of

---

[14] Knaplund, *Gladstone and Britain's Imperial Policy*, pp. 144–45.
[15] C. W. Dilke, *Greater Britain* (London, 1868), II, 151.

imperial defense was not entirely abated, and was to increase again as the costs of naval defense mounted. But this was largely in the future; for the moment it appeared that it might be possible to have empire without too great a burden of charges. Two astute students of nineteenth century British attitudes towards empire have discerned in the crisis over troop withdrawals from New Zealand and the general abandonment of garrisons in other parts of the Empire, a turning point in imperial relations.[16] It has been suggested that the apparently anti-imperial act of withdrawing the garrisons from the self-governing colonies made imperialism a safe political cause to espouse in Britain.[17]

No one was quicker to smell the possible shift in the wind, and to seek advantage from it, than Disraeli. His famous Crystal Palace speech of June, 1872, marked an official embrace of the cause of empire by a great political party. Disraeli charged that the Liberals had sought in recent decades the dismemberment of empire, and that the self-government granted to the colonies should have been part of a larger bargain, terms of which should have included definite colonial responsibility for their defense. He continued: "It [responsible government] ought to have been accompanied by an Imperial tariff, by securities for the people of England for the enjoyment of the unappropriated lands which belonged to the Sovereign as their trustee, and by a military code which should have precisely defined the means and responsibilities by which the Colonies should be defended, and by which, if necessary, this country should call for aid from the Colonies themselves."[18]

Of course, the so-called "revival of imperialism" of the eighteen-seventies, of which the Crystal Palace speech was an indication, was rooted in many factors of greater weight and significance than the fact that the British taxpayer had been emancipated from one of the more evident costs of empire. But of all the factors which enter into any consideration of the reasons for the apparent shift of attitude, the "withdrawal of the legions" is one of the more obvious. If empire as a political cry was now an election asset, it was because voters could regard empire itself as an asset. And empire was now felt to be an asset not only as a trading area and a new home for emigrating Britons, but also as a source of military power to Great Britain.

Gladstone's Secretary of State for War, however, was not overly concerned about a "military code of empire," or whether the colonies might ultimately be additions to the strength of Britain's forces. Cardwell's anxiety was to bring home the scattered imperial forces, so that he might

---

[16] C. A. Bodelsen, *Studies in Mid-Victorian Imperialism* (New York, 1925), pp. 89–94; Schuyler, *The Fall of the Old Colonial System.*

[17] Stacey, *Canada and the British Army, 1846–1871*, p. 259.

[18] George Bennett (ed.), *The Concept of Empire* (London, 1953), pp. 257–58.

have the manpower to carry out the necessary changes in the British army. The Cardwell reforns were the first great reforms in the British military forces since Waterloo. His three major measures—the abolition of purchase of commission, the introduction of short-term enlistment with the relatively early shift of trained men into the reserves, and the system of linked battalions—not only brought a higher degree of military efficiency but also assured greater economy. Yet much of this was possible only by having available at home, for the system of linked battalions, the forces withdrawn from the self-governing colonies.

Accompanying the recall of the imperial forces, and a minor part of the Cardwellian reforms, was the disbandment of several regiments that had been raised and maintained by the War Office in some of the colonies and had been localized for service there. The formation of these units had been prompted by several considerations. Local recruiting saved the costs of transportation which would otherwise have been necessary for the movement of purely British regiments in and out of the colony. Some regiments were formed substantially of veteran soldiers, who were less given to desertion than younger recruits and were more closely integrated to the life of the colony. In some instances, as in the West Indies, the existence of such a regiment could save regular forces from exposure to the health risks of the tropical climate.

One such regiment, the Royal Canadian Rifles formed in 1840, had been used largely for garrison duty along the frontier and in the territories of the Hudson's Bay Company. During the thirty years of its existence the regiment "did good service in keeping alive a martial spirit, and in providing militia regiments with professional instructors."[19] One of the heritages of this regiment and other units in the Northwest is the red tunic now worn by the Royal Canadian Mounted Police. The police hoped through the similarity of uniform to continue the goodwill of the Indians won by their soldier predecessors. When the imperial authorities disbanded the Royal Canadian Rifles, the same fate befell the 3rd West Indian Regiment—the regiment which had served in West Africa during some of the Ashantee troubles—and the Cape Mounted Rifles and Cape Artillery. Whether the disbanding of these local forces served the cause of economy, and the further cause of the encouragement of colonial self-reliance, was debatable. This was especially so in the Cape, where the constant threat of border troubles and tribal wars permitted no great diminution of imperial forces. But Cardwell maintained that the dissolution of such units in no wise diminished the influence of Great Britain.[20]

[19] George F. G. Stanley, *Canada's Soldiers, 1604–1954* (Toronto, 1954), p. 208.
[20] *Hansard*, 3d Series, CCIV, 330, Feb. 16, 1871.

However great the changes, the British Army remained what it had been through most of the nineteenth century, a colonial service army not designed to face the contingency of a European war. Under the system established by Cardwell, the battalion at home provided drafts for the battalion serving abroad. Besides supplying drafts for this service, the home army would furnish the potential expeditionary force needed to guard the imperial frontiers in remote parts of the world; it would provide the spear to be launched by Britain from behind the shield provided by the navy. The pace and vigor of army reform may have been accelerated by the events of the Franco-Prussian War, but the emergence of German military might did not bring any imitation of the German example. The preamble to the annual Army Act contained the statement that the army was needed for the preservation of the balance of power in Europe.[21] But when the question "What is the army for?" was asked, as it occasionally was, there was only one real answer: it was for service in India and in the colonial empire.[22]

It is difficult to think that the international security of any British colony was endangered by the withdrawal of the British garrisons. The true defense of the colonies rested primarily on the prestige of Britain. They were, as Cardwell said, under "the aegis of the name of England";[23] war with them would be war with England. It was recognized, however, that being under the English "aegis" was perhaps not protection enough in all instances. It might suffice to give security to English colonies from any predatory tendencies among other European powers, but did it suffice for the lesser breeds without the law? Evidently not, for even after the conferring of responsible government on the Cape, imperial forces were held in that colony and in neighboring Natal. The "aegis" needed a little reinforcement; British prestige with Boer and Bantu was not high.

There can be no denial of the strategic soundness of the withdrawal of the garrisons. Yet some concessions might have been made to imperial sentiment. It might have been of value to have kept small units of the British troops scattered throughout the self-governing colonies as a symbol of the companionship of arms and the unity of empire. The spirit of man throughout the ages has been nourished by the use of symbols, from the cross to the flag, and the retention of the red coat of the British regular in the colonies would not have been the sign of compulsion, so feared by the Liberals, but a visible token of the "aegis." It is a bit of an

---

[21] Removed in the 1866 revision.
[22] By Sir Wilfrid Lawson, for example. *Hansard*, 3d Series, CCXXVII, 1440–41, March 6, 1876. Lawson was a persistent champion of the traditional Liberal values of economy and non-intervention. Also by Sir William Harcourt, *Hansard*, 3d series, CCIX, 1819, March 11, 1872.
[23] *Hansard*, 3d series, CCXXVII, 390.

oddity that Gladstone's imaginative statesmanship, which could envision the future states of the British Empire as a community of free nations, could not also, on a smaller scale, see how the sense of common heritage and loyalty, and the shared traditions of valor, would have been evoked among the colonists by the sight of the Queen's uniform.

Yet, whatever the recriminations and piques aroused by the final withdrawal of the forces, and whatever the ignored opportunities, the wisdom of the policy was more than substantiated by subsequent developments. Certainly the Cardwell reforms, of which the ending of the garrison system was an essential part, made for greater efficiency in the British army; they also paved the way for the emergence of more effective units of colonial militia and for the creation of some small permanent military formations. There were, of course, mutterings in colonial circles about the apparent anxiety of the British government to concentrate Britain's might for the defense of the bathing machines at Brighton or the buoys and lightships on the Mersey. Demands were raised that imperial policy acknowledge no difference between the defense of Middlesex in Britain and Middlesex County in Canada.[24] In general, however, the *Sydney Morning Herald* reflected the situation accurately in its remark, "Any little hubbub over the determination to concentrate rather than distribute the Imperial forces has disappeared, and many wonder why so much fuss was made about so little."[25]

If the withdrawal of the garrisons removed the chief complaint of the anti-imperialists about the costs of empire, it did not end the debate on the proper share of the costs of defense to be borne by Britain and the colonies. While the costs of the garrisons had been the nub of the debate, there were other suggestions that it was inappropriate that the whole of the charge of the Royal Navy should be borne by the British taxpayer. Sir Charles Dilke, foe of the garrisons but no anti-imperialist, suggested that the Australian colonies ought to pay their share in the maintenance of the navy—a share to increase with the increase of their merchant shipping.[26] And a desire for greater colonial sharing had previously been manifest in the acceptance of the subsidy from India squadron of the Navy, and in the passage of the Colonial Naval Defense Act in 1865.

Even before the final departure of British troops from Canada, a member of the Commons had made the suggestion that there ought to be colonial contributions to imperial defense. Mr. R. A. Macfie, a Liberal, whose speeches introducing motions regarding colonial affairs usually had the

---

[24] These were views expressed by the *Volunteer Review*, Ottawa, Jan. 27, 1874, and Feb. 2, 1875. Quoted in John Colomb, *The Defence of Great and Greater Britain* (London, 1880), pp. 37, 42.

[25] *Ibid.*, p. 44, quoting *Sydney Morning Herald*, June 8, 1874.

[26] Dilke, *Greater Britain*, II, 150.

unfortunate effect of emptying the House, called for the creation of a Select Committee to consider what amelioration might be made in relations between Britain and the colonies "with a view of the most permanent maintenance of the best and most cordial inter-connection between all parts of the Empire."[27] He said that "if we were leaning, as we were entitled to lean, on the Colonies for support in case of war, we were leaning on what, in such circumstances, must prove a broken reed."[28] The general debate which followed included a strong statement from the government through the Undersecretary for the Colonies, E. H. Knatchbull-Hugessen, to the effect that while there were difficulties in the maintenance and defense of a colonial empire, the idea that a time would come when separation would be desirable was a belief which had never been avowed, and he hoped would never be avowed, by a British government. If colonies grew to be great and powerful, let them feel that there was nothing to be gained by separation.[29]

Macfie returned to the subject the next year, shortly before Disraeli's Crystal Palace speech. This time his resolution called for a commission to inquire into the ways and means and propriety of admitting the colonies "to participate in the conduct of affairs that concern the general interests of the Empire." Even though Macfie's resolutions were regarded as predictable and rather boring occasions—Adderley called them Macfie's "annual sentimental exercitation"—this one provoked a wide-ranging debate on colonial problems which touched on matters of defense at several points. It was asserted that without the colonies, Britain would be a third-rate power. The speakers referred to the usefulness of colonies as sources of supply in case of war, and of colonial ports as places of refuge for British ships. But nothing was said about the larger utility of colonial co-operation in war through manpower.[30]

The suggestion implicit in much of these debates became explicit in the resolution introduced by Lord Eustace Cecil in the Commons, March 7, 1873. He proposed that the colonies be invited to contribute to imperial defense in proportion to their population or wealth, with either contingents of men or grants of money. The amount of contribution in either form was to be agreed upon by consultation between the imperial and colonial governments. Lord Eustace argued that from 1815 to 1872 the colonies had cost the British taxpayer £103,000,000. None of this vast sum had been spent on the Navy, which he regarded as a proper charge on the British Treasury; all had been spent on the maintenance of the military defenses of the colonies. If the colonies were to have the privileges of empire, they should make a contribution toward its costs.

[27] *Hansard*, 3d series, CCVI, 750, May 12, 1871.
[28] *Ibid.*, p. 752.   [29] *Ibid.*, pp. 760–68.
[30] *Hansard*, 3d series, CCXI, 912–38, May 31, 1872.

Little support was won for this motion. Knatchbull-Hugessen said that now that the garrisons had been withdrawn, the colonies cost the imperial exchequer very little—aside from the true imperial costs such as the maintenance and defense of imperial fortresses like Malta and Halifax. The little they did cost, he said, was mainly spent in the effort to suppress the slave trade.

But there was some degree of sympathy with the general idea that the colonies might take a greater measure of defense on their shoulders. Adderley argued that the withdrawal of the imperial forces had made the colonies more prosperous, diminished the chances of native wars, and added to the general strength of empire. He hoped that an analogous naval policy would be followed—that naval forces in colonial waters would be withdrawn—to encourage naval contributions for defense. Gladstone paid tribute to the consistency of Adderley's views on colonial matters, and then went on to say that he trusted the true spirit of freedom in the colonial communities to lead them to take proper action. The habits of freedom in the colonies would prompt them to fulfill their duties and responsibilities as citizens of the Empire.

Lord Eustace withdrew his motion, thus closing the debate, but he had reason for satisfaction in the course the remarks had taken. The emphasis was no longer on the idea that the colonies should pay for purely local defense; rather, it was that in their maturing freedom colonial peoples and governments would perceive their duties and contribute from their wealth and manpower to the defense of the Empire as a whole. The issue was now whether formal approach should be made to the colonies for such support, or whether it was better to rely on the imperial patriotism of the colonies to lead their governments to make the offers of aid.[31]

Despite the Crystal Palace speech in 1872, charging that the Liberals were seeking the disintegration of the Empire, imperial relations were not a question in the 1874 elections. Nor was the larger issue of "imperialism." (The word was just coming into use in the new meaning which it was now acquiring: the extension of political power over non-European areas and peoples.) Following his election victory, Disraeli did little or nothing to remedy the conditions condemned in the Crystal Palace declaration. No vigorous effort was made in any of the areas specified in that utterance —tariffs, land policy, or defense—to undo the damage or remedy the neglect allegedly perpetrated by the Liberals. Indeed, in the realm of relations with the old-line colonies, with Australia, Canada, New Zealand, there was little constructive activity. The Colonial Secretary, Lord Carnarvon, was an idealistic and hard-working administrator, but the tone of the government was of course established by the Prime Minister,

---

[31] *Hansard*, 3d series, CCXIV, 1520–34, March 7, 1873.

and Disraeli's new-found concern for empire was not grounded in either interest for or knowledge of these colonies. Further, relations with these states called for arduous study and detailed administration, and these had little attraction for the Premier. Such matters held scant appeal for a mind which revelled in flights of imperial fancy, and rejoiced in a vision of a Britain that could hold the gorgeous East in fee. It was in the East that the *Imperium* of the *Imperium et Libertas* prevailed, and *Imperium* was by far the more engaging of the two to Disraeli.[32]

Carnarvon did make a minor effort to reverse the recall of the garrisons and to re-establish them in several of the colonies. In this he had the support of Disraeli, who had said that he regarded the restoration of military relations with the colonies as a question of high policy "which ought never to be absent from our thoughts." But if the Prime Minister's support was available for the project, that of the War Office was not. There Gathorne Hardy, continuing with the reforms that Cardwell had started, confronted recruitment problems which caused him to say that he could not even get enough men for the defense of Britain.[33] In fact, the defense of the British Isles themselves was not to be neglected at a time when the public was still excited by the events of the Franco-Prussian War, and by such fear-arousing pamphlets as Sir George Chesney's *Battle of Dorking*. The Secretary of War said that the self-governing colonies would get no British troops; the forces recalled home would stay home.[34]

While the Disraeli Cabinet was unwilling to reverse the policies of its predecessor with regard to the withdrawal of the garrisons, it did carry on a policy of imperial assertion and acquisition. The two most spectacular acquisitions made for the British Crown by the Disraeli Government reflect the Prime Minister's greater concern for the *Imperium* portion of empire, India and the East; they also reflect the strategic ideas which he had expressed during the debate on the cession of the Ionian Islands to Greece in 1863. Then he had said that "a country, and especially a maritime country, must get possession of the strong places of the world if it wishes to contribute to its power." In 1863 this had meant that Britain should retain hold of the protectorate it held over the Ionian Islands. In 1875 it meant the purchase of the shares of the Suez Canal

[32] The claim of Disraeli's early twentieth-century biographers that it was from his 1872 speech that the modern conception of the British Empire arose reads oddly today, when it is clear that the links which have survived the collapse of the European colonial empires were those forged from the spirit of freedom and voluntarism on which Gladstone leaned so heavily.

[33] Brian Bond, "Recruiting the Victorian Army," *Victorian Studies*, V (June, 1962).

[34] Sir Arthur Hardinge, *The Life of Henry Howard Molyneux, Fourth Earl of Carnarvon* (London, 1925), II, 96–98.

Company, and in 1878 the annexation of Cyprus. The same idea contributed to the annexation of Fiji in the remote Pacific.

The major concern back of these acquisitions was not the control of the Mediterranean for its own sake but control of the routes to India. Whether Suez or Cyprus were actually strong places is doubtful. In 1877 General Sir John Lintorn Simmons had prepared a paper on Britain's needs for a coaling station in the eastern Mediterranean, but in this Cyprus was not suggested as a possible location for it. The decision to annex Cyprus was made hastily, and mature consideration would have led to the choice of other possible sites.[35]

While the purchase of the Suez shares was a spectacular *coup*, flattering to British pride, it was also of doubtful strategic advantage. Both Suez and Cyprus presented a problem. In the narrow waters of the eastern Mediterranean they were really not the "strong places" of which Disraeli had spoken, for their strength was only that of the sea power which defended them. The route of their approaches in the Mediterranean was narrow, with several nations abutting upon it. It was made even more perilous by the political bargain which accompanied the taking of Cyprus. France was mollified by British assent to her taking of Tunisia, where France acquired Bizerte, one of the finest ports on the North African littoral and a position from which the vaunted sea route to India could be threatened. The relative uselessness of Cyprus was to be effectively demonstrated by the fact that when Britain acquired control of Egypt, Alexandria became the main naval base in the eastern Mediterranean rather than any of the relatively poor ports of Cyprus.

Gladstone was naturally highly critical of the Cyprus annexation on a variety of grounds, such as the immorality and injustice of the annexation, and the secrecy with which the "insane covenant" with Turkey had been negotiated. But he questioned also the usefulness of Cyprus. He did not feel that Britain's dominion in India rested on such uncertain foundations as her command of the communications with that land. Dominion, he claimed, was grounded on the assent of the people of India. If that acquiescence were ever withdrawn, then all the control in the world over the route through the Mediterranean and Red Sea would never assure the perpetuation of British power. The loss of the Suez route would be an inconvenience, no doubt, but it would not make "the difference between life and death in the maintenance of our Indian Empire."[36] Gladstone's attitude reflected the Radical-Liberal predilection for the open seas as

[35] Harold Temperley, "Disraeli and Cyprus," *English Historical Review*, XLVI (April, 1931), 274–79; (July, 1931), 457–60.
[36] Agatha Ramm, "Great Britain and the Planting of Italian Power in the Red Sea, 1868–1885, *English Historical Review*, LIX (May, 1944), 213.

the area of British power, and the distaste for long land frontiers, whose defense and security required "foreign policy," negotiations with foreign governments, and large military establishments. To this group, all these were devices for the oppression of the people and the denial of democracy.[37]

Annexation of Fiji rested on different grounds. The cultural shock of European penetration into the islands had brought lawlessness and racial tension in its wake, and the situation demanded British authority for the imposition of order. But there was great reluctance to take the action. Gladstone said that it might be the chill of age upon him, but he felt none of the excitement over the acquisition of new territory which seemed to animate proponents of the idea.[38] Sir Wilfrid Lawson, the authentic voice of Cobdenite liberalism, feared that one of the results of the annexation would be yet another native war, and the demand for British military units. Some people, he said, seemed to regard the army as a branch of the Society for the Propagation of Christian Knowledge. He was willing to allow the reported 150,000 Wesleyan Fijians and the 20,000 cannibals of the islands to fight out the question of their control among themselves.[39]

The Colonial Office of the Gladstone Government was of divided mind and unenthusiastic about annexation. In 1870 Undersecretary Robert Herbert suggested that Germany or Belgium might well be urged to annex the islands. He felt that Britain's only concern must be that the power taking possession should not be one that would be able to challenge British sea power in the Pacific. Knatchbull-Hugessen on the other hand favored annexation, perhaps too strongly for a member of the Gladstone Cabinet. And in the middle ground, the Colonial Secretary, Lord Kimberley, reflected the belief that the Australian colonies had more practical interest in the island groups than did Great Britain. He suggested that New South Wales, the senior Australian colony, should annex the islands herself and take the responsibility of their government. The suggestion that a colony lacking sovereignty and without standing in the community of nations should carry out an act of annexation was singularly inept. It might be pleaded, however, that under the spell of free trade liberalism and anti-imperialism, Britons had rather lost their touch in such matters.

Annexations came more easily under the Disraeli regime. Lingering doubts about the wisdom of assuming the task of ruling the remote Fijian island group were suppressed and annexation was authorized. In this, Carnarvon was prompted partly by the fear that unless Britain took the island, she might lose the opportunity of securing a needed base on the long sea routes between the Australasian colonies and British North

[37] A. J. P. Taylor, *The Trouble Makers* (London, 1957), ch. I–III, *passim.*
[38] *Hansard*, 3d series, CCXVI, 945, June 13, 1873.
[39] *Hansard*, 3d series, CCXXI, 1297, Aug. 4, 1874.

America. But strategic considerations in the motivation of the annexation were subordinate to the necessity of halting lawlessness. Fiji could no
more be regarded as a "strong place" than Cyprus.[40] Although it had
utility as a possible coaling station, any strength it might have could come
only from encompassing sea-power.

In spite of the histrionic embrace which Disraeli extended to the idea
of expansion, it is doubtful whether the strategic strength of empire was
augmented by his policies and annexations. Shortening the route to India
might be convenient, but the Mediterranean route was more vulnerable
to attack than the lengthier voyage around the Cape. A "forward" policy
in India like that pursued by Lord Lytton simply meant that the sub-
continent, which already demanded the services of one-third of the
British Army, absorbed still more of the limited trained manpower of
the Empire. Disraeli's imperialism was essentially rhetorical; it added
little to the Empire's power.

No effort was made to rouse colonial governments to greater activity
in imperial defense. And the withdrawal of the garrisons had not spurred
any of the colonies to any vigorous expansion of their own militia or
volunteer forces. The Canadian government gradually came to face the
fact of the withdrawal and to accept responsibility for the defense of the
Dominion, but this change occurred reluctantly and with some vexation.
On April 3, 1871, the Commons in Ottawa considered, without passing,
a resolution in which the Dominion was supposed to recognize "its
obligation to contribute to the utmost of its power towards its own defence
from whatever quarter." But the "utmost," even in this unpassed resolution, turned out to be pretty feeble.[41]

It must be acknowledged that there was little incentive for the Canadian
government to embark upon the vigorous building of Canadian military
strength. For one thing, the political situation changed much for the
better just about the time of the final withdrawal of the British units.
The successful negotiation of the Treaty of Washington with the United
States removed some of the exacerbating elements in Anglo-Canadian-
American relations, and feeling eased notably. The suppression of the
first Riel uprising, to which imperial forces made a substantial contribution, gave assurance that Canada was not likely to lose its national
inheritance of western lands. The reduction of the size of the American
army, and its general preoccupation with Indian wars in the western
plains, seemed ample evidence that the United States harbored no
aggressive designs against its northern neighbor. And if there were no

[40] Ethel Drus, "The Colonial Office and the Annexation of Fiji," *Transactions of the Royal Historical Society*, Fourth Series (London, 1950), XXXII, *passim*.
[41] Stanley, *Canada's Soldiers, 1604–1954*, p. 241.

real chance of American aggression, there would seem to be no need to worry about Canadian military organization. In addition, there were all the factors that incline against military preparations in a democracy, uppermost of which was the natural distaste of an aggressively democratic society for the formation of anything akin to a standing military force, the traditional enemy of the liberties of the people.

Even the militia, usually so favored by egalitarian societies, had little effectiveness. It was the victim of an excess of democracy, for staunch democrats tended to regard even its limited training and discipline as unnecessary. The "stake in society" theory, which had so long served as justification for keeping control of the armed forces of Britain in the hands of those who could afford the purchase of commissions, received an odd twist in the fervent democracy of the British colonies generally. There the purest form of volunteer tradition was espoused, in the firm belief that all that was necessary for the defense of the land was the ardent patriot who would rush to arms to defend home, farm, and family. This tradition, perhaps suggested most notably by William Jennings Bryan's comment that if the United States were endangered a million men would spring to arms overnight, was deeply embedded in the democratic traditions of the English-speaking peoples. It formed part of the profound distaste and distrust for both the professional military officer and the mass conscript army, the latter itself, ironically enough, a product of the democratic tradition of the Continent.

So Canadians confronted the problem of forming an effective defense with only vague ideas of why such a force was needed, and with a substantial distaste for all the methods and means which were needed to make any force effective. They were firm in the dubious conviction that, as the Toronto *Globe* commented, "Canadians can dispense with a standing army because they possess the best possible constituents for a defensive force in themselves. The finest soldiers are men whose own stake and interest in the conflict impel them to respond to a call to arms."[42]

At the time of the withdrawal of the British forces from Canada, the basic military legislation of the Dominion was the Militia Act of 1868. This established the conscriptive principle, holding all able-bodied males between sixteen and sixty, unless otherwise exempted, liable for military service in the defense of Canada. The Militia Act divided those eligible for service into two categories: the active militia and the reserve. The authorized strength of the active force was to be 40,000, with the expectation that there would be sufficient volunteers to meet this number. If there was a dearth of recruits, then compulsion might be resorted to, and

[42] Quoted in Stacey, *Canada and the British Army, 1846–1871*, p. 254.

sufficient eligibles would be required to serve to bring the force up to the authorized strength.

The Act divided Canada into nine military districts, which were sub-divided into brigade and regimental areas, and these in turn were sub-divided into company districts. The regimental districts were for the most part identical with the electoral districts or constituencies of the members of the House of Commons. The men joining the force were to receive arms, uniforms, and other equipment from the government; they were to receive fifty cents a day for the drill periods; and they were re-quired to spend eight to sixteen days each year in camp or at drill.[43] During the period when they were in camp or on other forms of service, they came under the provisions of the Mutiny Act of Britain. This, plus the fact that after the mid-eighteen-seventies the General Officer Com-manding the Militia was a British officer seconded for the duty, and that the manuals of drill and instruction were those used in the imperial forces, gave some degree of uniformity with the British army.

In 1871, when the British garrisons departed, the Canadian militia had 43,000 officers and men in its ranks. Of these, 34,000 had participated in the required annual camps or exercise and training. In 1871–72, some 22,000 had spent sixteen days in the brigade camp.[44] During the decade of the eighteen-seventies, the efficiency of the Canadian militia force declined. With a Liberal administration in office during most of the dec-ade, and with government revenues falling because of the prevailing depression, appropriations for the force were cut almost in half. The number of militia trainees in camp dropped down to 23,000, and the brigade camps, in which the force came together in greatest numbers, were discontinued. Training was limited to battalion and company levels.

The condition of the militia won no approval from the first of the British officers to command it. Major General E. Selby-Smyth said that it was evident that the withdrawal of the imperial forces had deprived the militia of a good example in military training and drill. He felt that the military spirit was languishing in Canada. As for the drill and encamp-ments, he remarked, "Certainly there have been camps of exercise, and very pleasant holiday gatherings they must have been. . . ." Selby-Smyth felt that the force was oversupplied with Lieutenant Colonels, and that too many of the uniforms revealed a most unmilitary taste for ornaments and lace. Under such conditions, the whole system of military distinction was in danger of being held in disregard.[45]

[43] Canada, Sessional Papers, 1869, IV, Paper #10.
[44] Canada, Sessional Papers, 1872, "Report on the state of the Militia," Paper #8, p. 3.
[45] Canada, Sessional Papers, 1875, Paper #6, pp. viii, xvi.

It is only fair to note that General Selby-Smyth revised some of his opinions and took a more favorable view of some of the force in later years, and indeed came to feel that it was perhaps not unworthy of the high responsibility which, in deathless prose, he assigned to it: "It is our duty, therefore, whether through the sunshine of peace or the darkness and gloom of war, still to advance shoulder to shoulder, helping the weak and cheering on the strong, until we have prepared for those who come after us a safe camping ground on the shores of a great future. . . ."[46]

Despite the antipathy existing generally among the Canadian Liberals toward the militia, it was the Liberal Cabinet of Prime Minister Mackenzie that took a major step in Canadian military growth: the establishment of the Royal Military College at Kingston. This was the first institution for military education established in any of the British colonies.[47]

Selby-Smyth's animadversions on the highly decorated state of the uniforms, and his feeling that the militia was too richly blessed in the number of its Lieutenant Colonels, suggest a problem which was the source of constant misunderstandings between the British officers seconded to the Canadian service and the Canadian parliamentary and political leaders who were responsible to the electorate for the efficiency of the force. As in the case of any large body of men in the service of a democratic state, political influences were powerful and pervasive. Even in democratic governments and societies it is rare to see the triumph of virtue simply because it is virtue. Usually more than a little finagling and manipulating, pressuring and logrolling are needed to get legislators to vote approval of what to others may be the essential good. Few British officers were sufficiently aware of this fundamental fact of the nature of the political process to accord politics and the politicians the role and duties which democratic institutions, expecially in the somewhat formless and inchoate colonial societies, placed on them. In the eyes of the officers, "politics" amounted to political interference, always detrimental to military efficiency. They did not sense the fact that politics might equally be a necessary way of securing political support for the militia. Since there was no tradition of professional military force, indeed a definite distaste for any such force, it was only by keeping the militia close to the people—and that, in effect, meant keeping it close to the politicians who led and commanded the votes of the people—that the force could run the gauntlet of the annual vote on the estimates. The British officers could have learned from the American experience in the then recent Civil War, when Lincoln purchased the support he needed in the early days of the war by the distribu-

---

[46] Canada, Sessional Papers, 1878, Paper #8, p. i.
[47] Stanley, *Canada's Soldiers, 1604–1954*, pp. 243–44.

tion of commissions to the right people—those with political influence—as a means of enlisting their support for the Union cause. It was only under the exigencies and pressures of conflict that such political generals could be put aside in favor of those who were able to win battles.

But the problems of command and leadership in the American Civil War were not at that time of as much interest to British military men as they became toward the end of the century.[48] Most of them came to command in Canada without the necessary preparation for dealing with the political realities of the military service in that state. And this was true not only in Canada but in the other colonies as well. For there was little in either the long-established tradition of aristocratic command or the emergent ideas of professionalism in training, to prepare any British officer for the vigorous democracy of colonial societies. Nor had the political education of British military officers generally been comprehensive enough to acquaint them with the facts of self-government in the colonies. That officers commanding the Canadian militia were servants of the Canadian government, not agents of imperial authority, and that they had no right to take an independent course when it seemed to suit them or to suit what they interpreted as imperial needs, was a fact which eluded many of them, and with consequent embarrassment to all. Thus, Major General Luard, Selby-Smyth's immediate successor, found it difficult to accept the fact that he had to follow policies laid down by a political superior who was not only a colonial, but a French-speaking colonial at that.[49]

Yet, with all these considerations, it is doubtful that even if the unfortunate officers seconded to the Canadian militia had possessed both the understanding of Tocqueville and the guile of Machiavelli, they would have been able to accomplish much. In a climate of opinion that was indifferent to defense, with as little liking for taxes as most, with no cadres of professional forces to assist them, and without anything remotely resembling a staff, it must be regarded as a triumph of personality and optimism that some of them managed to retain their good sense and a degree of Canadian good will.

Perhaps the situation in other colonies was not as persistently bad. New Zealand had learned, through the bitter experience of the Maori wars, the advantages of having some trained men; in 1862 the colony had established a small permanent force, the total not to exceed 500. The bulk of the defense force was enrolled as volunteers, the militia force orginally created having proved unsatisfactory. Small permanent forces were also created in the Australian colonies of Victoria and New South

[48] Jay Luvaas, *The Military Legacy of the Civil War* (Chicago, 1959), pp. 115–18.
[49] Creighton, *John A. Macdonald, the Old Chieftain*, p. 339.

Wales. In Victoria, they were formed for both land and sea service. With such small but relatively well-trained forces, the militia or volunteer units had cadres on which to build their own training.

But aside from this, the general conditions regarding the maintenance of the militia which existed in Canada also prevailed in other colonies. The same vulgar democracy, the lack of "tone" in government, which so distressed such a dedicated and capable imperial and colonial servant as Sir Arthur Gordon in his experiences in New Brunswick and New Zealand, existed throughout the colonial states. [50] Colonists were simply not schooled in the habits of discipline and rank and place so dear to the average military mind.

And so it was that after the withdrawal of the garrisons, and despite occasional brave words about meeting the challenge and taking up the burden, things jogged along much as they had before. The spirit of self-reliance and of initiative was there, but there was no urgency about arousing it to action. And London circles, in spite of all their clatter of imperialism, failed to give any strong lead for colonial collaboration in defense. The military relations between Britain and her senior colonies, for all of the suggestions in the Crystal Place speech about the creation of a military code for the colonies, remained much as they had been under the Liberals. Nor was much thought given to imperial strategy, despite the ideas tossed out by men like John Colomb. It took the breath of the bear who walked like a man to bring thought and activity to imperial defense.

[50] Paul Knaplund, *The Gladstone-Gordon Correspondence, 1851–1896* (Philadelphia, 1961), pp. 42–43, 85.

CHAPTER III

GROPINGS FOR AN IMPERIAL STRATEGY

If the withdrawal of the garrisons, foreshadowed by the adoption of the Mills Committee resolution, were to be implemented—as eventually it was—then those of British allegiance living abroad would have to look to two sources for their protection. Their colonial governments would have to provide security against internal disorders and possible tribal forays and native wars; and the Royal Navy would be their shield against external aggression. Canada, of course, would be the exception to such a division of responsibility. Otherwise, however, it had an engaging simplicity. It was, moreover, in line with the prevailing view of correct imperial relations, and it placed the main burden of imperial defense where it seemed rightly to belong: on the back of the Royal Navy rather than the army—that force which, according to Burke, was in its essence a danger to liberty.

The navy on which this greater responsibility devolved had, since the time of the Crimean War, lived "in the torpor of the long Victorian afternoon."[1] Nor had that torpor descended only in the years after the war. A certain absence of mind is suggested by this wartime reminiscence of one authority on imperial defense: "In 1854 a magnificent British fleet steamed away to the Baltic. Her Majesty bade it adieu, and with it went the great heart of England. The Admiral's signal of "Sharpen your cutlasses" is remembered by many, but the fact that the fleet went to one rendezvous while its coal went to another is forgotten by all."[2]

During much of the latter portion of the nineteenth century, the naval power of Britain was dispersed and scattered about the world as the military garrisons were. This dispersal was due in great measure to the

[1] Christopher Lloyd, *The Nation and the Navy* (London, 1954), p. 237.
[2] John Colomb, *Defence of Great and Greater Britain* (London, 1880), p. 19.

fact that the imperial navy of those days was largely a floating police force, a gunboat navy. It performed a hundred varying duties on the oceans of the world, but its command seemed to give little thought to the final vindication of sea-power: its successful use as an instrument of war. Sir William Molesworth's lamentations about the scattering of the military forces of Great Britain over the globe were paralleled by his similar complaints on naval distribution. In July, 1848, "he had linked the Navy with his proposal for an inquiry into colonial expenditure. He estimated that the colonies absorbed forty-five ships and 8,000 men, and apart from the expense, they dispersed the fleet and contributed to its weakness."[3] A Parliamentary committee of the same year noted the tendency for ships dispatched to a foreign station for emergency reasons to stay there permanently after the emergency had passed.[4] A First Lord later in the century grumbled against the "frittering away" of the naval strength of Britain on the "foreign stations"[5] that dotted the globe, and his successor complained that half the cost in the naval estimates went for police duties, for safeguarding of commerce, and for the protection of barbarous and semi-barbarous men against kidnapping and other outrages rather than for services related to war.[6]

This scattering of interests and ships contributed to the state of affairs described by one admiral in the twilight period of the Victorian epoch: "I don't think we thought much about war with a big W. We looked on the Navy more as a World Police Force than as a warlike institution. We considered that our job was to safeguard law and order throughout the world—safeguard civilization, put out fires on shore, and act as guide, philosopher and friend to the merchant ships of all nations."[7]

And so, "far called," the ships of the Royal Navy sailed away to show the flag in the ports of the world, to patrol the lanes of commerce, to check the depredations of the slave traders off the African coast and the

[3] C. J. Bartlett, *Great Britain and Sea Power, 1815–1853* (Oxford, 1963), p. 259.
[4] *Ibid.*
[5] For an imperial power with territorial and commercial interests throughout the globe, and for a naval power whose ships, while dispersed, operated everywhere out of ports or bases of the British Empire, the term "foreign stations" seems to reflect a singularly parochial outlook.
[6] Arthur D. Elliot, *The Life of the First Viscount Goschen* (London, 1911), I, 115–18. Sir William Clowes's famous work, *The Royal Navy: A History from the Earliest Times to the Present* (London, 1903), in a chapter on the "Military History of the Royal Navy, 1857–1900," suggests the nature of the duties and dispersal of the Royal Navy most clearly. He discusses the topic under the following headings: the Second China War, the Indian Mutiny, the Tai Ping Rebellion, the New Zealand War, Difficulties in Japan, the Ashantee War, Troubles in the Malay Peninsula, Troubles in South Africa, Bombardment of Alexandria, War with the Mahdi, the Conquest of Burmah. (Vol. VII, 91ff.)
[7] Vice Admiral Humphrey H. Smith, *A Yellow Admiral Remembers* (London, 1932), p. 54.

raids of the labor recruiting vessels in the "blackbirding" traffic in the South Seas, and to hunt down pirates in Asian waters.

A variety of reasons may be advanced to explain the apparent indifference to strategic principles suggested by this picture. But one fact overwhelmingly emerges. It is that the absence of any sustained naval threat to British sea supremacy in European waters made this dispersal of effort possible. For despite the occasional and recurring fears of invasion that swept over the British mind during the nineteenth century—largely based upon some naval innovation adopted or reputedly adopted by France—no European power seriously threatened Britain's mastery of the seas.

Even so, the invasion fears did point up the loose grasp of principles of naval warfare in the British official mind. There was a basic lack of understanding of the role of sea-power in the defense of the British Isles, a lack of secure faith in the capabilities of naval strength to defend the shores of Britain. This might be understandable among politicians, such as Palmerston, who feared that steam had bridged the Channel. But the war scare of 1859 revealed similar sentiments among naval officers. It was a naval officer, Captain Astley Cooper Key, who raised the cry of alarm and reported that the defenses of Portsmouth were inadequate to prevent the bombardment of the naval dockyard there "in the absence of our fleet." The assumption by a naval officer that the fleet might be absent from the place where it was needed was of course heresy of the first degree. But Captain Key compounded the offense, and significantly so, by joining in the recommendations of a Royal Commission to strengthen the defenses of the south coast by spending some £11,000,000 on the construction of land fortifications. The report of the commission stated that since the application of steam to the propulsion of vessels, "we can no longer rely upon being able to prevent the landing of a hostile force in the country."[8] Britain, the commission opined, could not be considered secure against invasion if it had to depend for its defense on the fleet alone.

Captain Key was not alone among officers of the naval service in accepting this report. Rear Admiral George Elliot, also a member of the commission, endorsed its report; and testimony given by several other ranking officers of the Navy showed that some of them accepted at least the possibility that the fleet might be absent from the place where invasion threatened.[9] It is a striking commentary that officers of the naval service should have placed their faith in "bricks and mortar" instead of

[8] Parl. Pap. 1860, Vol. XXIII (2682), p. x.
[9] Ibid., p. 323; Philip Colomb, Memoirs of Admiral the Right Honble. Sir Astley Cooper Key (London, 1898), ch. XIV passim.

fighting ships. Of the group associated with the commission, it is note-worthy that Captain Key later rose high in the service and closed his career as First Sea Lord during the eighteen-eighties.

If there was apparently no firm grasp of the principles of naval warfare and its effective use, this was in part due to the lack of any clear formula-tion or statement of such principles. Nineteenth-century naval warfare had no Jomini or Clausewitz to draw up a statement of creed to which honest naval men, when in doubt, might repair for instruction and guidance. It was, of course, not until late in the century that the name of Mahan emerged and acquired such authority that simply to mention it was to still all doubts about the dominant role of sea power in determin-ing the destinies of nations. Mahan himself commented on the lack of effective statements of principles of naval strategy, saying that prior to his lectures to the United States Naval War College, "reliance for princi-ples had to be entirely on works devoted to land strategy."[10]

Nor was the place of formal instruction filled by any lessons taught by "that most excellent instructor," war. To be sure, it was during the Napoleonic wars that the principles of naval warfare had been learned by British sea officers. But they were denied the "advantage" of such in-struction in the generally piping times of peace which followed, and lessons once learned were lost in the mists of memory. It is true that for decades positions of command in the Royal Navy were held by those who had served under Nelson.[11] Yet this made little difference. Old men forget.

The lack of instruction either from formal treatises or the school of experience applied to all naval forces. But there were other factors, some perhaps peculiar to the Royal Navy, which explain the widespread doubt and perplexity concerning principles of naval strategy. British naval authorities were slow to accept the idea that the naval officer was a full-time professional. In the early part of the century, many more officers held the King's commission than there were "posts" for them to fill, with the result that large numbers of them spent more than half of their span of working years at half-pay "on the beach." Adoption of an effective promotion system leading to something akin to adequate retirement pay came belatedly to British naval officers, and a "half-pay, hostilities only" officer was not likely to be the most effective student of the higher strategy.[12]

[10] Alfred T. Mahan, *Naval Strategy* (Boston, 1911), p. 12.
[11] John Fisher entered the Royal Navy in 1854 on the nomination of Admiral Sir William Parker, who had been one of Nelson's captains. Lt. Com. P. K. Kemp (ed.), *The Papers of Admiral Sir John Fisher* (London, 1960), I, xiii.
[12] Bartlett, *Great Britain and Sea Power, 1815–1853*, pp. 44–47, 316–18, 336.

In the Royal Navy, also, there was delay in accepting the place of formal education in the training of the future naval officer. For a large part of the century Britain had no equivalent of the United States Naval Academy, which had been founded in the eighteen-forties; in the British navy, therefore, "on-the-job training" at sea formed the major portion of the education of the naval cadet. The emphasis of that training was naturally on the practical aspects of the naval career, and it did little to encourage the naval tyro to win the approval of his superiors by study of principles of strategy. According to Admiral Humphrey H. Smith, "The general tendency of our training was to turn each ship and squadron into an efficient unit, without considering how these units should be used in time of war. Probably we thought that if war came, common sense would come again to our assistance as it had always come before, and that the cultivation of war doctrines in peace time might cramp individual initiative in war time . . . ."[13]

Smith cites the reliance on common sense. That, plus dash and courage, the "Nelson touch," and "bulldog breed" and "hearts of oak" tradition, with some mathematics on the side, were accounted sufficient to pull the naval officer through such trials as might confront him during his professional life. Under the impelling thrust of the swiftly changing naval technology, the theoretical content of naval education increased by the end of the century. On the whole, however, a notable lack of training in the philosophy of naval warfare remained. In 1899, the First Lord, Goschen, admitted that no effort was made to teach the elementary principles of naval science.[14] And according to a modern naval historian, "The naval officer knew how to fight a fleet action but had only very hazy ideas on how to conduct a war."[15]

This continuing deficiency must surely be ascribed in part to the bewildering changes occurring in naval technology. The increasing skills of the industrial age were moving into naval development, transforming it not once but over and over again during the course of the century. It was a mind-straining task to keep pace with a science and technology that had things constantly astir. Iron-clads replaced wooden walls, then iron ships the iron-clads, and iron ships in their turn gave way to steel. Sail was replaced by steam, and the steam was harnessed first to the paddle wheel and then to the screw. Round shot yielded to shell; and the torpedo was developed at a time when some officers still regarded the ram as an arbiter of naval conflict. Advocates of muzzle loading disputed advocates of breech loading—and while the argument went on, the guns grew heavier,

[13] Smith, *A Yellow Admiral Remembers*, p. 54.
[14] Arthur Marder, *The Anatomy of British Sea Power* (New York, 1940), p. 389.
[15] Russell Grenfell, *Sea Power* (London, 1941), p. 13.

their range longer, and their fire more accurate. Jomini might have claimed that changes in weapons affect practice and not principles, but in the midst of all the swirling currents of change in naval weapons it was easy to forget such aphorisms and to be thrown off balance by each innovation, especially since there was little effort to keep the principles clearly in mind.

In the prevailing uncertainty, one of the most fundamental precepts of sea power was forgotten: the idea that the sea is one, and that anything which tends to localize naval power robs it of the global mobility which is one of its essential strengths. Contrary to this principle, naval force tended to be attached to particular stations, ships designed for special services, vessels tied to particular coasts, and the strength of naval power scattered and fragmented.

Some of this fragmentation arose from the new technology. The limited operating range of the new steam-powered vessels, and their dependence on abundant coal supplies, limited the mobility of the ships. As one historian has pointed out, "When sails were abandoned, dependence on fuel bases became absolute."[16] The first completely sail-less British war vessel had a range of only 5,000 knots—some of its successors even less— and it must be borne in mind that for effective fighting, with the greater fuel consumption, the actual steaming range of warships was a great deal less than their theoretical optimum.

Further restrictions were placed upon the movement of the new ships by the greater complexity of their structure and the consequent need for a high level of skill, and a great complex of tools, materials and machines for their repair or periodic overhaul. The relatively simple skills sufficient in the past to keep sailing ships at sea for months no longer sufficed. Elaborate and costly installations had to be available for the maintenance of the vessels of the Royal Navy scattered all over the globe, for it was manifestly impossible for its ships to be constantly returning to British yards for repair. Yet there could be, after all, only a limited number of such installations, and ships could never be too remote from them.

In addition to the technical factors, there were political pressures for localization of naval forces. The very nature of the Empire, with its distribution of centers of political power, meant that there were governments able to voice demands for the retention of vessels in local waters as defense against possible commerce raiders. In the debates over the distribution of garrisons, suspicion was frequently expressed that colonies had vested interests to protect in seeking the retention of the forces; this argument was no less applicable to naval power.

[16] Bernard Brodie, *Sea Power in the Machine Age* (Princeton, 1941), p. 111.

The varied duties entrusted to the navy also contributed to localization, for they built up a sense of specialization which was partially reflected in naval building. Gunboats, for example, were a doubtful addition to the fighting strength of the navy, but they were most useful for the discharge of police duties. In the presentation of the Navy Estimates in 1881, G. O. Trevelyan, Financial Secretary of the Admiralty, told the Commons, "The call for gun-boats is incessant from the Foreign Office, from the British residents in ports abroad, who like the sense of security they feel at the sight of the British flag, and from other quarters where, without being bound by the ties of Treaty or even nationality, we are urged to yield assistance by the claims of humanity."[17] And outrage over the atrocities associated with the labor traffic in the Pacific led to the demand by Earl Belmore in the Lords in 1872 that the existing vessels on the Australian station be replaced by some more suitable for police work among the islands.[18]

In the second Disraeli Government, W. H. Smith was the "ruler of the Queen's Navee." In his first presentation of naval estimates to the Commons he spoke of the varied duties of the navy. Its ships were scattered all over the globe and subject to many contingencies. A ship useful in the Pacific might not be so in the Mediterranean, and one of service in the Atlantic might not be effective in the China Seas. "We require [he said] vessels which differ widely from one another, but all of which have some use and some purpose for the work they are intended to discharge."[19] The doubtful battle usefulness of such construction was pointed out by that informed and interested M.P., Thomas Brassey. He urged that the vessels constructed for the Royal Navy should be able to support and sustain each other in action; that they should be able to form effective fleet units around such larger fighting ships as the *Devastation*. But even he in effect conceded that the navy was in part an agglomeration of vessels built not around the central purpose of assuring mastery of the seas, but rather around a variety of purposes: coastal warfare around the British Isles, oceanic warfare, and protection of commerce.[20]

The concern for protection of commerce made it easy to fall into a defensive concept of naval strategy. The example of the *Alabama* was for a while much to the fore, and its depredations against Union shipping raised the fear that enemy shipping might cut the food lifelines which sustained the population of Britain. And as the memory of the *Alabama* faded, the advocacy of the *guerre de course* by some French naval theoreticians kept the fears alive. But as the foremost student of British naval

[17] *Hansard*, 3d series, CCLIX, 1392–93, March 18, 1881.
[18] *Ibid.*, CCXII, 89, June 24, 1872.
[19] *Ibid.*, CCXXXVIII, 1415, March 15, 1878.
[20] *Ibid.*, 1094–95, March 11, 1878.

policy during the later nineteenth century clearly suggests, no effective answer to the threat of irruptions into the lines of British commerce was ever formulated. Many of the solutions were of an essentially defensive nature—not the dogged hunting down of every single last enemy cruiser which might appear, but the patrolling of the sea lanes, or the distribution of cruiser squadrons at focal points of ship movement to furnish protection at the places likeliest to offer enemy raiders an abundance of victims.[21]

The influences leading to the localization of naval forces throughout the world were reinforced by the ideas of those who sought the larger participation of self-governing colonies in their own defense. This is suggested by the passage in 1865 of the Colonial Naval Defence Act, which was designed to permit such colonies to acquire and maintain ships of war and to recruit forces to man and operate them. Sponsors of such legislation urged it chiefly for the economies they though it would bring about; there seemed to be no strategic motive behind it, no idea of freeing the vessels of the Royal Navy for greater mobility.

The colonies were in no hurry to avail themselves of their new privileges. Despite the fact that the Act was couched in general terms, conditions made it more particularly applicable to the Australasian colonies than to any of the others. Canada certainly felt no need for any naval vessels of its own, for she was close enough to the heart of British naval power to be assured of its protective strength. And even had she wanted to engage in naval building or operations for protection against the United States in the region of the Great Lakes, treaty arrangements precluded that. So it was only in the southern hemisphere, among the Australasian colonies, that the Colonial Naval Act was likely to lead to any colonial maritime activity. There the sense of isolation, and the consciousness of the length of the lines of communication which connected them with Britain, might prompt some of the colonies to action.

Victoria, a colony so often foremost in her interest in defense matters, had already acquired a sloop of war, the *Victoria*, which had seen useful service in some of the Maori wars. The other Australasian colonies were content to leave naval matters to the Royal Navy. Yet however little might be done under the terms of the Colonial Naval Defence Act, its very existence, based on the well-known concern for colonial self-reliance in defense, tended to encourage the idea that sea defenses were something that might reasonably be tied to a particular coastline or sea frontier.

And there was further support for this in the acceptance of a subsidy of £70,000 from the government of India for the support of the naval forces in the bay of Bengal and the Arabian Gulf. The payment was

---

[21] Marder, *The Anatomy of British Sea Power*, ch. 4, *passim*.

established on the basis of a capitation fee of £70 per annum, based on the average number of men kept on service in the two areas mentioned north of a line drawn from Cape Guardafui to Ceylon and the Straits Settlements. India was to pay for the maintenance of a naval force essentially local in character, a successor force to the old Bombay Marine of the East India Company.[22]

The Colonial Naval Defence Act, and the negotiation for the subsidy from the Indian government, both of which reinforced, in colonial minds at any rate, the idea that naval defense was a local matter, were the works of Whig-Liberal governments. They can legitimately be regarded as part of a general naval policy that was a counterpart of the policy pursued with regard to the imperial garrisons. The withdrawal of the garrisons, the acceptance of naval subsidies from dependent governments, and the passage of the Colonial Naval Defence Act were all designed to ease the demands upon the British Treasury. But it should be noted in passing that there was no consistency in the effects to which these various courses of action tended. For whereas the withdrawal of the garrisons freed British soldiers for service elsewhere, the acceptance of naval subsidies had the opposite effect of tying down naval forces in waters adjacent to the colony granting the subsidy. And while the Colonial Naval Defence Act encouraged colonial governments to man and operate war craft, however small, in their own defense, the acceptance of subsidies had the effect of giving dependent governments the chance to hire the services of the Royal Navy, and this would hardly tend to encourage self-reliance.

With the coming of the first Gladstone Government, a new trend was discernible in British naval policy. H. T. Lowry Corry, First Lord during the preceding Disraeli Administration, had defended the policy of maintaining a large portion of the navy in foreign stations, and he later said that he did not see how an empire on which the sun never set could be defended by ships of war stationed mainly between the Foreland and Cape Clear.[23] But Gladstone thought otherwise. In his comments on naval defense to the Commons on August 1, 1870, at a time when British fears were aroused by the events of the Franco-Prussian War, he asked,

What is the use of a system of naval defence which dots your vessels of war over the whole globe, multiplying occasions of difference, of quarrel, of danger and of conflict, into which Parliament finds itself hurried by the act of some subordinate agent abroad, but which would never have been accepted on recommendation of a Cabinet? What is the use for the purpose of defending these shores, and of enabling you to assert the dignity of the United Kingdom, at a great European crisis, of that sporadic system which enables you, if you

[22] *Hansard*, 3d series, CXCIV, 885–86, March 8, 1869.
[23] *Ibid.*, CXCII, 36–37, March 11, 1868; CCVIII, 1148, Aug. 8, 1871.

think fit, to vaunt your strength in those parts of the world where the flags of the Queen's ships may be flying, but which, instead of adding anything, actually deducts from the real strength and energy of the country.[24]

And the chief Liberal naval spokesman, Hugh Childers, condemned the frittering away of naval strength on foreign stations, urging instead that there be a flying squadron stationed near Lisbon. This would be capable of hastening to any part of the Empire in need of stronger naval forces, and would be coupled with a withdrawal of some of the ships scattered about the globe on foreign stations.

Corry opposed the suggestion of the flying squadron. He stood by the existing distribution of naval vessels, arguing that it permitted the more immediate use of British sea-power where trouble was likely to break out. He also maintained that there was a continuing need for the widest possible distribution of British ships in order to give protection to British commerce.[25] But the Liberal victory at the polls in 1868 gave opportunity for the initiation of a program of retrenchment in expenditure and for reform in the distribution of naval vessels.

Hugh Childers, First Lord during the early part of the administration before ill-health forced his retirement, inaugurated what one of his civil service subordinates, John H. Briggs, Chief Clerk of the Admiralty, regarded as a memorable administration.[26] Prior to Childers, Briggs commented, "little or no attention had been paid to the composition and distribution of the fleet. Such matters were largely controlled by routine. At the expiration of three years ships were relieved, as a matter of course, by vessels of exactly the same type . . . . "[27] Briggs prepared for Childers a memorandum regarding naval policy which sounded the authentic note of sea-power, and which fitted in admirably with the policy of the withdrawal of ships and men from some of the overseas stations. "Success in war," Briggs urged, "depends upon the concentration of an overpowering force upon a given spot in the shortest possible time . . . . "[28]

In his first speech as First Lord on the subject of the naval estimates in March, 1869, Childers said that he planned a redistribution of vessels on foreign stations and the creation of the flying squadron which he had advocated before taking office.[29] It was disclosed later that the government had resolved upon the reduction of the naval manpower attached to foreign stations from the existing total of slightly over 17,000 to 11,000.

[24] *Ibid.*, CCIII, 1309, Aug. 1, 1870.
[25] *Ibid.*, CLXXXVI, 343, March 2, 1867; 969, April 1, 1867.
[26] John Henry Briggs, *Naval Administrations, 1827–1892* (London, 1892), p. 162.
[27] *Ibid.*
[28] *Ibid.*, p. 181.
[29] *Hansard*, 3d series, CXCIV, 885–86, March 8, 1869.

At the time Childers presented his second estimates to the House, that objective had been fully achieved. The number of men on foreign stations was down to 11,500 and the Indian government was paying for 400 of the 1,200 on the East Indian Station. But the limit of reduction had been reached; the demands on the navy allowed no further diminution. The slave trade was apparently increasing off the east coast of Africa, and a larger force was needed on the Australian Station because of the increase in blackbirding traffic among the islands of the South Pacific.[30]

The events of the Franco-Prussian War partly defeated the hopes of Gladstone and his associates for a reduction of armament expenditure. But when an extra £1,000,000 was voted for naval defense, the bulk of it was spent on the improvement of naval defenses based on the British Isles,[31] for the war reinforced Gladstone's belief in the desirability of greater concentration of naval power in British waters. He wrote to Viscount Goschen, who succeeded Childers as First Lord on the latter's retirement in 1871, "That for which I have been disposed to contend is that we are to have a powerful fleet in and near our own waters, and that outside of this nothing is to be maintained except for well-defined and approved purposes of actual service, and in quantities of force properly adjusted; and not under the notion that there are to be fleets in the various quarters of the world ready when a difficulty arises with a foreign country, or an offence to our ships, *then and there* [Gladstone's italics] to deal with it with a strong hand."[32]

If this statement had been strictly applied, it might have meant even the elimination of Childers' cherished flying squadron, whose terms of actual service were somewhat ill-defined. For under the policy as sketched by the Prime Minister, there would be no British sea-power outside the waters of the British Isles save those various vessels specially detached for such specific service as the suppression of the slave trade and the apprehension of the blackbirder. The statement never became policy, but it does show the trend of Gladstone's thinking.

The concentration of British naval power in European waters favored by Gladstone suggests the later concentration brought about by German naval rivalry. With Gladstone, of course, no such motive was involved. He wanted concentration for reasons of economy, and he wanted to keep his naval commanders on a shorter rein so that he would have a tighter grip on events and policies. Gladstone shared Cobden's distaste for the possibility that two drunken naval captains of frigates in the Antipodes might cause war between European powers.

[30] *Ibid.*, CC, 854–56, March 29, 1870.
[31] *Ibid.*, CCX, 429, March 21, 1872.
[32] Elliot, *The Life of the First Viscount Goschen*, I, 119, Gladstone to Goschen, Sept. 23, 1871.

But there were signs that after long years of sterility in defense thinking, a new spirit of inquiry was stirring. Attention began to be paid to ideas other than those emphasizing simply greater colonial self-reliance and therefore larger economies for the British taxpayer.[33] In part, these new stirrings of interest in an imperial defense strategy came from the growing dependency of Britain on imported supplies of food. The adoption of free trade, the growth of the world's network of transportation, the opening of the great new areas of extensive farming on the frontier fringes of Canada, the United States, Australia, and similar lands, were rapidly bringing the day when two out of every three loaves of bread baked in the British Isles would be made from imported grain. Any interruption of the flow of foodstuffs and raw materials to Great Britain would certainly cripple her, and if prolonged, defeat her in war. The sea lanes over which the increasing number of British merchant vessels moved were more than the highways of commerce; they were the lifelines of Britain. Gladstone might insist that the true strength of Britain lay with Britain herself, and not in the prolific scattering of blotches of imperial red over the globe, but this was true only as long as the world's shipping moved unimpeded in and out of the harbors of the United Kingdom. And it was the task of the Admiralty and the War Office, but especially the former, to furnish security for that shipping.

In the light of the depredations of the *Alabama* and the *Shenandoah* against Northern commerce during the American Civil War, there were those who claimed that no effective protection could be maintained. Voices of despair said that in time of war it was impossible to make the flow of food and raw materials to Britain secure by naval protection. Britain, they said, would have to resort to a massive shift of her vessels to foreign registry; she would have to depend upon regard for treaties to give wartime security to vessels engaged in peaceful commerce; she would have to adopt war risk insurance before shipping owners would venture to send their property to sea.

The ideas of the *Jeune École* of naval strategists in France encouraged the growth of these counsels of despair. Impressed by the success of the

---

[33] As to self-reliance, British governments did not always practice what they preached. The use of troops of the Indian army in the campaign in Abyssinia in 1868 was charged on the Indian budget, despite the fact that the cause of the campaign was concern for the safety of the envoys of European powers in the Emperor Theodore's land. When Sir John Lawrence, Viceroy of India, protested that India should not have to pay for the troops when they were on British service, Sir Stafford Northcote, Secretary of State for India, replied that India had many reasons to support the doctrine of the inviolability of envoys, surrounded as she was by barbaric states with which she had to have dealings. And if there were to be a strict accounting of costs, Northcote commented that India might be charged with the costs of a portion of the Royal Navy. Perhaps this presaged the later negotiations for the annual payment of £70,000 which the Indian government agreed to pay. Andrew Lang, *Life of Sir Stafford Northcote* (London, 1890), I, 309–11.

Confederate commerce raiders, the advocates of this doctrine maintained that the naval war of the future would be a war of ruthless commerce destruction, carried out by swift cruisers in the open waters and by torpedo boats in the narrow seas. Battleships would be useless to combat this menace and were therefore obsolete. Even the Admiralty absorbed enough of this to speak of further battleship construction in apologetic voice. In 1881, G. O. Trevelyan, Parliamentary Secretary to the Admiralty, expressed hostility to any further construction of large ships, not only on the ground of costs, but also because in the days of rams and torpedoes it was dangerous to put too many eggs in one battleship. Sir John Hay, former Admiralty official, agreed that "very large ships were of little use whatever . . . ."[34]

Another factor working to bring the problems of imperial strategy and defense to the fore was the influence of an ex-officer of the Royal Marine Artillery, John Colomb. Colomb devoted much of his life to the arousing of interest in defense problems and to the advocacy of what he regarded as sound principles of defense. In this he was seconded and supported by his brother, Admiral Sir Philip Colomb. The latter favored ideas of sea power which paralleled in many ways those of Mahan. Philip Colomb acknowledged his indebtedness for much of his thought to his brother.[35]

Perhaps it was his service in the Marine Artillery which kept John Colomb's approach to the problems of imperial defense free from too strong a dedication to the viewpoint of any one service. Certainly he took a broader view of these matters than was common at the time. Critical of the existing attitudes, he felt that there had been too great a growth of a purely military spirit in Britain, and that the army and military affairs generally attracted too much attention, to the detriment of the needs of the navy and of imperial defense. But the navy, he believed, had also been neglectful of general principles; it had made no effort to determine such principles and to make its strategic dispositions accordingly.[36]

In 1867, Colomb published a pamphlet, *The Protection of our Commerce and Distribution of our Naval Forces*, in which he listed the security priorities of Britain as the protection of the United Kingdom, the protection of British commerce at sea, and the occupation of India. As for areas of empire other than India, they had to defend themselves unless they were

---

[34] *Hansard*, 3d series, CCLXV, 58–61, Aug. 16, 1881. For a statement of the ideas of the *Jeune Ecole*, see Theodore Ropp, "Continental Doctrines of Sea Power," in Edward Mead Earle (ed.), *Makers of Modern Strategy* (Princeton, 1948), pp. 446–56.

[35] An important London newspaper stated in its obituary notice of John Colomb that he was the father of modern English naval strategy, and a pioneer in the field of imperial defense. *The Morning Post* (London), May 28, 1909.

[36] Colomb, *The Defence of Great and Greater Britain*, pp. 15–18.

to be regarded as military positions necessary to hold for the general welfare of the Empire.[37]

Colomb placed the weight of his arguments on the need to protect the lines of commerce and communication which bound the Empire together; Britain could be defeated as much by investment as through invasion by foreign armies. But for a later staunch advocate of sea power doctrines, he got off to a rocky start in his early writings. He was not a true "blue water" advocate. The fleet alone was not sufficient to protect Britain. True, the vessels bringing the products of the world to Britain could be secured in their passage through the Channel by British naval forces. But this did not preclude the possibility that these same ships might be attacked and destroyed in United Kingdom ports. Hence, the defense of the ports of Britain and of the Empire could not be left to sea-power alone, for the fleet might be absent at a critical time. What was needed were harbor defense vessels so designed that they could not be put off to sea; if they could not leave the port they were sure to be available when needed. Further, such vessels would release sea-going ships for free and unfettered action on the open seas.

In addition to arguing for the construction of harbor defense fortifications and vessels, Colomb also envisaged the need for a wide variety of types among the sea-going ships of the Navy. "The sea-going vessels adapted for the Channel and Mediterranean form a separate class; ships suitable for general service must be altogether different."[38]

At this stage of his thought, Colomb was certainly among those for whom "the ability of fast steamers to strike at isolated, vulnerable points was too often allowed to obscure the fact that overall command of the sea was the decisive consideration in imperial defence."[39]

In his later writings, Colomb abandoned the defensive doctrines of his first efforts in strategic analysis. In a speech to the Royal Colonial Institute in June, 1873, he maintained that forces existing for the defense of one portion of the Empire should not be so constituted as to preclude their employment elsewhere.[40] As to the role which colonies might play in imperial defense, Colomb urged that this determination might be the duty of a Royal Commission. He felt there was need for such a commission to consider the defense of imperial communications, and that this might well lead to a consideration of the just limit of imperial and colonial

[37] John Colomb, *The Protection of our Commerce and Distribution of our Naval Forces* (London, 1867), p. vi.
[38] *Ibid.*, pp. 12–24.
[39] Bartlett, *Great Britain and Sea Power, 1815–1853*, p. 246, note 4.
[40] John Colomb, "On Colonial Defence," Paper read to Royal Colonial Institute, June 28, 1873, p. 8.

responsibilities in defense. Further, from such consideration might come a scheme for the federation of the war forces of the Empire.[41]

Most important in Colomb's approach was, of course, his treatment of the Empire not as a group of disparate units, but as an interdependent complex of communities. Hitherto, discussion about defense had tended to fall into two separate categories: national defense (defense of the British Isles) and colonial defense. But the increasing dependence of British life on an uninterrupted flow of imports made any such division obsolete. National defense required a steady flow of needed supplies into the British Isles; but the protective screen of naval power necessary to maintain such imports would also furnish security from external attack for many colonial areas, Canada and India being the notable exceptions. Imperial defense embraced both the United Kingdom and the terminal points of the long lines of imperial communications. A firm grasp of these was the essence of defense.

Colomb's work was but one factor in bringing about a reappraisal of British ideas on imperial strategy; the use of troops from the Empire was another. There had been frequent occasions in the past when the widespread distribution of British troops on garrison duty throughout the world had proved to be a very present help. Troops from the Gibraltar garrison had been dispatched to Portugal at the inception of the Peninsular war. During the Indian Mutiny, forces had been sent to India from the garrisons in the Cape, Mauritius, and Australia. The force which had invaded Ethiopia in 1869 under Napier had been composed largely of troops from the Indian establishment. Some of the forces used in the Maori wars in New Zealand had come from the garrisons across the Tasman Sea in Australia. Indeed, so useful had these available reinforcements been in the past that Earl Grey, who had done so much to inaugurate the withdrawal and diminution of these forces, eventually stated that he felt the process had gone too far.[42]

But it was Benjamin Disraeli who made the most spectacular use of the military resources of the Empire when, in the midst of the crisis with Russia in 1878, he reinforced the garrison in Malta with substantial drafts of troops from India. The movement of these forces to the Mediterranean was announced while the jingo spirit was running high throughout Britain, but not so high as to cost the British their sense of humor. The jingo boast was twisted to meet the new vistas of imperial power thus revealed:

[41] *Ibid.*, p. 23.
[42] *Hansard*, 3d series, CCXXIV, 1115–16, May 31, 1875.

We don't want to fight,
But, by jingo, if we do,
We'll stay at home and sing our songs
And send the mild Hindoo.[43]

The announcement of the troop movement to Malta came while Parliament was in recess, but when the parliamentarians assembled vigorous debate broke out over many aspects of the maneuver. The use by the Crown in European affairs of military forces which were not within the controls of the annual Mutiny Act aroused the constitutional hackles of many of the Opposition and provoked a storm of criticism in both Houses. The Opposition charged that it was unconstitutional both in law and in spirit to go beyond the limits of the armed forces set in the Mutiny Act and in the passage of the army estimates. The numbers of the Indian army were not limited by the permanent Mutiny Act, and there were fears that the size of the force might be increased to permit the introduction of anywhere from 70,000 to 250,000 Indian troops from India into Europe to influence the course of European affairs, a prospect which provoked ministerial cheers.

The debate over the troop movement lasted three nights, with ample citation of precedent and law from both sides of the two houses. The essence of the government's argument was that there existed and had existed for some time a variety of forces under the Crown, forces which did not fall within the scope of the Mutiny Act. There were forces of colonial governments, forces of the Crown in India, forces of princely India. It was part of the prerogative of the Crown to move these forces, with the exception of those maintained by colonies with responsible government, from one part of the Queen's dominions to another. Of the forces of the colonial governments, Sir Michael Hicks-Beach, Colonial Secretary, said they were likely to expand for defense against any possible attack from the enemies of the Empire. He described them as liable for service not only in the colonies which raised and maintained them, but also for dispatch and service outside the colony according to regulations which might be drawn up by the Governor.[44]

The crisis of 1878–79 brought other actions affecting imperial defense besides the transfer of the Indian forces to the Mediterranean and the subsequent debate. Fear was expressed that a squadron of Russian war vessels could have found such ports as the Cape and Simons Bay without

[43] Sir Henry Lucy, *A Diary of Two Parliaments* (London, 1885–86), I, 419.

[44] *Hansard*, 3d series, CCXL, 288, May 20, 1878. For debate on the use of the Indian troops, see *Ibid.*, passim. There is an interesting parallel between the debate over the use of Indian troops and that concerning the employment of Hessian forces during the American Revolution. The latter is found in Cobbett's *Parliamentary History*, XVIII, *passim*.

adequate defense and, with coal seized from these ports, could have gone on to create even further damage—damage not only to British shipping, but also to the submarine cables, which were an essential part of the network of imperial communications. Anxieties about such possible depredations—there were 70,000 tons of coal at Singapore without protection—led to the formation of a small professional committee to consider pressing requirements of defense works in the more important colonial harbors and coaling stations. This was an *ad hoc* committee whose work was intended to be only temporary, and its life ended with the passing of the crisis. Two of its members recommended the creation of a permanent and more powerful committee, but this was not done at the moment.[45]

Hicks-Beach did bring about the creation of a Royal Commission to inquire into and consider the state of the defenses of British commerce and possessions abroad. Put in these general terms, the assignment given to this commission did not perhaps differ greatly from that which had been assumed by the members of the Mills Committee some years before. But the atmosphere had greatly changed meanwhile. The trend of events and thought since the time of the Mills report and the subsequent resolution had been running strongly against the "peace and retrenchment," free-trade liberal philosophy that had then been in the ascendant. Two new states had been created in Europe, mainly by means of war, and the British imperial connection, which some had thought was on the verge of disintegration, had shown a surprising longevity and vitality. A major political party through its leaders had openly espoused the cause of imperialism. Little of the supposed colonial ambition for separation and independence had manifested itself; indeed, colonists had taken a leading role in the founding of the Colonial Institute, a new rallying point for those interested in and concerned for the strengthening of the imperial connection. Europe, and Britain with it, stood at the beginning of a new age of imperialism when the new Royal Commission was established.

Hicks-Beach, after consultation with the War Office and Admiralty, and with the assent of the Cabinet, asked Lord Carnarvon, his predecessor in the Colonial Office, to be chairman of the proposed commission.[46] And since the labors of the commission were to be concerned with questions vitally affecting the colonies, the matter of colonial representation arose. Hicks-Beach suggested that any recommendations made by the commission were more likely to be accepted if some outstanding colonial

---

[45] John Ehrman, *Cabinet Government and War, 1890–1940* (Cambridge, 1958), p. 9.
[46] PRO, 30/6/52, Hicks-Beach to Carnarvon, July 26, 1879.

leader—he suggested such names as Sir Alexander Galt of Canada and Sir Julius Vogel of New Zealand—were a member of the group. If the selection of colonial representatives were rightly handled, he thought, the work of the commission might have some political effect, as representing the Empire.[47] However, no colonial representative was appointed and the murmurings caused by that failure, reported by Sir Henry Holland, a member of the commission, did not change the situation.[48]

Captain John Colomb wanted to be a member of the commission. He called on Carnarvon to push his claims, and Carnarvon reported that Colomb had been canvassing others in his own support. Carnarvon thought that he might make a useful witness, but Hicks-Beach certainly did not want Colomb for he regarded him as "pushing" and "mischievous."[49]

The membership of the commission when finally completed included Carnarvon, Childers, Sir Henry Holland, and the three professional members of the *ad hoc* body of the previous year: Sir Alexander Milne of the Admiralty, Sir Lintorn Simmons of the War Office, and Sir Henry Barkly, an old professional as a colonial governor, representing the Colonial Office interest. Thomas Brassey, M.P., and R. G. C. Hamilton completed the roster of the members. The latter represented the "Treasury interest" in the matter; he was Accountant General of the Royal Navy.

The work of the commission was interrupted by the change of government resulting from the election of 1880, and though there was some question as to whether its continuation was desired by the new Gladstone Administration, the commission continued with its work. When Childers and Brassey resigned, the new Colonial Secretary, Lord Kimberley, placed two of his own nominees on the commission: the Earl of Camperdown and Samuel Whitbread, the well-known brewer and political figure of liberal persuasion.

It had been thought at first that the commission might consider the state of defenses of the United Kingdom. But this was struck from its agenda, as was its consideration of what were termed the imperial garrisons of Malta, Bermuda, Halifax, and Gibraltar. These decisions naturably made the field of the commission's labors somewhat more colonial or imperial in character.

The three reports of the Royal Commission have been described as "voluminous" and "searching" by a leading British student of imperial

---

[47] *Ibid.*, Hicks-Beach to Carnarvon, Aug. 12, 1879.
[48] *Ibid.*, Holland to Carnarvon, Oct. 30, 1879.
[49] *Ibid.*, Hicks-Beach to Carnarvon, Sept. 12, 1879. Colomb later wrote *The Defence of Great and Greater Britain* as a supplement to the work of the commission.

defense.[50] The first report dealt mainly with the value of the commerce in which Britain and the colonies had an interest, and included a discussion of the defenses of the Cape and the armaments needed there. The second was concerned with the defense of the trade routes and the ways in which Britain and the colonies might contribute to this defense. The third centered largely about the problem of defense of the Australasian colonies.

On the matter of defense of trade routes, the report pointed out that command of the sea depended largely upon the maintenance of coal supplies. An enemy might get coal from his own or allied ports, from neutral ports, or from stock captured in British colonial ports or ships taken at sea. As for the Royal Navy, the greater the number of coaling ports at its disposal, and the more widespread their distribution, the greater the advantage. But it could not be the responsibility of the Royal Navy to stand guard over the entrance to each of these ports. Port facilities were there to assist the ships of the navy to function on the high seas, not to tie the ships down. The navy had to be free to act at sea. Such ports must therefore rely upon colonial governments for their defense. The commission quoted with approval the suggestion of Sir William Jervois, who had made a report on the state of the defenses of the Australian colonies in 1879: "That whilst the Imperial Navy undertakes the protection of the British mercantile marine generally, and of the highways of communication between the several parts of the Empire, the Australian Colonies themselves provide, at their own cost, the local forces, forts, batteries, and other appliances requisite to the protection of their principal ports."[51]

Yet the commission was not altogether content with this division of responsibility and expense. They thought that some of the richer colonies might "not unreasonably be called upon to assist in some degree in the naval defence of the Empire."[52] There were many objections to colonies owning sea-going vessels of their own. But they could see no objection to colonies making a modest contribution to the support of any naval squadron that was maintained by Britain for the protection of the interests common to the colonies and herself.[53] It would be undesirable that any such contribution should be coupled with any restriction on the free movement of the squadron, or that there be any suggestion that the contributions gave to the contributing colony a voice in the disposition of the vessels. A contribution from the Australian colonies, for example, should

[50] Unpublished and preliminary draft of an article on imperial naval defense by Sir Herbert Richmond, kindly lent to the author by Professor Gerald Graham, Rhodes Professor of Imperial History at the University of London.

[51] Parl. Pap., 1887, Vol. LVI, C5091-I, p. 315.

[52] Ibid.   [53] Ibid., p. 327.

be given as an aid in the defense of Australian commerce, but any hampering of the free movement of the vessels would defeat such a purpose. The members of the commission felt that the spirit of loyalty and the growing prosperity of the colonies would lead them to accept the contribution principle.

Though the commission was strongly opposed to any sort of localization of naval forces, Sir Alexander Milne, the naval member of the group, still expressed concern that some aspects of the commission's recommendations tended too greatly in that direction. He took particular exception to the suggestion that the defense of Ceylon would be dependent upon five separate squadrons based on five separate ports scattered about the periphery of the Indian Ocean. This seemed to imply acceptance of the idea, to him erroneous, that ships were for the defense of ports rather than for the command of the seas.

The commission obtained some colonial opinion with regard to the ways in which the colonies could properly participate in the defense of the Empire. Some eight or nine colonists testified, and some of them, such as Sir John A. Macdonald of Canada and Sir Henry Parkes of New South Wales, were the outstanding leaders of their communities. Macdonald indicated his belief that no common system of defense, embracing all the states of the Empire, could be established; the circumstances affecting the colonies were too various. He felt that Canadians would not feel bound to make large sacrifices in a war which might occur between Great Britain and a European power, since such a war was not likely to arise from disputes in which Canada had any concern. It was far better, he believed, to trust to the patriotism and imperial loyalty of Canadians in time of crisis than to raise hypothetical questions before an exigency arose. To seek grants of men or money in time of peace and without the stimulus of crisis would certainly arouse opposition, and politicians might find themselves bound by statements made in peacetime which in time of emergency they would wish unsaid.[54]

Sir Henry Parkes of the senior Australian colony of New South Wales said that if England were engaged in a war that seemed to commend itself generally to Englishmen, then the colonies would do all within their power to make their resources available for defense. But if the time came when they were to share with England the burdens of defense of empire, then the colonies would claim their share also in the making of policy. As to the sharing of naval defense, Parkes did not think that public opinion was ripe in the Australian colonies for this suggestion. England was expected to protect sea-borne commerce, since this was more important and necessary to Britain than to Australia.[55]

[54] PRO 30/6/126, Third Report, p. 623.   [55] *Ibid.*, pp. 591–94.

Other Australian witnesses were not as hostile to the idea of some form of naval subsidy. Sir Daniel Cooper, of New South Wales, suggested such a subsidy. He felt that it should be free from any ties, and that the Royal Navy should have a free hand in the movement of any vessels which the subsidy might help maintain. Frederick Sargood, the active Defence Minister of Victoria, also supported the subsidy idea. Sir Arthur Blythe of South Australia thought that his colony would fall in with any general understanding which the other Australian colonies might adopt for sharing the burdens of naval defense. He did feel, however, that such an idea would provoke a good deal of debate; it might raise the question of taxation without representation and demands for a voice in the declarations of war.[56]

The commission also asked, through the Colonial Office, for the opinions of various colonial governments as to the state of the defenses of their ports, the raising and maintenance of their local forces, and the amount of naval defense the local officials felt they needed. Reports were generally prepared by local committees, but such committees were frequently manned largely by British naval or military officers seconded to the local forces, or perhaps by personnel of naval vessels which happened to be in the vicinity. For example, the report forwarded from Mauritius was signed by two officers of the Royal Navy, among others, and the names of the same officers were appended to the report prepared in Ceylon. They seemed to constitute a sort of peripatetic committee. In the instance of the Cape, the Ministry said that there were no local officers whose opinion would be of value,[57] and the report was prepared solely by British officers.[58]

The surveys prepared and the recommendations made by these various local committees revealed that in several instances, aside from India's £70,000 annual payment, colonial governments made some monetary contribution to the Imperial treasury. Mauritius paid £70 per annum for each artillery and engineer officer and soldier stationed on the island, and £40 for each infantryman, up to a maximum of £45,000; the government of Singapore paid £50,000 a year to the imperial government for defense services.

The final recommendations of the Royal Commission stressed the paramount importance of safe coaling stations for the defense of the Empire, for there could not be full exertion of the power of the Royal Navy at sea until all the important coal stations had been made secure from attack. The commission made a series of suggestions for the improvement of the

---

[56] PRO 30/6/131, Second Report, pp. 11–21.
[57] PRO 30/6/26, p. 89.
[58] Ibid., pp. 118, 169.

defenses of the key ports and coaling stations, based on the reports obtained through the co-operation of the local committees. These suggestions envisaged substantial contributions by the various local governments to these improvements. The recommendations of the commission apportioned the costs on approximately a one-to-four ratio: slightly over £500,000 to be spent by local governments for barracks, roads, works, telegraphs, and the like, and about £2,000,000 by the imperial government for the same things plus armaments, submarine mines, gun and torpedo boats. In a distinct echo of the opinion of the Mills Committee, the Royal Commission said that the use of imperial troops on duties which were hardly distinguishable from police duties should be ended as soon as practicable, and that local forces should be raised where they were likely to prove trustworthy and efficient.

As to the whole picture of imperial and colonial co-operation on defense, the commission said: "It is not yet possible to define with accuracy the conditions upon which to determine the relative apportionment of the burdens as between the mother-country and her Colonies . . . ."[59] The maintenance of the navy had fallen upon the imperial funds and must for the present continue to do so, whatever the future might hold. But relations between Britain and the colonies as to the general defense of empire must alter from time to time. The capacity of colonies to share in imperial defense would be constantly on the increase. The commission recognized the value of the colonies to Britain, valued and appreciated their loyalty and patriotism, and saw no signs of colonial unwillingness to bear as large a portion of the burden as their strength would enable them to carry. Free and constant communication, if maintained with responsible colonial governments, would contribute to the development of a sense of partnership and mutual dependence.[60]

The creation of the interim committee of 1878, and of the subsequent Royal Commission, were not the only results of the war scare of that year. A sense of alarm existed in many parts of the Empire. In Canada, for example, " . . . wild rumours ran the length and breadth of the country: there was a Russian ship crammed with guns and men cruising off the east coast of Canada ready to bombard Canadian ports and convert merchantmen into armed raiders; a squadron of Russian warships was in San Francisco ready to descend upon the harbours of British Columbia!"[61] The scare stimulated a number of offers of service from Canadians, and also a suggestion from General Patrick MacDougall, commanding the imperial garrison in Halifax. MacDougall urged the

[59] *Ibid.*, p. 338.
[60] PRO 30/6/126, pp. 28–30.
[61] Stanley, *Canada's Soldiers, 1604–1954*, p. 246.

organization of a Canadian military unit for imperial service, which he hoped might inaugurate a *Bund* for the defense of empire, to which Britain and her dependencies might contribute *pro rata*. He thought the offer of such support at a time when India was rendering important service by furnishing troops for the Mediterranean would have peculiar and appropriate significance, and felt it would be feasible to raise some 8,500 men in Canada. The pay was to come from Canada; the arms, clothing and equipment from Britain.[62] MacDougall's suggestion won some support in Whitehall. The Commander in Chief, H.R.H. the Duke of Cambridge, approved the idea, but referred it to the Colonial Office with the suggestion that the views of the Governor General and Cabinet of Canada be sought. Hicks-Beach followed the suggestion, adding that perhaps recruiting for any proposed unit might be helped along if the Canadian government would promise land grants on retirement to those who enlisted.[63]

Lord Dufferin submitted the suggestion to the Canadian government, and a Cabinet committee considered the proposal. It reported that the government would facilitate in every way the formation of a Canadian force under any scheme the imperial authorities deemed best, though the details would have to be approved by the Militia Department. Both the committee of the Cabinet and Major General Edward Selby-Smyth, the officer commanding the Canadian militia, feared that Russian agents might be organizing Fenian raids from below the border. But the whole project, born in the excitement and tensions of the war scare, died with the settlement of affairs at the Congress of Berlin.

The idea of utilizing Canadian manpower was nevertheless kept alive by General MacDougall and the Marquis of Lorne, Dufferin's successor as Governor General of Canada. The latter sent to the Canadian government a memorandum of the General's which called for the creation of an imperial reserve. Troops were to be enrolled for six years of service, armed, clothed, and paid by the imperial government, and liable for service anywhere in the world when summoned. They would receive one month's continuous training each year. John A. Macdonald felt that the experiment was worth a trial.[64] General Selby-Smyth also gave it his support but warned that there was a "Canada for Canadians" feeling, and that imperial officers who might be sent to command any such unit would have only a limited usefulness because of that feeling. Nor must such a reserve seem to relegate the militia to second place in the military affairs of Canada. The militia had influence through both press and

[62] PRO, W.O. 32/120/7696, MacDougall to War Office, April 24, 1878.
[63] *Ibid.*, Hicks-Beach to Dufferin, May 9, 1878.
[64] Canada, Sessional Papers, 1880, Vol. V, #8, pp. 34–35.

parliament that would be used to prevent it from being thrust into any subordinate role.

But whatever the support secured in Canada for the project, it failed on the issue which was to kill many such proposals in various colonies: the issue of control. Hugh Childers, Secretary of State for War in the early period of the second Gladstone Government, raised the objection. Any such force as the proposed reserve would be liable for duty whenever summoned by the imperial government. But how was such a summons to be enforced? Since the British government had no authority in Canada, it would only be enforced by the local Canadian authorities. Would or could any Canadian government, fearful for its three thousand mile frontier, allow the most highly trained and best equipped military unit in the land to leave the country in time of imminent war? Would not the discipline of such a force break under the strain of such conflicting loyalties? But if the force maintained and paid by the imperial government could not be freely employed by the government, of what real value was it? Better to seek to strengthen the existing militia establishment in Canada; the reserve idea was impracticable.[65]

General Selby-Smyth sought to establish a Canadian naval militia in addition to the military forces which he led.[66] His efforts, plus those of Lord Lorne, persuaded the Admiralty in 1880 to lend Canada a sloop of war, HMS *Charybdis*. If this was done with the idea of encouraging the growth of a maritime spirit among Canadians, and of seeking the co-operation of Canada in the naval defense of the Empire, then it was badly done. The *Charybdis* was a decrepit craft which just managed to wheeze its way across the Atlantic. On reaching Canada it was found to be unseaworthy, and was subsequently returned to the Admiralty with precious little thanks. If the Lords Commissioner of the Admiralty were concerned to develop the naval aspirations and imperial loyalty of Canadians, they had to do better than that.[67]

The Australian colonies received somewhat better treatment from the Admiralty than did Canada, perhaps because of the influence of Hugh Childers in the government. When the replacement of the old sloop of war, *Victoria*, became necessary, the Admiralty gave the Victorian government HMS *Nelson* as a training vessel. This old line-of-battle ship had been launched in 1814, but was much reconstructed in later years. It was followed in 1869 by the *Cerberus*, a well-armed vessel which for a period was the most powerful warship in the southern hemisphere. The imperial government gave £100,000 toward the construction costs

[65] PRO, W.O., 32/120/7696, Childers to C.O., Dec. 10, 1880.
[66] Canada, Sessional Papers, 1880, Vol. V, #8, p. 37.
[67] George F. G. Stanley, "The Army Origin of the Royal Canadian Navy," *Journal of the Society for Army Historical Research*, XXXII (Summer, 1954), 69–70.

of the ship. Victoria coupled the acquisition of these vessels with the passage of a Discipline Act in 1870, which required that all persons serving on vessels placed in commission by the Governor of the colony should be subject to the enactments and regulations for discipline in effect in the Royal Navy.[68] Such an act was needed if there was to be any effective co-operation between the ships maintained by the colony, and the ships of the Royal Navy in Australian waters.[69]

Under the stimulus of the Jervois-Scratchley reports and recommendations for Australian defense,[70] and of the war scare with Russia, Victoria's neighboring colony, New South Wales, also made small steps in the direction of acquiring some naval experience. Acting on Jervois' suggestion, the Parkes Government in 1877 proposed to secure an ironclad for local defense. The colonial legislature wanted the vessel to be an imperial ship rather than a colonial one; but the cost of its maintenance would be borne by the colony. The Colonial Secretary, Lord Carnarvon, urged that the Admiralty give the suggestion earnest thought as a matter of grave importance, and as a project which might eventually lead to much larger results in the use of a system of imperial defense. But the Parkes Government was out of office too soon for any action to follow their suggestion, and the Admiralty said they would consent to the idea only if the colony would pay for the construction as well as maintenance of the ironclad.[71]

In 1881 New South Wales requested that the flagship of the navy's flotilla in Australian waters, HMS *Wolverene*, which was about to return to England, be retained in New South Wales in commission and maintained as an imperial vessel at the colony's expense, so that it might serve as a training vessel for a naval militia brigade. This time, the Admiralty and the colonial government were able to reach an agreement, with the Admiralty delivering the vessel over to the colony as a gift, after the colony had provided passage home for the officers and crew of the ship.[72]

During the remainder of the eighteen-eighties the Australian colonies maintained a high degree of interest in naval defense. Several small but modern vessels were purchased by some of the colonies, and these small naval forces were in operation by the close of the decade. Moreover, the colonies, combined with New Zealand, had obtained what they felt was a greater measure of naval security, by arranging for an annual subsidy to be paid to the imperial government for the enlargement of the forces of the Royal Navy in Australian waters.

[68] There was a permanent naval force of about 220, and a naval militia of a slightly greater number.
[69] PRO, C.O. 808/59, pp. 45–46.
[70] *Infra.*
[71] PRO, C.O. 808/59, pp. 11–12.
[72] *Ibid.*, pp. 13–24.

The war scare with Russia in 1878 did more than bring the word "jingo" into the English language; it brought about the first systematic study of the problems of imperial defense in the nineteenth century. Such a study naturally emphasized the central role of sea power. In the maintenance of that power, the colonies were assigned an essential place: the defense and upkeep of many of the seaports and coaling stations on which the power of the Royal Navy pivoted. The Royal Commission which made the study recognized, however, that the patterns of co-operation for defense would change with the changing conditions of the various colonies, and that some of the colonies might seek a large role in their own defense. This, indeed, was occurring while the commission was still laboring in the preparation of its reports. There was perhaps a good deal of error and miscalculation in the nature of the efforts which some of the colonies wished to undertake, and the imperial government did not always know how best to encourage the spirit which lay behind these efforts. But the roots of a working co-operation were there. If war tries the strength of a defense system, it is in peace that the framework itself is formed, and the decade of the eighteen-eighties saw the beginning of that formation. As a result of the increased need of Britain for the primary produce which the colonies could sell her, and of the growing interdependence between the metropolis of empire and the more mature of the colonies, a significant change had occurred: talk about colonial defense had yielded to the wider considerations of imperial organization for common defense.

CHAPTER IV

COLONIAL
WILLINGNESS TO SERVE

The imperial strategy espoused by Colomb, and largely accepted by the Carnarvon Commission, assigned a definite place to the self-governing colonies in the structure of imperial defense. The fear of invasion of the British Isles, which had dominated defense thinking at mid-century, had been supplanted by the fear of beleaguerment, of the loss of communications. The great seaways of the Empire were now the focus of concern. And to the maintenance of these seaways, the colonies with responsible government in Australasia, North America, and Southern Africa could contribute the necessary security of way-stations and termini.

This development in strategic thought was consonant with changing British thought about the Empire in general. The relations which Britain had with her white colonies were proving to be commercially and politically creative. To build on this success, especially when it might ease some of the British taxpayer's burdens, was surely a reasonable course.

The assignment of such responsibility was not, of course, a matter of formal agreement. Nor did it need to be, for the colonies of the eighteen-eighties, still only one or two generations beyond the establishment of responsible government, were in the main anxious to show that they were worthy of that responsibility, and that the "silken cords of kindred, tradition and self-interest"[1] made them more reliable partners in imperial affairs than did Colonial Office directives.

The optimism implicit in this attitude developed despite the fact that the decade opened with the resounding victory of Gladstone and the Liberals in the election of 1880. Winning on a platform which, if words had not lost their meaning, clearly indicated a return to the traditional Liberal ideas, they stood for nonintervention, a reduction of governmental

[1] Ronald Robinson, John Gallagher and Alice Denny, *Africa and the Victorians* (New York, 1961), p. 9.

expenditures, and opposition to the assumption of new responsibilities abroad. In the thundering Midlothian speeches, Gladstone raked the Tories fore and aft for their forward policies in the Mediterranean, the Pacific, South Africa, and the northwest frontier of India. And the Cabinet which he assembled after the election victory was dominated by the old-line Whig-Liberals, men whose political creed had been formulated in the period of pessimism about the future of empire. Once in power, they reversed the policies of their predecessors in at least two areas. The forward policy in India was stayed and Kandahar was returned to the Emir of Afghanistan. In South Africa, the 1877 annexation of the Transvaal was abandoned, unfortunately only after the defeat and death of Sir George Colley at Majuba Hill.

But for all the general anti-imperialist attitude of the government, the current of opinion and events was moving against the supporters of the old pessimistic doctrines. W. E. Forster, a member of both Gladstone Ministries, who had rebuked Disraeli for seeming to hold the white colonists in small esteem,[2] said in 1875 that there was no more popular cry than that of preserving the Empire. Indeed, he became an active participant in the formation and leadership of the Imperial Federation League. But new optimism regarding empire was more an interest in consolidation than in expansion. Where once it had seemed that Britain's interest lay in the direction of the emancipation of the United Kingdom from the burdens of empire by the encouragement of colonial self-reliance, now it seemed that the same British interest might be best served by the participation of those same colonies in imperial defense tasks. This new attitude was founded not only on the new strategical concepts, but also on the apparent willingness of some of the colonies to undertake responsibilities. Now that the pessimists had been disproved, anything seemed possible in the reordering of imperial affairs. "The colonies, which had barely ceased to fear imperial dismemberment, were suddenly invited to declare their views on imperial federation; they were haled forth, blinking, into the sunlight of Britannic favour; they were invited to sit in colonial congresses and to participate in the colour and splendour of the jubilees."[3]

This new faith and interest in empire, this belief that the colonies were now willing and able to make a contribution to the military and naval strength of the Empire, was rooted in a variety of factors, many of them the same as those that gave rise to the Imperial Federation movement. One was, of course, the demonstrated reluctance of the people and governments to see the dismemberment of the Empire. The prospect of

[2] A. P. Thornton, *The Imperial Idea and Its Enemies* (London, 1959), p. 46.
[3] Donald Grant Creighton, "The Victorians and the Empire," in *The Making of English History*, ed. R. L. Schuyler and Herman Ausubel (New York, 1952), pp. 562–63.

the severance of the imperial tie that had been envisaged by many at the time of the withdrawal of the garrisons, and the abuse which broke over the head of Lord Granville as the instrument of that policy, had revealed an unsuspected degree of imperial loyalty in the colonies. The prominent part which colonists took in the foundation of the Colonial Institute and the propagation of the new creed of imperial unity surprised many Britons and converted some to the idea that disintegration of the Empire was not the inevitable course of the future. The *Times* suggested something of the changed atmosphere.

> Of dismemberment there can be no question. There can be no question that English colonists and home-abiding Englishmen, of whatsoever party colour, have made up their minds once for all on one subject . . . The mother country would always have lamented the loss of a single colony, though the burden of retaining dependencies which insisted on continuing dependencies might have been unendurable. But it would assuredly never thrust from its family circle children that appreciate their duties to their parents and one another.[4]

The impression that colonies were an asset was accentuated and reinforced by the obvious eagerness of other nations to acquire some of their own. Why should Britons casually discard through indifference or pessimism that which others were so concerned to obtain? And more frequently than before, other nations came into contact with parts of the Empire which had hitherto been protected by the barriers of distance. The Pacific, an area in which Britain had for generations been the only sea power, was being invaded by other European countries. France was active in the New Hebrides and New Caledonia; and the fact that Germany had recently become a neighbor in Australia's near North could not but create concern for defense in both London and Australia.

The diminution of distances also made it possible to conceive of the Empire as an integrated unit in defense. The distances which the great Burke had seen as inevitably weakening imperial ties had been conquered. The seas still rolled, but months no longer passed between the giving of the order in London and its execution on the other side of the globe. The fragments of empire were no longer so scattered; greater unity was possible in defense as well as other aspects of imperial life.

Further, the sometimes rather despised colonies were growing up. With increasing populations and accumulating wealth, their usefulness as allies was not to be ignored in any marshaling of the strength of the Empire. The population of the colonies, some four million in Canada, two million in Australia, and about three-hundred thousand in New Zealand, may

---

[4] *The Times* (London), April 9, 1880.

not have been large enough to set the military planners of the great powers on their ears. At that time, however, when Britain shunned the idea of a mass army and depended on small professional forces, there were useful possibilities in such numbers if an effective lead were given.

The view that the Greater Britain which had emerged beyond the seas was an extension of the English state and not simply of the English nationality, encouraged also the idea that it was possible on such substantial bases to erect a political union. In Seeley's words, "Here too is a great homogeneous people, one in blood, language, religion and laws, but dispersed over a boundless space."[5] The United States was the best proof that a state might be immense and yet united and prosperous. And if those who sought union had been questioned as to the purpose of such a conception, defense would have been the reply of a large majority. *Zollverein* had its opponents, for the faith once delivered to Adam Smith was still strong in the land. But Bismarck and Moltke had won more disciples than had Friedrich List. Men of power were in the saddle, and more than ever, God was apparently on the side of the largest battalions and the biggest ships. In this period, the prelude to the age of violence, who could afford to neglect any asset which might come to hand?

Combined with these factors was the new faith in the power of positive action. Free trade still held a dominant position in the shaping of English fiscal policies, but laissez-faire in general had slipped in its command of the English public mind. The intruding power of the state, always implicit in the Benthamite utilitarianism, was both implicit and explicit in the activities leading to better housing, arbitrament of fair rents in Ireland, compulsory education, and *sanitas, omnium sanitas*. The administrative state, whose positive action was more and more deemed to be necessary for the public good, was emerging on the English domestic scene as an increasingly powerful force.

And in remoter lands touched by English power, nonintervention and "masterly inactivity" were also giving way before the power of positive thought and action. It is true that withdrawal from Afghanistan and abandonment of the annexation of the Transvaal were among the early actions ordered by the Gladstone Cabinet. But these withdrawals were followed by the bombardment of Alexandria, and Sir Garnet Wolseley's victory at the brisk little battle of Tel-el-Kabir, and by the beginning of the seventy-year period of English dominance in Egypt. Both in domestic legislation and in foreign affairs, policy seemed to depend upon the assertion of power.

Colonial societies were perhaps even better attuned to the demands of the new age than was England, where Cobdenite ideas still lingered on.

[5] Sir John Seeley, *The Expansion of England* (New York, 1931), p. 184.

There was no intellectual barrier against the exercise of state power in the colonies. In Canada and Victoria, for example, protectionism had reared its ugly head; there the power of the state had been used in the acquisition of capital for building railroads. John A. Macdonald's "National Policy" in Canada, Sir Julius Vogel's proliferation of public works in New Zealand, David Syme's domination of the public life of Victoria and his advocacy of protectionism revealed that laissez-faire had very shallow roots in the colonial world.

It was unlikely that the most dramatic political conflict in late nine-teenth-century British history would have been waged without affecting thought on imperial problems. Before the decade of the eighties closed, Irish Home Rule was the great issue, and the hopes and dreams of a federated empire seemed to clash with this divisive idea. The Gladstonian first Home Rule bill was an odd perversion of some aspects of Imperial Federation ideas. While Ireland was to rejoice under a system of respon-sible government, the imperial government was to keep in its hands a variety of reserved powers. This was an idea comparable to the reserva-tions for imperial authority which Durham had outlined in his famous report, and reminiscent of Disraeli's thought that responsible government should not have been granted without some understanding on matters such as an imperial tariff and military code. Among the wide range of powers which would have been reserved for the imperial government under the first Home Rule bill were foreign and colonial relations, and defense.

Ireland, however, would have to pay her share of defense costs and other charges. Her contribution was to be paid through taxes fixed by the imperial Parliament; approximately 40 per cent of Irish taxes would go to defray the imperial costs. And the fixing of taxes and the appropri-ation of the expenditures would be carried out by a Parliament in which Ireland had no representatives, for a feature of the first bill was the exclusion of the Irish representatives from Westminster. While this was subsequently modified, the changes came too late to destroy the bad impression created by the first version of the bill.

The Irish problem undoubtedly fed the fires of nationalism in some of the colonies, especially in Australia where there were many Irish migrants, and made the attainment of any form of imperial federation or even co-operation difficult to secure. But perhaps it would be equally true to say that British hostility to Irish Home Rule also contributed emotional support to imperial federation. To embrace broader union and closer association as a measure of protest against what seemed to be disintegra-tion and separation at home would be an obvious reaction. The Unionist label which opponents of Home Rule took unto themselves could easily inspire the conception of United Empire "as the greatest union of them all."[6]

Some Liberals, such as John Bright and Leonard Courtney, deserted Gladstone on the Home Rule issue because they saw in it a policy which would contribute to the disintegration of the Empire. Englishmen were so accustomed to using the term "Empire" while having little more than British affairs in mind, that too much should not be read into Bright's action; but in Courtney's case, his fear was that the talk of Home Rule for Ireland might encourage similar "foolhardiness" in India.[7] The *Edinburgh Review* discerned the issue of imperial greatness involved in the Home Rule dispute. "The real issue is whether Imperial England is to continue a dominant nation, or whether the old capacity for governing which made England what she is has gone down with the wreck of party . . . England will cease to be regarded as a dominant nation . . . . In India our authority will be shaken. In our colonial dependencies we shall become objects of ridicule . . . ."[8]

Lord Randolph Churchill adduced material considerations for opposing Irish home rule as running counter to the movement for a yet wider union among all the subjects of the Crown: "Let us go in for a party of Union, and it is not only to be a party of union for the United Kingdom . . . it is only by the union of all the subjects of the Queen in all parts of the world and by the reinvigorated co-operation, cohesion and consolidation of all parts of the widely separated British Empire that you can hope to restore to your commerce and to your industries their lost prosperity."[9] It was later to be the judgment of Salisbury that Gladstone's fight for Irish Home Rule "awakened the slumbering genius of Imperialism."[10]

Such considerations contributed to the emergence of the concept of the united or federated empire, and to the dream of the solidarity in defense of British governments throughout the world. The colonies themselves fed these dreams, by demonstrating an apparent willingness to participate in British military actions, and to assume, even though on a small scale, some share in the costs of imperial naval defense.

These manifestations of imperial unity had their beginnings, as did so much of the concern for defense, in the fears aroused by the war scare of 1878. The *ad hoc* Colonial Defence Committee, and the Royal Commission led by Carnarvon, were evidence of the concern felt in Britain. In the colonies, rumors of war ran wild as peace seemed to totter in the balance.

---

[6] J. E. Tyler, *The Struggle for Imperial Unity* (London, 1938), p. 80.
[7] Eric Stokes, "Milnerism," *The Historical Journal*, V, No. 1 (1962), 47.
[8] *Edinburgh Review*, CLXV (April, 1887), 579–85, quoted in *ibid.*, p. 48.
[9] Eric Strauss, *Irish Nationalism and British Democracy* (New York, 1951), p. 178.
[10] *C.H.B.E.*, III, 157.

Even the "penny pinching" Mackenzie Government in Canada took some steps for the improvement of defenses, and new interest was shown in the generally undefended naval base at Esquimalt in British Columbia.[11]

In the Australian colonies, defense activity at this time was associated largely with the activities of Sir William Drummond Jervois. This officer of the Royal Engineers had, to a considerable degree, become the principal adviser of colonial governments on their defense problems. He had been active in the preparation of reports on Canadian defenses during the eighteen-sixties, and in the late seventies was the chief adviser on defense to the various Australian governments. Being an engineer, he was very fortification-minded. Sir Robert Meade, later Chairman of the Colonial Defence Committee, said that Jervois' recommendations had led to many millions of pounds being sunk in fortifications, "which have turned out a gt waste of money, tho' highly applauded at the time."[12]

Jervois wrote from Australia to Meade, then Undersecretary in the Colonial Office, that progress in defense in Australia was satisfactory. But with the passing of the war scare, he apparently found governments reluctant to spend the funds voted for defensive purposes. He felt that the Colonial Secretary would be justified in prodding the various colonial governments into greater defense activity. British expenditures on the general naval defense of the Empire, he felt, gave justification for such prodding.[13]

Not many in Australia agreed with Jervois, however. The political leaders of the colonies felt that the prodding should go in the opposite direction. A conference of the premiers of colonial governments in 1881 expressed grave concern over the relatively defenseless state of British interests in the Pacific, and urged the strengthening of British naval power in Australian waters. They were careful to say, however, that they felt that this increase of naval strength was something that should be accomplished without Australian contribution. The defense of empire against external attack was the responsibility of the imperial power; the contribution of the colonies was to guard their own ports, and to deny their use to enemy vessels.[14] This notion was not to the liking of Lord Derby, Secretary of State for Colonial Affairs, who said that he could not "express satisfaction at the suggestion to increase the naval defence and that it should be an exclusive charge on the Imperial Treasury."[15]

[11] Stanley, *Canada's Soldiers, 1604–1954*, p. 246.
[12] British Museum, Add. MSS 43556, Meade to Lord Ripon, Oct. 19, 1892.
[13] C.O. 201/590, Jervois to Meade, Dec. 1, 1879.
[14] Victoria, Legislative Assembly, *Votes and Proceedings*, Vol. IV (1880), Paper 62.
[15] Sir Herbert Richmond, unpublished MS.

But the Australian colonies did take some steps in naval defense. Victoria purchased a large torpedo boat and two gunboats in 1882; New South Wales had taken charge of the *Wolverene* as a training ship for a naval militia force; and the northern colony of Queensland placed orders for a torpedo boat and two gunboats in 1883.[16]

These manifestations of interest in naval defense did not necessarily meet with the approval of the Senior Naval Officer of the Royal Navy's Australian Station. Commodore James E. Erskine felt that there was great danger in the maintenance of seagoing vessels by colonial governments. It meant a misdirection and waste of defense efforts and funds by such governments, and it complicated the activity of the local naval commanders. An example of such complication came in 1884, when the Queensland government wished to place one of their gunboats into service with the Royal Navy squadron. It had to be rejected by Commodore Erskine, for Queensland had not yet passed a Discipline Act, and without such legislation, placing the local vessels under the same discipline and regulations as those of the Royal Navy, it would be impossible for him to establish effective command over such vessels.[17]

There were hurt feelings in Queensland over the refusal. The Governor of the colony, Sir Anthony Musgrave, felt that the colony was providing a good example in offering the co-operation of her own forces. Other colonies might imitate her, and a useful squadron of five or six colonial vessels might form a unit under the command of the local Royal Navy S.N.O. At any rate, the colony took the lesson, and before the end of the year the necessary legislation was passed.

Another officer of the Australian Station, Captain Cyprian Bridge, prepared a report on the naval defenses of New Zealand at the request of the indefatigable, defense-minded Jervois, who was now Governor of that colony. Captain Bridge recommended that the colony acquire four "short voyage cruisers" as part of a fleet of vessels for the defense of the colony and its trade routes.[18] A lack of agreement among the naval officers on the Australian Station was evident. While Commodore Erskine deplored the idea of any colony acquiring seagoing ships, Captain Bridge suggested that New Zealand acquire several such vessels. But however the officers of that station might disagree about the proper role of the colonies in their own naval defense, the Australian station and colonies were a hive of activity in naval matters compared with Canada. In general, the Colonial Office was lucky if it managed to elicit any reply from the Canadians to letters dealing with naval affairs. Communications from the

[16] C.O. 808/59, pp. 25, 30.
[17] *Ibid.*, pp. 45–46.
[18] P.R.O. Adm. 116/68.

Carnarvon Commission went unanswered, as did letters from the Admiral commanding the North American and West Indian Station.[19]

The vague fears in Australia concerning possible Russian attack during the crisis of 1878 were supplanted in the next few years by fears of another power's activities in the South Pacific. Rumors concerning possible German annexations in the Pacific prompted in part the attempt of the northern Australian colony of Queensland to annex the unclaimed eastern portion of New Guinea to the British Empire in 1883. It was a move which found little support in British official quarters. The former High Commissioner in the Western Pacific, recently also Governor of New Zealand, Sir Arthur Gordon, wrote his friend Gladstone that he opposed the annexation. He was hostile to any further extension of British sovereignty to "several millions of savage and semi-civilized natives," and he could not conceive of a government more unfit to the task of governing such natives than Queensland.[20]

The general hostility toward Queensland's annexation found justification in the assurances furnished by the Foreign Office that Australia's fears of German moves in the Pacific were unfounded, and the annexation was disavowed. But assurances of the Foreign Office turned out to be ill-advised. Germany did establish a protectorate over large areas of the northeastern part of New Guinea, and belatedly, Britain created a protectorate over the southeastern area, the part of the island closest to Australia. This British hesitancy in taking action to protect what most Australians regarded as a legitimate Anglo-Australian interest in the South Pacific resulted in a good deal of criticism in Australian circles.[21]

The New Guinea issue aroused a more general interest among Australians than any other question since the agitation to end transportation. There was considerable agreement among colonial governments over the need for the annexation of the island to the Empire, and general indignation over the dilatory British action. And out of this common concern came a step toward the unification or federation of the Australian colonies. Several colonies formed a compact, the Federal Council of Australasia, designed to speak on their behalf in matters which concerned Australia in the South Pacific. According to Graham Berry, a prominent political leader in Victoria, "It was at that time that the idea of federation

[19] Public Archives of Canada, Governor-General Numbered Files, No. 165, Vol. V.

[20] Knaplund, *Gladstone-Gordon Correspondence, 1851–1896*, pp. 88–90. Typical of British opinion of the character of Australian political life was the tenor of the comments of an Australian correspondent of *The Times* (London). He complained of the low moral and political tone of the Legislative Assembly of Victoria. *The Times* (London), March 31, 1880. See also Marjorie G. Jacobs, "The Colonial Office and New Guinea, 1874–1884," *Historical Studies, Australia and New Zealand*, V (May, 1952), 112.

[21] Donald C. Gordon, *The Australian Frontier in New Guinea, 1870–1885* (New York, 1951).

took a real and substantial hold upon the people—that the colonies began to understand that in order to speak with a united voice, which would be heard in Downing Street, in regard to what were then called 'our foreign relations,' it was necessary that we should have a central representative body . . . ."[22]

The unity represented by the Federal Council was far from complete. New South Wales, the senior colony, did not join. But the whole matter of the annexation, and the concern displayed in colonial society over the intrusion of European powers in waters adjacent to Australia, made the Australian public the readier to increase the contributions which they made to their own defense, and thereby indirectly to the defense of the Empire.

If there was excitement in Australia over the activities of European powers in the Pacific, there was more than comparable excitement in Britain at the same time over the apparent weakness of the British navy. The naval scare of 1884, whipped up by W. T. Stead's *Pall Mall Gazette*, stirred up a public already excited by tension with France over Egypt and by Russian activity north of India. In this state of tension, any cry for the enlargement of the navy was bound to meet with ready response.

The First Sea Lord, Admiral Sir Astley Cooper Key, welcomed the agitation, and urged an increase in naval expenditure. He also prepared a memorandum on the role colonial governments might take in naval defense. Admiral Key recognized that many of the colonial governments, especially in the Australian colonies, were seeking ways in which they might supplement the work of the Royal Navy and furnish protection for their shores. He also noted that they were encountering great difficulties in securing officers and crews, especially those with the necessary skills for handling torpedoes and submarine mines. Further, they had difficulty with discipline, since colonial naval forces did not come within the scope of the Naval Discipline Act unless the service of the vessels they manned had been specifically accepted by the Admiralty, under an Order-in-Council. And where that was done, there arose the touchy question of the relative rank of those in the colonial naval force compared with Royal Navy personnel.

Any effective co-operation between the Royal Navy and colonial forces for defense of colonial ports must, the Admiral felt, be based upon guidance furnished by Admiralty instruction, and must use Admiralty signal books. Few colonists would have the necessary knowledge, especially in view of the complexity of naval signaling systems at the time.[23]

[22] Victoria, *Parliamentary Debates* (1885), pp. 48, 111.
[23] Fourteen thousand variations of signals were considered the minimum requirement of a fleet in daytime. Richard Hough, *Admirals in Collision* (Ballantine Edition, New York, 1959), p. 39.

Since it was the duty and interest of the Admiralty to assist the colonies, the First Sea Lord had a number of suggestions to make. The number and description of vessels for local harbor defense should be considered by the local government in consultation with the Admiral of the Station. The Admiralty would superintend the construction and maintenance of such vessels. While the colonies were to provide the maintenance of vessels and crews, including pension contributions, the Admiralty would furnish, with few exceptions, the officers and crews themselves. Thus the troublesome issues of discipline and relative rank would be removed. In both peace and war, these ships would be under the command of the Senior Naval Officer of the Station.

Lest the vesting of command in the Royal Navy create the fear in colonial minds that the vessels for which they paid might vanish from their ports when they were most needed, Admiral Key's memo said that such vessels were to be "especially appropriated to the defence of the port to which they belong," even though they would be under the orders of the commander in chief for any service for which they might be suitable. In the case of the Australasian colonies, for which the memorandum was largely prepared, Admiral Key felt it would be particularly useful if those colonies were to combine their efforts in naval defense.

During the excitement of the 1885 Sudan campaign, Lord Derby in the Colonial Office sent a circular letter to the governors of the major colonies, commenting favorably upon the steps in naval defense taken by the Australian colonies, and suggesting that the opportunity seemed favorable for presenting to colonial governments the ideas contained in Admiral Key's memorandum.[24]

The Australian command of the Royal Navy had been raised to flag rank in 1884, and Rear Admiral Sir George Tryon was named as the first to hold the command at the new rank. Admiral Tryon was one of the most aggressive and able of the naval officers of the day, and his previous career had nicely balanced sea duty and shore administration. In the course of his career on land, he had been private secretary to Goschen when the latter was First Lord during the Gladstone Government, and he had recently been Secretary to the Board of Admiralty.[25]

Before he left for his new post as Commander of the Australian Station, Tryon himself had drawn up a memorandum, "With reference to Colonial Vessels of War," dated November 28, 1884. As he summarized its principles, the Admiralty were to supply, man, and maintain the ships, with the colonies reimbursing the Admiralty. Any such vessels so maintained would be kept in Australasian waters, even in time of war.

[24] C.O. 808/65 and Public Archives of Canada, Ottawa, Gov.-Gen. File No. 165,4b have the Key memorandum and Lord Derby's letter.
[25] Hough, *Admirals in Collision*, pp. 29–36.

Admiral Tryon's proposals were scrutinized by Lord Northbrook, the First Lord, and by Admiral Key. Tryon understood that these men accepted the principles of his statement, and that he was entrusted with the task of presenting them to the governments of the Australasian colonies. He was to try to ascertain their wishes, and to ask them for any proposals they might want to make.[26]

The principle of naval subsidy by the colonies suggested in Tryon's memo was no novelty. It had already been adopted on a small scale with India, and it had been suggested on a number of occasions as a means of securing better defense in the various colonies. Though the Australian Intercolonial Conference of 1881, which had sought greater British naval power in the Pacific, had rejected the idea of colonial subsidy toward that end, the South Australian delegation, apparently at the instance of Sir William Jervois, had supported the idea of colonial contribution. And the New Zealand government, which had been seeking to have an armed cruiser of the first class assigned to New Zealand waters, was offering in 1885 to pay $3\frac{1}{2}$ per cent of the original cost of a cruiser, and two-thirds of the costs of crew and maintenance of the ship each year. Also, the Carnarvon Commission had urged that a "modest contribution" be made by the Australian colonies.[27]

Once he reached his Australian command, Tryon found himself deeply involved in discussions about Australian defense, and he threw himself into the negotiations *con amore*. Sir Henry Loch, Governor of Victoria, first sought his advice concerning the state of the defenses of Port Phillip Bay, the harbor on which the capital of the colony, Melbourne, was located. Later, on March 21, 1885, Loch wrote asking the views of the Admiral on the subject of the protection that the colony and its trade might expect to receive from the Royal Navy in time of war with a European power. Specifically, he asked about the possibility of the assignment of a number of first class vessels not to be withdrawn from Australian waters. He hoped for an arrangement whereby such ships, while they would come under the control of the Senior Naval Officer in time of war, would have as their primary task the protection of the Australian coast.

The Admiral's reply in effect conceded the soundness of a localization of naval forces. He admitted that it was possible that the Australian colonies might be attacked by a small squadron of ironclads, for, he said, "Squadrons and fleets have escaped the most vigilant admirals." If this were to happen in Australian waters, the most damaging effect would be the destruction of Australian commerce, for the defenses of the local ports,

[26] Adm. 1/6785, Tryon to Admiralty, July 8, 1885.
[27] C.O. 808/65, F. D. Bell, Agent General of New Zealand, to Colonial Office, April 7, 1885.

which seemed satisfactory, would suffice to keep such raiding squadrons from bombardment. Admiral Tryon felt that what he called cruiser catchers were the vessels needed to cope with such elusive raiders. Six such ships would be substantial added protection to trade and commerce, and they would be a most useful addition to the ships of Her Majesty's squadron usually stationed in Australian waters.

Such ships would naturally be sea-going craft. Should it be agreed that the highest interests of the colonies and Britain would be served if the colonies defrayed the costs of such additional ships, while the Admiralty supplied the ships and the crew, he then suggested that the following terms be considered.

1. Any such agreement should run for ten years; it should be terminable on three years' notice.

2. Ships should be equipped and manned as were other vessels of the Royal Navy.

3. The agreement should be ratified by the various colonial governments.

4. At no time should the ships be removed from Australian waters without the assent of the governments of those colonies supplying the subsidy.

Loch sent Tryon's memorandum embodying these ideas on to the governors of the other Australian colonies. Ironically, it was the government of Loch's own colony, Victoria, that displayed the greatest hesitancy about the Admiral's suggestions. In the other Australian colonies, despite some jealousy aroused by the lead taken by Loch in the affair, there was a favorable reception to the ideas of the Tryon memorandum. Premier Alexander Stuart of New South Wales commented that it appeared that the wisest course for Australia to follow would be to come to some definite agreement with Britain as to the size of the naval forcess to be maintained in Australian waters, and to offer to meet the costs of any force greater than that which had been customarily maintained in the past. He was fearful, however, of the difficulties that might arise if any form of dual control were to be written into such an agreement. Disastrous consequences might result if colonial governments refused to permit subsidized vessels to go out of their jurisdiction.[28]

The Premier of Queensland, Samuel Griffith, urged that however great, in the abstract, was Britain's duty of furnishing protection to Australia and its commerce, there was every reason to suppose that until the colonies took the matter of defense into their own hands to some degree, they would not feel as secure as they would wish. He felt that the pro-

[28] C.O. 808/65, p. 73, Stuart to Lord Loftus, June 3, 1885.

gram outlined by Admiral Tryon contained the basis of a possible agreement.

If the ideas of Tryon seemed to elicit considerable approval, it was because they departed substantially from those of the Key memorandum. The latter had aroused many objections. There was nothing in it concerning the protection of the floating trade in Australian waters. Further, the scheme of Admiral Key would require substantial imperial control over local defense, since the local harbor defense vessels would be brought under the control of the Royal Naval command. In the main, existing methods of harbor defense were based on some scheme of interlocking action between land fortifications and artillery, and such marine activity as submarine mines. The Key scheme would break up this interlocking pattern by the introduction of a divided command.[29]

In the event, the Key scheme was abandoned by the new Board of Admiralty that was selected by the First Lord of the Admiralty in the short-lived Salisbury Cabinet of 1886. Lord George Hamilton, the new First Lord, felt that Admiral Key had been taxed too greatly by the difficulties of his period of office. Lord Northbrook, Hamilton's predecessor, had been out of the country a great deal, and much of the labor of the Board had fallen on Key, who with his "omniverous love of work," had been practically a one-man Board of Admiralty.[30]

The change in the Board led to the formulation of a new plan of imperial-colonial co-operation in naval defense. The Key memorandum was supplanted by another of September 9, 1885, and Admiral Tryon was authorized to negotiate with the Australian colonies on the basis of its suggestions.

The differences between the two schemes were substantial. The plans of Admiral Key had been concerned with local harbor defense only. The new formulation, on the other hand, returned to the traditional view that defense should be purely a colonial responsibility, and that colonial governments should raise, maintain, and command local forces. The emphasis of the new memorandum was therefore on the protection of the floating trade in Australian waters. For the greater protection of such trade, the Board suggested that five light cruisers and two seagoing torpedo boats were needed. In time of peace these vessels were to be employed on the usual routine duties of the station. In time of war they were to be allocated to the protection of Australian floating trade. The memorandum stressed that the ships must be under the sole control of the Commander in Chief of the Naval Station. It said that the creation

[29] C.O. 808/65, pp. 90–93, Loch to Stanley, Aug. 7, 1885.
[30] Lord George Hamilton, *Parliamentary Reminiscences and Reflections* (London, 1916), I, 292.

of such additional strength on Australian waters would not lead to a reduction of the usual strength of the imperial squadron. But it proposed that the costs of the additional vessels be met by the colonies jointly. The Admiralty suggested, more specifically, that the colonies pay the original cost of the additional vessels to be put on the Australian station, and the annual gross liability for their maintenance.[31] The revised scheme was forwarded to Tryon with instructions to present it for the consideration of the Australian governments.[32]

There was more than a change of emphasis in the ideas of the new memorandum. The principles of the Key memorandum, if adopted, would have enlarged the authority of the imperial naval officer in a colonial area by extending his control to local defense vessels. Under the new memo, such defenses were to be left strictly in the hands of the local governments; but more than that, the colonial governments were to have a voice in the disposition of vessels of the Royal Navy, for in the later statement, there was a strong suggestion of localization of naval forces. The additional vessels were designated specifically for the defense of the Australian floating trade. Despite the reservation of control of the flotilla in the hands of the local commander in chief, if the Australian governments were to pay for the ships, and if they were assigned to Australasian water, then localization was certainly apparent.

What led the Board of Admiralty to accept an idea so subversive of the mobility essential to the effective use of sea power? Perhaps the basic factor was the preoccupation with seamanship and "polish," the general indifference to strategy and the neglect of the study of basic problems of imperial defense that still characterized the Royal Navy. As John Fisher said when he looked back over the distribution of British naval power during the nineteenth century: "The Navy and the country have grown so accustomed to the territorial nomenclature of our distant squadrons that their connection with the sea is considerably obscured, and their association with certain lands has led to a tacit belief that those particular squadrons are for the protection of the lands they frequent, and not generally for the destruction of the enemy's fleet wherever it may happen to be."[33]

Then, too, there may have been concern that the Australian governments might take action on their own and acquire a fleet of vessels which would be a cause of embarrassment to the imperial authorities. From his position on the Australian Station, Tryon had reported his feeling that the people of the colonies would not long accept from Britain that

[31] C.O. 808/65, pp. 89–90.
[32] Adm. 1/6874, Col. Stanley to Loch, Dec. 1, 1885.
[33] P. K. Kemp (ed.), *The Papers of Admiral Sir John Fisher* (London, 1960), I, 36.

which in their own opinion they could do as well themselves. He further commented that it would be desirable to defer the day when the colonies would have seagoing vessels of their own,[34] and Sir Henry Loch took much the same view. The latter relayed to the Colonial Office his opinion that unless the Royal Navy squadron in Australian waters was improved, the colonies would acquire ships of their own, and having such vessels, "there are many men in these colonies who would not hesitate, under certain eventualities, to despatch them to seize Samoa, the New Hebrides, or any other place or island on which they had set their desire."[35] The recent example of Queensland's attempt to annex New Guinea indicated that Loch's fears were amply grounded, and justified the "if you can't beat 'em, join 'em" attitude which he shared with Tryon.

On the basis of the new directive, Tryon pushed vigorously forward in his negotiations with the Australian governments. Difficulties arose in certain aspects of the negotiations; resentment arose, for example, over the fact that much of his correspondence was with the governors of the colonies rather than with the leaders of the various ministries. But Tryon whipped most of the problems in a meeting which he held on his flagship in Sydney harbor on April 26–27, 1886, with the premiers of New South Wales, Queensland, and Victoria. The New Zealand premier had also been invited to the gathering, but an impending session of Parliament held him at home. Tryon's memorandum for the conference with the premiers defined the main concern of the gathering as the bringing about of "a naval seagoing force localised to the Australian seas."

The haggling over the terms of the agreement was more over the distribution of the costs than over its principles. The Victorian premier was hesitant about entering into any contract for payments which stretched over a ten-year period. What if there were to be a depression? There was also a suggestion that since the floating trade in Australian waters, the object of special concern in all the negotiations, was largely British-owned, British merchants and insurance firms were being benefited at the expense of the Australian taxpayer.[36] Victoria offered to pay only the annual maintenance charges of the additional vessels on the station. The other governments, particularly Tasmania, South Australia, and Western Australia, offered to pay 5 per cent of the costs of construction of the ships each year plus costs of maintenance.

During most of the period of Tryon's negotiations with the Australian colonies, noises of exasperation were to be heard from New Zealand. If Australians wanted to have a portion of naval strength localized in their

[34] Adm. 1/6785, Tryon to Admiralty, July 8, 1885.
[35] C.O. 808/65, Loch to Stanley, Aug. 7, 1885.
[36] Victoria, *Parliamentary Debates*, Session 1881, LVI, 2188.

waters, New Zealanders were equally inclined to insist that they have their share of any ships which were allocated to the Australasian area.

There was a general feeling in New Zealand that far too much attention was being paid to the trade route which ran westward from Australia. The trans-Pacific route, New Zealanders maintained, was just as important as the route through the Suez or around the Cape. The New Zealand government felt that the islands of the Pacific could be much more advantageously and effectively patrolled by vessels from Auckland than from Sydney. In the main, the prevailing view was that the interests of New Zealand were sufficiently distinct from those of the colonies across the Tasman Sea to justify a demand for vessels stationed in their waters and a direct agreement between New Zealand and Great Britain, rather than one in which the colony was simply another in the catch all of the Australasian colonies. Tryon's delay of some months in paying a visit to Auckland added to New Zealand's irritation. That the colonial premier found it difficult to attend Tryon's conference of April 25–26 in Sydney may have been grounded in part on this irritation.

New Zealand was not going to hold aloof from any general scheme for strengthening defense in the South Pacific, however. Its government offered £20,000 a year toward any scheme, with the proviso that in time of peace a New Zealand port would be the headquarters of at least two vessels.[37] Tryon rejected the demand. He said that the proffered amount, although a useful sum, would not cover the costs of two ships. Further, he did not feel that any agreement should tie up two ships in New Zealand ports. The spirit of the New Zealand demand could, however, be met in part by the promise of more frequent Royal Navy visits to New Zealand harbors. And Tryon acknowledged the justice of the wish that the people of New Zealand should see more than just an occasional glimpse of the ships they helped pay for.

The process of seeking agreement on naval affairs in the South Pacific was assisted by the general atmosphere of euphoria created by the demonstrations of imperial loyalty over the Sudan. The death of General Gordon at the hands of the followers of the Mahdi at Khartoum sent a shock throughout the British colonies quite parallel to the shock in Britain itself. In the anticipation that the military expedition sent to rescue Gordon would be transformed and enlarged into a punitive force, offers of military assistance came from many British colonies.

Indeed, the services and skills of the Empire had already been drawn upon for the force which had been dispatched to the relief of Gordon. Lord Wolseley, the commander of that force, had served in Canada and had commanded the men sent to Red River in 1870 for the suppression

[37] Adm. 1/6815, Memorandum of Premier Richard Stout, March 27, 1886.

of the first Louis Riel uprising. His experience with Canadian rivermen, and the fact that the approach to Khartoum was largely up the Nile, led him to seek the service of Canadian *voyageurs* for the handling of his river craft. The *voyageur* was a dying race in Canada, but 386 woodsmen were recruited, some of them Indians, for service in Egypt and the Sudan. These men, however, were civil employees of the British forces, not soldiers, and they did not participate in any combat activity of the Nile campaign.[38]

The military assistance offered in the aftermath of the Khartoum disaster was of a different character, however. Offers for the recruitment of fighting units came from individuals in Canada and New Zealand, and more significant tenders of aid came from colonial governments who were able to volunteer the services of existing and reasonably effective units. First in tendering such an offer was the government of New South Wales, but several other Australian governments speedily joined in the offer of contingents of troops.[39]

The recruitment of the New South Wales contingent of some 700 men accompanied by some hundreds of horses was rapidly accomplished, and on March 3, 1885, the unit sailed from Sydney. Their march to the place of embarkation was lined with cheering crowds, which the *Sydney Morning Herald* placed at 200,000, and the *Herald* commented that the day marked a new departure in the relations between Britain and her colonies: "Hitherto the colonies have been regarded by many politicians as a drag upon the home country, and statesmen have been heard to say that the colonies of England were a source of weakness to her and not of strength. The fallacy of such a statement was demonstrated beyond dispute March 3."[40]

But there were voices of dissent in the colony. Sir Henry Parkes, the leading figure in the political life of the colony, criticized the action in numerous letters to the press. The decision to send the contingent, he pointed out, had been made by the Attorney General and Acting Premier of the colony, William Bede Dalley, while the Premier was on vacation in New Zealand. It had been taken without consultation with the full Cabinet and without the approval of one of the major members of the Cabinet, the Colonial Treasurer.[41]

Parkes was not able to carry his opposition into Parliament, having "retired" from political life a short while before. Eventually, the govern-

---

[38] Stanley, *Canada's Soldiers, 1604–1954*, pp. 270–71.
[39] Offers were made by Victoria, South Australia, and New Zealand, and in Canada a Colonel Williams of the Canadian militia offered to raise a unit of a thousand men for Sudan service. But nowhere was the offer as immediate, tangible, and accompanied by reassurances of speed as in New South Wales.
[40] *Sydney Morning Herald*, March 11, 1885.
[41] *Ibid.*, Feb. 27, 1885; Sir Henry Parkes, *Fifty Years in the Making of Australian History* (London, 1892), II, 139–46.

ment summoned a special session to approve the expenditures it had entered upon and to win approval for its actions. For a week the debate was staged before packed galleries of the Legislative Assembly.[42] Most of the debate was on the Address in Reply to the Governor's speech which had expressed approbation of the Government's course. The legislative result was the passage of the Australian Military Contingent Bill, which was intended to remove any legal difficulties in the way of the command and control of the force while overseas.

Dalley said that New South Wales had not only astonished the world, but also itself, both in the willingness to dispatch the force and in the speed and effectiveness with which it had been organized and embarked. He also conceded that in what they had done, the Government had undoubtedly "strained the law."[43] The opposition centered its attack less on the sending of the contingent than on the haste with which the Government had acted, and on its failure to consult the legislature. But the Government's course was upheld by a large margin.

The contingent which had departed in early March to the sound of such enthusiastic cheers was back in Sydney by June 23. It had seen little action in the Sudan, though it had engaged in a few skirmishes and contributed labor to the building of the Suakim railroad which was designed as a support line from the Red Sea to British forces in the Sudan theater. But in the midst of this playing at war in the Sudan, the outlook had changed sharply. Deteriorating relations with Russia now aroused concern in Australia for Australian defenses. The Penjdeh crisis on the borders of India suddenly made the Sudan issue seem rather unimportant, for British forces were needed in India. As the crisis seemed to mount, Dalley, the man largely responsible for the dispatch of the Sudan contingent, said that the purpose of the colonial government had been "to assert the arms of England wherever our help was needed. . . . Wherever our contingent can be useful it should be available to the mother country."[44] Sir Saul Samuel, the Agent General of New South Wales in London, regretted that the great patriotic gesture seemed about to run into a dry spot if the forces sent to assist were not to be used in securing revenge for Gordon's death.[45] But the colonial government assented to the idea that the force might be used in India.

The suggestion that the contingent was available for general service, that it was at the disposal of the imperial authorities for use elsewhere than the Sudan, was not accepted happily in the colony. Penjdeh and

[42] Frank Hutchinson and Francis Myers, *The Australian Contingent* (Sydney, 1885), p. 118.
[43] New South Wales, *Parliamentary Debates*, 11th Parliament, 1st Session, p. 9.
[44] *Sydney Morning Herald*, April 29, 1885.
[45] W.O. 32/129/7700/1932, Samuel to War Office, April 27, 1885.

the Indian frontier carried little of the emotional appeal of the martyred Gordon. And unlike the forces of the Mahdi, those of the Czar might conceivably be able to strike at Australia. The *Sydney Morning Herald* said that the people of the colony would not have assented to the dispatch of the contingent in the case of a war with Russia, "not because they would have been lacking in sympathy for the mother-country, but because the men's presence would have been required here, and because the interests of the Empire could have been best served by keeping them here."[46] Wry comment might have been made about colonial aid which was available for wars against disorganized native tribes, but not for conflicts against a major power when it might have been of some real assistance. But the attitude of the *Herald* only reflected the realities of the situation. Admiral Tryon admitted that Russian cruisers might get through to raid the Australian coasts.[47] Any such raid in the absence abroad of even a small portion of the colonies' defense forces would place a considerable strain on imperial ties.

When the excitement of the Sudan was over, and the apparent Russian threat on the northwest frontier subsided, there remained the fact that Admiral Tryon and the Australian premiers had made a good start toward a naval agreement between Britain and its Australasian colonies. But while the framework of agreement had been built, much remained to be done before it could become effective. Some of the work was carried forward at the first of the Colonial Conferences, in April, 1887. The projected Australian agreement was the main defense business of that conference.

As in other instances during the previous two decades, it was the colonial members of the conference who were more imperial-minded, and more concerned for vigorous expression of opinion on imperial matters. Alfred Deakin of Victoria, who was later to be the outstanding political leader in the first decade of the Australian Commonwealth, attacked imperial policy strongly for its hesitancy in supporting British and Australian interests in the Southern Pacific. And the project of some form of commercial union among the states of the Empire was introduced and pushed by Jan Hofmeyr of the Cape, who tied the idea of imperial *Zollverein* to that of a *Kriegsverein*. He suggested that all imports be taxed at 2 per cent *ad valorem*, and that the revenue thus obtained be used for imperial naval defense.

But while there was much advocacy of closer imperial co-operation, the tangible result of the conference was the approval in final form of the Australian naval agreement. Under the terms finally hammered out, the

---

[46] *Sydney Morning Herald*, April 30, 1885.
[47] Adm. 116/68, Tryon to Admiralty, April 6, 1885.

Australasian colonies were to pay £126,000 per year toward the support of an auxiliary squadron of ships which was to be maintained in Australian waters by the Royal Navy. These were to be fully equipped and manned ships, in every respect fighting ships of the Navy. They were to be assigned without diminution of the regular forces, which were to be maintained as they had been in the past. As for the vexing question of control, the Admiralty surrendered some of its freedom of control over the vessels of the proposed auxiliary squadron. Command of the force was, of course, to be in the hands of the naval commander in chief of the Australian Station, but the vessels subsidized by the colonial governments could not be moved from the waters of the station without the assent of those governments. Both Colonial Office and Admiralty made somewhat of a grimace over this necessity. The First Lord, Lord George Hamilton, protesting that the Admiralty could ne'er assent, assented, admitting that if Australia wished to add to the British establishment by a special contribution, she might legitimately claim some control over the force to which she thus contributed. He felt it unlikely, however, that the limitation of the movement of the ships would survive under the strain of war.[48] Sir Henry Holland, Secretary of State for the Colonies, noted that this was the first time that Britain had agreed to tie down any of the navy to a particular portion of the globe. Ratification of the agreement by the various colonial legislatures and the imperial Parliament was necessary to bring it into effect, and the debates over the ratification suggest that within the agreement there were fruitful grounds for discord. To the British way of thinking, the colonies were making a contribution to imperial defense, while to Australians it was a means of augmenting their own defense. The Australians felt that they were buying a larger degree of security from the only agency capable of supplying it for them: the imperial government.

That British opinion should have regarded the agreement as a step toward imperial union or federation was natural. Few in Britain had much knowledge of colonial life. "The truth is, as we must confess to our shame, that in the mother country very little indeed is known concerning the realities of colonial life,"[49] was the complaint of the *Times*. By way of explanation of that ignorance, the *Times* might well have scrutinized its own columns. Such information as there was frequently came from expatriate colonials, or those who visited Britain often. Many of the Australians seen about London, such as Edward Wilson, proprietor of the Melbourne *Argus*, Francis P. Labillière, William Westgarth, and others, were enthusiastic imperial federationists. Palmerston's statement

[48] Hamilton, *Parliamentary Reminiscences and Reflections*, I, 77.
[49] *The Times* (London), March 27, 1880.

that if he wished to be misinformed about a country he sent for a man who had lived there for thirty years may have been too clever by half, but certainly these Australian voices misrepresented the Australian willingness to embrace any form of imperial federation. It was rare for Britons to hear a forthright expression of Australian opinion. In the prevailing ignorance, it was not surprising that such seeming manifestations of imperial loyalty as the Sudan contingent and the naval agreement were taken as indications of a colonial willingness to contribute to imperial as opposed to a distinctly Australian defense. A reading of the debates in the various Australian legislative bodies over ratification of the agreement might have been illuminating to many in Britain. All parties concerned ultimately ratified, but not before delays and the exchange of bitter and heated words.

Sir Henry Parkes, his brief period of "retirement" from political life being over and once more leader of the government, introduced the naval agreement bill into the legislature of New South Wales. Twitted somewhat by his opponents for the apparent contradiction between his opposition to the Sudan contingent and his present support for the naval agreement, Parkes defended the latter as a contribution to the coming of Australian federation. The co-operation of the colonies here, he felt, presaged united action in other areas. Further, the colonies could not at such a small cost provide in any other way so effectively for their defense.[50]

While the opposition did not seek the defeat of the bill, it directed a wide range of criticism at it. Much of this was based on the regret over the loss by the Australian colonies of any possibility of remaining neutral in a great European war. [51] Such a possibility, if it ever had any reality, was diminished by the dispatch of the contingent, and now by the naval agreement. It was charged that the agreement yoked the colony to the "juggernaut of imperialism,"[52] and that with its ratification, "we shall . . . accept responsibility of all quarrels between Great Britain and other powers."[53] It was also charged that when the time came for the colony to seek its independence, the British naval force would be used against it, and that the colony was being invited to contribute to a force which would eventually be used to subjugate it.[54]

[50] New South Wales, *Parliamentary Debates*, 1st series, XXIX (Session 1887), 1532.
[51] The prospect of colonial neutrality had been expressed nost notably in Australia by Sir Charles Gavan-Duffy, distinguished jurist and Premier of Victoria. Cf. *C.H.B.E.*, VII, 525. Nourishing such hopes were the remoteness of the Australian colonies, and the considerable strain of social protest and idealism in Australian life. All of this contributed to the hope that under the Southern Cross, Australia might be a "fortress built by Nature for herself against infection and the hand of war."
[52] New South Wales, *Parliamentary Debates*, 1st Series, XXIX (Session 1887), 1572–73.
[53] *Ibid.*, p. 1578.
[54] *Ibid.*, p. 1537.

Sprinkled through much of the debate was the scorn of the true-born Australian democrat for the manners and behavior of the effete citizens of the Old World. The auxiliary squadron would be a "high-bred force, with the epauletted darlings who would be brought out from home." Another critic wanted no "curled darlings" to "cast their foul breath on fair Australian maidens." As for the Colonial Conference, it was described as a "hole and corner conference in London" at which the whole agreement had been "humbugged up and concocted." But despite the heat and passion of some of the debate, the New South Wales government and the supporters of the agreement had an overwhelming majority, and the agreement passed with ease.

There was rougher going in Queensland. Queensland was usually regarded as the most radical and egalitarian of all the Australian colonies. Certainly the debate on the naval bill revealed a strong colonial bias against the aristocratic *hauteur* and exploitation of the working class associated with the Old World. The situation in Queensland was complicated by the fact that the current session of Parliament was in its closing days. Sir Samuel Griffith, the Premier, would have preferred the postponement of the ratification debate until another session, but for the sake of a show of unity among the various colonies, it had been generally agreed that the bills of ratification would all be presented to the respective legislatures on the same day. Victoria had set the time, to the general embarrassment of Griffith and his government.

Opponents of the bill charged that the imperial government had driven a disgraceful bargain, [55] one that not only presented Queensland with a large bill, but that also involved the contentious issue of taxation without representation. The opposition quoted the view of the *Daily Telegraph* of Sydney:

> It is indeed virtually the same demand which is preferred against the colonial now which, in a different form somewhat over 100 years ago, precipitated the American revolution and changed all modern history. The great difference between what was done by a Tory English Government then and what is being attempted by a Tory English Government today is that then England claimed the right to tax the colonies for Imperial purposes now she asks the colonies to tax themselves . . . . The essential point to consider is that though they differ in their methods their end is the same. [56]

Others elaborated on the same theme, saying that after the wars with France in North America, England had attempted to get the colonies

---

[55] Queensland, *Parliamentary Debates*, LIII, 1628.

[56] *Daily Telegraph* (Sydney), Nov. 18, 1887, quoted in Queensland, *Parliamentary Debates*, LIII, 1697.

of that day to pay for British armaments; the subsidy was an effort on her part to compel Australia to pay for British armaments.[57]

Despite the wide-ranging attack on the bill, it passed the second reading. The margin was so narrow, however, that in the prevailing state of parliamentary affairs Griffith did not think it advisable to push it through to finality. Nor was he in a position to appeal to the electorate on the issue, for the Queensland Parliament had recently passed a redistricting bill, and the process of drawing the boundary lines of the new constituencies would not be finished for some time. It was not until the agreement had been brought into operation by the approval of other colonies that Queensland finally ratified it in 1891.

In Victoria, the agreement was ratified, though regret over the diminishing chances of Australian neutrality was also expressed. John Woods, a leading figure of the radical group in Victorian political life, said that up to the time of the Sudan affair, Australian colonies had always occupied a neutral position. If the colonies approved the naval agreement, they would inevitably be part of every quarrel in which the Empire might become engaged.[58] The bill was passed with enthusiasm, however.

In New Zealand, the Legislative Assembly also gave approval to the bill in the closing hours of debate before a Christmas recess, and with fully half of the members absent. Perhaps the sourest note there was the comment of that venerable figure of New Zealand and imperial history, Sir George Grey, that he regarded the whole thing as a "futile measure."[59]

Imperial ratification of the agreement came in 1888 with the passage of the Imperial Defence (Expenses) Bill. In introducing the measure, which called for an appropriation of £850,000, the initial costs of the new vessels to be put on the Australian Station, W. H. Smith said: "We have in this Agreement recognized the principle of a common duty by the people of this country and our cousins, friends and children in the Colonies in connection with the protection and defence of the Empire."[60] And Lord George Hamilton said that the agreement established the great principle of financial partnership between the colonies and Great Britain.[61] Henry Labouchere, still strongly the Little Englander, bitterly opposed the agreement. Britain had made a bad deal, one which could only lead to further "sponging" on Britain by the other colonies.[62] But the agreement was ratified by a thin house and by a margin of about two to one.

[57] *Ibid.*, p. 1715.
[58] Victoria, *Parliamentary Debates* (Session 1887), 2192.
[59] New Zealand, *Parliamentary Debates*, 1st session, 10th Parliament, LIX, 1005.
[60] *Hansard*, 3d series, CCCXXVI, 364, May 15, 1888.
[61] *Ibid.*, pp. 382–83.
[62] *Ibid.*, pp. 397–98.

It was perhaps natural to overemphasize the contribution which an intangible such as imperial loyalty made to the creation and ratification of the naval agreement, but that it did play a part is incontestable. There was a stronger streak of such loyalty than ever would have been imagined by the separatists of a generation or so earlier. But imperial loyalty was not the only factor working toward the consummation of the agreement. Irritation with imperial policy, annoyance with the indifference, as it was regarded in Australia, with which the imperial government had treated their interests in the Pacific, also contributed. Australians had noted with increasing concern the instrusions of European powers into the Pacific area, and had reacted strongly against them. The Queensland effort at the annexation of New Guinea, the fear of French activities in New Caledonia and the New Hebrides, the efforts to assert a form of Australian Monroe Doctrine in the Pacific, all had been expressions of this sense of alarm, and all had been treated by the imperial authorities with a casual air, which to Australians seemed to reveal an almost total disregard of their interests. The irritation of Australians had been most clearly conveyed to Britons by the statements of Alfred Deakin at the Colonial Conference in 1887. This irritation led some to resent the agreement; it led others, such as Deakin, to support it, in the belief that it was better to have some British power in the Pacific, even if it required subsidy, than not to have it at all.

The difference between the strong Australian nationalists, who wanted to reject the agreement, and moderate nationalists such as Deakin who would accept it until Australian growth and development permitted something better and something more Australian, allowed the passage of the various bills of ratification. The moderate nationalists were allied for the nonce with the imperial-minded element of Australian thought, those who saw the naval agreement as the prelude to a yet larger unity in defense, or as the First Lord put it in Britain, "a good stepping stone towards the gradual establishment of an Overseas Fleet being maintained by our distant Dominions."[63]

There were few such complicating factors in New Zealand. There the phylacteries of imperial loyalty were more widely distributed, for New Zealand lacked Australia's vocal Irish minority, with its radical, anti-imperialist tradition. The naval agreement, frequently referred to as the prelude to closer unity in the Empire, passed through the Parliament with ease.

In this attitude New Zealand differed from Australia. Though the passage of the agreement might encourage the faith of the imperial

---

[63] Hamilton, *Parliamentary Reminiscences and Reflections*, I, 121.

federationists, it was for the most part more a matter of convenience to Australians, a stopgap until colonial federation permitted the exercise of a larger and more effective Australian initiative. For by the time of the passage of the various bills of ratification of the agreement, the limited enthusiasm in Australia for imperial federation was dying out. The apogee of the imperial federation idea had been reached in the middle of the decade of the eighties.[64] The agreement, which to federationists in Britain had heralded the coming of the dawn, was a false dawn in the Antipodes as Australian nationalism waxed.

---

[64] Charles S. Blackton, "Australian Nationalism and Nationality: the Imperial Federationist Interlude, 1885–1901," *Historical Studies, Australia and New Zealand,* VII (Nov. 1955).

CHAPTER V

THE COLONIAL
DEFENCE COMMITTEE

The dispatch of the Australian contingent and the Canadian river-men to the Sudan, and the naval agreement between the Australasian colonies and Great Britain, were earnests of the willingness of some of the colonies to collaborate in the duties of imperial defense. For such collaboration to be effective, however, some coherence would have to be brought to the entire system of colonial defense arrangements; some agency would have to see that the efforts made were reasonably well directed and proportionate to any perils which the respective colonies might confront. The establishment of such coherence was undertaken by the Colonial Defence Committee, the first permanent agency created by the imperial government to furnish the colonies with guidance on matters of defense. Its task was to secure information on the state of colonial defenses, to formulate basic principles of defense and educate colonial governments in these principles, and to warn and prompt them into action when they seemed remiss or neglectful of their duties.

Heretofore, advice given to colonial governments about defense had been of the most sporadic character. Occasional recommendations for local defense arrangements had been made by such fortification specialists as Sir William Jervois, who had served as adviser to governments in Canada and Australia, and by others of lesser fame. In addition, itinerant officers of the Royal Navy had been consulted by colonial officials, but there had been nothing systematic in such consultations. And while the Carnarvon Commission had managed to assemble a good deal of information on the state of defenses of the various colonies, such material would need to be kept continuously up to date if it were to be of any lasting value. As it was, authorities in London had no established or effective means of learning about the state of defense of colonial ports, or about the military potential of the colonies.

The moving spirit in the creation of the Colonial Defence Committee was Robert Meade. Meade was Assistant Undersecretary and about mid-term in his years of service in the Colonial Office in 1885. He had entered the department with Lord Granville's tour of duty there, and remained in the Colonial Office for the rest of his life; at the time of his death in 1898 he was Permanent Undersecretary. A man of considerable charm and tact, Meade was perhaps happier in the more relaxed atmosphere of his early years than in his latter days under the strenuous Chamberlain leadership.

Meade urged the creation of the Defence Committee in the spring of 1885, during the exciting days following the melancholy news from Khartoum, when offers of military assistance for the avenging of Gordon's death were flooding in from the colonies. What spurred Meade to action was not the Sudan, however, but rather one of the recommendations of the Carnarvon Commission. That body had suggested that the small remaining imperial forces be withdrawn from Barbados, and the Inspector General of Fortifications, Sir Andrew Clarke, had concurred in the recommendation. But Meade was concerned lest the contemplated withdrawal lead the local government and people to misguided efforts in the fortification of their ports. Weak fortification might only invite attack, he felt, and furnish an enemy with a cheap victory. The Barbadians needed guidance in any defense projects they might undertake, and the Colonial Office was not equipped to furnish it. In a minute of April 14, 1885, Meade commented, "We can scarcely deal here satisfactorily with questions of this kind, and to refer by ordinary correspondence to the W.O. and the Admiralty will be a long and unsatisfactory affair."[1]

Meade consulted with Sir Robert Herbert, then Permanent Undersecretary of the Colonial Office, and with various military and naval officers, and there was agreement that it would be a good idea to establish a small standing committee of the Colonial Office to which matters of colonial defense arrangements could be referred. The Colonial Defence Committee, thus approved, met for the first time on April 22, 1885. The business at hand was to discuss proposals of the imperial officer commanding the forces in the West Indies concerning the future defense of Barbados.

The committee's initial membership included, in addition to Meade, several men who had been associated with the two earlier groups concerned with colonial defense: the *ad hoc* committee of 1878 and the Carnarvon Commission. Its first chairman, despite the Colonial Office origin of the group, was a military man, Sir Andrew Clarke, the Inspector

[1] Public Record Office, Cabinet Office (henceforth cited as Cab.), 8/1/1.

General of Fortifications. And within three months of its establishment, the committee profited from the appointment of Captain George S. Clarke as its secretary.

George Clarke, later Lord Sydenham, who shared with men like Viscount Esher the distinction of being among the major "back room boys" of British defense planning before World War I, has been called "the first of that line of expert secretaries to committees of defence who in due course were to leave a mark on British constitutional practice."[2] Despite his military background, he was an avid supporter of naval power and, later in his career, of the ideas of Admiral John Fisher; he often sought to confute naval heresies by letters to the press generally signed "Navalis." Later, he became the first secretary of the Committee of Imperial Defence. There he fell out with Fisher, who expressed the wish that a way might be found to send him to die of yellow fever as Governor of some West Indian island.[3] As things worked out, he was relegated to the Governorship of Bombay. But there can be little doubt that Clarke left the mark of his strategical concepts on the work and the traditions of the committee.

The concern for defense in Barbados was the beginning of one of the continuing interests of the Colonial Defence Committee: the evaluation of plans for defense drawn up in the colonies. One of the first aspects of this job was the gathering of information about such plans and arrangements. During the negotiations conducted by Admiral Tryon in Australia, the Admiralty had received a collection of reports on the conditions of the shore defenses of some of the colonies there. The minute of the Admiralty official receiving the reports noted that this was the first authentic information on these defenses it had received. One of the first concerns of the Colonial Defence Committee was to put an end to the widespread ignorance in this field, and to see that an adequate knowledge of colonial defense arrangements was available to imperial authorities in London. To this end the Committee circulated a request to the colonial governments in August, 1885, asking for reports from colonial authorities on such matters as local floating defenses, the number of submarine mines in store, the amount of cable available for use in mining operations, the reserves of telegraph wire in the colony, and the number of troops in the colony, both colonial and imperial. The committee also asked for information about the reserves of small arms, munitions supply, existing fortifications, and the number of artillery pieces—requests that suggest clearly the lack of any effective knowledge in London concerning colonial defense matters. Another early request to colonial governments

[2] John Ehrman, *Cabinet Government and War, 1890–1940* (Cambridge, 1958), p. 10.
[3] Arthur J. Marder, *Fear God and Dread Nought* (London, 1956), II, 83.

was that they should formulate defense plans and forward them to London for the security of the committee.[4]

Once launched upon its labors, the committee kept busily at its work over the next few years. By the time of the first Colonial Conference in 1887, it had prepared twenty-six memoranda, most of them concerned with specific local defense issues, and in addition had made recommendations in some fifty-three other local defense matters. By October, 1891, it had held fifty-eight meetings at which it had considered some 470 items. The defenses of some thirty-seven colonies had passed under its security in one way or another. Nineteen of the colonies had drawn up plans for their defense with the assistance of advice from the Committee; six colonies had been written off as either being too small or having too meagre resources to be able to undertake any effective defense measures of their own. In carrying out its duties, the committee had prepared memoranda on some forty general aspects of local defense.[5]

Among the early dispatches of the committee to the colonies was a memorandum to colonial governors which stressed the importance of preparations to be made at times when war might seem imminent. In this, only guidance of a most general character could be given, since conditions in the colonies varied so greatly. But the governors were warned that any break in the cable connections of the colony, coming at a time when political tension was known to exist, should be taken as a probable indication of the outbreak of hostilities. The memorandum further dealt with the general nature of any landing operations which might be directed against colonial areas. It urged the importance of proper placing of submarine mines in harbor waters, and of making cable landing sites secure. Lights, buoys, and beacons in the harbor should be rendered useless to any enemy. The committee also sought to inform the governors of the likely effects of any bombardments which might be directed against seaboard towns. And advice was given about the disposition of supplies of food, coal, and the colony's specie.[6]

Since there were 107 instances between 1700 and 1883 in which either a European state or the United States had commenced hostilities without a declaration of war, the committee sternly warned colonial governors against allowing more than two warships of any one foreign power into a colonial harbor at the same time. Further, no more than one troop transport should ever be permitted. This last warning was prompted by a recent incident in which about 500 Germans had been landed on the Danish West Indian island of St. Croix and had engaged

[4] Cab. 8/1/1, C.D.C. #10, Aug. 12, 1885.
[5] Cab. 8/1/1, C.D.C. #41, Dec. 28, 1891.
[6] Cab. 8/1/1, C.D.C. #19, Nov. 1, 1886. The memorandum was prepared by Clarke; see Lord Sydenham of Combe, *My Working Life* (London, 1927), p. 71.

in military drill and exercises. The local Danish Governor had been powerless to raise any objections and had reluctantly given the German commanders permission for the landing. Occasionally British governors of isolated colonies had been approached with similar requests.[7]

Not everyone was happy with the work of the committee. Edward Stanhope, Secretary of State for War, suggested that the committee be reorganized, or rather, that it be replaced by one composed of officers of the highest rank in the Admiralty and War Office. This suggestion was opposed by Lord Knutsford, the Colonial Secretary, on the grounds that such a reconstruction of the committee would end its essentially "colonial" character. If the War Office did not wish to continue co-operation, he said, then there were enough retired officers qualified to act as advisers to the Colonial Office to allow the committee to function.

Sir Robert Meade felt that the life of the committee was precarious. In September, 1892, he urged Lord Ripon to seek another term for Clarke as Secretary of the committee, but he did not think that Clarke's work with the committee should be extended for any specific period of time, "as the existence of the C.D.C. is by no means assured."[8] There was open opposition to the committee in the War Office, and personal dislike of Clarke by some of the War Office generals because he was both a Liberal and a Home Ruler, and was generally regarded as "too big for his britches."

Ripon's intervention was not able to secure the extension of Clarke's service with the committee, although the committee itself survived the War Office dislike and opposition. But Meade recommended a K.C.M.G. for Clarke in the 1893 Honors List, saying, "I do not suppose that any candidate could be found who has done more for the defences of the Empire or for this office than him."[9]

The Colonial Defence Committee frequently tried to prod colonial governments into action, not always with success. Efforts to collect and collate information on the defenses and military resources of the various colonies were generally successful, as were the attempts to get colonial governments to prepare defense schemes. Increasingly, colonial authorities forwarded the reports on their military posture to the Colonial Office for the committee's perusal. But perhaps the committee's greatest failure to secure action in defense planning was in Canada. Despite the prodding and exasperation of the Colonial Defence Committee, it was not until the powerful pressures of Joseph Chamberlain were added to the com-

[7] Cab. 8/1/1, C.D.C. #26, Oct. 19, 1885.
[8] British Museum, Add. MSS, 43556, Meade to Lord Ripon, Sept. 2, 1892, Oct. 14, 1892; Add. MSS 43517, Henry Campbell-Bannerman to Ripon, Oct. 20, 1892.
[9] *Ibid.*, Meade to Ripon, Dec. 13, 1892.

mittee's efforts that Canada at last asked for the assistance of a group of imperial officers in the shaping of a defense scheme.[10]

Not all of the needling or inquiring of the committee was directed at colonial governments, however. On occasion it would seek action or clarification of policy from the imperial government. In 1896, at the time of the Venezuelan crisis with the United States, the committee felt that events testified to the wisdom of abandoning the Esquimalt naval base on Canada's west coast, and it sought to obtain a decision on the matter. Other questions directed to the imperial government concerned the enlargement of the area of the colony of Hong Kong, and yet another sought permission to publish some of the reports and comments of the committee.[11]

The committee does not seem to have sounded the tocsin for colonial governments over the recurring possibilities of war. It did not issue telegrams on impending states of war, or take any action to alert colonial defenses. But it could not avoid being affected by the shifting events of international relations. It is easy to sense the note of urgency, probably caused by the pressures of the Venezuelan affair, in the secret dispatch #59 to Canada, concerning the state of the Canadian militia: "Canada, alone of the many parts which make up the British Empire, is absolutely without any organization for utilizing its splendid personnel in war. The Colonial Defence Committee view this condition with dismay . . . . "[12] The dispatch quoted the long standing pledge of the imperial government to aid Canada in case of aggression, but emphasized the time which would necessarily elapse before any such assistance could be effectively brought to Canadians. During that time, it pointed out, they would be on their own: therefore let Canada get on with the job!

While the above was a secret dispatch, the committee on occasion sought to influence public opinion by the more or less open expression of its opinion. It proposed, for example, to give publicity to its comments on the advantages to be drawn from the federalization of Australian defenses, in the hope that opinion in the colonies would respond, and that action toward federation of the colonies there would be hastened.

It was not until the Colonial Defence Committee had been in existence for several years that it ventured to draw up a statement of general principles of colonial defense. The committee was called upon by the Colonial Office to prepare a memorandum which would, to quote from a minute of Admiral Lewis Beaumont, have the effect of educating

[10] Cab. 8/2/1, C.D.C. #147.
[11] Cab. 8/1/2, C.D.C. #79, #85.
[12] Cab. 8/1/2, C.D.C. #59.

colonial public opinion in the right principles of defense.[13] The memorandum was to be confidential rather than secret, so that it might have circulation and influence among colonial leaders.

The statement which the committee prepared appeared as Memorandum #57M. In its first form, it was dated March 3, 1896, and was to be issued for the general information and education of officers of colonial governments concerned with defense matters; it was not intended to get into the hands of the press. Another version of the same document, dated May 19, was later prepared. As was to be expected, the central argument of the memorandum stressed the importance of sea power:

> The maintenance of sea supremacy has been assumed as the basis of the system of Imperial defence against attack from over the sea. This is the determining factor in shaping the whole defensive policy of the Empire, and is fully recognized by the Admiralty, who have accepted the responsibility of protecting all British territory abroad against organized invasion from the sea. To fulfil this great charge, they claim the absolute power of disposing of their forces in the manner they consider most certain to secure success, and object to limit the action of any part of them to the immediate neighbourhood of places which they consider may be more effectively protected by operations at a distance. . . . [14]

There were certain places where the Navy required absolute security for coaling, refitting, and repairing. These included the imperial fortresses of Gibraltar, Bermuda, Halifax, and Malta. In addition, several coaling stations were listed. In the defenses of these stations and other ports, the committee said that works without troops were useless and delusive, while troops without works could often defeat an enemy. Fortifications sometimes gave only an illusory security. The memorandum went on to remark that the defense schemes submitted by the various colonies, and the reports of their defense conditions, seemed to reveal an increasing grasp of strategic principle by colonial authorities.

Reconciliation of the absolute freedom of the Admiralty to move its vessels where they thought best, with the terms of the existing naval agreement with the Australasian colonies, would have been difficult at best; it would have been impossible if the colonial governments proved obdurate. This was not, however, what aroused some hostility on the part of the Admiralty to the statement. Rather, the details given in the memo caused the Admiralty to fear that the statement was too explicit in the listing of coaling stations; and there was objection also to the statement of the committee that the small arms reserves for the colonial

[13] Adm. 1/7340 B.
[14] Cab. 8/1/2, C.D.C. #57M.

military forces should be at least 500 per man. Viscount Goschen was also somewhat annoyed over the implication, in the paragraph concerning sea supremacy, that the Admiralty's acceptance of the responsibility to defend all British territory against invasion was in some way a new undertaking on its part. But efforts to secure a substantial revision were checked by the fact that the Duke of Devonshire, chairman of the Standing Defence Committee of the Cabinet, quoted extensively from it in a speech delivered at the Guildhall on December 3, 1896. Another version of the document, #90M, was prepared, and this version omitted some of the details to which the Admiralty had objected. But it was #57M which Joseph Chamberlain had ordered dispatched to the colonial governors in July that year.

From time to time the Colonial Defence Committee issued memoranda designed to bring colonial governments abreast of strategic developments, and to apprise them of changes in the over-all strategic picture. In the wake of the changes in the distribution of British naval forces in 1905 made by Sir John Fisher, the committee issued #348M, which explained the scrapping of so many of the over-age vessels, and the greater concentration of naval power in waters adjacent to the British Isles. This memorandum said that the changes were due more to the evolution of naval technology, especially the recent improvements in communication, than to any alteration in the strength and distribution of foreign fleets, though this was a factor in the changes.

The committee's memorandum went on to say that the principles of sea command were now generally so well understood that any enemy was unlikely to undertake organized attacks on commerce or commercial ports until at least one major attempt had been made to cripple British naval power. If there were to be regular and systematic attacks on British commerce, they were more likely to come during the later phases of any naval war, when the enemy's battleships had been reduced to inactivity by British naval superiority. Then they might resort to such commerce raids, for only at that stage, with their battleships immobilized, would their cruisers be relieved of the necessity of furnishing escorts for those ships.

It is notable that however much these memoranda enlarged upon general strategic principles and sought to inform colonial governments about them, they were still dealing only with defense. Nothing in the nature of offensive operations were considered; the overwhelming concern of the committee was still simply the state of colonial defenses. Nor was there any effort to create a comprehensive system of imperial defense, with, for example, allocation of various tasks of defense to different parts of the Empire. One memorandum of 1890 dealing with the advantages of federation in the defenses of Australia did suggest that these colonies were not likely to be content with the passive defense of their ports. They would doubtless desire that solid guarantees for their future security should be taken by organizing their land forces on a common basis so that they might take concerted action if necessary. The memorandum remarked, "The possibility of being able to take a vigorous offensive against points which might subsequently prove menacing would be a strategic advantage of the first importance."[15] And Sir George Clarke, not in his capacity as Secretary of the Colonial Defence Committee but as an authority on the defense problems of the Empire, suggested that plans might be developed for using colonial forces within the area of the encompassing or adjacent naval station, under the authority of the naval commander in chief. The results, he thought, would be the first commencement of a federation of the Empire by groups for the purpose of defense, and this principle, once established, could be extended.[16]

Occasional doodling of this nature also appeared later in some of the papers of the committee. For example, Captain Nathan, one of Clarke's successors as secretary of the committee, encouraged perhaps by the participation of the colonies in the Boer War, sketched out a possible use of colonial military forces in case of war with various powers, such as Russia, Germany, or the United States.[17]

But while the committee took heart from various signs of a willingness on the part of colonial governments to assume a larger role in imperial defense than that simply of the defense of their own shores, the whole problem was usually approached in the spirit of the language of the general memorandum #57M:

> Doubtless a time will come when the increasing strength and resources of the self-governing Colonies will enable them to materially assist the mother-country, by placing at her disposal for operations in any quarter of the globe bodies of troops formed from the excellent material of strong, self-reliant Colonists, but at present, the development of their own vast territories in time of peace, and the effective protection of them in time of war is undoubtedly the best contribution the Colonies can offer to Imperial defence. To this, however, there is an important exception. England may be engaged in the future, as she has frequently been in the past, in a war which carries with it no danger of attack on the Colonies. In such a case, the offer of assistance from them would be prized, not only for its real value, but also as evidence of that real solidarity on which the greatness of the British Empire must ultimately rest.[18]

[15] Sir George S. Clarke, *Imperial Defence* (London, 1897), p. 208.
[16] *Ibid.*, pp. 220–21.   [17] Cab. 11/121.   [18] Cab. 8/1/2, C.D.C. #57M.

The efforts of the committee were not always effective in eliciting action from the colonial governments. The delays in getting Canada to draw up plans for its defense have already been mentioned. It was not until 1899 that New Zealand began turning in an annual report on the condition of its defense. And when later the Commonwealth of Australia embarked on a course that was to lead to the creation of a quasi-autonomous Australian naval unit, all the persuasive efforts of the committee were of no avail in holding Australia to what the committee regarded as the path of strategical rectitude of the "One Empire, One Fleet" doctrine.

Despite such failures, however, the Colonial Office found the committee to be a useful tool. This is revealed in the reaction to Stanhope's suggestion that the committee be abolished or else greatly reorganized in membership. There would undoubtedly have been great advantage in the creation of a more imposing committee. The Colonial Defence Committee was, after all, essentially a subordinate body of a department which had not yet attained the prestige it did later in the decade. None of the members of the committee was of the highest political or military rank; nor was the committee in any way an embryonic general staff. The range of its deliberations was strictly limited to colonial affairs, and aspects of imperial defense which included the United Kingdom did not come within its purview.

Nevertheless, the Colonial Office persisted in its view that the work of the Colonial Defence Committee should continue in the same general form and remain under its supervision. Even after the creation of what was to be a much more powerful agency of defense planning, the Committee of Imperial Defence, there was resistance to the idea of loss of Colonial Office control of the C.D.C., with Sir Montagu Ommaney, Permanent Undersecretary of the Colonial Office, strongly objecting to the C.D.C. becoming a subcommittee of the C.I.D.[19]

There can be no doubt that within the range of its limited power, and in an unobstrusive fashion, the committee did a lot of useful work. First of all, it fostered the habit of thinking about defense. In a government in which comparatively little energy was expended upon thought about such matters, there was at least one agency trying to create some order and coherence in colonial defense planning. Furthermore, it established to a greater degree than ever before the exchange of ideas between the imperial government and colonial authorities with regard to defense. Such exchange did not necessarily lead to greater co-operation, for that depended upon circumstances which generally lay far beyond the control of the committee; but the pattern of consultation established by the

[19] Cab. 17/93, Ommaney to Sir George Clarke, Feb. 28, 1905.

committee contributed to the later formation of the Committee of Imperial Defence.

The Colonial Defence Committee also sought to establish a habit of considering defense more in "imperial" than in "colonial" terms. Despite its reluctance to go beyond the scope of purely defensive considerations, the occasional memoranda dealing with general principles of imperial defense, and the committee's appraisals of defense risks confronting such outposts of empire as New Zealand or Australia tended to encourage an outlook broader than the purely colonial. So also did the labors of the committee in scrutinizing the state of the military forces of the various colonies, as when it examined the colonial laws under which the militia forces and the small permanent military units existed, and when it sought to secure greater harmony of legal status among them.

While the Colonial Defence Committee sought to bring greater rationality and order to colonial defense arrangements, defense problems were also contributing to the coming of greater political order and coherence in one of the most important of the colonial areas. For the negotiation of the 1887 naval agreement with Britain had not exhausted Australian interest in defense. The sense of insecurity that had in part prompted the Australian concern for New Guinea was certainly not lessened by the annexations of Germany and other European states in the islands of the Pacific. At the 1887 Colonial Conference, Samuel Griffith, Premier of Queensland, had urged that there be periodic inspection of the military forces of the various Australian colonies by an imperial officer of General rank. And Sir James Lorimer, delegate from Victoria and minister of defense of the colony, had talked to Lord Wolseley about the possibility of a visit to the Antipodes for that purpose, and had found the famous soldier not unwilling.

The matter was raised again the next year by the Victorian Premier, Duncan Gillies, in correspondence with his fellow colonial premiers. Gillies felt, however, that more than inspection was needed; the colonies required highly authoritative military advice from someone familiar with their affairs. For the most part, the other premiers assented. Sir Henry Parkes of New South Wales alone showed signs of dissent, feeling that the colonies should act for themselves and rely on their own wisdom in defense as in other aspects of self-government.[20]

The inspection of their defenses was subsequently made by Major General Bevan Edwards, and the contribution of his report urging the federalization of Australian defenses is well established. General Edwards

[20] Victoria, Legislative Assembly, *Votes and Proceedings*, Session 1889, Vol. III, Paper #57, Parkes to Gillies, March 30, 1888. Other correspondence on the matter of such inspection and advice is also found here.

made several reports to the various governments on their defense arrangements, but accompanying these was a series of recommendations concerning the defense of Australia as a whole. It would be "quite impossible" to put the defense system of the colonies on a proper footing without a federation of the forces of the different colonies, General Edwards wrote in his report. "The Colonies have now been brought face to face with the fact, that an effective system of defence cannot be established without federation."[21]

The federation of military forces, which the General urged as an immediate goal, could be obtained by the adoption of a common defense act, which would place all the forces under one law and permit them to function without legal hindrance throughout all of the Australian colonies. (At the 1887 Colonial Conference, Griffith had said that his colony of Queensland was the only one whose law allowed its forces to operate outside its borders for the defense of the rest of Australia in time of danger or war.) There should also be, Edwards urged, a federal military college, a federal system of supplies and stores, plus manufacturing of arms, and an imperial officer of General rank appointed to command.[22]

The Colonial Defence Committee was not altogether happy with the military emphasis of the Edwards report to the Australian colonies. General Edwards had urged the completion of certain defensive works at Sydney and Melbourne as necessary to provide against the possibility of an attack by a "powerful fleet" in the case of Melbourne, and a "powerful squadron" in the case of Sydney. The committee felt that no part of the British Empire was so little liable to the danger of such aggression as Australia. No full-scale attack like that envisaged in the Edwards reports could be made until the British fleet had been worsted, and even if this were to occur, great difficulties would remain to bar any large-scale attack on Australia. There were no naval bases or ports from which the type of attack conceived of by Edwards could be launched. Recurring fears of possible Russian attack had swept the Australian colonies, but Vladivostok was almost 5,000 miles away and ice-blocked a good part of the year. The most likely menace to which Australia was subject was an attack upon its trade routes, and this could be countered only by naval means.[23]

If later it was sometimes remarked in Britain that the Australians seemed to have no clear grasp of strategic principles, the apparent confusion in the Australian mind might reasonably have been ascribed to the conflicting advice which they had received from British officers.

[21] W.O. 32/911, Edwards to Adjutant General, War Office, Nov. 16, 1889.
[22] *Ibid.*, Paper #139.
[23] W.O. 32/911, May 16, 1890.

Men like Sir William Jervois, Colonel Peter Scratchley, and General Bevan Edwards had come to Australia, worked and lived there, and encouraged Australians to build fortifications against the possibility of attack by a powerful fleet. Yet the advice which they received from afar, from the remote officialdom of Whitehall through the Colonial Office, deprecated the idea that any such fortification was necessary. The weight of the argument was undoubtedly with the remote officialdom, but the argument for fortification was supported by all the pressures arising from local fears, by the fact that such projects were within the measure of colonial competence, and further by the fact that it fitted in with the overwhelmingly military character of colonial defense forces.[24]

Despite a distaste for certain aspects of Edwards' recommendations, however, the Colonial Defence Committee tried to shepherd this movement for the federation of Australian defense forces to a successful conclusion. It approved a general plan for Australian defense developed by a committee of military commandants and officers in October of 1894, and forwarded its comments to the colonial governments concerned. New South Wales presented them to the Inter-Colonial Military Committee that met in Sydney in 1896. The local plans were revised in accordance with the suggestions made by the imperial committee, and a draft agreement to put the plans into effect was considered by the colonial premiers in March, 1896. By that time, the project of political federation came first. But while agreeing that such federation was essential for any complete scheme of colonial defense, the premiers felt that the various colonies should in the meantime amend their militia and defense acts to allow their military forces to serve in any part of Australia in time of war, and to achieve as much uniformity in organization as possible.

The Inter-Colonial Military Committee had also suggested defining a large area for Australian defense activities. The growth of a Pacific consciousness in Australia, already suggested by the effort at the annexation of New Guinea and by Australian alarm over European activities in the south Pacific islands, was further indicated by this proposal of the military commandants. Instead of thinking purely in terms of the continent and Tasmania, they recommended that the defense region of

---

[24] The confusion in the Australian mind was paralleled by a similar confusion prevailing in British military circles. There a similar clash existed between the fortification, "bricks and mortar" school, and the "blue water" ideas of the navy. Two years after the adoption of the Naval Defence Bill of 1889 in which the two power standard had been adopted into law as the standard to be sought in British naval supremacy, the Stanhope memorandum recommended the construction of an elaborate system of fortifications around London and some of the main British ports. Nor did the creation of a Joint Naval and Military Committee designed to co-ordinate the defenses of the British Isles do much to iron out the fundamental confusion existing between the two policies, as Ehrman, *Cabinet Government and War, 1890–1940*, pp. 22–23 indicates.

Australia be extended to include New Zealand, New Caledonia, the New Hebrides, New Guinea, and portions of Borneo and Java.

This ambitious planning was pregnant with the possibility of embarrassment for imperial authority. It was quite likely, for example, that an Australian federal military commander might use troops in the area outlined in a manner inconsistent with imperial policy and with the orders of a naval commander in chief. But the Colonial Defence Committee thought it unwise to suggest any changes in the geographical definition of the scope of Australian defense. The possible gains from having the power to use Australian troops, under an imperial officer, for the capture of places which might be used as hostile bases against the Australasian colonies, was most valuable. To suggest changes might create irritation and lead to a return to the limitation of Australian military action to the island continent, or might even cause the Australians to formulate plans which they might try to keep to themselves, away from the prying eyes of imperial officialdom.[25]

The growing impetus of the movement toward a federal Australia made the purely military federation unnecessary. Political federation was the overarching necessity, and when that was accomplished, military unification would follow. When federation did come, the scope of Australian action in the Pacific was somewhat more sharply defined than in the statement of the military commandants. The powers of the new Commonwealth government were limited to the naval and military defense of Australia, and to relations with the islands of the Pacific.

Aside from the gentle prodding given to Australian federation by the Colonial Defence Committee and other agencies of the British government, the decade of the nineties was notably lacking in any major development in collaborative imperial defense planning. More than ever, the matter of the relations of the colonies to the problems of imperial defense seemed to have slipped to the periphery of defense thinking. The Colonial Defence Committee continued its quiet labors, but it was the only body in the entire structure of imperial or colonial authority which was concerned with the over-all defense of the Empire, and its modest though useful work was not of a kind likely to ruffle the dovecotes of those in command.

Paralleling this general trend was the decline of the formal movement for imperial federation. This movement encountered such difficulties in the pursuit of its goal that its leaders professed to be satisfied simply with the awakened interest in the subject; this, they claimed, was all they had been out to accomplish all the time. The constitutional problem of finding a suitable legal framework for the united Empire, and the differ-

[25] Cab. 8/1/2, C.D.C. #72, July 20, 1896.

ences in the ranks of the federationists themselves between those who wished to give priority to the *Zollverein* and those who sought a *Kriegsverein*, seemed to be insuperable obstacles. In 1892 Lord Brassey, one of the leaders of the movement, said that it had been the aspiration of the leaders to "cultivate the sentiment of unity." Once that had been done, they were then content to leave it to the statesmen of the Empire to translate that sentiment into legislation.[26]

The split in the ranks of the federationists between those who sought primarily a unity of trade and those more anxious for unity in defense led to the formation of the Imperial Federation (Defence) League. Those who placed priority on defense unity had more to encourage their hopes than did the adherents of empire preference. They at least had what Lord Brassey called the "happy augury for the future" in the naval agreement of 1887. But they had precious little else to give them courage. Nothing in the decade of the nineties occurred to give them hope; there were no stirrings of events equivalent to the Sudan contingent or the shaping of the naval agreement in the previous decade.

There were several reasons for this. The decade was not, after all, a happy one for the commodity and raw material producing countries of the globe, and the major British colonies fell into that category. The long drawn out depression of the decade was felt in all of the colonies from which defense co-operation might have been forthcoming. In Canada, the early years of the decade were bleak and meagre ones; there was little economic cheer until the beginning of the rise in commodity prices toward the decade's close. In Australia, all of the colonies were hit hard by the depression, and none more so than Victoria, which had hitherto been so much to the fore in Australian defense activity. In Victoria's principal city, Melbourne, twenty-one building and loan societies folded in 1891–92. And also in Australia the issue of federation tended to put all other issues aside, due to the natural feeling that until that fundamental question was disposed of, all other matters would have to wait. Across the Tasman Sea, things were no better. In the words of a leading historian of New Zealand, "The problem facing the Liberal ministry which took office in January 1891 may be summed up in one word: misery."[27] And under the promptings of the depression, the ministry advanced that program of social reform and reconstruction that made New Zealand the object of so much reformist interest in the last decade of the century. These were not, however, activities likely to be associated with any great concern or initiative in defense matters. In this realm the

[26] Lord Brassey, "Imperial Federation for Naval Defence," *The Nineteenth Century*, XXXI (Jan., 1892), 90.
[27] Keith Sinclair, *A History of New Zealand* (London, 1959), p. 169.

spirit of adventure shown in the eighteen-eighties was markedly lacking in the nineties.

There was one colony with responsible government in which things concerning imperial defense and military matters developed with remarkable vigor during the eighteen-nineties. That, of course, was the Cape, where Cecil Rhodes's drive and ambition were rapidly involving Britain and the other colonies in a march of events leading inevitably to war. Never, perhaps, have the old liberal precepts warning against allowing colonial governments to involve imperial power in war received more ample justification. And yet the old line which they drew between British and colonial interests seemed like a doctrine from the neolithic past, something certainly remote from the thoughts of the brisk age of expanding empires. The long and tangled skein of relations existing between Bantu, Boer, and Briton, an entanglement reaching back to such things as the 50th Ordinance, Schlagter's Nek, and the filio-pietistic Boer memories of the Great Trek, was now further complicated by the overflow of British investments into the South African mining industry, and by the now firmly established imperialist faith that the possession of superior civilization carried with it the obligation to spread it to the lesser breeds without the law.

But with all the potential for trouble which was accumulating in South Africa, and even with the resort to violence in the ill-fated Jameson Raid, there was no effort to create co-operation in military relations between imperial and colonial governments. Despite the fact that of all of the colonies with self-government, the Cape and Natal lived closest to a threat of war on and within their borders, less was done there than in any of the other major colonies to create military forces of any kind, either permanent or militia. The commando system of the Boer republics had no counterpart in the British colonies, and the Cape Mounted Rifles and Mounted Police were both more police than military forces. Since British military forces had never been withdrawn from the Cape as they had from the other self-governing colonies, the colonial inertia seemed amply to justify the arguments of the advocates of troop withdrawal that this course was a necessary stimulus to colonial self-reliance in defense. At any rate, whatever the cause, and despite the atmosphere of imminent war, the springs of colonial military organization seemed paralyzed.

This inaction and apparent lack of concern about imperial defense on the part of the colonies during the eighteen-nineties was surely not due to any lack of stimulus from abroad. More than enough was happening in the fields of both empire and defense to arouse activity by colonial governments had they been so inclined. The volume and costs of the world's armaments mounted yearly. The decade of the eighties closed in Britain with the passage of the Naval Defence Bill of 1889, which adopted into law the maintenance of the two power standard. The following year brought the publication of Mahan's *The Influence of Sea Power on History.* The tempo of acquisition in Africa mounted; there were diplomatic brushes with great powers, some of which might easily have led to war. And there lurked in the background, and not always in the background, the cantankerous matter of Britain's relations with the Boer republics. The British army still patrolled the frontiers of the Empire, had numerous skirmishes, and left temporary resting places, in the words of one well known participant and observer, on the Indian frontier or on the African veldt marked by race courses, polo grounds, and cemeteries.[28]

But with all the panoply and pomp of empire still intact, and indeed, about to reach its apogee in the Jubilee celebration of 1897, it was also apparent to the discerning that the halcyon age of Britain's comparatively effortless world supremacy was rapidly passing away. The days of Victorian self-assurance—when it seemed that all the world might embrace the doctrines of free trade, the institutions of parliamentary government, the liberal traditions of voluntarism and the goods produced in Birmingham and Sheffield—seemed to be drawing to a close. Of course, the age had never been as halcyon as the true believers in peace, retrenchment and reform had hoped for. There were recalcitrant elements who had to be brought to see the virtues of collaboration with British commercial or humanitarian enterprise. The Maoris had to be persuaded to accept freehold land patterns. The tribes of the northwest frontier needed the discipline of the occasional punitive expedition. It had been necessary to check the predatory impulses of the Kaffirs. Indeed, as the Colonial Secretary was to claim, the doors of the temple of Janus were seldom closed through the wide domains of the Queen. But all of this had called for little in the way of strenuous national effort; the muscles of British power had not been strained by any of these exercises. Britons had not derived from them any real instruction in the costs of power, or the amount of blood it might take to run an empire. The army could do what was needed without placing any great demands upon either the manpower or wealth of the state, and without recourse to any powers of leadership other than those uncovered by the normal processes of promotion. The margins of safety were wide indeed, allowing the Navy to slumber in the long quiet of the Victorian afternoon, working on spit and polish, still concerned that seamen should receive training in sails, and in its business on the great waters chasing the slave trader off

[28] Winston S. Churchill, *The River War* (London, 1899), p. 455.

Africa or Arabia, or seeking out the Pacific island labor kidnapper among the atolls and reefs of the island groups.

But the long period of much empire with little effort was threatened by ominous intruding events. The unification of Germany, and with it the apparent triumph of militarism as a national way of life, were the most obvious aspects of the new "toughness of mind" and purposive national effort which seemed to have sprung into existence. And underlying this, of course, was the rejection by other peoples.of many of the virtues so long espoused and cherished by the Victorian liberals. The assumptions of constitutional government, of government by consent within the law, and of the continuing decline of force as a factor in human and international relationships, gradually gave way before the onslaught of events; the glorification of conflict for either national or class ends, which Europeans learned from such mentors as Marx and Treitschke, supplanted the old faiths.

In the new age of toughness, none had been better instructors than the Prussian "schoolmasters" of Gravelotte and Sedan. The Germanic system of military conscription was justified by victory, at least to the satisfaction of the defeated, for France adopted conscription in 1872, and Russia and Italy followed suit two or three years later. Britain did nothing so drastic, but neither was she content solely with putting the *Pickelhaube* on the heads of some of her soldiers. Impetus was given to the Cardwell reforms designed to give Britain a more effective military posture, even though they had to be sold to many of the Liberals on the basis of the economies resulting, rather than the greater military efficiency obtained.

In 1851, the year of the great exposition to celebrate the triumphs of peace, Edward Creasy wrote in the preface to his *Fifteen Decisive Battles of the World* that it was "an honourable characteristic of the Spirit of this Age, that projects of violence and warfare are regarded among civilized states with gradually increasing aversion."[29] Fifty years later Herbert Spencer saw many signs very contrary to Creasy's happy reading of the auspices. All about him he discerned the signs of re-barbarization and militarism, one of which was the considerable popularity of Creasy's book. Life had increasingly taken on the note of militancy and combat. Athleticism held a higher and more respectable place than ever among Britons. Movements of Christian evangelism and reform went forth in the militant guise of the Salvation Army, under the banner of Blood and Fire, and with the exhortation of a journal called *The War Cry*. And the followers of General William Booth were not alone, Spencer pointed out: " . . . in the Church-services held on the occasion of the departure of

---

[29] Edward S. Creasy, *Fifteen Decisive Battles of the World*, ed. Robert H. Murray (rev. ed.; Harrisburg, Pa., 1943), p. xi.

troops for South Africa, certain hymns are used in a manner which substitutes for the spiritual enemy the human enemy. Thus for a generation past, under cover of the forms of a religion which preaches peace, love and forgiveness, there has been a perpetual shouting of the words 'war' and 'blood', 'fire' and 'battle', and a continual exercise of antagonistic feelings."[30] Considering the temper of the times, it was perhaps natural that on occasion the "soldiers of the Queen" managed to get themselves confused with those militant Christians hymned by Sabine Baring-Gould and Sir Arthur Sullivan in "Onward Christian Soldiers."

The year in which Sullivan gave a new marching song to the forces of militant Christianity was 1872. That year also saw another portent of the new age of "antagonistic feelings," for it was then that the first English translation of Clausewitz's *On War* appeared. Englishmen might now learn from the master himself of the manner in which violence might effectively be pushed "to its utmost ends" in the interests of the state. And the appearance of *On War* had been preceded the year before by Chesney's brilliant *Battle of Dorking*,[31] the first of what was to be an increasing number of invasion alarm stories.

Such cries of invasion and alarm were naturally reinforced by the growth of the popular press, which often seemed to work on the assumption that in the army of new readers created by the growth of popular literacy (given great impetus by the Education Act of 1870), there were many who found fun and satisfaction in "having a good hate," especially if the hated were foreign. They were reinforced also by W. T. Stead's campaign in the columns of the *Pall Mall Gazette* in 1884 for the enlargement of the Navy. There was a new popular interest in the Navy. A leading historian has pointed out that "from the conclusion of the Napoleonic Wars until late in the century the subject of naval defence was almost foreign to English thought."[32] But if this were so, it did not remain so. The naval scares of 1884, engineered by Stead, and that of 1888, plus the Naval Review of 1887 on the occasion of the Royal Jubilee of that year, were climaxed by the Royal Naval Exhibition in 1891, visited by more than two and one half million Britons. And armed with the doctrines of Admirals Philip Colomb of Britain and Alfred Mahan of the United States, supporters of the Royal Navy founded the Navy League in 1894. Members must have seen much to make their hearts glad in the Naval Review of 1897, for 165 modern ships, drawn entirely from British waters, the fruit of the "two power standard" law adopted in 1889, were spread

[30] Herbert Spencer, *Facts and Comments* (New York, 1902), p. 178.
[31] The *Battle of Dorking* first appeared in *Blackwood's Edinburgh Review*, May, 1871.
[32] Arthur J. Marder, "The Origin of Popular Interest in the Royal Navy," *Journal of the Royal United Service Institution*, LXXXII (Nov., 1937), 763.

out for the edification of the visitors, British and foreign, who graced the occasion.[33]

Although the vessels in the 1897 review came entirely from British home waters, some of the military contingents came from the remotest corners of empire. In the disciplined pageantry of the military reviews and parades, alongside the ancient regiments of the British army were to be found mounted riflemen from Australia, and units from Canada, New Zealand, South Africa, West Africa, Hong Kong, and Burma.

But if the presence of colonial contingents, and of the leaders of the colonial governments which raised and maintained such units, was a token of widespread loyalty to the Crown, there was still the difficult and tangled problem of translating that loyalty into something the military planners could rely upon in moments of crisis. To put the co-operation implicit in the presence of the colonial forces in London on to a contractual basis seemed to be the particular need of the hour.

[33] *Ibid.*, p. 768.

CHAPTER VI

CHAMBERLAIN AND ENERGETIC IMPERIALISM

As the decade of the eighteen-eighties drew to a close, the somewhat ramshackle military system of Great Britain was passing through the opening phase of the managerial revolution. There were discernible at this time the preliminary stirrings of those who were intent upon making the British military apparatus as efficient as vested interests, inertia, and the traditions of a profoundly unmilitary people would allow. The Cardwell reforms of the eighteen-seventies had freed the British army from many of the obligations of colonial service in the self-governing colonies, and also from the long-term service enlistment which checked recruitment and made the provision of a military reserve impracticable. But enormous changes were still needed before Britain would have an effective military system. The division of power between the Secretary of State for War and the commander in chief continued to exist; recruiting lagged, and the quality of recruits obtained was unimpressive. The military establishment was not abreast of industrial and scientific developments on which much of its fighting power would ultimately depend. There was no general staff, no co-ordination of effort in the planning of the defense of the British Isles and of the vast territory that looked to Britain for security.

Things were much worse in the militia, despite its high place in the regard of those who looked for defense to the sturdy manhood of the realm, rather than to the hirelings of the regular army with their gilded coxcombs of commanders. The militia remained what it had always been, a home defense force. No militia unit could be dispatched from Britain without the assent of the men in the unit.[1] The yeomanry were

[1] During the South African War, three Irish and one Scottish battalion of militia refused service abroad, a situation reminiscent of the conduct of the fashionable New York militia force which balloted and refused to join the campaign in Cuba. J. K. Dunlop, *The Development of the British Army* (London, 1938), p. 90.

even more localized. Up to 1888 such units could not be required to serve outside their county; after 1888, they could be required to serve in Great Britain, but not in Ireland.

A number of efforts were made to improve things, but perhaps the most effective of all centered in the activities of the Hartington Commission of 1889. This was another in what had been a long series of inquiries into the management of one aspect or another of British defense organization and posture.[2] The responsibility of the commission was to examine the operations of the War Office and Admiralty. It was basically a probe into administration rather than policy. But in its final report it suggested the advisability of the "formation of a Naval and Military Council, which should probably be presided over by the Prime Minister, and consist of the Parliamentary Heads of the two services and their principal advisers."[3]

There was little imperial content in the work of the Hartington Commission. The labors of the Colonial Defence Committee do not seem to have attracted the attention of members of the commission. If its work has been called a "landmark in the history of imperial defence,"[4] it was not because the commission dealt with any aspect of harnessing the resources of the Empire as a whole to the task of imperial defense. The "imperial defence" to which it contributed was still that which was imperial in the range of its responsibilities, and not in the marshaling of the assets of empire. Imperial defense was defense controlled by the imperial government; not defense based on the co-operation of the governments of the Empire.

Nor did those who took an unofficial but articulate interest in the problem of imperial defense contribute much to the development of imperial co-operation. The Imperial Federation (Defence) Committee, one of the successor groups to the Imperial Federation League, continued to seek the wider sharing of the defense burdens among the colonies. Sir John Colomb, one of their leading figures, asked if anyone really thought that adequate naval security for a world-wide empire could be furnished by one small corner of that empire, and urged the summoning of a colonial conference to deal with the problem.[5] But a weakness of the position of Colomb and of the Imperial Defence group generally was of

---

[2] From the later sixties to 1880, no fewer than seventeen Royal Commissions, eighteen Select Committees, nineteen Committees of officers inside the War Office, and thirty-five Committees of Military Officers had considered matters of policy affecting the army. The commission of 1887 to 1890 was thus the latest example of a practice which had been thoroughly familiar since the reforming decade following the Crimean War. Ehrman, *Cabinet Government and War, 1890–1940*, p. 7.

[3] Parl. Pap., 1890, Vol. XIX, Cmd. 5979, p. viii.

[4] *C.H.B.E.*, III, 253.

[5] John Colomb, "Wanted, an Imperial Conference," *The Nineteenth Century*, XXXVI (Dec., 1894), 943.

course that Britain showed no disposition to diminish the armed forces even if the colonies made no contribution to them. The army was still largely an army of colonial and Indian service, but the area of its duties lay outside the borders of any of the self-governing colonies. It was the dependent part of the Empire, not the responsibly governed colonies, which set the size of the British military forces. And the naval strength was determined not by the dimensions of the colonial empire, but by Britain's need to maintain its naval strength on the world's ocean highways and in European waters. For generations, Britons in colonies had drawn dividends from Britain's naval power; there was no indication that those dividends were now to be denied if the colonies did not chip in on the costs.

While the Imperial Federation (Defence) Committee ploughed their unrewarding furrow, others interested in Britain's defense position and strength were more concerned with administration and planning, in leadership and organization of the British forces, than they were in seeking to harness the strength of empire to the tasks of defense. Even as empire-conscious and alert a man as Sir Charles Dilke paid no attention to this aspect of potential British strength. In the collaborative work with Spenser Wilkinson, *Imperial Defence*, published in 1892, he made no real reference to the contribution of self-governing colonies to imperial defense, beyond a brief and most general statement that the true policy of England should be to organize the military resources of her empire as a whole. And the weight of discussion in this regard was given only to the Indian army as a source of imperial strength.[6]

In his advocacy of the creation of a British General Staff, however, Dilke put forward the argument that establishing such a staff would be a major step in the development of a true form of imperial defense. Britain, he argued, needed a body of men whose duty it would be to work out the problems of imperial defense. "The problem is more difficult for the British Empire than for any other state, and yet we are the only power spending vast sums who have no General Staff." There was little hope for any form of military co-operation or federation without the planning and leadership of a general staff, and indeed the existence of such a staff would itself constitute a form of military federation. Dilke felt that several of the colonies would be willing to take a share in a military scheme which could be shown to be a part of an all-embracing organization of imperial defense. Each of the co-operating colonies, he suggested, should have a general staff of its own to interlock with the British staff.[7]

[6] Charles Dilke and Spenser Wilkinson, *Imperial Defence* (London, 1892), p. 61.
[7] Charles Dilke, *Problems of Greater Britain* (London, 1890), II, 560–64.

There were, however, no colonial parallels to the reviving interest in defense manifested in Britain. While this was due in great degree to the paralyzing grip which speculative collapse and commercial distress had upon many of the colonies in the eighteen-nineties, preoccupation with domestic problems was not the only cause of the prevalent inertia. The changing character of strategic doctrines, and the shifting technology of war seemed to put any effective participation in imperial defense further out of the reach of colonial governments than ever before. Among the many doctrines propounded by the influential Mahan, that which perhaps most affected the possibility of colonial action in imperial defense was his emphasis on the folly of naval defense anchored to the coast. Naval power, said Mahan, should be exerted far from shorelines; the enemy should be kept not only out of the ports, but also far away from the coast. The true object of naval power was to drive the enemy's vessels from the sea by the possession of overbearing naval might. And such overbearing power was to be found in the great ships, those which carried the great guns. Mahan disposed of the *guerre de course* nightmare which had troubled the dreams of British naval men; in the long run the speedy, lightly armed vessels would be driven from the seas by those with less speed but with the great guns.

All of this tended to cast a considerable blight over any colonial aspirations to participate in the naval defense of the Empire. What they had done in the past, and what they might build for in the future, were just the sorts of things which Mahan condemned. The small vessels acquired under the authority of the Colonial Naval Defence Act of 1865 were for coast and port defense; the small gunboats that had been purchased and were operated by colonial governments could contribute nothing effective to the defense of either colonial or imperial interests, if the new authority in naval doctrine were to be believed. The Naval Agreement of 1887 seemed equally unsound. It was based on a directive which stated that it was designed for the protection of the "floating trade in Australasian waters"; thus the agreement embodied the heresy of tying up and localizing the auxiliary force which it created. The formidable authority of Mahan seemed to proscribe the continuation of such patterns of the past. It posed a nice dilemma for those colonial leaders who combined a concern for colonial maritime aspirations with a sense of responsibility for the general defense of empire.

Of course, Mahan left colonial leaders the avenue of supplementing the work of the navy by defending their ports and harbors. These were essential for the maintenance of the stations along the highroads of the seas, and these highroads were the internal communications of the Empire. But the manner or degree in which colonies could make any contribution to the security of such ports was affected by the downgrading of fortifications and fixed guns as military weapons. This downgrading was implicit, of course, in the emphasis on the decisiveness of the actions of great battle fleets far at sea. In view of this assumption, it was of no significance that the defenses of an Australian port were greater than those of Malta or some of the other imperial fortresses. The most that far-distant ports would ever need would be guns of sufficient weight to repel the approaches of a raiding cruiser.[8]

Another and most practical barrier to colonial participation in naval defense was the mounting cost of all naval craft. Each passing year brought about higher and ever higher costs in naval construction, putting even the smallest type of naval vessel into a class of expense which few colonial governments could contemplate. The small colonial ships that had been ordered in the eighties for Australian ports did useful service in some cases, and were occasionally modernized; when they became obsolete, however, colonial finances did not allow their replacement by newer and more costly types.

Under these circumstances, even colonies with growing populations and expanding economies apparently could do little in the defense of empire. Thus they were back to the condition which had prevailed some decades before. New doctrines and technologies made even the small participation in naval defense allowed by the 1865 act virtually useless, and the new theories of naval conflict belittled the importance of their activities in the fortification and defense of their own harbors.

Nor was there any pressure on the part of imperial authorities to enlist a wider measure of colonial co-operation in imperial defense. In an age that had been generally regarded as the apogee of imperialism, and in which the world's future seemed to rest with the great states, it is remarkable how little effort was made in any way to secure the constructive co-operation of the colonies in the maintenance and support of empire. Things moved on much as before in relations between Britain and her major colonies; the impulses of imperialism were directed more toward the acquisition of new land and alien peoples than toward cultivation of the imperial estate which already existed. The old precepts, the old and tested principles of laissez-faire and responsible government, continued their commanding authority, along with the generally prevalent ignorance of colonial life. This combination of acquisition and inertia nicely combined the ideals of *Imperium* and *Libertas*. The *Imperium* marched formidably forward in Africa, while the *Libertas* which governed relations with the older colonies was undisturbed by any effort to create

[8] George S. Clarke, *Fortification* (London, 1890), pp. 216–17, 250, 257.

either through consolidation or organized co-operation a greater degree of unity in imperial defense.

There were, however, occasional exercises of the *Imperium*, which, had they become widely known, might well have destroyed much of the growth of sense of imperial collaboration or co-operation founded on *Libertas* between Britain and some of her senior colonies. Lack of understanding of the realities of colonial life, and of the essential nature of the pattern of responsible government, is illustrated, though slightly out of chronology, by the military and naval planning which occurred as a result of the Fashoda incident of 1898.

In October of that year, the Admiral commanding the North American Station of the Royal Navy, Sir John Fisher, informed the imperial officer in command of the garrison at Halifax that he had been instructed by the Admiralty to concert measures with him for the seizure of the islands of St. Pierre and Miquelon in case of war with France. The seizure of the islands would cut the French cables and thus isolate French forces in the western hemisphere. General Lord Seymour, who commanded the British at Halifax, was mindful of the French heritage of one-third of the Canadian population, and inquired of the Governor General of Canada, then Lord Aberdeen, if he thought any such move against the French islands would lead to reactions in Canada which might affect the disposition of British troops. He also inquired if units of the Canadian militia might be used to assist the British regular forces in the seizure and occupation of the two islands.

Lord Aberdeen replied that while there might be some trouble from rowdies in Montreal and Quebec, he expected no real signs of protest. But it was left for Aberdeen's successor, Lord Minto, to answer the latter portion of Seymour's inquiry. Minto thought there would be no problem in the use of Canadian forces to garrison Halifax while the regulars were on the missions against the islands, but he advised against stationing of the Canadian units on the islands. He also felt that any such use of Canadian forces in the French islands would be a new departure and contrary to the intentions of the Canadian Militia Act.[9]

Lord Minto raised the matter of the possible use of the Canadian forces with Laurier and the Canadian Cabinet, and found himself in conflict with them on the interpretation of the Canadian law. Prime Minister Laurier, Minister of Justice, David Mills, and the Minister of Militia, Dr. Frederick Borden, were all of the opinion that the language of the Militia Act allowed the imperial government to move Canadian forces both within and without the Dominion. The imperial government could order Canadian forces to St. Pierre, Miquelon, Martinique, or wherever

[9] W.O. 32/275B/266/191, Seymour to War Office, Dec. 14, 1898.

the exigencies of war might demand, though the Canadian Prime Minister did advise that it might not be wise to use predominantly French-Canadian units.

Lord Minto was not overborne by this body of Canadian opinion. His own view was based largely on an earlier period of service in Canada, when he had been a military aide to the then Governor General. He recalled that at the time of the Sudan affair, John A. Macdonald had felt strongly that a suggestion of Canadian forces being used in the Sudan— as were those of New South Wales—was out of the question. Macdonald was perfectly clear in his mind that, all other considerations aside, the Canadian law did not allow the use of Canadian forces on any such foreign service.[10]

All of this was relayed to the War Office by Seymour, along with the opinion which he shared with Minto, that there was no regiment in the militia efficient enough to justify consideration for any type of foreign service.[11]

The War Office minute to Lord Seymour's dispatch, signed by Assistant Adjutant General Sir William Everett, said that the War Office had been anxious to clarify the situation and to satisfy doubts arising from Minto's initial reply to Seymour's first inquiry. There had been concern in the War Office, since the whole basis of the defense of Canada in time of war depended on the movement of Canadian forces across international frontiers.

Apparently relying on the reported opinion of the Canadian Cabinet, the War Office asked Lord Seymour to make definite arrangements with Lord Minto to have Canadian troops replace the British regulars in Halifax in case any move against the two St. Lawrence islands was necessary. Seymour was also asked to send to the War Office a definite plan for the seizure and occupation of the two islands. Everett, in an accompanying private letter, stressed that Seymour should impress upon Minto the necessity for secrecy.

Seymour had difficulties in carrying out his instructions. Making the necessary arrangements with Minto took a great deal of time; Fisher's successor as Commander of the North American Station did not share his predecessor's enthusiasm for the plan; and there were doubts whether the operation was necessary if its principal objective was simply to cut the French cables—there was surely a much easier way of doing that than by seizing the landing sites of the cables.

In reply to Seymour's complaints about these difficulties, and to the consequent failure to prepare the plans as ordered, the War Office

[10] *Ibid.*, Minto to Seymour, April 1, 1899.
[11] *Ibid.*, Seymour to Undersecretary for War, April 11, 1899.

abruptly informed Seymour that the whole scheme was cancelled. He was to tell this to the Canadian ministers and any officers with whom he might have conferred. And he was provided with a "public" letter which he might confidentially display in order to announce the abandonment of the plan to seize the islands. But the War Office people were not happy with Seymour's conduct. They regretted his consultations with various Canadian officials, and also his failure to carry out instructions.

Major General Sir John Ardagh, Director of Military Intelligence, commented that Seymour had done things he ought not to have done and had left undone the things he was asked to do. Ardagh now counselled a follow-up of the "public" letter with another letter containing fresh —and secret— orders. These orders were duly sent, and in them the now thoroughly bemused Seymour was told that whether St. Pierre and Miquelon were seized or whether only the cables would be cut would depend on the circumstances of the moment. But plans for such eventualities were to be prepared for the Naval Commander in Chief and with the G.O.C. of the Canadian Militia, Major General Edward Hutton. No other person in Canada was to be informed or consulted. The necessary details of the arrangements were to be discussed only with Hutton, and nothing was to be put into writing.[12]

In defense of Ardagh in this extraordinary venture in military planning and imperial relations, it may be argued that the matter had become largely a routine military exercise, of less immediacy now that the Fashoda alarm had been abated. Further, the number of Canadian troops which might be involved was thought likely to be small. But when all this has been said, the whole idea of planning a military enterprise which would use colonial transport and rail facilities and require the co-operation of at least some colonial forces, while leaving all colonial personnel in total ignorance of the whole project, is surely remarkable—the more so, when one realizes that the sole Canadian officer who was to be consulted was actually a British imperial officer who had just run afoul of Canadian officialdom.

The whole plan placed Seymour squarely in the midst of a mess. On the basis of the earlier "public" letter, he had intended to destroy his original plans, and he had written Minto to that effect. Further, by the time he received the later secret orders, Hutton had been recalled from his post of G.O.C. of the Canadian Militia under circumstances which made it all too clear that the Canadian government would bitterly resent anything like the independent action contemplated, should it conceivably become known.

[12] *Ibid.*, Sir John Ardagh to Seymour, Feb. 15, 1900.

The whole situation verged on the bizarre, however, when Lord Seymour was ordered to duty elsewhere, and replaced in command by Colonel V. R. Briscoe. Colonel Briscoe was completely ignorant of all that had gone on before his assumption of command, and yet he had the duty of drawing up the plans required by the War Office. He formulated some rather rudimentary plans in consultation with the naval commander in chief, which involved the use of the Intercolonial Railroad to Sydney, Nova Scotia. Since any planning for the use of the road would inevitably involve consultation with the road's officials, the difficulties of planning any British military move from Halifax without co-operation from Canadians would seem most pronounced. Colonel Briscoe's laments about the difficulties he had encountered seem to have put the end to this rather extraordinary attempt in military conspiracy. But one can only contemplate with a wild surmise the state of mind of Laurier and his Cabinet colleagues had they known of the secrecy, and worse, of the deception, which accompanied the affair. The use that Henri Bourassa, Israel Tarte, or indeed any Canadian anti-imperialist might have made of the deception, had it leaked out, can be imagined. Fortunately for the sake of imperial co-operation, no word of the fantastic episode seems to have leaked, and the waters of imperial relations were untroubled, at least from this quarter.

The Government of Lord Salisbury which had come to power in 1895 was substantially better equipped to deal with imperial problems than that of the supplanted Liberals. Gladstone had deplored upon his retirement in 1894 that the world then was "not the world in which I was bred and trained, and have principally lived."[13] And the party which Gladstone had led for so long, shattered by the split over Home Rule, was still too firmly anchored to the old faith to be able to respond with anything but a dragging reluctance to the changing times. "Traditionally reluctant to face the responsibilities or yield to the excitements of Empire, it was reduced to peddling reforms for which there was no general or hearty demand. . . ."[14] These might seem extravagant words for a party whose governments had occupied Egypt, annexed Uganda, and launched Britain upon a large program of naval rebuilding in the mid-nineties, and whose nominal leadership after Gladstone's retirement was in the hands of as staunch an imperialist as Lord Rosebery. But there can be little doubt that the Conservative Unionist Government breathed more easily in the new atmosphere of power and of toughness of mind than their Liberal rivals would have done.

[13] Paul Knaplund, "Great Britain and the British Empire," in *The New Cambridge Modern History* (Cambridge, 1962), XI, 408.
[14] G. M. Young, *Victorian England, Portrait of an Age* (London, 1936), p. 173.

No member of the new government was more at home in this new world than Chamberlain, the Colonial Secretary, who with Lord Salisbury and Balfour formed the heart of the Cabinet. The facts of power held no terrors for the former Radical, and he would use the instruments of power for both reform and empire. Like the Empire itself as hailed by the Poet Laureate in 1897, he was "panoplied alike for War or Peace," seeking either a *Kriegsverein* or *Zollverein*, or both. But the union for war came first. Imperial defense, the greatest of common obligations, came before imperial trade, the greatest of common interests.

If any practical results were to emerge from his labors, however, they would be more likely in military than naval co-operation, since the previously mentioned changes in naval technology and strategic doctrine left little opportunity for the colonies to collaborate in the naval field, other than by the stultifying method of making monetary gifts or grants to the Royal Navy. Fortifications, harbor defense vessels, small coast-hugging men-of-war, were all condemned by the new strategic canons, and along with them, any possible contribution that the colonies might make to their own naval defense.

The idea of using the military manpower of the colonies for the defense of their own areas was, of course, as old as the defenses erected around the little settlement at Jamestown, or as the small bands of men who took training under the leadership of Miles Standish at Plymouth. But during the latter portion of the nineteenth century the growing concern was not that colonials should undertake the defense simply of their own areas, but rather that they should share in the defense of empire beyond their frontiers.

There had been regiments raised for imperial service from colonial populations before. The Royal Americans and similar groups raised from those elements of the American population which were loyal to the Crown during the American Revolution were one example; the Royal Canadian Rifles, raised to man the posts of Canada, were another. And there were various forces of the Crown raised in the colonies without responsible government, such as those in Malta, Ceylon, Hong Kong, or other dependencies.

Another development in the utilization of the manpower of colonies for imperial defense came with the formation of the 100th Royal Canadians in 1858. The establishment of this unit was "the first occasion on which a regiment was raised in Canada for service abroad in the Imperial interest."[15] The command of the force was given to a British officer then serving in the Canadian militia. But despite the fact that both ranks and officers of the regiment were mainly Canadian, it was only in that limited

[15] Stanley, *Canada's Soldiers, 1604–1954*, pp. 215–16.

sense that it could be called a Canadian force. It was a part of the British military establishment, and its organization and equipment were paid for by imperial funds; Canada was simply the recruiting area.[16]

The 100th Royal Canadians were definitely exceptional, however. For while the Crown colonies might continue to be used as recruiting grounds for such distinctively named regional regiments as the West Indian Regiment, the colonies which had been granted responsible government were in the main closed as recruiting areas, even had there been in Britain any great desire for the use of their manpower. But the chief British concern had always been that such colonies should organize effective militia forces of their own.

The war scare of 1878 had revealed some of the military potential of the Empire. Disraeli's movement of the Indian troops to Malta was the most apparent of the suggestions that "they little knew of England who only England knew" when it came to any reckoning of military strength. Of course, Indian troops had been used before for imperial causes, as in the case of Lord Napier's Ethiopian invasion, but this was the first instance in which such forces had been used as an element of European diplomacy. The scare of the time also prompted a number of Canadians to offer their services to the Crown, and there had been the suggestion of General Patrick MacDougall for the creation of a Canadian military unit for imperial service.[17] Yet, whatever the political possibilities of such action, the legal difficulties, the matters of the control and command of any such force, were a substantial barrier to its creation.

The legal difficulties which Hugh Childers had discerned, and which led him to put an end to the discussion arising from MacDougall's suggestion, arose again with the dispatch of the New South Wales military force to the Sudan in 1885. This was a colonial force raised by a colonial government and serving under conditions established by colonial law. The troops were essentially volunteers; they constituted no part of any scheme of an imperial reserve or anything of that character. Premier Dalley of the colony had consulted neither its Parliament, nor indeed, the troops of the units which he offered for service. But his action was sustained by a great wave of patriotic and imperial enthusiasm, which swept through the colony despite the criticism from the Nestor of Australian political life, Sir Henry Parkes, who argued that Parliament should have been consulted.

The dispatch of these Australian forces highlighted certain legal problems, however. British subjects, wherever they lived throughout the

---

[16] *Ibid.* Canada was not to be the recruiting area for long, for with the Cardwell reforms, the regiment was given an Irish domicile and renamed the Prince of Wales Leinster Regiment (Royal Canadians). It was disbanded in 1922.

[17] Cf. *supra.*

Empire, on entering any branch of military service of the Crown, came under a law establishing the code of discipline and law for that force. The British regular and auxiliary forces served under the terms of the Army Act, which was renewed each year by the passage of the Army (Annual) Act; those in the Indian Army were under a permanent army act. But the forces in the self-governing colonies were raised under the powers granted to the various colonial governments, expressed in the acts establishing militia or other defense services. Colonial governments had no power to make their laws binding on their citizens outside of their own territorial limits. Such forces could not be dispatched outside the colony and still be under colonial military law and discipline, for such law ended at the border of the colony.

Substantial efforts had been made to cope with this difficulty. Many of the colonies wrote into their military law the provision that forces enlisted under it came under British law as well. Thus, the New South Wales Military and Naval Forces Regulation Act of 1871 made the men enlisted under that act subject also to the Army Act, the Naval Discipline Act, the Articles of War, and the Queen's Regulations. The neighboring colony of Victoria took similar steps, placing its volunteers under the Army Act and the Naval Discipline Act.

But this was of dubious validity in overcoming the lack of extraterritorial legislative power. If colonial governments could not legislate for their citizens outside their own borders, if they could not, as the courts affirmed, punish one of their citizens for entering into a bigamous marriage while out of the territorial limits of the colony, then it was difficult to believe that they could place their people under the terms of imperial legislation.

The Army Act of 1881 tried to overcome this problem by the inclusion of Section 177. This in effect conferred on the colonial governments the right to make their military law binding on their forces while serving either within or without the colony. It further sought to supplement such colonial law by stating that in cases where any colonial force was serving with regular British units, where the colonial law had not adequately provided for the government and discipline of the force, the terms of the Army Act were applicable.

At one time or another, substantial doubts were entertained as to the adequacy of this act also to cover the legal *lacuna*. Dalley admitted that he might have "strained the law" somewhat, and secured the passage of a special act by the Parliament of the colony placing the force sent abroad under the British Army Act, though one would have thought that this had been done already as well as it could be done. And Lord Derby, the Colonial Secretary, shared some doubts also. He sent two dispatches to colonial governments, April 15 and 27, 1885, suggesting the passage in each colony of a discipline act designed to apply to any future contingent serving with imperial forces beyond the borders of the colony. From at least one of the colonies circularized, Victoria, the reply was that the colony did not have the power under its constitution to enact any such extraterritorial legislation.[18]

The Judge Advocate General of the army in Britain also felt that Section 177 was not quite sufficient to cover the circumstances. He felt that an Imperial Act could not in itself be binding on troops raised in and belonging to colonies. Perhaps Section 177 should be amended to make certain of covering all such possibilities. If this were not done, then colonial volunteers would have to have the import of Section 177 explained to them individually, and agree to be bound by its terms.

Although the War Secretary, W. H. Smith, brushed aside these reservations and accepted Section 177 as adequate, there were continuing instances in which both colonial and British law officers felt that they were on shaky ground in relying on the language of Section 177 to overcome the limitations of colonial legislative power. Among those sharing such doubts was Sir Henry Jenkyns, one of the prominent contributors to the Manual of Military Law published in 1899. But despite such concern, the niceties of law yielded, if such yielding was in fact needed, to the pressures of public opinion. After all, no colonist was required to serve abroad. Those who did so were volunteers, and in nearly every instance of such service were supported by pulsating currents of public emotion, which were indifferent to the technicalities of the law. The basic colonial force was and remained the militia, and in the tradition of the constitutional force, it could not be required to serve outside the home territory. At the time of the outbreak of the World War in 1914, Canada was the only state which could require its militia force to serve outside its boundaries. And of course the same principle of militia service existed equally in Britain.

Nor were the legal difficulties the only problems to be surmounted in securing some effective collaboration between imperial and colonial forces. An essential aspect of the problem was naturally the quality of the colonial forces, and the reports of British officers and governors in some of the colonies made gloomy reading. During a period of financial retrenchment, the commander of the defense forces in New Zealand was saddled with the additional duties of Commissioner of Police and Inspector of Prisons. Lord Glasgow complained that Premier Seddon of New Zealand was full of "spread-eaglism and twaddle" about defense, but actually was doing nothing. The defense forces were in a state of demoralization; Seddon and his ministers hated everything and every-

[18] Adm. 116/69; also New Zealand Parliamentary Papers, 1887, A-6.

body not entirely under their control. Defense orders were a matter of political patronage, with orders for rifles being placed with one whom Lord Glasgow called a "third-rate ironmonger in Wellington."[19]

A survey of Australian defense organization made on the eve of federation among the Australian colonies revealed lamentable deficiencies which had accumulated because of the financial stringencies of the decade, and because the approach of federation paralyzed any state interest in what was soon to be a federal responsibility. A précis of the survey made in the War Office touched on lack of support establishments for the militia units, lack of ordnance, veterinary establishments, engineer and medical units. There were no permanent units to deal with supply and transport problems. Lack of small arms ammunition was general; Victoria, once in the lead in Australian defense interest, had only seventeen rounds per rifle.

The fixed defenses, on which much attention and money had been spent in times past, were obsolete strategically, and useless in practice, for their guns were outmoded, and frequently there were mountings without guns, and guns without mountings. New South Wales had ammunition which could not be used in any of their guns. Queensland had recently bought black powder for guns which could use only cordite.[20]

Things were perhaps a little better in Canada. There "the first stirrings of reform" had begun with the assumption by General Ivan Herbert of the post of Commander of the Canadian forces. He initiated administrative reforms, including the adoption of the regimental system for Canadian forces. A step toward both greater efficiency of the Canadian forces and wider imperial co-operation was the dispatch of several officers and non-commissioned personnel of the Canadian permanent establishment for special instruction in England. As described by one historian, "although several officers had gone to England when the first permanent schools were organized in 1883, the dispatch of these men in 1893 marks the real beginning of the system of sending Canadians abroad to improve the standard of professional training of the Canadian Army and to assimilate, to some extent at least, the military training methods of Great Britain and Canada."[21]

But the improvements were limited. A report by General Herbert's successor, Major General Gascoigne, to Sir Redvers Buller in the War Office in 1896, enlarged upon the difficulties of his post. Political influence and intrigue in the militia organization made a mockery of efforts to secure efficiency; the current Minister of Militia was a Frenchman whose

[19] British Museum Add. MSS 43560, Lord Glasgow to Ripon, May 12, May 29, Aug. 9, 1894.
[20] W.O. 32/911/092/733.
[21] Stanley, *Canada's Soldiers, 1604–1954*, pp. 266–67.

knowledge of English was indifferent, whose business interests took him from Ottawa two days each week, and who, further, knew nothing of the militia. The British commander had no power to effect any real reforms. There was no proper supervision of the arms issued to the militia; the forts had fallen into decay. If England expected Canada to play any real part in its own defense, real authority would have to be placed in competent hands. Gascoigne suggested that perhaps the commander of the imperial garrison at Halifax was the man for the task.[22] The small permanent force was not in much better shape. It was specially afflicted with a high rate of wastage, one British officer reporting that for 1890–91 out of slightly less than a thousand men in the force, the loss of men during the year was 497.[23]

But the idea of empire was at its zenith, and the air full of projects of imperial confederation. And so it was almost inevitable that Chamberlain should have moved energetically to make some of the magnificent fighting manpower potential, which existed in the colonies despite the lack of effective military structure, available to the larger cause of imperial defense. In doing so he fulfilled admirably Bagehot's definition of a "constitutional statesman" as "a man of common opinions and uncommon abilities." In the age of imperialism, who better than he could bring reality to "the dream," which his biographer describes as "an empire better organized by degrees, both for trade and defence. . . ."[24] It was the long awaited opportunity of power for one who had early read Seeley and Dilke, and had taken them into his mind, seeing in the colonies, as they did, a Greater Britain overseas.[25] In the age of challenge, it was inevitable that he should try to draw such strength as they might afford to the Empire and its occasions.

The first opportunity which presented itself was the Colonial Conference of 1897, held at the time of the Diamond Jubilee of the Queen. This was the first colonial conference to come under the dominating personality of the new Colonial Secretary, and at it a more resounding imperial note was struck than at the first conference of ten years before. Unlike the earlier gathering, invitations were extended to the leaders of government of the self-governing colonies only. They all accepted, for the invitation was couched in "Disraelian terms," meaning that the imperial government under Chamberlain's influence was willing to entertain the colonial politicians with a fairly lavish hand. They were guests of the state. They had carriages of the Royal Household placed at their disposal. They were accompanied by military contingents, and

[22] W.O. 32/275A/266/4, Gascoigne to Buller, Feb. 5, 1896.
[23] P.A.C., Governor-General's File, #165, Vol. 6b.
[24] J. L. Garvin, *The Life of Joseph Chamberlain* (London, 1934), III, 28.
[25] *Ibid.*, p. 9.

invited to share in the pomp and parade of the Jubilee. The colonial premiers had a prominent part in the ceremonies of the hour, and the colonial forces marched with the ancient regiments of the British army in honor of the Empress-Queen. The whole affair, indeed, had all the aspects of imperial display which were regarded as so fatal to staunch national values by such sturdy moralists as the editors of the *Bulletin* in faraway Australia, and Goldwin Smith in Canada.[26]

It was noted during the ceremonies that the colonial military units were the representatives of forces totalling about 70,000, roughly equivalent in size to British forces in India, and as a writer in the *Times* said, it was an almost certain corollary of the British imperial system that Britain would place these forces, trained and disciplined, at her side.[27]

The Colonial Defence Committee had made its preparations for the conference, and had drawn up a long list of subjects for inclusion on the agenda. It proposed discussion of colonial assistance toward the maintenance of the Royal Navy, uniformity of military laws, regulations and conditions of service, and uniformity also of arms, equipment, and stores. It suggested that colonies should be encouraged to follow the example of Canada and establish their own military colleges, and that they should attempt to establish factories for the manufacture of some of their basic military needs. With Australian conditions more especially in mind, the committee urged that the restriction on the use of naval vessels on the Australian Station under the 1887 agreement be ended, and that without waiting for the creation of a federal government in Australia, where necessary the colonies amend their militia laws to allow use of their forces outside their own borders in defense of other colonies. The committee also hoped that there might be some informal discussion at least with Laurier of Canada on the possible exchange of military units between Canada and Britain, in line with a suggestion which had been made a few years before by Colonel I. J. C. Herbert, then the officer commanding the Canadian militia.[28]

If there had been any inclination on the part of the delegates to make defense a prominent issue in their discussions, Chamberlain gave them a strong lead. In his opening statement, he said that every war fought by Britain during the Queen's reign had had at bottom a colonial interest, or if not colonial, the interest of a dependency such as India. And he urged on the members of the conference the greater military efficiency

[26] Goldwin Smith said that Laurier had been spoiled by the Jubilee, which had been an imperialist and militaristic demonstration, and by the knighthood conferred on him. R. Craig Brown, "Goldwin Smith and Anti-Imperialism," *Canadian Historical Review*, XLIII (June, 1962), 99.

[27] *The Times* (London), July 8, 1897.

[28] Cab. 8/1/3.

which could be effected by the interchange of military units between Britain and the colonies.[29]

During a discussion of naval defense, Admiral Lewis Beaumont, Director of Naval Intelligence, appeared before the delegates as representative of the Colonial Defence Committee and, as indicated above, pressed for the removal of the restrictions placed on the movement of ships of the Australian Auxiliary Squadron by the terms of the 1887 agreement. He met with a hostile reception from the Australian leaders present. George Reid of New South Wales said that in 1887 the agreement had been regarded in Australia chiefly as an extension of local defense, and not as a contribution from the colonies to imperial defense as a whole.[30] And Premier C. C. Kingston of South Australia put forth an even more local view. He said that his government believed that the subsidy paid by the colonies should be spent locally in the maintenance of the crews and for colonial naval reserves. Sir George Turner of Victoria said that there was an agreement among the Australian members of the conference that there would be no objection to the enlargement of the area of the Australian naval station. But he stressed the view that there was a fear in Australia that without the existing restriction on the movement of the vessels, they would be removed from Australian waters in time of war. As for the thought that the Australian colonies should be more generous in their subsidy, Turner commented that other colonies got the advantages of British naval protection without contributing a shilling to the imperial treasury.[31]

All the Australian delegates insisted that the subsidy was not to be regarded as a contribution to imperial defense. It was a means of securing purely local security for Australian interests. Both Reid and Sir John Forrest, Premier of Western Australia, said that they would be unable to obtain any funds for the subsidy from their legislatures if the admirals were given absolute control over the movements of the subsidized vessels.

The strong statement of these opinions carried the day against the effort to remove the restrictions. On July 8, Viscount Goschen, First Lord, accompanied by Admiral Sir Frederick Richards, the First Sea Lord, attended the conference session. He had read the previous discussions and said that he was convinced of the difficulties which would beset efforts to secure colonial contributions in any other form. The Admiralty therefore proposed to leave the agreement in its existing form. While he would be happy to see the Admiralty given a free hand in the disposition of the vessels, Goschen said that he hoped from the political viewpoint to

[29] Parl. Pap., 1897, Vol. LIX, C. 8596, pp. 7–10. And Cab. 18/9, Misc. 111 contains the minutes of the 1897 Conference, not in C. 8596.
[30] Cab. 18/9, Misc. 111, p. 55.
[31] Ibid., pp. 57–59.

see the present arrangement continued. He stressed, however, that this
in no wise qualified the general obligation of the Navy to come to the aid
of any portion of the British Empire which might be attacked. Agreement
or no, he could think of no case other than the loss of British sea supremacy,
in which it would not be the duty of the Admiralty to defend Australia
and New Zealand.

Sir George Turner and Richard Seddon of New Zealand expressed
concern over the Duke of Devonshire's Guildhall speech of December 3,
1896, in which he had spoken of the need for full Admiralty authority
over all naval vessels. Goschen said that he knew of the speech, and felt
that it was primarily a protest against any naval policy based on hugging
the shoreline. The policy of the Royal Navy must be aggressive; it must
aim at attacking the possessions of those powers at war with Great
Britain. Within the waters of the Australian station, for example, it must
either attack possessions of the enemy power, or seek out the vessels of
such a power.[32]

To one delegate at the conference, much of this discussion between the
British and the Australians must have seemed rather remote from his
concerns. Wilfrid Laurier, recently installed in office as Canadian Prime
Minister, took little part in the discussion about defense. When he did
express an opinion, it was not what one might have expected from the
man who perhaps more than any other colonial leader was the architect
of the later commonwealth relationship, and who more than any other
was the inheritor of the mantle of Gladstonian liberalism in his advocacy
of full self-government. For Laurier did not accept the Australian views
on the nature of their subsidy payments for the auxiliary naval force, and
he kept insisting that the issue involved was not one of colonial contribution for a particular purpose, but rather one of a contribution for the
general purpose of imperial defense. Along with the rest of the colonists,
however, he did seem agreeable to the idea of interchange of military
units, and also to the possibility of recruiting men from Canada for the
regular army.[33]

To the ardent imperialists of Britain, the hero of the conference was
the Premier of the Cape, J. Gordon Sprigg. The head of an insecure
government in his colony, and fearful of the intransigeant President of
the Transvaal, Paul Kruger, Sprigg laid offerings on the altar of imperial
patriotism in the form of a gift of a cruiser to the Royal Navy. The offer
was hailed jubilantly in London. A delegation from the Imperial Federation (Defence) League headed by Sir John Colomb and H. O. Arnold-
Forster, accompanied by Sir Charles Dilke, waited on Sprigg to thank

[32] *Ibid.*, pp. 140–48.   [33] *Ibid.*, pp. 75–76.

him for the leadership he had displayed.[34] The First Lord of the Admiralty, Viscount Goschen, hailed the gift and the *Times* said that this was the first gift from a colony which could be freely applied for the defense of empire in all waters and in all conditions. The Cape had learned the sound and solid theory of naval warfare.[35]

The *Times* felt, however, that no such gratifying view could be taken of the achievements in defense of the conference as a whole. The remainder of colonial governments all too clearly did not share the sound views which prevailed in governing circles in the Cape. The statement of the First Lord to the conference members should, the *Times* thought, help dissipate some of the misconceptions of naval strategy which seemed to prevail, both at home and in the colonies. But for all its strategic limitations, the existing agreement with the Australian colonies was far too valuable politically to be lightly set aside or jeopardized.[36]

The project for the exchange of military units got no further than the efforts to secure naval contributions. While there was much general approval, the project bogged down in a discussion of the military laws of the various colonies, and the possibilities of sending the personnel of the units formed under such laws abroad with their own consent.[37]

The limited degree of approval given the idea at the conference, however, sufficed to encourage Chamberlain to push ahead with the project in correspondence with the governments of the self-governing colonies after the conference had ended. This was done with the support of the War Office, which saw in the project at least the possibility of raising the standard of military efficiency of the colonial forces. The military authorities did want assurances that any such forces would be brought under the authority of the Army Act, however.[38]

After correspondence between the War and Colonial Offices, the suggestion of the exchange was finally transmitted to the colonies in a letter of August 3, 1898. This proposal was circumscribed in its effect by the fact that the forces to be exchanged were to be limited to the regular military units of the colonies; militia were not to be included. This confined the project almost completely to the possible exchange of artillery units, since this arm of service was about all that any of the colonists maintained on a regular basis.

The responses from the various colonies raised all manner of difficulties. The Cape pointed out that their only regularly organized force was the Cape Mounted Rifles, and this was more of a police than military unit.

[34] *The Times* (London), July 10, 1897.
[35] *Ibid*. Sprigg's ironclad, which had been so joyously hailed, never materialized. A succeeding government changed the gift into an annual subsidy payment of £30,000.
[36] *Ibid*., Aug. 26 and 27, 1897.
[37] Cab. 18/9, Misc. 111, pp. 70–71.
[38] W.O. 32/908/091/2126, War Office to Colonial Office, July 22, 1898.

Its members were scattered throughout the colony on police duties. As for the sister colony of Natal, it had no regular military forces at all to put into an exchange.[39]

A mixed bag of responses came from the various Australian colonies. The Tasmanian government thought the idea an excellent one—but they had no forces. The South Australian government had a small force of artillery, but did not approve of the idea. New Zealand had neither the troops nor the power under its defense act to send men abroad for any military service. Victoria also raised the question of the legal power of the colony to send any forces abroad. The Attorney General of that colony said that the colonial government had no power of extraterritorial legislation under the colonial constitution, nor was Section 177 of the Army Act sufficient to cover the circumstances, since that would be an unconstitutional delegation of the power of the colonial government to make law for its people.

Only in New South Wales and Queensland was there an affirmative response to the suggestion. The Military Commandant of New South Wales, Major General G. A. French, suggested that they combine with Queensland to send a battery of field artillery to Britain. But this suggestion met with a poor response from the other proposed partner. The Queensland authorities regarded such a combination of units as impractical; the differences between the two colonies in pay and terms of enlistment were as great as those between British and colonial forces. The best that Queensland could offer was the proposal that two Queensland officers and two N.C.O.'s of her artillery force go to England for duty there, in return for four of equal rank to serve in the Queensland unit. Evelyn Wood in the War Office approved the suggestion; there was a shortage of artillery officers in Britain at the moment, and the colonials would be welcome. But some delay would occur before British officers could be sent to Queensland for the other part of the exchange.[40]

As far as the Canadian government was concerned, their response was largely in the form of a question: since their permanent officers of artillery were mainly employed in instruction of the militia, would British officers on exchange be willing to carry out these same duties?[41]

"And they all with one accord began to make excuses" is the text which springs most rapidly to mind. Certainly these reactions to the exchange proposal suggest strongly the limited nature of the machinery of law and the size of forces available for colonial collaboration in imperial defense. The bulk of such forces were militia, and limited by the traditions of that "constitutional" arm to service within the borders of their

[39] W.O. 32/908/091/2132.
[40] W.O. 32/908/091/2132–40, 2153.
[41] *Ibid.*, 2152.

own state or colony. And the professional forces were so limited in size, and involved in such duties that they could not be spared. Even Queensland, which had displayed a firm intention to join in at least some exchange of personnel, backed away with the threatening war scare in South Africa, not because there was any drying up of the well-springs of imperial loyalty, but simply because if those springs were to be drawn on, and volunteers dispatched to South Africa, the colony would require the services of every trained man she had.

The whole probability of any effective colonial collaboration in the Empire's defense took on an entirely new complexion when the colonies rallied so staunchly by Britain's side during the South African war. British opinion about the war was seriously divided, much more so than was opinion in the colonies. Of course, colonial participation in the war was not without some opposition, but it paled in comparison with the venomous feelings prevailing in Britain between the anti- and pro-Boer elements. In New Zealand there was almost unanimous support for the imperial cause. In Australia there was some nationalist, left-wing opposition, much of it expressed by the brilliant and powerful voice of Australian nationalism, the *Bulletin*. And in Canada the whole problem was naturally confounded by the dualistic character of Canadian society, with opposition to participation in imperial wars centering in French-Canadian voices such as that of Henri Bourassa and Israel Tarte. But however powerful these voices of dissent, they were not able to prevent the various states of the British Empire from presenting a substantially united front to the rest of the world during the war.

The overwhelming bulk of the offers of volunteers came spontaneously from the colonial governments and people. There were, however, occasional promptings to get the sluggards into action, so that the united front might be secured. Laurier in Canada was of all empire leaders the most embarrassed politically by the growth of the crisis in South Africa. As the pre-war tension there tightened, demands were heard from English Canada that its government take steps to lend assistance to the imperial cause. The offers that came from other colonial governments added to the embarrassment of the Canadian government, and Minto reported to Chamberlain that Laurier and the Cabinet were irritated by the irresponsible offers of aid coming from empire-enthusiasts throughout Canada. Laurier approved of the imperial actions in South Africa, but was opposed to offering troops because it would be a new departure in colonial responsibilities. Discussion in the cabinet on the matter was extremely heated.[42]

[42] C.O. 42/869, Minto to Chamberlain, Oct. 13, 1899.

As the issue developed and Canadians took sides and debated the matter, Chamberlain tried to guide it to what he hoped would be a happy conclusion. In July, before the outbreak of the war, and before the offer of services from any of the colonies, he had written to Lord Minto in Canada saying that the possibility of war offered the chance of showing the solidarity of empire, and that if "a really spontaneous request were made from any Canadian force to serve with H.M. troops on such an expedition it would be welcomed by the authorities. . . ."[43] Was such an offer probable? If so, it should be made soon, though Chamberlain did not want it to be the result of external pressures or suggestion.[44]

Since the Governor General showed the letter to Laurier, the hope of there being no external suggestion was speedily lost. Laurier noted especially the sentence concerning the really spontaneous offer, and for the rest was noncommittal. Chamberlain sought more than volunteers for British units; indeed, he said that he was unwilling to accept these, for the whole point of the offer would be lost unless it were endorsed by the Canadian government, and applied to an organized body of colonial forces.[45]

In the meantime the Canadian Cabinet worried over the issue, and rumor, reinforced by the news of the increasing tension in the Transvaal and of offers of contingents from other colonies, dominated the land. Laurier wrote Minto that "the present case does not seem to be one in which England, if there is a war, ought to ask us, or even expect us, to take a part. . . ."[46] But General Edward Hutton, the energetic British officer commanding the Canadian militia, had other views, and was busy making arrangements for the dispatch of a contingent, and supporting the cause by statements and speeches. The Cabinet was eventually forced into action by the public clamor, abetted by another telegram from Chamberlain, expressing thanks for the offer of forces—as yet unmade officially—and laying down the guide lines on which such forces should be organized. The publication of this jostling telegram in a garbled version left no time for further havering, and the offer of a contingent was finally made.[47] Hutton's preparations now paid off, for the unit was assembled and dispatched in about three weeks' time, and no sooner had the hulls of the transports dropped out of sight down the St. Lawrence from Quebec than the government offered a second contingent. The imperial government received this offer with thanks, but

[43] Public Archives of Canada, Minto Papers, Box MM #30, Chamberlain to Minto, July 3, 1899.
[44] Garvin, *The Life of Joseph Chamberlain*, III, 529–33.
[45] P.A.C. Minto Papers, Box MM #30, Chamberlain to Minto, Oct. 7, 1899.
[46] Garvin, *The Life of Joseph Chamberlain*, III, 530.
[47] C.O. 42/869, Minto to Colonial Office, Oct. 20, 1899.

refused, with the proviso that it would be borne in mind by the War Office. News of this offer and its refusal was released in part to the press; the declination was made public, but not the thanks which accompanied it. Lord Minto felt that this was done to embarrass the imperial authorities; indeed, he felt that the offer of the second contingent was made solely for its political effect.[48]

No such difficulties beset the other colonies whose governments decided to send forces. Offers of such assistance started to flow into London well before the outbreak of hostilities on the veldt. The first offer came from the northern Australian colony of Queensland in July. It came from the executive of the colony, during a legislative recess. The offer was made spontaneously, but stimulus was given by concern in Australia over affairs in South Africa, by the fact that many of the miners in the gold fields there were Australians, and by the appeals which they, along with others of the so-called Uitlanders, sent for support for their cause.

When such appeals were made in the form of a telegram sent to Premier George Reid of the senior colony of New South Wales, however, there was no great reaction on his part. Reid entered into correspondence with the premiers of the other Australian colonies, but his own thought on the matter was that if there were to be a war between Britain and the Boer republics, the preponderance of power was so greatly in Britain's favor that colonial troop offers would serve little purpose. When the Premier of South Australia suggested that the Australasian colonies might offer the services of the vessels of the Auxiliary Squadron attached to the Royal Navy, Reid felt that there was little likelihood that they would be of any use.

Yet by the end of October the situation had changed greatly, and all the Australian colonies with any military units available had offered troops for service in Africa. Perhaps the main element in the change was the welcome given by the imperial government to any such offers. This was made clear in the circular letter of October 3, which Chamberlain dispatched to the colonial governments. For the practicing politician in Australia there was a strong imperative to get on the bandwagon of the imperial cause. For there can be little doubt that among the general populace the support of the war was a popular cause, and that opposition to the dispatch of Australian contingents waned rather than waxed during the course of the struggle.

Such opposition as there was centered in the ranks of the newly emerged Labor Party. Nearly all the votes cast in the colonial legislatures against

[48] C.O. 42/869, Minto to C.O., Nov. 1, 1899. Minto to C.O., Nov. 21, 1899. Actually the War Office did accept the offer of the second contingent in December of the same year.

the dispatch of the initial contingents came from the Labor members. There was no party line on the issue; the matter was left substantially to a free vote of the party members, which perhaps was evidence of the fear among their leaders that a strict party approach to the matter would put it into deep political trouble. And by the time, a few months later, when the dispatch of a second contingent was to be voted upon, the initial opposition had diminished to only four votes in all of the legislative bodies of the colonies together. Influencing this vote was of course the fact of the defeats of the "Black Week" and the apparent need for the display of all the imperial solidarity which could be mustered, but it is hard to believe that more than four opposition votes could not have been assembled had the dispatch of the troops not been a genuinely popular cause. Certainly there were many more volunteers than there were places in the various units to be filled. With any real effort at recruiting, it is apparent that the Australian colonies could easily have provided more than the 16,000 they sent to Africa during the course of the war.

Perhaps as significant as the fact that the opposition to aid to Britain waned during the war was the ground on which such opposition was based. Unlike Canada, where much of the criticism was founded on the fear of further involvement in the tasks of empire, and the reluctance to contribute to the growth of the habits of collaboration, the Australian opposition was confined largely to those who felt that the only good war was the class war. The war was criticized as a capitalist-inspired attack upon the freedom and independence of liberty-loving European settlers. The basic criticism was that the war was unjust, and that therefore Australians should not volunteer for participation in it. In contrast, the position of Laurier was that the war was essentially a just one, but that Canadians should participate only to a limited degree, lest the habit of such participation become too ingrained in Canadian life.

Few, if any, such reservations or qualifications emerged in New Zealand. There the zeal for the war ran higher than in the other major dominions. Such opposition as did develop was based on grounds similar to the Australian opposition: the injustice of the war. Much of the support for the conflict, on the other hand, was in the form of a hysterical imperialism, an unthinking imperial loyalty and "Soldiers of the Queen" patriotism that was worlds removed from the calculated imperial loyalty of a man like Laurier. Somewhat representative of this was the dominant figure in New Zealand political life at the time, Prime Minister Richard Seddon, "King Dick." A strident and at times somewhat uninformed imperial loyalty was one of his principal stocks in trade, both in the Parliament and on the hustings. But Seddon was an empire defender in order that he might be an empire builder. One of the reasons for the enthusiasm with which he supported the imperial cause was his hope that by so doing he might acquire virtue in British eyes, and thus lead the imperial government to grant the long-standing New Zealand desire for control over the Fijian and other islands in the Pacific. Seddon could reinforce his claim that New Zealand stood ready to act as Britain's partner in bearing the burdens of empire in the Pacific, by demonstrating her willingness to share these burdens in Africa.[49]

Before the close of the conflict, New Zealand had sent ten contingents, totaling 6,500 men, to South Africa. And the initial enthusiasm for the struggle showed little signs of abating. Governor General Lord Ranfurly attributed the sweeping successes won by Seddon and his Liberal party in the election late in 1899 to the popularity of the government's action with regard to the contingents.[50] And he was able to report later that there were over 4,000 volunteers for the eighth contingent, and that volunteers offered their services for the ninth at a rate of 1,000 per day.[51]

The excitement of the war, and the imperial enthusiasm suggested by the rush of colonial volunteers to join the colors in so many different corners of the Empire, formed a congenial background for consideration of Seddon's proposal that an imperial reserve be established in the colonies, available for summons to imperial service when needed. Seddon made the proposal to the New Zealand House of Representatives in July, 1900. The force suggested was to be both an imperial and a colonial one, to be supported by both imperial and colonial funds. It would be available for such duty in various parts of the world as would be agreed upon by the two governments. Seddon felt there would be little difficulty in recruiting a force of about eight to ten thousand men for such service, and in view of the enthusiasm of the volunteers for South African service, this may well have been a reliable judgment.

But the constitutional and legal difficulties alluded to before still remained; the proposed reserves were neither militia nor volunteers as those serving in South Africa were volunteers. The proposed reservist would be much more a man under authority than the militiaman, for the purpose of the reserve was to have a reliable force which could be readily mobilized and then dispatched to any threatened area. Such units could be relied upon to a degree that volunteers could not. But such units would exist only by virtue of colonial law; colonial governments had no power of extraterritorial legislation and could not bind their

[49] D. K. Fieldhouse, "New Zealand, Fiji and the Colonial Office, 1900–1902," *Historical Studies, Australia and New Zealand,* VIII (May, 1958), 113–14.

[50] C.O. 209/260, Ranfurly to C.O., Jan. 1, 1900.

[51] *Ibid.,* Ranfurly to C.O., Dec. 26, 1901, Feb. 9, 1902.

citizens to serve outside their limits. Nor did the fact that recruitment for the proposed reserve would be voluntary get around the problem, for such men when sent abroad would be bound only by authority based on the somewhat uncertain foundation of Section 177 of the Army Act.

This lack of extraterritorial power of legislation was not the only legal difficulty in the way of the formation of the contemplated reserve force. There was also the matter of command of such forces when and if they might serve abroad, and the whole tangled matter of relative rank and precedence. Section 71 of the Army Act gave the imperial government the power to regulate officers vested with command over Her Majesty's forces. The power of such command was limited to Her Majesty's forces. Were colonial forces in that category? Were Her Majesty's forces not those raised by the authority of the imperial Parliament? Colonial forces were raised under the authority of the colonial constitutions and legislatures. At least one leading authority thought that such forces did fall under the classification of Her Majesty's forces. Sir Henry Jenkyns, Assistant Parliamentary Counsel in 1886, and a prominent contributor to the War Office's *Manual of Military Law*, said that they were not. The Queen, he said, had no constitutional power to raise any forces without the consent of Parliament, and colonial forces were not so raised. The fact that colonial forces were of a different category than those raised either in the United Kingdom or India was suggested by the separate consideration given them in Section 177 of the Army Act.

Other authorities disagreed. Sir Courtney Ilbert, Parliamentary Counsel in 1894, took an opposite view, as did other law officers of the Crown.[52] But despite the legal doubts or confusions which befogged the matter, Seddon's proposal, reinforced by similar suggestions from other colonial military quarters, came to form a central issue at the Colonial Conference of 1902. It constituted the main effort to translate the colonial military support of the Boer War into a reliable and coherent pattern of military collaboration among the major states of the Empire.

[52] Cab. 11/143.

CHAPTER VII

THE COLONIAL
CONFERENCE OF 1902

The Colonial Conference of 1902 assembled in an atmosphere vastly different from that of its predecessor of five years before. The previous gathering had met in what now seemed supremely peaceful times, despite the great naval review and the general bawling of the militant strains of "Soldiers of the Queen." But now the Queen was dead, and her soldiers were just getting their first respite after the bitter and long drawn out conflict on the South African veldt, six thousand miles away. The victories which followed Lord Roberts' assumption of command had atoned in part for the grueling early defeats, but these victories had not brought the war decently to an end. Instead there began a phase of prolonged pursuit of Boer guerrilla bands which continued almost to the time the representatives of the various colonies assembled in London. And at the same time charges and revelations of military stupidity, ineptitude, and inefficiency continued to pour out.

The enormous display of anti-British feeling abroad, stirred up by the war, also colored the atmosphere. Surrounded by the hostility of the great powers, the United States and Japan excepted, Britain seemed to dwell in a world of increasing peril. It is true that the various suggestions for the formation of a coalition of continental powers against Britain never got off the ground.[1] But the vitriolic attacks of the continental press, especially the German press, were warning enough that if the German government was not willing to go too far in its condemnation of British policy, German opinion was. Much of the scurrility of the German press campaign of lies and filth against Britain, against the war, against the morals of the British Royal Family, against British commanders and troops in Africa, was concealed from the British public. With one or two

[1] William L. Langer, *The Diplomacy of Imperialism* (2d ed.; New York, 1960), pp. 651–72.

exceptions, the correspondents of the British press in Germany took the tone of their dispatches from the attitude of the German government rather than from the press. But even so, few Britons could have harbored the thought that they were popular abroad.[2]

If the German government was not receptive to the idea of a coalition of powers against Britain for the sake of the Boers, it was succeeding in rallying German public opinion behind the cause of naval expansion. The Boer War and the lead of the Kaiser had enabled the naval authorities to follow the passage of the first naval bill in 1898 with the introduction of yet another such bill in the following year. Admittedly there was confusion as to the value and purpose of all this, but that did not diminish the stark fact of naval power which was emerging on the other shore of the North Sea. There was much apparent justification for Chamberlain's statement that the Empire was under attack from all sides, and for his inference that Britain and the Empire had better look to its interests.[3]

In the midst of the hatred and contumely of other nations, the staunchness of the colonies shone forth like a good deed in a naughty world. Colonial contingents were fighting side by side with the British troops in Africa, and there were more available where those had come from. Only in Canada, among the major colonies, was there some restraint; but while the Canadian government withdrew to some extent from the recruitment and formation of contingents, Canadians in numbers still sought African service in one way or another. In Australia and New Zealand there were more volunteers than places in the units formed; this despite the fact that by the spring of 1900, according to population, the New Zealand contingent in South Africa was the equivalent of a force of 107,000 men sent from more populous Britain.

And the attacks made by the foreign press on the conduct of British soldiers aroused much the same indignation in the colonies as in Britain. While there were many who shared the forthright opinion of a leading Australian paper that "never was it more conspicuously true than now that the British army is largely led by asses . . . ,"[4] it was definitely not cricket to attack the men they commanded. The Australian House of Representatives passed a resolution—followed, as such resolutions frequently were, by three cheers for King and Empire—deploring such attacks and defending the martial honor of the British warrior. The resolution also affirmed the readiness of the new commonwealth to give all requisite aid to the mother country in order to bring the war to an

[2] Oron J. Hale, *Publicity and Diplomacy* (New York, 1940), ch. VIII.
[3] Julian Amery, *Life of Joseph Chamberlain* (London, 1951), IV, 405.
[4] *The Age* (Melbourne), Jan. 1, 1902.

end.[5] There was some demur over the sweeping nature of the pledge of continuing collaboration in the war effort; one member said that Australia had very few young lives to spare.[6] But the resolution passed without difficulty.

Such manifestations of imperial loyalty were naturally most warmly received in Britain. Balfour said that the offers of the contingents indicated that Britain had with it the conscience of the Empire.[7] Lord Charles Beresford said that of all the incidents of the war, the greatest was the line and view that the colonies had taken of it.[8] And the *Times* thought that the issue of the war had never been better put than in Laurier's speech to the first contingent on its departure, when he told its members that the cause for which they were going to fight was the cause of justice and humanity, of civil rights and religious liberty.[9]

To the Irish Nationalists and Home Rulers, all of this fervent imperial loyalty, this demonstration of the use to which Home Rule was put by colonies which had it, was most distressing. Indeed, it made them waver in their faith. Michael Davitt admitted that the fact that Irishmen in Canada and Australia were siding with Britain because they had Home Rule there made him question the value of Home Rule. If he thought that the concession of this right to Ireland would make him give his sympathy to a war of cowardly injustice and tyranny, he would cease to be a Home Ruler.[10]

With Britain at war, and with colonial support shown mostly through military assistance, it was natural that hopes for placing the Empire on a business footing, as Lord Rosebery put it, should center on defense. Of course, when Englishmen of the day talked about imperial defense, and of the need for placing it on a sounder footing, it is sometimes difficult to discern whether they were really concerned about the Empire, or about some social scandal involving officers of the Brigade of Guards. "Empire" and "imperial" shrank remarkably at times and seemed to be terms largely applicable to the affairs of some Lesser Tolpuddle on the Wold. The foes of Irish Home Rule could refer to that idea as causing the disruption of the Empire, just as if John Bull's Other Island were all the world; and it was possible for some to refer to "imperial" contributions to local taxation, when they were discussing Treasury grants to local governments in the United Kingdom.[11] This confusion of Empire with one's own back yard had its colonial counterpart, but since the colonies were more dependent than Britain on the imperial connection, there was somewhat less of it.

[5] Commonwealth of Australia, *Parliamentary Debates*, VII (Melbourne, 1902), 8739. The passage of the resolution was perhaps spurred by the fact that there had been some aspersions in the German press also against the courage of the Australian forces.
[6] *Ibid.*, p. 8754.　　[7] *The Times* (London), Oct. 18, 1899.
[8] *Ibid.*, Nov. 6, 1899.　　[9] *Ibid.*, Nov. 1, 1899.　　[10] *Ibid.*, Oct. 18, 1899.
[11] *The Economist* (London), March 1, 1890.

It was natural that before the Colonial Conference assembled, plans were made by some of the service chiefs as to the suggestions and recommendations to be presented to the gathering. In April of 1902 an informal meeting of Admiralty officials was held, including the First Lord, Lord Selborne, the First Sea Lord, and the Director of Naval Intelligence, Admiral Reginald Custance. Much of the discussion centered on the question of further colonial subsidies for the Navy, in line with the agreement of 1887 negotiated with the Australian colonies. But dissatisfaction with that agreement was widespread, for it was felt to be out of harmony with newer strategic thought. The conclusion was that the word "defence" should be dropped from the agreement, and that a new statement of the requirements of the Australian Station and its costs should be drawn up. It was further decided to seek a *pro rata* contribution per head from Australia and New Zealand, and it was determined that under no condition would the Admiralty agree further to any terms which bound them to tie the vessels of the Squadron to the waters of the Station. Yet despite all the dissatisfaction with the Australian agreement, it was decided to seek a modified agreement of the same kind with Canada.

These decisions formed the basis of the memorandum entitled "The Colonies and the Navy," initialed by Lord Selborne in May of 1902.[12] The memorandum enlarged upon what the Admiralty regarded as the major defects of the agreement with the Australian colonies. One of these was the limitation on the Admiralty control of the vessels; the other the failure of the agreement to attract Australians and New Zealanders to a naval career, for it was felt that the agreement had created no personal interest in the naval service in either of the Australasian colonies.

There were, of course, other weaknesses stemming from the terms of the agreement as it stood. The locking up of the vessels was but part of the "ludicrous"—the word was John Fisher's—distribution of ships around the globe. Further, the fact that the Admiralty to some degree did lose control over the ships on the Station led them to see that nothing very good or modern in the way of vessels went there.

The Intelligence Department worked out a statement setting forth the optimum size of the naval forces in Australasian waters, in view of the size of forces in the adjacent East Indian and Chinese stations, and of French and Russian naval power in the Far East. While rejecting the idea of limiting the movement of the subsidized vessels to the Australasian area, the Admiralty was willing to limit them to that and the other two neighboring stations. It further hoped that the contribution of the colonies might be increased from the existing £126,000 to £410,000.[13]

Chamberlain was not altogether happy with this preparation. A conference with him in June prompted Lord Selborne to ask Custance for

[12] Adm. 1/7610.   [13] *Ibid.*

a general statement of the naval problem. It should get down, he said, to the elementary principles of the case, and should also be pointed so as to elicit an inquiry of "What do you propose?" from the colonial representatives. The answer, of course, would be larger and better subsidies.

The military were also making their preparations for the conference, and these centered around the stimulating suggestion which had come from faraway New Zealand: Prime Minister Seddon's proposal, previously referred to, of a force of New Zealanders which would stand as part of the reserve forces of the British army. After his sweeping reelection in December, 1899—an election victory which the Governor attributed to the popularity of Seddon's vigorous sponsorship of the contingents to South Africa—Seddon sent a memorandum on defense to the Governor.[14] He stressed the lack of capital in the colony for defense forces and equipment and suggested the possibility of a British loan, at the relatively low rate of 3 per cent. He went on to suggest the creation of a joint colonial and imperial reserve force, composed of trained men and available for service in areas agreed upon by the two governments. Seddon made the same proposal to the New Zealand House of Representatives in July, and the legislature accepted the scheme by the adoption of the Defence Act Amendment Act of 1900.

The passage of this legislation in New Zealand inevitably meant that the possibility of creating a system of imperial reserves in the major colonies would be a central consideration at the forthcoming conference. The fact that a colonial government had taken the initiative would give to the discussion an edge which had never previously attached to the idea. The colonial action met the first requirement laid down by Lord Lansdowne for consideration of any such plan: that the initiative must come from the colonies.

Of course, the suggestion that there be imperial reserves in the colonies had cropped up before from time to time. Perhaps the most notable advocate of the idea, before Seddon, had been Lord Brassey. While serving as Governor of Victoria in the mid-nineties, Brassey had urged that it would be possible and advantageous to create a force of about 5,000 riflemen for such service. He had estimated that a subsidy of £20 per man each year from imperial funds would suffice to attract recruits and to maintain such a unit at a high level of discipline and training.

The Colonial Defence Committee had reacted coolly to the suggestion, seeing considerable difficulties in the way of any such scheme. It would be hard to secure a permanent supply of officers for any such force. The costs of such a force maintained in Australia would be much greater than a similar force in the United Kingdom, because of the expense of

[14] C.O. 209/260, Earl of Ranfurly to C.O., Jan. 1, 1900.

the proposed subsidy and the higher rates of pay and other charges in the colony. (The committee estimated the cost of a force of 5,000 at £1,050,000 per year, compared to £640,000 for a comparable body raised and maintained in Britain.) Further, because of Australian conditions, the men would be far too scattered to be trained effectively. And there was the strong possibility that in time of actual combat, the Australian governments would resist the withdrawal of their most highly trained force from the continent for service elsewhere.[15]

Brassey, not silenced by the committee's objections, tried to argue the case. But the committee held to its position, although it did suggest the recruitment of an Australian regiment for the regular army, which would co-operate in the manner of the linked battalion organization of the Cardwell system. The committee hoped that the opportunity for travel and service abroad might be regarded as compensation for the low rates of pay which prevailed in the British forces. Most of the colonial governments felt, however, that such pay would be an almost insuperable barrier to any recruitment.

Yet in the wartime atmosphere and manifest imperial unity of the hour, more seemed possible than in the piping times of peace. Thus Major General G. A. French, commandant of the military forces of New South Wales, noting that "few who had not resided in these colonies during the past six months could realize the intense enthusiasm and desire among all classes to take part in the war . . . ," suggested yet another scheme for imperial subsidy of reserves. Lieutenant Colonel E. A. Altham, Assistant Quarter Master General, reacted to this suggestion, observing that the past twelve months had demonstrated that the regular army was not sufficient to meet the military needs of the Empire, and that the colonies were both willing and able to offer military assistance of great value. But there should be a definite contractual relationship entered upon beforehand, rather than a reliance upon spontaneous offers; for unless a colonial government could point to some such long-standing agreement, it would be difficult if not impossible for them to resist an outcry to keep the troops at home.[16]

Colonel Altham drew up a set of considerations governing the use of the proposed reserves. Two conditions, he felt, were essential: the United Kingdom must be able to rely with certainty on any such force being of definite size and available for service anywhere on the globe; and the contingents had to be efficient in both training and equipment. Altham outlined what he thought the various colonies might be encouraged to do. The Australian colonies might well raise a force of 9,000 men, New

[15] W.O. 32/275A/266/45; CDC Memo. 126M, Feb. 25, 1898.
[16] W.O. 32/275A/266/59.

Zealand 4,500, and Canada 3,000. The strategically weak position of the latter made it unwise to consider plans that would entail the withdrawal of any large numbers from her local forces: for the defense of Canada in a war with the United States would be the most difficult military problem the Empire could ever face.[17] Altham was willing to consider the idea that some form of imperial subsidy was perhaps necessary to bring any reserve forces into being. The amount of payment per man would depend on the length of time spent in training each year.

The Colonial Defence Committee, however, remained lukewarm to the whole idea, reflecting some of the concern of the Admiralty over the possibility of paying imperial subsidies to colonial governments for military defense just at the time when the Admiralty was seeking larger subsidies from the same governments for naval defense. The recent legislation in New Zealand was applauded. The scheme was conceived in a broad and patriotic spirit; it gave promise of knitting together the land forces of the Crown and marked a distinct step toward a comprehensive system of imperial defense.[18] But with all this, the committee was by no means as hospitable to the idea as Colonel Altham had been. Captain Nathan, the current secretary of the body, said that he was averse to all such plans. Recent experience in the Boer war had shown that they were not necessary. They would throw an additional burden on the British taxpayer, who was already charged with the cost of the Royal Navy, coaling stations and garrisons, and the regular army. Formal agreements were likely to lead to disputes; it was far better to rely upon the spontaneous loyalty of the colonies than to demand troops from them under the terms of an agreement.

Even so, an unidentified member of the C.D.C. apparently thought it worthwhile to sketch out roughly the various areas of the world in which any possible imperial military reserves raised in the colonies might be used. A minute in the War Office files records a number of suggestions. In case of a war with the United States, Canadians would be held to a defense of their own frontier; Australians and New Zealanders might be used in operations along the Pacific seaboard; and troops from South Africa would be used in the main theater of war, wherever that might be. In case of war with France, the Canadians could be used against the French West Indies, the Australasians against the French islands in the Pacific, and the South Africans could be used in Egypt and the Indian Ocean area. Various other contingencies were mentioned and planned for, including a war with Germany in which the Australian and New Zealand forces would be utilized against German Southwest Africa.

[17] Cab. 8/3/2.   [18] Cab. 8/3/1.

There was apparently no place for Canadians in a conflict with Germany, for they were ignored in these hypothetical assignments to combat.[19]

But the memorandum of the Colonial Defence Committee on the possibility of subsidized reserves in the colonies reflected nothing of this strategical "doodling." It omitted the question of subsidies altogether, dwelling instead on the possible gains which might be realized from some definite agreement between Britain and the colonies. It recognized that Britain possessed great advantages in its ability to draw upon the large communities of white subjects outside of Europe for military assistance. But plans for ensuring combined military exertion by all parts of the Empire depended on voluntary co-operation on the part of the self-governing colonies. The committee hoped that these colonies would be able and willing to give some assurance regarding the strength of the contingents which they would be able to place at the disposal of His Majesty's government for extra-colonial service in the case of war with some European power. In return, the imperial government might be able to inform the colonial governments of the nature of the duties which might be assigned to their forces—a faint and muted echo of the assignment of hypothetical colonial forces in the case of the hypothetical conflicts suggested above.[20]

Little was new in any of this. There was no apparent realization that the war had revealed the existence of a great imperial patriotism, which might now be effectively drawn upon for the better defense of the Empire. The programs and suggestions of both the Admiralty and the Colonial Defence Committee ran along entirely conventional lines. The most notable military topic, the matter of colonial reserves, had reappeared on the agenda as the result of colonial initiative. To speak of this limited program of defense collaboration as a "dead set . . . to take advantage of the supposed wave of imperial enthusiasm following the Boer War,"[21] as Laurier did later, is surely exaggeration. In view of the emotions of the hour, and the existing evidence of colonial willingness to give aid, a smaller program could scarcely be conceived.

To be sure, there were certain intractable problems, perhaps sometimes more apparent to Whitehall officialdom than to colonial politicians, that limited the possibilities of defense collaboration. To the Admiralty, the need for one fleet operating under one command seemed imperative for the effective defense of the Empire. It followed that the only practical manner in which the colonies could contribute to that defense was by bigger subsidies with no strings attached, a clause regarded as particularly

[19] Cab. 11/121.
[20] W.O. 32/908, C.D.C. Memo. 293M.
[21] O. D. Skelton, *Life and Letters of Sir Wilfrid Laurier* (New York, 1922), II, 300n.

important by an Admiralty already contemplating a sweeping redistribution of its forces.[22]

As for the military forces, any project for the creation of colonial forces to act as imperial reserves ran counter to decisions made long ago, decisions on which the constitutional structure of the existing Empire was built. With the granting of responsible government, the imperial government had abandoned the power of coercion over citizens of these colonies. Ability to command the services of these people depended solely on the co-operation of their governments, and such co-operation was more likely to flourish in an atmosphere of freedom; loyalty could not be secured by contract.

The cautious nature of the proposals put forward by the imperial authorities was to be more than justified by the results of the conference. As would soon be argued by the acute student of imperial relations, Richard Jebb, the assistance rendered by the colonies in the form of the military contingents was based more on a growing self-respect, akin to nationalism, than on an imperial patriotism. It was national sentiment in Canada and Australia which demanded that they share in the dangers of empire as well as the benefits which they had long known. Self-appreciation would no longer permit colonial peoples in such advanced areas to feel that they could make no significant contribution to the war in which Britain was engaged. Further, Jebb felt that the course of the war had reinforced this self-appreciation and had helped to exorcise from the colonial mind the attitude that things colonial were in all respects inferior to all things British.

By the end of the war, colonial opinion on the military question had become crystallized. It may be summarized as follows. Officers and men alike proved superior in this war to their British brethren; more adaptable to the business at hand; more used to life in the open; handier to make shift under difficulties. They were horsemen, not men on horses. They have eyes and can use them, having been reared in countries of big distances and dazzling mirages. They are not intellectually fettered by rule of thumb, nor by red tape. The officers are not hampered by aristocratic habits and mannerism, but are more in sympathy with their men. The men are not mere machines without individual intelligence; but being used to think for themselves make better use of cover, and are less liable to panic when deprived of their leaders.[23]

There are limits to the acceptance of such a view as Jebb's. He was describing what might be called the cautious nationalist, not the extremist

---

[22] In Feb., 1902, the Admiralty advised the Colonial Office that "in view of the great development which is taking place in certain Foreign Navies, it has become necessary for strategic reasons to concentrate more than is the case at present the Naval force in commission." C.O. 42/889, Admiralty to C.O., Feb. 11, 1902.

[23] Richard Jebb, *Studies in Colonial Nationalism* (London, 1905), p. 127.

viewpoint as expressed, for example, by the *Bulletin* of Sydney. That eloquent spokesman for an aggressively Australian nationalism did not hesitate to condemn the war out of hand as Jewish-inspired, sneering at those whom it called the "Cohentingenters."

But the extremism of the *Bulletin* was not typical of the general circumspect combination of national and imperial loyalties suggested in Australia by such men as Alfred Deakin, and in Canada by Wilfrid Laurier. The *Bulletin's* nationalism lacked the element of imperial feeling; as in contrast, the imperialism of New Zealand's Richard Seddon lacked nationalist content in its devotion to all things British. Both were extremists, out of touch with the mainstream of development of British imperial relationships.

Foremost among those representing the moderate combination of national and imperial loyalties was, naturally, Laurier. With his attachment to the British tradition based on intellect rather than emotion, and with a deep consciousness of his duties in the creation of a united Canada out of the disparate elements of its population, he approached all matters with a native caution, a caution strongly reinforced in matters imperial. He had approached the clamor for the dispatch of forces to South Africa in just such a manner, later taking pride in his refusal to be carried away by "passion or prejudice or even enthusiasm."[24]

But Laurier had been jostled about in the making of his policy toward the war, and he had been called upon later to defend his policy from attacks of both imperialist and French-Canadian groups. The Canadian government's nationalist feelings had been revealed at that time by its demand that the contingents sent overseas stay together and maintain their Canadian identity, rather than being absorbed as individuals into British units.

It was natural that Laurier would be opposed to any commitments which might limit the discretion of future Canadian governments, or assist in dragging Canada into the "vortex of militarism" which was the curse of Europe. He could see little use in any discussions of schemes for imperial defense collaboration at the conference.[25] The prospect of closer connection with the imperial military structure and personnel through any such plans as the projected reserve was also likely to arouse his apprehensions; for the recollection of the ebullient General Edward Hutton could not have faded from his mind.

General Hutton was one of the unfortunate British military officers picked to hold the position of General Officer Commanding the Canadian militia (G.O.C.). He already had some experience with colonial military

[24] Skelton, *Life and Letters of Sir Wilfrid Laurier*, II, 98n.
[25] *Ibid.*, p. 293.

forces, for he had been commander of the military forces of New South Wales. But as he and others before and after him found, the post of G.O.C. was something special in its trouble-making potentials. For one thing, the position itself was a difficult one, fraught with all the hazards of divided loyalty and responsibility. Of course, such a division of loyalties existed not in the terms of the law, but rather in the limitations of human nature. The Canadian militia act was clear enough: the officer commanding the militia was a Canadian officer, holding a Canadian commission and responsible to the Canadian government. But the chief qualification for the job was that one must be an officer of His Majesty's regular forces, with the rank of colonel or higher. It was imposing too great a strain on most men reared in the service of the Crown to ask them to serve the Crown solely through the Canadian government, rather than in a wider and more imperial sense.

Hutton was one who had not been equal to the strain. An active and effective leader in many ways, he lacked the tact necessary to understand and appreciate all of the constitutional subtleties of his position and all of the niceties of Canadian politics. The approach of war in Africa, and the possibility of a Canadian force being sent there, had been too much for him. Without waiting for the decision of the government by whose commission he held authority, he busied himself in preparing for the formation of a contingent, and in encouraging public opinion to expect such a contingent.[26]

Hutton's activities had naturally done little to endear him to the Canadian Cabinet, and when he gave forth a blast against what he regarded as political interference in the management of the militia, the Cabinet asked that he be relieved of the command. Lord Minto, while acknowledging Hutton's lack of tact, sought to have him retained. But the Cabinet took the high line of ministerial responsibility (which Minto had not contested). They maintained that imperial officers seemed to be under the delusion that they served in the Canadian forces as imperial officers, and therefore were not really under the control of the Canadian minister. This was, they asserted, a wholly erroneous position; such officers were subject to and under the control of the policy laid down by the advisers of the Crown in Canada. Further, the position of the minister concerned was not that simply of a supervisor; he was the active head of administration, with the G.O.C. simply his expert adviser.[27]

[26] Hutton later stated that he began his preparation for the dispatch of a contingent several months before the decision for its formation had been made. "The boots alone with which the men were provided had to be made, which took at least six weeks." *Journal of the Royal United Service Institution*, L (July–Dec., 1906), 885.
[27] C.O. 42/875. The views of the Canadian Cabinet were appended to Minto to C.O., Feb. 8, 1900; John Buchan, *Lord Minto: A Memoir* (London, 1924), pp. 123–49.

Following the termination of Hutton's command, there were other irritants. The choice of Hutton to command forces including the Canadian contingents in South Africa was regarded as a snub by some of the Canadian officials. The lack of zeal in Canada for further contingents annoyed some in London. And the suggestions that command of the Canadian militia should properly belong to a Canadian also generated irritation in one or another officer concerned with Anglo-Canadian relations. Lord Minto was so aroused by some of these disputes, and so suspicious of ministerial and political interference in the affairs of the militia, that a calming influence had to be exerted from London. Chamberlain and Sir John Anderson both urged that it was impossible to treat Ministers as if they were not to be trusted.[28]

In view of the Hutton episode and subsequent irritations, it was not remarkable that Laurier's views on imperial federation, as reported by Minto in June, 1901, had in no way changed. Laurier still held to the view that Canada's future would lie in the assumption of greater national responsibility rather than in any imperially centralized schemes, political or military. "In fact," reported Minto, "he would appear to expect more good in an imperial sense from sentimental connection with the old country, than from any official participation in the central councils of the Empire." Minto also passed on Laurier's statement that the time had not come for Canada to undertake any great expenditure for imperial defense; any increased outlay in that direction would be neither understood nor approved.[29]

Nor had Laurier changed his views in any way as the conference date approached. On the eve of departure he wrote to his friend J. S. Willison of the Toronto *Globe*, that

> With regard to the question of Imperial Defence, I am prepared for a storm, but this is a thing as to which I have my mind firmly made up. I am not disposed to go into military expenditure any more than we have done in the past. There is a movement on foot to bring the Colonies into the vortex of expenditure which Great Britain [sic] situation and warfare make incumbent upon her. The principal item of expenditure in Great Britain's Budget is land and marine armaments; the principal item of Canada's Budget is public works and we have as yet so much to do in that line that to divert any portion of that expenditure to throw it into armaments would seem to me like suicide.[30]

[28] The issue which so aroused Minto was the proposal that the choice of the graduates of the Canadian military college who were to receive imperial commissions should be taken from the G.O.C. and given to the Minister of Militia. Minto regarded this as a pure patronage proposal. C.O. 42/875,, Minto to C.O., April 6, 1900.
[29] C.O. 42/883, Minto to C.O., June 4, 1900.
[30] Public Archives of Canada, Laurier MSS, Vol. 229, 64256, Laurier to Willison, April 14, 1902.

The Australian representatives to the conference were Edmund Barton, Prime Minister, and Sir John Forrest, Minister of Defence of the newly established commonwealth. Their new status of nationhood had been secured after a decade of hard work and negotiation, and their most recent recollections of imperial negotiation were of the general receptivity in Britain toward Australian federation. There had been some disagreements, chiefly over the right of appeal from Australia's High Court to the Judicial Committee of the Privy Council, with but that exception the proposed Australian constitution, certainly one of the most democratic then written, had received cordial support from Chamberlain in its passage through Parliament.

The Australian Commonwealth had taken over the organization of some of the later contingents sent to South Africa, superseding the colonies (now became states) in that task. In addition to this, the new government also confronted the job of trying to weld into shape the various military units which it had inherited from the colonies. Burdened with these duties, and with all of the other tasks of any new government, the Australian representatives had every reason to play it cosy and to avoid anything in the way of a bold and vigorous stand. This attitude was reinforced by one of the limitations on the new government written into the new constitution, the so-called "Braddon blot." Written to ease the transition of the states into the new federal structure, the clause required that for a number of years, three-fourths of the customs revenue collected by the Commonwealth was to be turned over to the states. Since customs were one of the main sources of revenue, this was a crippling limitation of the powers of the new government, sufficient to plant caution in the minds of any of its ministers.

Of course, defense had been one of the main factors pushing Australians into the formation of the Commonwealth. The creation of the new union had stemmed to a great extent from the recommendations for federalization of defense in the report of General Bevan Edwards; this report had triggered off the federation drive climaxed by the establishment of the Commonwealth. But the concern for defense was Australian in focus; it was, after all, Australian federation, not imperial, which was the object of all the sweat and labor. And with the assistance of a lengthy series of reports and recommendations from the Colonial Defence Committee— extracted from the accumulated knowledge in their files—and under the leadership of the ubiquitous General Edward "Curly" Hutton, the shaping of a Commonwealth military establishment was underway.

From the previous colonial governments, the Commonwealth also inherited the existing naval agreement. In naval defense, the ministers of the new government had sought the advice of Admiral Lewis Beau-

mont, since 1901 Admiral of the Australasian Station, before their departure for London. There seems to be substantial evidence that even
though the Admiral was not altogether orthodox in his views, at least
in the eyes of the Admiralty, it was he who substantially suggested the
line of argument of a memorandum on the naval defense of Australia which
Forrest carried with him to London. Nothing could have been more
satisfactory to the Admiralty pundits than this, for it gave complete
acceptance to the continuing need for the "one ocean, one fleet, one flag"
doctrine, and to support by colonial governments of the naval pre-
eminence of Britain through subsidies. Forrest's education in naval
matters, from Admiral Beaumont in Australia and other naval officers
whom he met in Britain during the conference, apparently went forward
apace. In Australia he had expressed to Beaumont some fears that the
local existing reserve naval brigades were not being used, and he had
urged that they be given a chance for some service, with the object of
gradually building up an Australian navy. It was during this discussion
that Beaumont had sought to put before Barton and Forrest the principles
of naval defense as he saw them. After reaching London, Forrest had
meetings and exchanged letters with Admiral Reginald Custance,
Director of Naval Intelligence, and it became evident that Beaumont's
persuasive efforts must have effected a conversion in Forrest. For in
this exchange of letters Forrest rejected the idea of allocating certain ships
to be paid for by Australia, on the grounds that this gave support to those
who advocated an Australian navy. This, he said, would be useless for the
imperial cause and would encourage the establishment of petty navies
in each part of the Empire. Forrest was not inclined towards any large
increase in the Australian payments towards the Royal Navy, however,
and he quoted Barton as saying that Australia could do no more unless
Canada also made some contribution. "Laurier has been breathing forth
loyalty, unity and Empire but the keystone of unity and Empire is
command of the sea . . . . " How, Forrest wanted to know, did Laurier's
refusal to help maintain that command fit in with his eloquent after-
dinner speeches?[31]

The Australians came to the conference with few of the nationalist
concerns which governed Laurier's thought, and, in the case of Forrest,
with a willingness to accept a greater measure of centralization of power
for defense. But the limitations of their new constitutional arrangements,
and the problems which the new government faced, preoccupied them.
Further, Barton was of a quiet temperament, unlikely to take a strong
lead in any such gathering. His was the judicial disposition, and he was

[31] Adm. 1/7610, Forrest to Custance, Aug. 2, 1902.

happier in his eventual post on the bench of the High Court of Australia than in one of political leadership.

Few of these problems affected the exuberant Premier of New Zealand, Richard Seddon. The proponent of the one innovative idea in military collaboration, Seddon was the representative of the most imperial-minded of the major colonies, the colony which had been most receptive to the idea of imperial federation.[32] A loud and clamorous imperialism was one of Seddon's favorite political devices. In this stand he was motivated in part by a keen knowledge of the electorate, and in part by the desire to give New Zealand a larger role in settling the affairs of the Pacific. A bluff, hearty and genial man, he could display a streak of ruthlessness for his own advancement, as he did in the process of becoming Premier in 1893.[33] Having found the support given in the South African war a popular cause, Seddon had followed it with his suggestion for the formation of a colonial military reserve. In this, New Zealand was to stand in singular isolation from the other colonies, and Seddon apart from his confreres.

Although the Colonial Conference opened in the exuberant atmosphere of the impending coronation, the excitement was soon turned to gloom by the illness of the monarch and the postponement of the celebration. But in the brief period before the interruption caused by the royal illness, Chamberlain opened the meetings with the statement of his "very great anticipations…as to the results which may accrue from this conference."[34]

On July 4, when the conference was finally able to proceed, Lord Selborne opened the discussion of defense matters with the assembled Prime Ministers. He expressed his hope for a contribution to the Navy from all parts of the Empire, and of the existing Australian agreement he said that there would be no difficulty about the vessels subsidized by the colonial governments in Australian waters in peacetime, provided that they were allowed to combine in training exercises outside of Australian waters with the ships from other adjacent naval stations.

Selborne found Seddon his most receptive auditor. The New Zealand leader staunchly denounced anything tending to the localization of naval forces; efforts of an enemy to destroy Australasian commerce would, he said, center at the Cape and not off colonial coasts. New Zealand acknowledged its dependence on the imperial navy, and had no intention of building or buying any war vessels of its own. As for further assistance, however, Seddon shifted to a more cautious tone, telling the conference

---

[32] J. E. Tyler, *The Struggle for Imperial Unity*, (London, 1938), pp. 159–65.
[33] R. T. Shannon, "The Liberal Succession Crisis in New Zealand, 1893," *Historical Studies, Australia and New Zealand*, VIII (May, 1958), 30.
[34] Cd. 1299 contains a brief summary of the proceedings of the conference. I have used the full report of the gathering found in C.O. Misc. 144 (in Adm. 1/7611).

that New Zealand gave substantial help to Britain by the preferential tariff rates which she accorded British goods. The favor amounted to £150,000 a year—equal, said Seddon, to the interest on the costs of five battleships.

The other premiers were more forthright and less equivocal. Laurier declared that the costs of Canadian internal development precluded any contribution. And Barton took substantially the same position. He referred to the problem presented to the commonwealth government by the "Braddon blot," and said that Australia could not go as far in the contribution as Lord Selborne hoped. Like Canada, Australia faced the task of constructing a transcontinental railroad.

As to naval defense, Barton felt that Australia could not face the costs of constructing a naval nucleus of her own. It would be very difficult to keep any such force up-to-date. A proposal along the lines of that submitted by Lord Selborne, but one less costly to Australia, would present less difficulty. But any new agreement must provide more modern vessels, and there must be some arrangement which would allow the employment of Australian naval reservists on the ships of the auxiliary force. The recent debate over defense legislation in Australia had revealed the unpopularity of compelling any such reservists to serve outside the waters of the Commonwealth. Barton did acknowledge, however, that too great a localization of naval forces was not in the general interest.[35]

When Secretary of State for War St. John Brodrick spoke to the assembled Premiers on July 25, one of the first points he made was designed to dispel the prevalent suspicion that the war in South Africa had proved the effectiveness of the citizen soldier over the regular. While critics of the British regular were comparing him to his disadvantage with the Boer, Brodrick stated that had the Boers been formed into a really organized army they would have been able to take much greater advantage than they did of the British reverses early in the conflict. He further held that despite the excellent qualities of both British and colonial volunteers in Africa, no British general would be willing to pit them against European forces without further training, indeed a great deal more training. Brodrick ended with a plea for the establishment of a trained reserve in the various colonies, with a liability for overseas service.

Sir Frederick Borden, the Canadian Minister of Militia, wanted no part of any such idea. He raised the argument that the creation of such a force would make it a *corps d'élite*, whose existence and special training and equipment would have a damaging effect on the rest of the Canadian

[35] *Ibid.* See also Australian National Library, Canberra, Prime Minister's Department, Correspondence and Papers, Vol. 32, for Barton's Report to the Australian Cabinet on the Colonial Conference.

militia. The best thing that Canada could do, he felt, would be to seek the steady improvement of the existing militia forces.[36] Barton also expressed dissent. He did not agree with the opinion of some, drawn from the war, that marksmanship was the only requirement for a soldier. But this was a widely held belief, and one that tended to increase the diversion of defense money, better devoted to the militia, to volunteers and rifle clubs. Further, Barton felt that to set aside a force especially for service abroad would run contrary to sentiment in Australia. In recent debates on a defense bill in the Commonwealth Parliament, not one voice was raised in favor of a clause in the bill which would have allowed service outside the Commonwealth, even though it was made clear that any such service would be subject to the consent of the Commonwealth government.[37]

Naturally enough, since it was largely of his inspiration, Seddon supported the proposal made by Brodrick. But the opposition of the Canadian and Australian members had put the quietus on the scheme. While Chamberlain gave some support to Brodrick, saying that it was desirable that a reserve force should be maintained in the colonies, he recognized that the state of public opinion in the colonies did not seem to make the scheme practicable. He did allow himself the comment that if this were so, public opinion in the colonies must be very backward. "I think it will have to progress," said the Secretary, and he hoped that the example set by New Zealand would be helpful.[38] Chamberlain restated this idea in a letter to Brodrick on that same day, telling him to assure Seddon that great importance was attached to his proposal. Through it, the hands of the Dominion and the Commonwealth might be forced, since they could not with decency remain behind after New Zealand had taken the initiative.[39] But despite the efforts of both Chamberlain and Brodrick, nothing was accomplished, and Seddon withdrew the resolution which he had presented to the conference in support of the proposed reserve scheme.[40]

The failure was irritating. Chamberlain expressed the assurance that Britain was "perfectly satisfied with the results of the voluntary, purely voluntary, and spontaneous offers. We trust entirely to them in the future." But there was annoyance in his regret over the attitude of the two senior dominions, and in his statement that if the United Kingdom were engaged in a future war, " . . . it is almost certain to be in connection with

---

[36] C.O. Misc. 144, pp. 81–86 (in Adm. 1/7611).
[37] Ibid., pp. 87–90.
[38] Ibid., p. 99.
[39] Amery, Life of Joseph Chamberlain, p. 427.
[40] Adm. 1/7611 (C.O. Misc. 144, p. 197).

some question in which the Colonies, or one of the Colonies, is primarily interested."[41]

That Chamberlain was not content to leave the matter where it rested is indicated by the further private discussions which he had with Laurier and other members of the Canadian delegation.[42] But this got him nowhere. Apparently Laurier had simply become more firmly rooted in his views as a result of this major War Office and Admiralty offensive for increased contributions from the colonies.[43]

This attitude is strongly suggested by the deletions which Laurier requested from a memorandum of the discussions drawn up by W. S. Fielding, a member of the Canadian delegation. Fielding was Minister of Finance in the Canadian government. He prepared a memorial stating that the Canadian delegation regretted their inability to accede to the suggestions put forward by Lord Selborne and Mr. Brodrick. He tempered this, however, by suggesting that as Canada grew in wealth and population, she would be able to make a more liberal outlay on measures of defense. And he dwelt at some length on recent measures which had been taken for the improvement of the militia. Fielding's memorial also stated that recent experience had shown that in case of need, Great Britain could rely upon substantial aid from the Dominion. That aid, he asserted, would be even more cheerfully given, if, in the future as in the past, it was entirely voluntary in character. Laurier wished struck from the document anything which could be interpreted as establishing a departure from established policy, and he particularly took exception to the statement about Great Britain being able to rely on aid in case of need. He felt that this implied, though it did not formulate, a pledge that in any war that might take place, Canada would take a part.[44]

If the defense projects submitted to the conference had been meager, the results were even more so. With Canadian reluctance to enter upon anything in the way of a binding commitment, and with Australia's concern to keep her obligations commensurate with the strength of the infant Commonwealth, no bold new ventures in "empiremanship" were forthcoming. The high hopes engendered by the war had proved illusory; the conference had revealed a stubborn reluctance on the part of the colonial governments to share in any of the major enthusiasms of the Colonial Secretary. "His idea of a Council of Empire had been ignored. His appeals for Colonial contributions to Imperial Defence had been rejected. The trade negotiations remained inconclusive."[45] In defense,

[41] *Ibid.*, p. 98.
[42] Skelton, *Life and Letters of Sir Wilfrid Laurier*, pp. 298–99.
[43] Amery, *Life of Joseph Chamberlain*, p. 424.
[44] P.A.C., Laurier MSS., Vol. 240, 67182.
[45] Amery, *Life of Joseph Chamberlain*, p. 447.

the two South African colonies had agreed to a small subsidy payment for the Admiralty, and the naval agreement with the Australasian colonies had been renewed, with the colonies agreeing both to a slightly larger payment and to the ending of the restrictions of Admiralty control over the vessels subsidized. But in view of the hopes, these gains were rather "Like to the apples on the Dead Sea's shore, / All ashes to the taste."

Even the manifest willingness of Seddon to join in an agreement for the creation of an imperial reserve force in New Zealand came to nothing. After the conference, despite the discouragement there, Seddon carried forward the discussion of this idea with St. John Brodrick, and they agreed on certain fundamentals of the plan. The troops in any such reserve force were to be trained up to the standards of European forces, and furnished with complete and effective modern equipment and arms. It would consist mainly of mounted infantry; there would be regular inspection by an imperial general officer to guarantee efficiency. The force would be available to the imperial government for service within the limits of China, South Africa, Canada, and the islands of the western Pacific. The imperial government would pay £9 for each efficient man in the force, and in addition, much of the cost of the equipment. Seddon felt that there would be no difficulty in recruiting 4,500 men for the projected unit.[46] In view of the enthusiastic response in the colony to the call for volunteers for South Africa, this would seem to be a reliable judgment.

Brodrick discussed these matters with Chamberlain, and also the apparent need of securing amendments to the Imperial Reserve Forces Act in order to provide legal basis for the contemplated Imperial-Colonial reserve unit, so that it could be paid for as an imperial force. But by this time Chamberlain had apparently lost any enthusiasm which he may once have had for the project. Sir John Anderson represented the Secretary of State in the discussions on the Reserve Act amendment, and Chamberlain's instructions to him were to deprecate any proposals for such a force as Seddon—and the proposed amendment—envisaged.[47]

The indifference of the Colonial Office to the project is further suggested by the fact that the letter of October 2, 1902, to that office from the Secretary of State for War, outlining the terms of the agreement reached with Seddon, went long unanswered by the Colonial Office, despite a reminder some months later. More than a year later, the War Office passed along the word that Seddon was still awaiting some news con-

---

[46] C.O. 209/264 Seddon to Brodrick, Sept. 6, 1902, enclosed in W.O. to C.O., Oct. 2, 1902.

[47] C.O. 209/266. Minute by Sir John Anderson for Secretary of State Alfred Lyttelton on the reserve proposal. Sir John suggests that Chamberlain never had much regard for the scheme.

cerning the contemplated arrangement. Search indicated that the Colonial Office had replied, but a letter of May, 1903, had gone astray in the War Office. In the letter, Chamberlain had opposed the projected scheme on the grounds that the imperial treasury should not be called upon to pay for reserves raised in the colonies. Further, the Secretary felt that once Seddon's strong personality was removed from the scene, it would be found that public opinion in New Zealand would not be markedly different from that of the other colonies, where there was opposition to any reserve scheme.

Brodrick's successor at the War Office, H. O. Arnold-Forster, found these arguments persuasive. He also felt that in time of any real crisis, the colonial government would be hesitant to allow the most highly trained force at its disposal to leave the country, despite any agreements to do so. But since the War Office was loth completely to abandon the possible reliable use of colonial manpower, and since there was a natural reluctance to give such a generally dusty answer to the only government which had shown any genuine interest in sharing military burdens, the rejection was tempered by the suggestion that New Zealand might raise two battalions for imperial service. One would serve at home, and the other in India. The latter would be paid from Indian funds and would be on the same footing as the British regiments serving there. There was nothing doing, however. Lord Plunket, Governor of New Zealand, wrote Alfred Lyttelton that whatever the merits of Seddon's plan, the delay in considering it was foolish and chilling to one of his ardent nature.[48]

Little improvement in the organization of defense of empire had come from either the 1897 or the 1902 conference.[49] Brodrick might complain of being "checkmated" by the determination of the colonies to keep things as they were, but in view of the colonial willingness for sacrifice displayed in the Boer War, the failure to issue a summons awakening the energies of the states of the Empire to the duties of defense seems to rest with imperial officialdom, rather than with the colonial leaders. The latter were far from indifferent to the imperial claims on their loyalties and resources; they too heard the drum beats calling them to their imperial tasks. But they also heard a different drum, that of their own national self-respect and self-reliance. The task of bringing the different beats into collaborative rhythm was yet to be done, and it would require more than exhortation by those with minds and ears attuned to one drum alone.

[48] W.O. 32/909, 091, 2247, 2275, 2311.
[49] B.M., Balfour MSS, Add. MSS, 49720, 238–39.

CHAPTER VIII

CANADIAN ALARUMS
AND REFORMS

The failure of British officials in 1902 to obtain any collaboration from the colonies, other than a modification and renewal of the naval agreement with Australia and New Zealand, was not due simply to colonial recalcitrance. Collaboration must be based on confidence, and colonial leaders might well ask what confidence could be placed in a defense system which had been reduced to such disarray by the embattled farmers of the veldt. The ink was not yet dry on the Treaty of Vereeniging when the conference members were assembling in London; memories of the humiliations of the war were still fresh. But even more important, there was no general imperial strategy which would give colonial peoples and governments any significant role in imperial defense. As the later Esher Report stated, "The scientific study of Imperial resources, the coordination of the ever-varying facts upon which Imperial rule rests, the calculation of forces, the broad plans necessary to sustain the burden of Empire, have, until quite recently, found no place in our system of government."[1] Without such strategy, to ask colonial governments to engage their resources for imperial defense was like asking them to buy shares in an unnamed enterprise of unspecified purpose whose plans were yet to be disclosed.

Had the conference met a few months later, however, discerning members might have felt the winds of change blowing through the musty cobwebs of British defense planning, and might have been stirred to more generous views of their role in it. For 1902 was the beginning of the end of the long period of unplanned British defense. Indeed, a year in which the Committee of Imperial Defence was initiated, in which the labors of the great investigative Elgin and Esher Commissions were begun and Admiral John Fisher was appointed a member of the Board of Admiralty

[1] Parl. Pap., 1904, Vol. VIII, Cd. 1932, p. 1.

might well rate as an *annus mirabilis* in the history of British strategical planning.

The years following the close of the South African war saw a marked falling away from the exuberant and optimistic imperialism which had prevailed at the war's beginning. Much of the emotion of former years had been spent in the struggle on the veldt; imperialism was drained of its emotional appeal,[2] and this was reflected in the generally negative attitude taken by the colonial premiers at the 1902 Colonial Conference. But the colonial governments and peoples obviously could not ignore the pressures for a better organization of British and imperial defense arrangements, pressures now stronger than ever since the bitter trials of war had revealed the deficiencies of the British military structure. The colonies were going to feel, though in less direct manner, the same impulses that led the Balfour Government to initiate the notable reforms in the organization of British defense.

In previous years Canada, as compared with the Australasian colonies, had been more laggard and indifferent in matters of imperial defense collaboration. In the early years of the new century, however, a variety of factors tended to make Canada central in such activity. There was, of course, a reflection of the re-awakening interest in defense problems in Britain, but other operative factors were the reaction of the North Atlantic community to the rise of German naval power, and the personal misfortunes of some of the British commanders of the Canadian militia. Basic, of course, was the new stature of the Canadian state. With the terms of trade turning so substantially in favor of the raw material-producing states of the world after the mid-nineties, the financial clouds which had been so ominously and fretfully present over much of the final quarter of the century lifted. Canada benefited from the new conditions as much if not more than any other state of the Empire. People poured into the prairie provinces to settle on the great unclaimed lands, and Canada launched upon a railroad-building program of dimensions unparalleled in her history. In the first decades of what Laurier hailed as Canada's century, it was manifestly impossible to be content with the bedraggled defense organization with which one had got by in the bleak decades just passed.

Further, it was all too apparent that British power in the western hemisphere was declining, both absolutely and with relation to the power of the United States. The founding of the modern American navy, the truculence displayed by the United States in the Venezuelan boundary matter, the Spanish-American War, and most especially the manifest

---

[2] William Langer, "Farewell to Empire," *Foreign Affairs*, Vol. XLI (Oct., 1962); Thornton, *The Imperial Idea and Its Enemies*, p. 110.

British anxiety to avoid controversy with the United States over the proposed Panama arrangements and the Alaskan boundary controversy, all revealed to discerning Canadians that the great safeguard of its evolving nationhood was now diminishing. With the British "aegis" weakening, Canadian nationhood would have to evolve more quickly; the daughter in her mother's house would have to move more rapidly to become mistress of her own in this world of new power alignments into which she was being impelled.[3]

The forces leading her to change might be national rather than imperial, and the resolution to avoid being involved in the "vortex of European militarism" as strong as ever, but the change was under way nevertheless. Laurier might claim for Canada, as he did, that she should "be at liberty to act or not to act, to interfere or not to interfere, to do just as she pleases, and that she shall reserve for herself the right to judge whether or not there is cause for her to act."[4] But this was a claim to a wider measure of freedom and choice than is the lot of most men, especially the leaders of states; sovereign necessity makes folly of the sovereignty of nations. And increasingly, without realizing it, Canada found herself committed to the assumption of a role in imperial defense.

Superficially, Canadians frequently seemed bent on continuing to do things in their own willful way. In 1898, they had finally succumbed to the exhortations and admonitions of the Colonial Defence Committee and other Whitehall officialdom, and had invited a British commission to make a survey and offer recommendations regarding Canadian defense. This commission had been headed by General Sir Edward Leach. But the recommendations of the Leach report were not put into effect, despite the fact that the current Minister of Militia, Dr. Borden, had been a member of the group; and this failure was a matter of deepest distress to both Colonial and War Offices. A committee of the Canadian Cabinet appointed to consider the report brought no results, if indeed it ever met. Borden confessed to Lord Minto that he lacked the expert knowledge necessary to appraise many of the recommendations. And then came the South African war and the approach of the Colonial Conference as excuses for further delay.[5]

In the light of the still-existing pledges by Great Britain to come to the defense of Canada if attacked, the state of the Canadian militia remained a matter of considerable concern to the Colonial Office. Sir John Anderson, Permanent Undersecretary during part of the Chamberlain regime, felt that Britain had a moral right to know that Canada was

[3] W. L. Morton, *The Canadian Identity* (Madison, Wis., 1961), pp. 64–68.
[4] Quoted in J. Bartlet Brebner, *Canada: A Modern History* (Ann Arbor, Mich., 1960), p. 371.
[5] C.O. 42/892, Minto to C.O., April 25, 1903.

doing its part in its own defense, and that if it were not, that fact ought to be made known to the Canadian people. If then they did nothing, Britain would be justified in reconsidering the pledges given.[6]

Canada caused irritation in other ways. Despite hand wringing in the War Office and appeals from the Colonial Defence Committee, the Canadians adopted their own Ross rifle as standard equipment for their infantry forces. The use of this weapon set their forces apart from those of Britain and the rest of the Empire. The Canadians also talked much of severing one of the most important ties which linked their militia with the regular United Kindgom forces, by opening the command of the militia to a Canadian officer rather than reserving it for a British regular officer. Indeed, the Canadian government, or rather Dr. Borden, displayed in many instances a most tender sense of Canadian *amour propre*. War Office nominations for commandants of the Royal Military College, recruiting in Canada during the Boer War, the relative rank of officers holding Canadian commissions as opposed to those holding imperial commissions, and the relations between the imperial officer commanding the Halifax garrison and the commander of the Canadian militia: in all of these matters Dr. Borden manifested a sensitivity sorely trying to the Governor General, Lord Minto.[7]

Nevertheless, for all of these accumulating irritants, the Canadian militia went through an important period of growth and development. During the latter years of the nineties, and the first few years of the new century, the size of the permanent forces was doubled, staff courses were offered at the Royal Military College, medical units were established, engineer, signal and ordnance units were created. And the organization of the militia into brigades and divisions began to give an air of verisimilitude to the claims of the militia to be a military force.[8]

At least some of these innovations and reforms must be credited to two British imperial officers who fell into the bad graces of the Canadian government, and were forced out of the post of General Officer Commanding the Canadian Forces: General Edward Hutton and General Lord Dundonald.

As suggested previously, the existing militia laws of Canada reserved the command of the Canadian forces for officers of general rank in the British regular army. But certainly to any conscientious imperial officer the position must have been one of the most frustrating and difficult in the entire British military structure. The basic difficulty, as Prime Minister Laurier later remarked in the midst of the controversy, was that the

[6] C.O. 42/895, Minute of Anderson, Dundonald to War Office, March 26, 1903.
[7] C.O. 42/875–883 contains most of Minto's correspondence with the Colonial Office on these matters.
[8] Stanley, *Canada's Soldiers, 1604–1954*, p. 290.

British officer was essentially a stranger. The Canadian militia was, of course, a force of citizen soldiers, and was, as such bodies were likely to be, rooted in the life and politics of the state. Politics and patronage played a part, and perhaps a necessary part, in securing parliamentary support for the militia from the legislators of a profoundly unmilitary people. "Parliamentary colonels" might be a military handicap, but they were a political necessity. And yet British officers rarely revealed any awareness of these political realities. They blundered ahead in search not only of military efficiency, but also of closer linkage of the forces they commanded with those of Britain, a matter naturally of greatest political sensitivity in dualistic Canada.

Of course, a normal amount of jockeying, of pushing and shoving between civil and military, was to be expected even without the conflict of loyalties which was incorporated in the post. The Canadian militia act attempted to delineate the respective areas of authority of the Minister of Militia and the Commanding Officer, but the basic issue was whether the military officer was adviser to the Minister, or an officer with a quasi-independent command.

Sir John Anderson of the Colonial Office went into further detail about the hapless job of the British commander of the Canadian militia. He was, Anderson pointed out, powerless without the support of his political head and of Parliament. If he complained to the War Office, the British government could not use the complaint as the basis of criticism of the Canadian forces without revealing him to be guilty of insubordination. If he sought to educate Canadian opinion, without the consent of the minister, he was equally guilty. Those in Britain had no means of letting the Canadian public know how wrong and rotten things were with their militia force, save through complaints to a minister who might himself be the cause of the mischief. Anderson felt that perhaps the best arrangement which could be made would be to have an annual inspection of the Canadian force by a British officer. If Britain could publish his report, it would get to the Canadian public. This might produce better results than the existing conditions, and at the same time let the Canadians have their own military commandant. Colonial Secretary Chamberlain also thought that Britain would have to find some way of informing the Canadians of the unsatisfactory nature of their defense arrangements. The Canadian electorate were simply not educated to the necessities of the situation, and were not inclined to pay much for defense. The politicians had no courage and would not tell the people what their duty was.[9]

[9] C.O. 42/895. These comments were appended to a report from Lord Dundonald to the War Office, March 6, 1903, forwarded by the Director General of Military Intelligence to the Colonial Office, May 4, 1903.

Under the circumstances, it was rather remarkable that any of the British officers seconded to the command of the Canadian forces were able to stay out of trouble; remarkable, and also a tribute to the strength of the imperial tie. But for "Curly" Hutton, as we have seen, the pressures were too great. As indicated previously, Lord Minto had argued that the recall of Hutton, added to the well-known record of difficulties which other British officers had had in their dealings with the Canadian militia, was likely to bar any high-minded British officer from accepting the post of G.O.C. in the future. The Laurier Cabinet's comment on this was that imperial officers seemed to feel that they served in the Canadian forces as imperial officers, and as such, were not in any way under the control of the appropriate minister of the Crown in Canada. This was, in the Cabinet's view, a wholly erroneous opinion. Their imperial service was simply a qualification for the Canadian office to which they were appointed. They were subject to Canadian authority, and were controlled by the policy of the government of Canada.[10]

If Lord Minto was disturbed over the Hutton affair, he was even more worried by subsequent indications from Borden that the latter was considering amending the Militia Act to throw open the position of command to those who had served only in the militia forces. Minto felt that this would be disastrous for the militia.[11] Sir John Anderson of the Colonial Office agreed with this. But there was fear that Minto had lost some of his customary urbanity and good sense in the violence of his reaction to another suggestion by Borden, to the effect that he might in future designate the students of the Royal Military College who were to receive imperial commissions, rather than having them selected by the militia commander.[12] Minto assailed this idea as simply another example of political patronage.[13] Sir John Anderson and Chamberlain both feared that Minto was carrying things too far in his comments on Borden's policies. Anderson noted that "we cannot treat Ministers as if they were totally unfit to be trusted." And the upshot of the dispute was that the graduates of the R.M.C. to be granted imperial commissions were selected by the Governor General with the advice of the responsible minister.[14]

The Canadian authorities continued to show substantial hostility towards Hutton even after his departure from their shores. They con-

---

[10] C.O. 42/875, Minto to the Privy Council, Canada, Feb. 3, 1900. Privy Council to Minto, n.d., enclosed in Minto to Colonial Office, Feb. 8, 1900.

[11] *Ibid.*, Minto to C.O., March 26, 1900.

[12] *Ibid.*, Minto to C.O., April 6, 1900. Since there were so few opportunities in the Canadian forces, a high proportion of the R.M.C. graduates had for years availed themselves of the opportunity to take imperial commissions. The War Office had started granting such commissions in 1880 to members of the first graduating class. Stanley, *Canada's Soldiers, 1604–1954*, p. 244.

[13] *Ibid.*, Minto to C.O., April 6, 1900.

[14] *Ibid.*, Minto to C.O., May 12, 1900.

sidered, for example, a remonstrance to the British government on the decision of the War Office to appoint Hutton to the command of some colonial forces in South Africa, feeling that this suggested a rebuff to the Canadian government.[15]

One oddity of the Hutton affair, in which the Canadian authorities were upholding the principle that the officer commanding the Canadian militia was a Canadian officer and subject only to the Canadian government, was the fact that Borden and another Canadian cabinet member appealed to General Lord Seymour, commander of the imperial garrison in Halifax, to use his authority as Hutton's superior to restrain Hutton's impetuosity.[16]

The War Office reacted strongly against the possibility that the command of the Canadian militia might go to Canadian officers, or rather, to those whose military experience had been confined to the Canadian service. To open the command to colonels of the Canadian militia would be disastrous, for the War Office was doubtful whether the militia could produce an officer competent to command the whole force. It was also important that the commanding officer of the militia should be a man who was in touch with military authorities in Britain, and a man free from associations with local politics. Lord Lansdowne, the Secretary of State for War, hoped that no such measure would receive the "sanction" of the Colonial Office, an odd view, for a high imperial officer, of the nature of responsible government and the powers of the Colonial Office.[17]

Coupled with the War Office fear about the possible change in command arrangements for the militia was annoyance, plus some degree of ignorance, on the matter of the relative rank of imperial officers seconded to the Canadian militia. Under Canadian law, such officers held command by virtue of Canadian commissions, and took their place on the table of seniority according to the date of such commission. This put experienced imperial officers in a position of inferiority to inexperienced Canadians with no service outside of the militia. General Hutton, for example, had appointed a Lieutenant Colonel Stone to the command of the Canadian artillery. In this position, Stone, an imperial officer, found himself subordinate to several Canadian Lieutenant Colonels with little of his experience or professional competence.

The War Office took an imperious tone on this, and asked the Colonial Office to point out to Lord Minto that "no act of the Canadian Ministry should be allowed to override the Queen's Regulations."[18] The War

[15] C.O. 42/876, Minto to C.O., June 13, 1900.
[16] *Ibid.*, Seymour to Selborne, Sept. 18, 1900, enclosed in C.O. 42/876, Minto to C.O., Oct. 29, 1900.
[17] *Ibid.*, Lansdowne to Chamberlain, April 5, 1900.
[18] C.O. 42/879, Lansdowne to Chamberline, May 11, 1900.

Office sought the assent of the Colonial Office to a proposal that in future it should be made a condition of the employment of imperial officers in Canada that they would not receive local commissions, but would have rank and seniority by virtue of their imperial commission. The Colonial Office people, however, took a dim view of the whole idea. The proposal was clearly contrary to Canadian law, and Canadian law in this matter was similar to that in other colonies, such as the Cape, Natal, and New Zealand. (The Australian situation was changing with the establishment of the Commonwealth.) Further, the Canadian regulations were practically identical to the British regulations concerning the authority which regular officers had over militia and volunteer units.[19]

And so, while the Colonial Office agreed with the position of the military about the possible disastrous consequences of the possible amendment of the Canadian law, there was distress over the somewhat "cocksure" attitude of the War Office. Sir John Anderson noted with some asperity that the Canadian militia existed by virtue of Canadian law, and that neither the Queen's warrant nor the Regulations governed there.[20] He fully agreed with the Canadian opinion than an imperial officer seconded to the Canadian forces was, for the time being, an officer of that force, and not of the British regular army.[21]

While the Canadians did not then abandon the practice of reserving the command of their militia for an imperial officer, the passage of legislation which allowed the promotion of officers of the militia to the rank of colonel was a preliminary step to full Canadian command of its forces. Eleven of the Lieutenant Colonels of the militia were promoted to the higher grade. But a minute of the Canadian Privy Council gave assurances that as far as possible the Minister intended to be guided in promotions by the usages of the War Office.[22]

Despite their assurances, however, the sensitivity of the Canadians was evident in the dispute over the command of the royal review during the visit of the Duke and Duchess of York to Halifax. The decision of St. John Brodrick, who had now succeeded Lord Lansdowne at the War Office, was that the imperial officer at Halifax, Colonel Briscoe, should command during the review. The Canadian ministers were sufficiently incensed at this to formulate a minute to the Governor General, protesting the decision, and asserting that the honor of the command should have gone to the General Officer Commanding the Militia. The Colonial Office, in an effort to calm the waters, suggested that since there was not room

[19] C.O. 42/886, Minute to War Office to C.O., April 16, 1901.
[20] C.O. 42/879, War Office to Colonial Office, May 11, 1900.
[21] Ibid., Minute to War Office to C.O., Aug. 31, 1900.
[22] C.O. 42/883, Minute Sept. 10, 1901, with Minto to Colonial Office, Sept. 10, 1901.

under the circumstances for both, the militia officer should absent himself from the ceremonies.[23]

Underlying this Canadian sensitivity was, of course, the basic philosophy of Laurier and his Liberal Party associates. In 1901, Lord Minto reported to the Colonial Office on a wide-ranging discussion which he had had with Laurier concerning imperial federation and imperial defense. Laurier, Minto recounted, did not regard the time as ripe for any form of imperial federation. He still adhered, Minto felt, to his former views that the Canadian tendency should be toward greater assumption of national responsibility rather than toward participation in imperial councils: ". . . in fact he would appear to expect to derive much more good in an Imperial sense from sentimental connection with the old Country, than from any official participation in the councils of the Empire." Minto reported Laurier as saying that one of the first questions which would be brought to the fore in any imperial council would in all probability be that of imperial defense. This would involve an increased outlay of Canadian funds, which would neither be understood nor approved in Canada.

During the course of the discussion, Minto had reminded Laurier of what Canada owed to the general support of British arms in the past, and urged that if Canada were to hold an important place, not only in the Empire, but also in the world, she would have to accept greater responsibility for her own defense. Much of this Laurier conceded, but he insisted that the moment had not come for Canada to undertake greater expenditure for imperial defense.

Minto wondered in his letter to the Colonial Office whether Laurier was reading aright the public mind of Canada. He doubted the Prime Minister's appraisal of Canadian sentiment on sharing imperial responsibilities. His own experience convinced him that the existing government could scarcely be regarded as really being in touch with much of the pro-British sentiment existing in Canada.[24]

The pro-British sentiment had an opportunity for demonstration and parade a couple of years later in *l'affaire* Dundonald. Douglas Cochrane, the twelfth earl of Dundonald, came to the post of General Officer Commanding the Canadian Militia with the distinction of a fine military career. He had been one of the heroes of the relief of Ladysmith in the recent war, and had in the course of that conflict commanded some of the colonial forces. Unfortunately, however, the professional competence of the man was not balanced by the traits of personality which would have given him the skill to move through the mine-strewn fields of

---

[23] *Ibid.*, Minto to Colonial Office, Oct. 3, 1901.
[24] C.O. 42/883, Minto to C.O., June 4, 1901.

Canadian militia-political life. Candid to the point of brusqueness, yielding on occasion to his flair for the dramatic, and with a soldier's contempt for the politician, Dundonald was really ill-equipped for one of the most politically sensitive posts in the whole structure of British-imperial military relations. His sense of urgency about putting Canadian military affairs in order, his strong sense of imperial mission in doing this, and his total lack of appreciation of the caution needed in the political leadership of a dualistic society were all qualities well calculated to create trouble.

One of Dundonald's first encounters with the political leadership was with Laurier, and the experience must have been chilling to one of Dundonald's ardent military spirit and imperial impulses. Laurier advised him "not to take the militia seriously . . . it will not be required for the defense of the country, as the Monroe Doctrine protects us from enemy aggression."[25] But Dundonald had every intention of taking the militia seriously and set to work to right what he regarded as an almost hopeless situation. A report on the state of the Canadian militia was a catalogue of failure and omission. There was no military organization on which plans could be based, no regiments up to a reasonable strength. There had been no field training, no adequate preparation, and regimental officers were deficient both in numbers and training. The list of particulars was long and inclusive, with much to condemn, and little or nothing to praise.[26] (Dundonald also felt that Borden had a personal grievance against imperial officers, for he apparently believed that they had discriminated against his son in the distribution of awards for South African service.)[27]

The efforts of the British G.O.C. to remedy these unhappy conditions led to the so-called "Dundonald incident," and if any further justification for the abandonment of the old arrangements was necessary, it was abundantly available here. In the two years during which he served in Canada, Dundonald did much good in the purely military system, but he accomplished this at a cost of growing estrangement with Borden and the remainder of the Cabinet. Smarting because of Borden's editing of his annual reports, Dundonald "blew his top" when some of his recommendations for the officer personnel of a new regiment were denied by the Acting Minister of Militia, for the political reason that they were too strongly Conservative in flavor.

At a banquet in Montreal in June, 1904, Dundonald threw all constitutional caution aside and denounced what he called "flagrant political interference," saying that it was intolerable that his recommendations

[25] Stanley, *Canada's Soldiers, 1604–1954*, p. 294.
[26] C.O. 42/895, Dondonald to Major Altham, March 6, 1903.
[27] *Ibid.*, Dundonald to General Sir William Nicholson, Nov. 25, 1903, enclosed with Minto to C.O., Jan. 15, 1904.

should be so grossly tampered with.[28] It took a few days for the story of the speech to reach the press, and when it did, Dundonald was the center of a political controversy which was bitter but short. After ascertaining that the news summary of the speech was essentially correct, Borden telegraphed Dundonald immediately that he was dismissed, and an Order-in-Council drawn up by Borden and a committee of the Privy Council charged him with "a regrettable failure to appreciate the principles of British constitutional government, . . . and a grave act of indiscretion and insubordination."[29]

Dundonald was naturally the hero of the moment to all Conservative and imperialist elements in Canadian life, and his dismissal was a convenient club with which to beat the Laurier Government over the ears in the approaching Fall election. But the hero got no support from London. Secretary of State for War Arnold-Forster ordered him home and commanded him to take no further part in political controversy.[30] And Lord Minto, no longer Governor General, said that Dundonald's attitude had been "unreasonable" and "most regrettable."[31] When later the Army Council acceded reluctantly to the request of the Canadians that they be permitted to publish papers on the controversy, Lyttelton said he had hoped the affair had blown over. It had been a "foolish matter for wh. Ld. D. has only himself to blame."[32]

However foolish Dundonald's actions may have been, there is still justice in the comment that he was more influential after his dismissal than before. As one of his journalistic supporters put it, "If Lord Dundonald makes a speech or two more, the panic-stricken Ministers will not stop until they have completed his whole program of reform. As ex-Commander his influence is accomplishing more than they would allow him to do in office."[33] Perhaps the Toronto journal was a little hasty in this observation, but it would have been apt a few years later. Of course, many of the reforms in the Canadian military structure which were put in train in the decade after Dundonald's enforced retirement had been advocated by many of his predecessors; many were demanded by the pressures of the hour, and many were due to the effective workings of the new command structure. But whatever may be the correct ascription of credit, most of the changes which Dundonald had advocated, and with which he was identified because of all the excitements attendant on his going, were put into effect in the following years.[34]

[28] *The Citizen* (Ottawa), June 8, 1904.
[29] Canada, Sessional Papers (Ottawa, 1904), Vol. 38, Paper #113.
[30] *Hansard*, 4th series, CXXXVIII, 495, July 19, 1904.
[31] Frank H. Underhill, "Lord Minto on His Governor-Generalship," *Canadian Historical Review*, LX (June, 1959), 130.
[32] C.O. 42/904, War Office to C.O., July 19, 1905.
[33] *The Mail and Empire* (Toronto), July 21, 1904.
[34] Stanley, *Canada's Soldiers, 1604–1954*, p. 287.

During the period when Dundonald was thus unangelically troubling the waters in Canada, his political superior was bringing to fruition the suggestion made during the Hutton days, that the command of the Canadian militia should be opened to a Canadian officer. On April 13, 1903, Minto telegraphed the Colonial Office about the Canadian Cabinet's intention to seek amendments to the Canadian Militia Act which would strike from the act the delegation of the King's authority to command this militia to the Governor General, and which would open the post of General Officer Commanding the Militia to Canadian officers. Minto urged that the British government should request the Canadians to consult with the imperial authorities before introducing such radical changes into Canada's basic military legislation.[35]

Minto discussed the matter himself with both Laurier and Borden. Both assured him that they were prepared to delay the bill for the present, and both were agreeable to an exchange of views with the imperial government. But Colonial Office personnel were not as exercised over the matter as Minto. A. B. Keith was not sure that there was any delegation of the royal authority to the Governor General outside of the language of Canadian law. And in great measure the Colonial Office had about given up on the usefulness of the existing system. While Sir Montagu Ommaney felt that it was desirable to retain the existing arrangement, since it at least furnished the United Kingdom with a means of knowing what was going on in the Canadian militia, Sir John Anderson characterized the position of the British commander of the militia as "hapless." And the Colonial Defence Committee was thinking along the lines of accepting a Canadian in command of the militia, with some degree of supervision exercised by the imperial general commanding the imperial garrison at Halifax. If there should be any dissent from this by the Canadians, which the committee regarded as a fairly likely contingency, then an acceptable alternative might be periodic inspection of the Canadian forces by a high imperial officer.[36]

Even Minto admitted the failure of the existing system. In a private letter to Chamberlain, he said that any attempt to continue the arrangement could not long succeed. Friction and Canadian public opinion would force the imperial government to give up what little control the British had over the militia forces. Nor could the failure always be attributed to the Dominion. "It is very difficult," he wrote, "to find a soldier capable of looking beyond purely military needs and of dealing tenderly with political necessities. . . ." Minto suggested an amalgamation of the imperial command at Halifax with the command of the militia as a possible solution, a scheme somewhat akin to the first alternative of

[35] C.O. 42/892, Minto to C.O., April 13, 1903.
[36] C.O. 42/893, CDC Memo. #306, enclosed with Minto to C.O., Sept. 15, 1903.

the Colonial Defence Committee, though it did not concede the command of the militia to a Canadian officer.[37]

A system so universally found wanting could not long endure, especially in the face of the opposition of the Canadian government. But the promise of Laurier and Borden that there would be consultation with the imperial government was fulfilled. By the time Borden actually reached London for the consultations, Chamberlain had resigned from the government and had gone off on his crusade for imperial preferential trade. In his stead as Colonial Secretary was Alfred Lyttelton, a man of staunch imperial convictions, though without the bravura of his predecessor.

Lyttelton and Borden met with the newly created Committee of Imperial Defence on December 11, 1903, and there it was agreed that the Canadian Militia Act should be amended to allow the appointment of a Canadian officer to command, subject to the right of the Government of the United Kingdom to appoint in time of war a senior general to supreme joint command of both regular and Canadian troops in North America.

It was further agreed that in the event of a Canadian officer being appointed, and during the time when Canada lacked fully qualified officers with staff training, three officers of the regular army would be appointed as Quartermaster General, Assistant Quartermaster General, and Deputy Assistant Quartermaster General. Under the command of the General Officer Commanding the Militia, and the Minister of Militia, they would have the duty of preparing the war plans of the Dominion. Borden also agreed to amendments to the Canadian law ensuring that British regular officers employed in the Canadian militia would suffer no derogation in rank while serving with the Canadian forces.

In the larger field of general military co-operation, Borden agreed with the C.I.D. that a general defense scheme for Canada should be prepared, and that Canada would maintain and revise it annually. Canada would forward these plans to London for expert criticism, and would also forward all the reports of the commander of the militia, including those classified as confidential. It was also agreed that it would be advantageous to consider the possibility of raising a Canadian regiment of two battalions, one for service in Canada and the other for India, and of providing for the inspection of the Canadian forces by a high British military officer.

This meeting of the Committee of Imperial Defence also considered the possibility of transferring the responsibility for the maintenance and defense of the naval bases of Halifax and Esquimalt to Canada, under

[37] C.O. 42/895, Minto to Chamberlain, April 15, 1903.

conditions which prescribed that the necessary technical troops of the garrison of Halifax—units of the Royal Artillery and Royal Engineers— would be furnished by Britain until Canadian units had attained similar standards of efficiency.[38]

There was, however, a certain tentativeness in Borden's understanding with the C.I.D. He was apparently apprehensive about possible political reaction to this discussion, for he did not want the minutes of the meeting, which would be circulated to responsible officials in both countries, to contain any reference to the possibility of Canada taking over the two naval bases, or to the raising of a Canadian regiment for service in India.[39]

Borden's meeting with the Committee of Imperial Defence could not be counted a conspicuous success. Though it was the first occasion on which a representative of a dominion government conferred with the C.I.D., and though there was agreement on the matter of the command of the Canadian militia, there were drawbacks which might discourage the making of such consultations a normal procedure. For one thing, Borden came to the meeting with authority to commit his government on one issue only, and that was the matter of the command of the militia. Further, there was subsequent disagreement about the exact nature of things agreed upon: the minutes could not be accepted or issued until they had been approved by all participants, and Borden's remoteness from London delayed this.

When Borden finally introduced the amendments to the Canadian Militia Act in the Commons, Lord Minto noted with alarm that the bill did not include a clause setting forth the right of the Crown in time of war to appoint a senior British military officer to supreme joint command. Borden also alarmed Minto by his statement to the Commons that a Canadian might be appointed if senior in rank. Despite Borden's promise that amendment to the legislation would be put forward during the second reading of the bill, Minto felt that he could no longer put any faith in the promise.[40]

But the whole question of the militia command was affected by the recommendations which, early in 1904, were emerging from the labors of the Esher Committee. That body, acting with a remarkable promptness, had urged a series of sweeping changes in the administration of the British army, including the creation of an Army Council, and the establishment of a General Staff. And the speed of the committee's labors was matched by the swiftness with which its suggestions were adopted. King Edward VII, who had followed the work of the committee with great

[38] C.O. 42/895, War Office to Colonial Office, Dec. 22, 1903.
[39] C.O. 42/986, Borden to Minto, March 1, 1904, with Minto to C.O., March 4, 1904.
[40] C.O. 42/896, Minto to C.O., March 19, 1904.

interest, issued the Letters Patent for the Army Council early in February, 1904. These moves in Britain led Borden to introduce a clause in the pending militia legislation enabling him to adopt some device similar to the Army Council if it seemed desirable. And following the suggestions made for Britain by the Esher group, he resolved finally on the creation of a Militia Council of seven members, with functions in Canada roughly comparable to those of the new British Army Council. The Minister of Militia was to be chairman, and there were to be four military and two civilian members. The first military member of the council, the Chief of Staff, was to be an officer of the regular army for some time to come. The new system also made provision for an Inspector General of the Militia. Borden would have preferred that the commander of the imperial garrison at Halifax might add that to his other duties; perhaps his correspondence with General Sir Charles Parsons, currently G.O.C. in Halifax, encouraged him in that idea, for Parsons had urged upon him the creation of the Militia Council system, and also the post of Inspector General.[41] But the two positions were not combined, and the first Inspector General under the new system was another imperial officer.

The new ordering of militia affairs brought about a marked improvement in the direction of Canadian military activity. The basic adjustment, of course, was in the political field. The new arrangements ended what Sir John Anderson of the Colonial Office called the incompatibility of a quasi-independent militia command with complete ministerial responsibility. The new system left no doubt about the final authority of the responsible minister; the military members of the Militia Council were to be his expert advisors, but clearly his subordinates. The built-in antagonisms and political suspicions of the old system were abated, and the way was opened for more intimate collaboration between the civilian chief and his military experts. And while it clarified that issue, the new system also more clearly than ever placed the responsibility for Canadian military defense in Canadian hands. As long as the G.O.C. of the Canadian militia was an imperial officer with somewhat of an independent status, that ultimate responsibility was obscured.

The new system was fortunate in its first Chief of Staff, Percy Lake. Lake had first served in Canada in the nineties as Quartermaster General of the Militia and, in 1898, had represented Canada on the Leach Committee. From 1899 to the time of his appointment to Canada again, he had served as Assistant Quartermaster General in charge of the Mobilization Division of the War Office. The Canadian government was urgent in its request that Colonel Lake be seconded to the new post, and although the War Office was reluctant, since Lake was low in seniority on the list

[41] *Ibid.*, Minto to C.O., April 11, 1904.

of colonels, the appointment was eventually made. Lake was not particularly eager to go to Canada, and as a condition for his going stipulated that he be raised to the rank of Major General. To do this, it was necessary to promote him over some 280 officers who outranked him, but this was done, Lord Minto interceding with War Secretary H. O. Arnold-Forster to help bring it about.[42]

Once in his new post as Chief of Staff, Lake displayed all of the qualities necessary for the job: professional competence combined with tact and a sense of the political realities. Lake defined the golden rule for one in a position such as his: it was to bear in mind that a responsible government had to answer to the people for the use of the money voted by the legislature. The wise course for the military authorities was to make things as easy as possible for the political head of the military department from a parliamentary point of view. Much could be accomplished by the effective use of regulations; a minister would be only too glad to avoid responsibility by sheltering under the regulations.[43] With such political common sense, it was natural that the Canadian government sought to prolong Lake's tour of duty with the Canadian forces.[44]

In the midst of the wild excitement which had marked Dundonald's farewell parade in Ottawa, he had shouted repeatedly, "Men of Canada, keep both hands on the Union Jack!" On the occasion and in the spirit in which it was said, this cry was certainly inimical to everything that Laurier and his government stood for in imperial relations; it was clearly remote from the Canadian leader's vision of the Empire evolving into a league of free nations. But even as Laurier defended that ideal against the advocates of imperial centralization, and enlarged the claims of Canada over her own military system, Canada was being pulled inexorably, in fulfillment of her new national stature, into the "vortex of militarism" which Laurier so volubly deplored.

In February, 1902, during the closing months of the Boer War, and before the Colonial Conference of that year, the Board of Admiralty informed the Colonial Office that "in view of the great development which is taking place in certain Foreign Navies, it has become necessary for strategic reasons to concentrate more than is the case at present the Naval force in commission."[45] This statement is indicative of the changes which were beginning to occur in the upper levels of British naval command. Unchallenged for so many decades, hampered by inadequate education for higher command among its officers, and frequently more

[42] Cab. 17/44, Minto to George S. Clarke, Jan. 12, 1905.
[43] C.O. 42/929, Lake to Colonel Aston, Oct. 20, 1908, enclosed with Lord Grey to C.O., Jan. 15, 1909.
[44] C.O. 42/900, Grey to C.O., Feb. 10, 1905.
[45] C.O. 42/889, Admiralty to Colonial Office, Feb. 11, 1902.

handicapped than strengthened by the consciousness of its great traditions, the Royal Navy was still in the same rut in which it had been running for nearly a century. "Though numerically a very imposing force,"
says one authority, "it was in certain respects a drowsy, inefficient, moth-
eaten organism."[46] And he adds, "The ablest minds in the Navy lived
in the day before yesterday."[47]

The "Foreign Navies" of the Admiralty statement were chiefly those of
Germany and the United States. For Canadians, the latter was, for the
moment, the more important. And the root of the matter was, as Sir
George Clarke said a few years later, that the United States Navy would
soon be beyond rivalry in its own waters.[48] As he had told J. S. Sandars,
Balfour's secretary, "What it is best not to say is that we believe that the
idea of opposing the navy of the U.S. in the Caribbean & the W.
Atlantic close to its bases must be abandoned."[49]

Certainly the Admiralty was becoming increasingly pessimistic about
the possibility of the naval defense of Canada. A memorandum of
February, 1905, stated that the ability to come to the aid of Canada
depended on command of the Western Atlantic, where the United States,
with a rapidly growing navy, could apply all of her strength. Great
Britain was 3,000 miles away, and the exigencies of European politics
did not allow her to denude home waters of naval strength.

There were political aspects to the Admiralty document. In view of
British interest in the maintenance of cordial relations with the United
States, it was urged that Britain should not undertake any preparation
for the defense of Canada which might arouse suspicion in the republic.
Canada should have borne home to her that in any war with the United
States, she would have to rely mainly on her own resources, and she
should be cautious about provoking any squabbles over petty questions.
Britain, as the Admiralty saw it, had no special obligation to counter
the growth of American naval might. Canada had no moral claim to any
additional naval effort on Britain's part, since she contributed nothing
to the maintenance of the British navy. Naval support would be given
freely to Canada as far as available in time of war, but only after command of the sea had been fought for and won. But the limited usefulness
of any such British naval aid was pointed out. The United States, because
of its self-sufficiency and relatively small merchant marine, was fairly
invulnerable to the usual pressures exerted by sea power. Finally, the
Admiralty had to point to the "incurable optimism" of Canada in regard
to her own defense. The lack of any effort at defense showed all too

---

[46] Arthur J. Marder, *From the Dreadnought to Scapa Flow* (London, 1961), I, 6.
[47] *Ibid.*, p. 11.
[48] Cab. 17/47, 75th meeting C.I.D., July 13, 1905.
[49] B.M., Balfour MSS, Add. MSS, 49701, Clarke to Sandars, March 31, 1905.

clearly that Canadians did not consider war with the United States as a real possibility.[50]

The General Staff took exception to the tone of the naval statement. It commented that apparently the Admiralty was not only resigned to the loss of control of the waters of the Great Lakes, but also of the tideway of the St. Lawrence. And in defense of the Dominion, the General Staff said that Canada contributed more proportionately to its own defense than any other self-governing colony. In view of the fact that any danger to Canada was from overland invasion, it felt that the Dominion should be discouraged from making any contribution to the Royal Navy, and should be encouraged instead to devote all its efforts to improving its military organization. But the General Staff wanted a ruling on certain questions. Was the Royal Navy responsible for securing control of the waters of Lake Ontario on the outbreak of war between the United States and Great Britain? Was the Navy responsible for securing control of the tideway of the St. Lawrence to Montreal? And did the pledge given to Canada and the other colonies in the C.D.C. memorandum #57, that the Royal Navy accepted the responsibility for the defense of all British territory against invasion, still hold good for Canada?[51]

The Admiralty's reply to these questions was that it could not do anything about either the Great Lakes or the St. Lawrence, and as for the pledge to protect Canada, the basic fact was that Canada was not likely to be invaded in any manner which the Navy could oppose.[52]

The pessimistic tone of the Admiralty observations concerning aid to Canadian defenses, and the talk of the withdrawal of the imperial garrisons from Halifax, led the Colonial Secretary to seek assurances from the Committee of Imperial Defence that the pledges of British aid given to Canada in the past still stood. He referred the members of the C.I.D. specifically to Cardwell's pledge of June, 1865, and Chamberlain's of July, 1896. The committee agreed that if necessary he could give Canada the reassurances he desired. But the War Office representative was not satisfied about the position of the Admiralty concerning Canadian defense, and at the committee's meeting in July, he pressed for greater certainty as to the Navy's role. Fisher for the Board of Admiralty stood by the position previously set out in their memorandum. The Navy could not accept the responsibility for the security of Lake Ontario in case of war with the United States, nor could it guarantee to bar the passage of all hostile vessels up the St. Lawrence to Montreal. One of the members of the committee felt that Canada might be urged to maintain submarines

[50] Cab. 5/7, Admiralty Memo., "Defence of Canada."
[51] Ibid., General Staff memo, March 17, 1905.
[52] Ibid., Admiralty memo, 25–C.

and torpedo boats at Halifax to guard the river, but Chancellor of the Exchequer Austen Chamberlain opposed this strongly. He said that he looked forward to the time when Canada and the other self-governing colonies would have navies of their own which would be available for service with the British fleet in a great naval war. He would not favor any scheme which tended to encourage the idea among Canadians that their duties to the Empire were limited to local defenses; that would be a retrograde and disastrous step. Balfour agreed with the general line of Chamberlain's argument, but felt that submarines and torpedo craft might constitute the beginnings of a sea-going Canadian fleet.[53] The C.I.D. thus continued the acceptance of the long standing British obligation to come to the defense of Canada, though the strategic possibilities of any real British assistance were rapidly diminishing. But in the light of the limited possibility of any conflict with the United States, the renewal of the pledges was not as paradoxical as the strategic circumstances might indicate.

Obviously, the Committee of Imperial Defence would not have accepted this paradox of the obligations to Canada and the practical impossibility of fulfilling them, had there been any sense of menace or threat from the United States. The committee had things of greater immediacy to think about: the general need for greater military efficiency, the threat in the rise of German naval power and the possibility of invasion of the British Isles, and the continued need for vigilance on the Indian frontier. The latter was still regarded as of major importance, even after the deflation of Russian military power by the Japanese. In the light of these larger considerations, H. O. Arnold-Forster proposed to the C.I.D. the withdrawal of the small existing garrison of imperial forces from Halifax. Sir George Clarke noted that the discussion that followed concerning colonial garrisons was most important; it implied a new departure and a reaction against the unsound principles which had long prevailed and added so greatly to British military costs. There had been in the past an exaggerated role given to fixed defenses. As to Halifax, there was no more reason for maintaining a garrison there than in Sydney, Australia. The withdrawal of the garrison would bring home a sense of responsibility to the Canadian government and people.[54]

Strategic considerations certainly justified the proposed withdrawal of the imperial forces. It was also consonant with the growth of Canadian nationalism that Canada should fall heir to the control and maintenance of the ancient imperial citadel guarding the approaches to the St.

[53] W.O. 106/40, Minutes of C.I.D. Meetings, April 5, 12, and July 13, 1905, Jacket Bi–4.

[54] Cab. 2/1, 38th meeting of C.I.D., July 8, 1904; Brit. Mus. Add. MSS 49700.

Lawrence. During the South African war, the imperial garrison had been withdrawn for duty on the battlefields, and Canadian militia units had taken over the duty. Borden had told the C.I.D. in 1903 that Canada was willing to consider taking over the garrison duty permanently. But the situation was, nevertheless, one of some delicacy, for the imperial authorities proposed to abandon Halifax regardless of the course taken by Canada. What it amounted to, then, was that the Canadians were to be encouraged to take over the defense of a position which the imperial authorities regarded as unimportant, and which at least some of them regarded as indefensible against the one state which had been the *raison d'être* for most Canadian defense activity, the United States.

The situation caused some discomfort in the Colonial Office. Sir Montagu Ommaney, the Permanent Undersecretary, said that he was at a loss as to what to do when the War Office notified the Colonial Office that the Army Council had decided upon the immediate withdrawal of the battalion of regular infantry stationed at Halifax, in line with the recent decision of the Committee of Imperial Defence. Ommaney felt it was important that the military should do nothing until the Colonial Office had time to prepare Canada for the change. But unfortunately the War Office had supplied no reasons for the contemplated withdrawal which were suitable for the Colonial Office to pass along to the Canadians. Ommaney was keenly alive to the difficulties of framing a dispatch that would give plausible grounds for the change of policy, and which while maintaining that garrisons were no longer necessary, would at the same time invite the Canadians to furnish such garrisons.

Fortunately, however, the Canadian press came to the aid of the Colonial Office. The *Morning Post* of December 8, 1904, carried a dispatch from Canada saying that the Toronto *Globe*, a ministerial organ, had begun a campaign for the withdrawal of all imperial forces from Canada. Taking the offering so agreeably presented, the Colonial Office telegraphed the new Governor General, Lord Grey, to inquire whether the views of the *Globe* were those of the Canadian Cabinet.[55] Grey replied that Laurier had said that there was no objection to Canada taking over the fortress and its duties.[56] But Ommaney was not satisfied; he felt that Grey had missed the point. The Colonial Office wanted the Canadian government to make a proposal to take over the garrison duties, not simply to agree to a British request that they do so. Under further prodding, Grey eventually wired that he anticipated an offer from Canada to take over responsibility for Halifax and Esquimalt.[57] Further en-

[55] C.O. 42/899, appended to War Office to C.O., Nov. 29, 1904.
[56] C.O. 42/897, Grey to C.O., Dec. 15, 1904.
[57] *Ibid.*, Grey to C.O., Dec. 29, 1904.

couragement was given in a speech by Borden, in which he was reported
to have said that the Canadian government and people were prepared
to relieve the British taxpayer of every dollar of taxation arising from
the protection of Canadian territory, at least in time of peace.[58] Ommaney was able to report to Sir Edward Ward of the War Office, after
the Canadian government made a formal offer to take over the Halifax
duties, that this news "happily relieves H.M.G. from the invidious duty
of telling Canada that without consulting the Dominion Government it
had decided to withdraw the garrison."[59] It was, Ommaney felt, rather
a triumph to have got the Canadian government to make the offer.

There were further, though minor, problems to be disposed of. The
War Office would have liked to have had Canada take over the post at
the beginning of April, 1906, while the Canadians stated that July 1 was
the earliest date possible. The Laurier Government proposed that imperial
troops stay on until Canada was able to replace them, and that Canada
pay for their services after the July 1, 1906, date. It further proposed that
these forces come under the Canadian command to be established at
that time.[60] The Army Council in Great Britain accepted the date, but
could not consent to placing British troops under Canadian command
until the vexing matter of the relative rank of officers with imperial and
Canadian commissions had been more definitively settled.

These problems were disposed of, and the Colonial Office hierarchy
was somewhat surprised at the general speed with which Canada was
able to find recruits for the units to be stationed at Halifax. The long-
standing and irritating matter of relative rank had apparently been settled
on terms proposed by the Army Council. These were designed to place
the regular army and the Canadian permanent forces in a definite relationship with each other. The Canadian government, proposed the Army
Council, should recognize the imperial commissions of British officers
serving with the Canadian militia, thus enabling them to exercise command over Canadian units without the granting of Canadian commissions unless for the purpose of conferring higher local rank. In return,
the United Kingdom would recognize the substantive rank of Canadian
militia officers as the equivalent of British militia rank. Canadian militia
officers were to take rank with British regulars and Canadian permanent
forces as "the youngest of their degree." Canada was to require the same
educational requirements for officers of her permanent forces as those
imposed on army officers in the United Kingdom. Qualified Canadians
were to be offered facilities for employment on staff work in Britain.

---

[58] *Ibid.*, Grey to C.O., Dec. 30, 1904.
[59] C.O. 42/900, Ommaney to Ward, Jan. 21, 1905.
[60] *Ibid.*, Minute of Canadian Privy Council, Feb. 28, 1905.

The Canadians accepted the proposal as containing a "generous recognition" of the services and reputation of officers of the Canadian forces.[61] Some further words were exchanged between the War Office and the Colonial Office, however, for the former felt that for the arrangements which they had proposed to be fully legal, it would be necessary for the Canadian commissions to be signed by the monarch. The Colonial Office took strong exception to this. This was not reciprocity, they urged, for the responsibility of the King's signature rested with the home government. Further, the exercise of the royal prerogative in granting commissions was limited to forces raised by authority of Parliament. Canadian forces were not so raised; the issue of commission in Canada was a matter between the Governor General of the Dominion and his advisers.[62]

The Colonial Office also resisted an effort of the War Office to put some of the costs of the transfer of forces and of the facilities and supplies which the Canadians were inheriting on the Dominion. Such consideration was perhaps largely to be attributed to a guilty conscience on the part of some of the Colonial Office people; they were aware that the Canadians had been lured into assuming a charge and responsibility that the imperial authorities felt was wasted. As Lyttelton remarked, the imperial government had taken every precaution to prevent the Canadians from knowing that if they did not provide a garrison for Halifax, there would be none.[63] The Canadians had the happy consciousness of assistance to the Empire, while the Colonial Office was uneasily aware that the assistance was actually neither necessary nor wanted. This is perhaps part explanation of the generally protective position which the Colonial Office assumed towards Canada during the Halifax negotiations.

Analogous to the shift of the responsibility for the garrison at Halifax was the later transfer of the maintenance of the naval facilities at that base and Esquimalt to the Canadian government. The Admiralty's reasons for the transfer were, of course, implicit in the whole policy of the concentration of forces which had been carried out in the Fisher regime. And the negotiations for the transfer were marked by an indication of the growth of political understanding on the part of the naval authorities. In the light of previous cases, where detailed, but in practice unenforceable conditions, had been established for colonial governments, the Admiralty was willing to accept only a minimal number of conditions for the transfer. These were that if the existing facilities of supply and repair were not maintained, then equal ones would be provided; that adequate coal supplies would be kept on the base; that all facilities re-

[61] C.O. 42/904, War Office to C.O., June 13, 1904; Grey to C.O., July 21, 1905, C.O. 42/901.
[62] C.O. 42/904, War Office to Colonial Office, Sept. 16, 1905.
[63] C.O. 42/904, Draft C.O. to Treasury, Oct. 5, 1905.

quired would be given to the Royal Navy whenever wanted, free of cost with the exception of labor and materials; and that the Admiralty would be informed beforehand of any plan or intention of the Dominion government to use the facilities of Halifax and Esquimalt for other than naval or military purposes.[64]

By the time that the whole transaction had been legalized by an Order-in-Council of 1910 turning the ownership of the bases over to the Canadian government, the naval picture had been substantially changed. A blaze of excitement, the "we want eight and we won't wait" excitement of the 1909 dreadnought crisis, had swept through Britain, Canada, and much of the rest of the Empire. In this crisis Canada felt better prepared to act, for she had by then made substantial strides in her defense arrangements. She was in control of an improving militia organization, a permanent military force that, though small, was taking on an increasingly professional character. And she was about to come into the ownership of two naval bases which, however useless in the eyes of imperial authority, were to Canadians part of the guardianship of the seas which they and Britain shared together.

[64] C.O. 42/914, Admiralty to C.O., Oct. 2, 1907.

CHAPTER IX

AUSTRALIAN NATIONALISM, DEFENSE, AND ALFRED DEAKIN

The Commonwealth of Australia came into existence on the first day of the new century. It was the child of political pragmatism, and yet the new continental commonwealth was informed with a measure of idealism, a combination of nationalism and egalitarianism that had emerged out of the "mateship" of the bush. This awakening Australianism had been fanned to brighter flame by the efforts of the *Bulletin*, the nearest thing in Australia to a truly national newspaper. Coarse, strident, clever, and intensely readable, the *Bulletin* gave voice to a nationalism that rejected the values of the European and British life from which Australia had developed. It struggled:

> . . . angry and striving
> against the blindness
> ship-fed seas bring us
> from colder waters.[1]

Part of the blindness against which the *Bulletin* fought, with good reason, was the so-called "colonial cringe": the idea that anything Australian was necessarily inferior to the same thing "at Home" in England, that all that was bravest, fairest, and wisest was gathered together within the limited area of the British Isles, and that before all this concentrated pre-eminence Australians were only fit to bow the head and bob the knee.

But for all of the editorial labors of the *Bulletin*, and for all its not inconsiderable achievements, the currents of Australian life were, by 1901, flowing in broader channels than those dug by that journal. Australian nationalism was developing in a more moderate and temperate

[1] Ian Mudie, "Underground," *Modern Australian Poetry*, ed. H. M. Green (2d ed.; Melbourne, 1952), p. 5.

fashion. Trading on the tension in the Australian mind between the claims of national loyalty and the traditional loyalties to Britain[2] (or what the *Bulletin* derisively called the "Hempire"), might still be a profitable furrow for the journal, but the responsible leaders of Australian political life were seeking to define the proper relations between the two allegiances without doing damage to either. Inevitably, the future lay with the developing Australian nationalism rather than the traditional British connection; but this was a matter of gradual growth and maturation, and could not be done by the hothouse forcing which the *Bulletin* so stridently advocated.

To some degree, the *Bulletin's* influence had passed its peak by the time the Commonwealth was formed. The achievement of Australian federation drained away some of the political and emotional enthusiasms which might otherwise have gone into the cause of imperial federation, and thus deprived the *Bulletin* of one of its chief targets. Further, British officialdom had been almost universally friendly to the aspirations of Australian nationalism in the creation of the Commonwealth, and this fact had not escaped notice in Australia. An imperial loyalty which enabled Australians to order their own affairs as they pleased, and yet at the same time gave them assurance of defense in an uncertain world, seemed to most a very good bargain indeed.

Of course, it was not only a sense of such advantage which led 16,000 Australians to volunteer for service in South Africa. Love of adventure, the novelty of strange scenes, all of the forces were present which in the past had led men to arms and battle. But some sense of attachment to "Home" and Britain played its part too. Though the *Bulletin* might rage and, regarding the war as growing from the greed of international Jewish capitalism, sneer at the "Cohentingenters," it was not able to diminish the flow to the recruiting offices. Nor was it able to check Australian celebration of Empire Day, though it dubbed it "Vampire Day" in the attempt.

One of the first occasions on which the Parliament of the new Commonwealth came to grips with the problem of reconciling the two loyalties was in the passing of legislation creating a new Commonwealth Department of Defence. The proposed defense act called for the creation of a small permanent force and for a militia establishment, the latter to be kept up to strength by ballot selection from the male population if necessary. But the chief debate centered on the clause of the bill that would have permitted the employment of these forces outside the bounds of the Commonwealth. There was strenuous objection to this—in some cases extending even to a refusal to allow the use of the permanent force

[2] *The Bulletin* (Sydney), Jan. 24, 1903.

in New Guinea—and the clause eventually was rejected. This happened even though the Barton Government, which had introduced the bill, had a nominal majority in the House.

The debate also reflected some of the irritations arising in the Australian mind from the conflict then being fought out on the African veldt. Annoyance was expressed at the loss of Australian control over the forces dispatched abroad; the occasional use of Australian troops as firing squads in military executions was cited as a case in point.[3] There was also a pronounced hostility to anything suggestive of a professional military caste. The idea of the citizen soldier, deeply rooted in the democratic tradition, was frequently lauded, with suggestions that the Swiss military system provided Australia with the most applicable example. If there had to be an officer corps, it should be open to all; the idea of a closed officer caste was most abhorrent.

In all of the discussion, there was little residue of the old separatist spirit of a decade back. A Labor member, Charles McDonald of Queensland, came closest to the old feeling in his opposition to "any attempt to tax the people of the Commonwealth in order that we may assist in the defence of the Empire,"[4] and his assertion that England sent her forces abroad only to enlarge the market for English goods. In general, however, the protestations of attachment to empire were all that the most ardent imperialist might desire.

The tenor of this debate on the defense bill was in Prime Minister Barton's mind during his attendance at the 1902 Colonial Conference, and it formed part of his general resistance to efforts of Chamberlain, First Lord of the Admiralty Selborne, and War Secretary Brodrick, to get a greater contribution from the colonies for imperial defense. The debate was especially pertinent to New Zealand Premier Seddon's pet project, the creation of an imperial reserve. Barton remembered that not a single voice in the House of Representatives in Melbourne had been raised in favor of the clause which authorized service outside the Commonwealth.[5] But Barton agreed to the prolongation of the existing naval agreement with the United Kingdom, though with modifications that were substantially in accord with Admiralty desires. The amount of the subsidy, a comparatively unimportant matter, was increased: the Commonwealth was to pay £200,000 per annum. More important to the Admiralty, the control of the Australian government over the movement of the subsidized vessels in time of war was ended; such ships would be

---

[3] Commonwealth of Australia, *Parliamentary Debates* (C.P.D.), III, 2963, 2979.
[4] *Ibid.*, p. 3522.
[5] Australian National Library, Canberra, Prime Minister's Department, Correspondence and Papers, Vol. XXXII, Barton's Report to Cabinet on 1902 Colonial Conference.

fully under the discretionary control of the Royal Navy. In return for these concessions, the Admiralty agreed that more modern vessels would be placed in Australian waters.

Barton had gone along with this, feeling that the new Commonwealth could not face the costs of establishing a naval nucleus of her own. (The vessels inherited by the Commonwealth government from the states had long since lapsed into such a degree of obsolescence as to be militarily useless; though the South Australian ship *Protector* had been of some service during the Boxer Rebellion in China.) Further, the costs of keeping any small naval force up to date were too great for the Commonwealth government. The renewal of the agreement seemed the most available and expedient course. [6]

This was not, however, a course which was agreeable to the more ardent spirits among the Australian nationalists. The *Bulletin* naturally directed some of its sharpest salvos against Barton's decision. Among its other efforts, it showed him returning from the conference saddled with the heavy burden of the agreement. [7] It subsequently said that Barton had been glorified and banqueted while in England, and that the new agreement had been fixed up while the glamour of the soup and the radiance of the salmon were still upon him. [8]

The *Bulletin* was not alone in attacking Barton for the renewal of the naval agreement. The same line of strong opposition, though couched in more moderate language, was taken by the Melbourne *Age*. This journal was the strongest voice of moderate liberal nationalism in Australia. It was the property of David Syme, the foremost advocate of protectionism in Australia, and a man who had been a power in the political life of the state of Victoria. Alfred Deakin, Attorney General in the Barton Cabinet, also had associations with the *Age*. Deakin had once worked for the paper and was still in many ways identified in the public mind with its policies. The *Age* established its opposition to the renewal of the agreement from the time when the first London news dispatches suggested that this was the policy that Barton would follow. The paper was opposed to any effort on the part of London authorities to bring all the defenses of the Empire under one central control, arguing that events in Africa had demonstrated that neither the Admiralty nor the War Office had any monopoly on wisdom. [9]

Barton was able eventually, at the close of a debate lasting some three weeks, to get the new naval agreement approved by the Commonwealth House of Representatives. But the debate revealed substantial dissatis-

[6] *Ibid.*
[7] *The Bulletin* (Sydney), Oct. 18, 1902.
[8] *Ibid.*, Jan. 24, 1903.
[9] *The Age* (Melbourne), March 13, 1902.

faction with the arrangements and suggested that in all likelihood this would be the last such agreement made with the Admiralty.

The Commonwealth Prime Minister based much of his defense of the agreement upon the idea that so long as Australians had the advantage of the imperial connection, they had obligations to the Empire as well: "While we remain part of the Empire, there will arise questions of Imperial rather than local importance, and they will arise even if we turn away and shut our eyes. But it is our duty to have regard to these questions so long as we remain in the Empire, and to recognize what our position requires of us, not to the extent of slavish adherence to everything done by others, but to the extent of realising that with participation in the advantages of the Empire comes reciprocal obligation."[10] Barton also pointed out that there were distinct benefits in the terms of the new agreement. For with the new mobility allowed to the subsidized vessels came the advantages of concentration of force, and Australia would have greater security because the new arrangements allowed a wider freedom for concentration of British naval forces of the Australasian, China, and Far Eastern Stations.[11]

There was little of the old anti-imperialism in the criticism of the agreement, as there had been little in the debate over the first defense act. There was, however, a prevailing sense that British and Australian interests were not in all instances likely to be identical. While some of the opponents of the bill recognized the advantages of concentration in war, they also expressed the fear that in global conflict Australia might succumb while Britain concentrated her power for the defense of the heart of empire. They felt that Australia should take at least the first steps toward ensuring that in such a circumstance, her maritime trade and her seacoasts would not be left defenseless. In time of a great war, it was felt, there would be no naval vessels available for Australian defense unless Australia provided them. Along this line, William Morris Hughes, a leader of the young Labor party in the Parliament, and a future Prime Minister, argued that the most efficient manner in which Australia could aid Britain was to free British sea power for concentrated operation in other parts of the globe by furnishing the assurance that whatever might come, Australians would render a good account of themselves in their own defense either on land or at sea.[12]

Among the party leaders, J. C. Watson, leader of the Labor party members of the House, opposed ratification on the grounds that the defense of Australia should not be merged with the general defense of the Empire. On the other hand, George Reid, the former Premier of New South Wales, voted for the agreement. Reid, however, who was leader

[10] C.P.D., XIV, 1799.   [11] *Ibid.*, pp. 1779–81.   [12] *Ibid.*, p. 2318.

of the free trade element in the House and therefore leader of the Opposition to the government, managed in the debate to live up to the nickname "Yes-No" Reid, which he had won by his ambiguous attitude on federation. This agreement, he said, was grounded on the idea of imperial partnership. The 1887 agreement had made the Royal Navy and the colonies partners in Australasian defense, while the new one made them partners in imperial defense. But this partnership he argued, was beyond the existing capacity of Australia: "We cannot pretend to be competent to rule the affairs of India or South Africa." And he saw in this effort by Britain to secure such partnership not statesmanship but a failure of nerve on the part of the imperial government. Nevertheless, Reid announced his intention to vote for the agreement.

To Barton and his Minister of Defence, Sir John Forrest, the waves of criticism seemed to buffet the agreement so roughly as to make its ratification doubtful. Feeling that something should be done to mollify the strong desire for some form of local defense, they asked for six small torpedo boat destroyers as substitutes for one of the cruisers called for in the agreement, suggesting that these would be locally manned and officered. Even two of them, they urged, would help allay some of the opposition.[13]

The Colonial Office reaction was typical of its firm and inflexible attitude toward all Australian views on naval defense over the next few years. Sir Montagu Ommaney, Permanent Undersecretary, minuted on the request that "the Australians do not seem to be able to grasp the principles of naval defence." The vessels they had proposed would give no security to Australia; they would give them only a sense of false security that might lead to neglect of coastal defenses.[14]

The Australians' original request was reinforced by a telegram saying that without some concession on the part of the Admiralty it would be hard to obtain passage of the agreement. Sir John Anderson took the matter up with the Admiralty, and Admiral Prince Louis of Battenberg formulated the Admiralty's views. He held that to add destroyers to the force to be provided under the agreement could be taken as an admission that the sea-going fleet was insufficient, and that the principle on which the agreement was based was unsound. From a purely naval viewpoint, the Admiralty felt it would be best if the agreement were rejected anyway. But the Admiralty might be willing, for imperial reasons, to make some concessions in order to aid ratification, and he suggested that some torpedo boats might be substituted for one of the cruisers provided under the agreement. When the Admiralty's reply to the Colonial Office inquiries was finally formulated, it pointed out the uselessness of torpedo boat destroyers when there were no torpedo boats within 4,000 miles of

[13] C.O. 418/26, Tennyson to C.O., April 24, 1903.   [14] *Ibid.*

Australia, and it took refuge in the tripartite nature of the agreement as a barrier to any modification.[15]

If the Admiralty accepted the agreement only as a token of a greater imperial unity in defense which it hoped would follow, the Admiral on the Australian Station also could see little virtue in it. Admiral Lewis Beaumont, former D.N.I. in the Admiralty and after that Commander in Chief of the Australian Station, said on his retirement from the latter duty that apparently nothing would change the belief of the Australian people that the payment of the subsidy gave them a proprietary right in the ships on the station. He regretted that there was apparently no understanding in the Australian mind as to what the true naval needs of their country were. The mass of the people remained ignorant of the true principles of naval power, and continued to be misguided in this by their public men. Moreover, the terms of the new agreement, that opened the way for the recruitment of Australians into the Auxiliary Squadron, would, he felt, lead to trouble, for Australians would not accept the discipline, and would desert. They were used to moving from one job to another with casual ease, and would not be content to stay in the naval service if they found it onerous.[16]

Beaumont's successor on the Australian Station, Admiral Fanshawe, did not take such a dismal view of the agreement and tried to assist in its ratification. He discussed the matter with George Reid and felt that, if the latter fulfilled his promises, the agreement would get sufficient votes despite the opposition of the Labor party and those who hankered for the establishment of an Australian navy.[17]

In the end, Admiral Fanshawe had the right of it, for the agreement was ratified, though its passage through the Senate of the Parliament was not less bitterly contested than it had been in the Representatives. But the political correspondent of the *Age* said that the debate in that body indicated "clearly enough that the Senate will never again assent to an agreement, naval or otherwise, which emphasizes the position of Australia as a dependency."[18]

H. F. Wyatt, an emissary of the British Navy League, had been going about the Empire at this time, seeking to enlist popular support for colonial aid to the Royal Navy. To him the whole tenor of the debate was dismally bleak.[19] And the *Times* of London remarked of his mission: "The *Times* had noted the departure of Wyatt on this missionary journey around the globe, and while it deplored the notable laxity of strategic thought among

---

[15] Adm. 1/7670; C.O. 418/31, Admiralty to C.O.
[16] P.R.O., Adm. 1/7654, Beaumont to Admiralty, Jan. 12, 1903.
[17] Adm. 1/7670, Admiral Arthur Fanshawe to Admiralty, April 27, 1903.
[18] *The Age* (Melbourne), Aug. 28, 1903.
[19] *Ibid.*, July 15, 16, 1903.

the Australians, it felt that if Sir George Clarke, Governor of Victoria, and Admiral Harry Rawson, Governor of New South Wales, were not able to bring them back to the path of naval rectitude, Mr. Wyatt was not likely to do so either."[20]

One of the best summaries of the causes of the opposition to the naval agreement came from Sir George S. Clarke, then serving as Governor of Victoria. It was more moderate than some of his later observations on the Australian position regarding their defense. Sir George traced much of the difficulty to the flaws which he felt had existed in the original 1887 agreement. This had encouraged an acceptance of the notions that the colonial subsidies were for vessels earmarked for local defense; that the distribution of the naval power of Great Britain was done on political rather than strategic grounds; and that Australia's interests had some special and peculiar right to Admiralty consideration apart from other areas of the Empire. Further, under the terms of that agreement, there had been no real chance for Australians to serve in their own naval defense, to learn the ways of the sea, and to gain some familiarity with naval problems. Hence there existed in the Australian mind a tendency, arising from ignorance, to entertain exaggerated views of Australian potentialities. A large body of Australian opinion, Clarke said, favored the establishment of an Australian navy. "In so far as this opinion is genuine, it must be respected and taken into account. It is quite natural in a community which is much inclined to overrate its capabilities, and is profoundly ignorant of the function which the Royal Navy discharges and of the principles of naval defence."[21] Unfortunately there was really no method of educating the people on this, since those who could speak with knowledge and authority—and Sir George surely included himself among these—were obliged to remain silent. And even in England narrow views on naval defense prevailed in some quarters.

The criticism of the agreement in Australia had been observed with a considerable degree of irritation in London. Ommaney's comment about the inability of Australians to grasp the principles of naval defense is strongly suggestive of the Colonial Office line. And the *Times*, dismally sneering at the colonial efforts to think through an imperial problem, took patronizing exception to the views of the *Age*. It called the financial argument over the agreement "shabby," the constitutional argument "flimsy," and its strategic conceptions "childish." The whole approach of the *Age* and others who opposed the ratification of the agreement was "nothing less than a direct negation of all sound principles of Imperial defence." If the colonies repudiated the agreement, the *Times* could only

[20] *The Times* (London), Sept. 27, 1902.
[21] Adm. 1/7670, Clarke to C.O., March 30, 1903.

say with Burke that the age of chivalry was gone, and a new age of "sophisters, economists and calculators" was established in its stead.[22]

While things were sticky in Australia, there were no sophisters, economists, and calculators discernible across the Tasman Sea. None of the difficulties and foot-dragging evident in Australia appeared in the New Zealand Parliament when it was called upon by "King Dick" Seddon to ratify the agreement. There the ratification passed without opposition, and with protestations of imperial attachment and loyalty.[23]

Of course, the agreement was practically stillborn. Surviving the rigors of birth with difficulty, it was immediately faced with a host of grim-visaged bad fairies, clustering about its cradle heaping curses upon it, pressed down and running over. It had never been a child of love from its conception. The Admiralty cared nothing for it, except as it exemplified the principle of colonial contribution to imperial defense. The actual contribution was too small—about 1 per cent of the annual naval estimates of the time—to be of any real value. And the new contract with the colonies, despite the clause which gave the Admiralty greater freedom in the movement of the vessels, still carried the birthmark of localization about it. For example, when the Admiralty proposed in December, 1904, to make some changes in the vessels on the station, in the light of the recent decision to employ in peacetime only vessels which would be effective fighting machines in time of war, the Colonial Office felt that colonial legislation on the matter would be necessary as well as politically desirable.[24] The whole arrangement smacked of the strategic thinking before the "enlightenment" and the spread of the true faith in naval doctrine; the odor of the gunboat era of British naval history hung about it.

The new naval doctrines soon received ruthless and remorseless reinforcement with the coming of Admiral Sir John Fisher to the post of First Sea Lord. The Fisher era began with the redistribution of British naval forces and the coming of the dreadnought, and the first of these dealt a severe blow to the agreement. One of the selling points on which Barton had placed great emphasis in seeking ratification of the agreement was the availability of British naval power on the China Station for the defense of Australia if needed. The co-operative action of the forces of the China, East Indian, and Australian Stations of the navy was to be assisted by the enactment of the agreement, and thus the defense of the Commonwealth would be strengthened. But the props of such co-operation were knocked away with the withdrawal of the five battleships that

[22] *The Times* (London), Jan. 2, 1903.
[23] New Zealand, *Parliamentary Debates*, 3rd Session, 14th Parl., CXXII, 507–26.
[24] C.O. 418/34, Admiralty memo, Dec. 7, 1904.

had heretofore been the truest embodiment of British naval power in Pacific waters.

The withdrawal of these vessels and other changes in the distribution of British fighting ships were based on the shifting circumstances of international diplomacy. The increasing menace confronting Britain in the growth of German naval strength, the development of the Anglo-French entente, and the creation of the Anglo-Japanese alliance in 1902 and its subsequent renewal after the demonstration of Japanese fighting effectiveness in war with Russia, were all elements contributing to the change, though the memorandum of the Colonial Defence Committee which went to the colonial governments to explain the changes laid them to the shifting technology of naval warfare.

The redistribution involved also the destruction of about 150 ships of so little fighting capacity that Fisher referred to them as belonging to the "Snail" and "Tortoise" classes.[25] These were just the small, police-duty vessels which had been frequently utilized in Australasian waters and some of which had been subsidized by the colonial governments. Now they were withdrawn from naval service as useless, and were headed for the breaker's yards. For the *Bulletin* it was a glorious chance; it pointed out with glee that H.M.S. *Boomerang* and *Karrakatta*, just a short while before part of the fleet protecting Australia, for whose support the Commonwealth paid £200,000, were now out of the fleet and sold for £1,900 and £1,875 respectively.[26] And the language of the *Age* was no less bitter. "Fisher's new broom has also swept away the type of vessel seen so much in Australian waters as embodiments of British sea power. The Australian Station is evidently like a paddock to which old and worn out animals are sent in ignorance of their approaching end. This is the sort of squadron for which Australia has been paying a subsidy."[27] The *Age* drew the lesson that Australia had better start acquiring some viable vessels of her own.

Nor was the nationalist element of Australian political life, whether of the moderate stripe of the *Age* or the more belligerent view of the *Bulletin*, happy with the substitute for British sea power in the Pacific which was offered by diplomacy: the Anglo-Japanese alliance. To many in Australia, the most notable achievement of the new Commonwealth Parliament had been the enactment into law of the "White Australia" policy. The need for such a policy was a major item of faith with the *Bulletin*, and with most Australians in general. The ignominy of being assured that the alliance with the Japanese gave security to a state which

[25] Adm. 116/942, note by Fisher, dated simply Feb., 1907; Kemp (ed.), *The Papers of Admiral Sir John Fisher*, I, 30.
[26] *The Bulletin* (Sydney), Nov. 9, 1905.
[27] *The Age* (Melbourne), Feb. 21, 1905.

would not permit Japanese to stay any length of time within its borders was galling to many, especially the militant nationalists. The *Bulletin*, which complained that the Australians had had no voice in the making of the treaty, said that Australia was not morally bound by it, and lamented that it was not easy to remain white in an Empire which grew blacker every day.[28]

New Zealand was officially more content with the naval agreement than Australia, as we have seen. But even so, Lord Plunket, newly arrived in New Zealand as Governor in 1906, detected an undercurrent of irritation over it, which he summarized in a lengthy statement to the Colonial Office. Though he admitted that the agreement was not as unpopular there as it was in Australia, he felt that were it not for the implication in the agreement that the colonies accepted some responsibility for imperial defense, the agreement would be better done away with. It led, he declared, to bickering and irresponsible criticism in both press and Parliament, with no one satisfied. It brought little financial aid to Britain, created criticism in the colonies of what Britain furnished in return for the subsidy, and compelled the Admiralty to tie up ships in Australian waters. And it led to a form of guilty conscience in both Australia and New Zealand, for in both lands there existed a realization that what the colonies gave was of little assistance to Britain, and this made the colonies somewhat ashamed. But the colonies were not likely to contribute more, said the Governor, for the agreement annoyed them by its flavor of taxation without representation. And they also had a craving for some ships of their own, no matter how small.[29]

There were, of course, defenders of the agreement in Australian life. Against the opposition of the *Age* might be balanced the support of the conservative Melbourne daily, the *Argus*. And in the other major Australian cities there was always a major daily that supported the agreement. Further, the agreement could always find backing within the conservative membership in the Parliament. In 1908, for example, after the agreement had been in force for half of its ten years, both Sir John Forrest and George Reid were still staunch in its defense. Reid argued that under the agreement Britain was furnishing adequate naval defense for Australia, and if this was so, why duplicate simply "for the sake of hoisting our own flag?"[30] Further, he argued, the idea of having Australian naval vessels would raise grave constitutional issues. The British government would be legally responsible for the acts of colonial officers. In language which echoed Cobden, he urged that it would be dangerous

[28] *The Bulletin* (Sydney), Feb. 22, 1902.
[29] P.R.O., C.O. 209/268, Lord Plunket to C.O., Sept. 7, 1906.
[30] C.P.D., XLVII, 852.

for Britain to have a situation in which the blundering act of an Australian ship's captain could compromise the British Empire.[31]

Forrest also stood by the agreement and the memorandum he had sponsored at the 1902 Colonial Conference. He felt that the constant sniping which had been directed at the agreement had denied it a chance to prove its merit, and that efforts to undo it would result in a great deal of damage.[32]

Although Forrest and Reid were not alone in their stand, the thrust of political action was against them. True, the eroding forces of circumstance that had condemned the agreement to such general unpopularity might not alone have brought it to a premature end. But these forces of erosion received strong reinforcement from the political leadership of Alfred Deakin, and from the intruding events of the 1909 naval scare and the "we want eight and we won't wait" agitation which swept through much of Britain.

Alfred Deakin was perhaps the most distinguished personality in Australian federal politics during the first ten years of the Commonwealth. He was also the most distinguished looking,—six feet tall, with heavy black hair and beard, he was fastidious in dress, manner, and speech. Deakin had built his career through his mastery of words. After a legal education, he had gone from the law into journalism and then into political life. But he never forsook journalism, for during the years in which he was a leading figure in the political life of the Commonwealth, he was also working as the Australian correspondent to the *Morning Post* of London, a fact which was known only to a most restricted circle of the paper's directorate.[33]

When Edmund Barton resigned as Prime Minister in 1903, Deakin, who had been Attorney General and Deputy Prime Minister, succeeded to the leadership of the government. It was a position which the inchoate state of the parties in the Parliament made infinitely difficult. The Labor party held the balance of power between the two conservative groups, protectionists and free traders. Deakin led the protectionists, and in sub-substantial measure shared the more nationalistic attitudes which prevailed within the ranks of Labor. Dependent upon Labor votes, he was in no way antagonistic to much that Labor stood for. This was as true in defense as in fiscal policy.

Deakin had not been one of the ministers who had defended the naval agreement in its passage through the Parliament. Had he done so, it would have been the triumph of Cabinet solidarity over his own convic-

[31] *Ibid.*, p. 853.
[32] *Ibid.*, pp. 1136–42.
[33] J. A. La Nauze, "Alfred Deakin and the *Morning Post*," *Historical Studies, Australia and New Zealand*, Vol. VI, No. 24, May, 1955.

tions. For Deakin, as he soon disclosed, thought the agreement inconsonant with the status and dignity to which the new Commonwealth should aspire. Most of Deakin's efforts in defense planning were directed toward replacing the agreement with something more agreeable to Australian opinion.

Another man who shared Deakin's hostility to the agreement was Captain William Rooke Creswell. Captain Creswell, once of the Royal Navy but invalided out while yet a young man, had spent much of his later career in the naval service of various of the Australian colonies before federation. Shortly after the creation of the Commonwealth, he became its Director of Naval Service. Sir George Clarke, while functioning as secretary of the C.I.D., blamed the agitation for an Australian navy on two disgruntled officers of the Australian service. Creswell was certainly one of these, for along with Deakin he became a leading figure in the effort to create an Australian naval force. The two men worked in parallel channels, agreeing on their main objective, but frequently differing on the nature of the forces which might be appropriate for the commencement of such a unit. In the technical aspects of the problem, Deakin was essentially a seeker after truth, hoping even that some guidance might be forthcoming from the Admiralty; he did not lean on Creswell, though both men labored in the same cause.

As long as the Admiralty retained even its limited acceptance of the principle of subsidy as the most effective means of colonial collaboration in imperial defense, it was naturally reluctant to give any form of technical advice to the Commonwealth government. And without such technical skill, Deakin and other Australians floundered about from one suggestion to another, coming up with nothing that was in any way likely to appeal to the Admiralty mind. Actually, what was essential was that the political aspirations of the Australian leaders should be gently directed by the Admiralty technicians along channels where the money and effort which the Commonwealth might be willing to expend would contribute both to the security of Australia and the support of British sea pre-eminence. The Admiralty had, in other words, to face the political facts of life; to understand the conflicting loyalties of the Australians,[34] and to guide them into effective naval collaboration.

The reconciliation of these conflicting elements, and the meshing of the Admiralty's concern for control and efficiency of naval forces with Australian concern for a larger role in its own defense, was a task which the Colonial Office and the Colonial Defence Committee might well have

[34] This mingling of loyalties created uncertain geopolitical views among some Australians. In discussing naval and defense problems of Australia, Prime Minister Barton, for example, had referred to France as "our nearest neighbour across the Channel." C.P.D., XIV, 1778.

confronted. Yet they failed to do so for some time, adhering generally to the line of strategic orthodoxy, and displaying little interest in or understanding of the Australian position on the matter. Indeed, there was a general tone of hostility in many of the minutes and comments on the appeals and letters from Deakin. This was rather in contrast with the growing esteem in which Canada was apparently held during these same years.

A variety of factors lay behind this muted anti-Australian attitude in official circles. Basic to the whole situation, of course, was the great geographical distance between London and Melbourne. The southwest Pacific was an area of primary interest to the Australian government, if not to many of its people; but for the imperial government—Admiralty and Colonial Office—it was remote and peripheral to their main concerns. The Australians pressed their views over matters about which London cared little. Australian trading privileges in the German-held Marshall Islands, for example, and a dispute with France over the condominium in the New Hebrides, were matters which gravely concerned Australians, and they complained of British neglect in standing up for Australian interests in these areas, to the irritation of British officialdom.

Again, the "White Australia" policy, the "dog in the manger" attitude of some four million people holding a great national estate which they were not able to develop effectively, struck many in Britain as absurd. The *Times* felt that Australians had hindered the diplomacy of the imperial government, had put barriers in the path of their own economic progress, and had revealed an inadequate sense of obligation toward their fellow subjects of the Crown. And yet, complained the *Times*, Britain was ultimately responsible for any high-handed action which the Australians might attempt.[35]

The Australian addiction to protectionist tariffs, the large role played by the state in economic activity, and the substantial borrowings of public authorities in Australia, sometimes raising questions in London about Australian credit, all caused doubts about the fiscal responsibility of the Australian government and the leaders of the Australian economy. And there was no one in the Colonial Office who had actually travelled to the Antipodes. It was not until 1909 that C. P. Lucas ventured as far afield from Whitehall as Australia and New Zealand, and this lack of actual experience also formed one of the barriers against mutual understanding. Certainly, however, the occasional "arrogance" and "brusquerie" which one authority has discerned in the tone of the Colonial Office was to be found in its dealings with the Australian government.[36]

[35] *The Times* (London), April 4, 1908. For survey of relations between Britain and Australia, see Henry L. Hall, *Australia and England* (London, 1934).
[36] *C.H.B.E.*, III, 763.

The general attitude of the Colonial Office and the C.D.C. is perhaps less explicable when the record of colonial forces in recent British difficulties was considered. The Royal Commission on the conduct of the South African war (the Elgin Commission) reported that the colonial contingents, of which the Australian forces were a significant segment, had been of great value; such forces, it was suggested, could be an important adjunct to the army in any future war.[37] It is true that certain British officers felt that the colonial units needed better trained leaders. Lord Roberts felt that the efficiency of such units was materially increased when officers of the regular forces were attached to them.[38] And Major General H. C. O. Plumer stressed the need for more highly trained officers in the colonies. But it was generally agreed that colonial elements, when commanded by regular officers, were outstanding.[39]

Of course in all of this type of criticism there was much to arouse the fighting spirit of the *Bulletin*, which discerned in it only the anxiety to keep Australians in subordinate positions while the perfumed darlings of the War Office lorded it over them. But to the politically discerning eye, which Colonial Office leadership might reasonably have been expected to possess, the general lesson to be gleaned from this record of colonial participation should surely have been the Scriptural one: that those who had been faithful in small things would be equally faithful in large.

The record of the colonial contingents in South Africa was reinforced also by the excellent service which Australian units rendered during the Boxer uprising. Naval brigades from New South Wales and Victoria, and a coastal naval vessel from South Australia, the *Protector*, acquitted themselves admirably. According to General Gaselee, the commander of the British forces, the Australians were the mainstay of the British garrison at Tientsin, and were the nucleus of the police force in the British concession. Their appearance on so remote a field as North China had had an excellent political effect.[40]

Yet on the part of the Colonial Defence Committee, as well as the Colonial Office, the tendency was to speak down, as if to intellectual inferiors. The C.D.C. held to the sweeping assumption that the concepts of naval warfare adhered to by the Admiralty had a universal validity, and were recognized by all, and that therefore the conduct of war by any possible foe was highly predictable. This was apparent in a widely distributed memorandum of the committee. According to the C.D.C., the vital importance of command was now so well understood

[37] Parl. Pap., 1904, Vol. XL, Cd. 1790, p. 80.
[38] *Ibid.*
[39] Parl. Pap., 1904, Vol. XLI, Cd. 1791, p. 336.
[40] Commonwealth of Australia, Parl. Pap., 1901/02, Vol. II, p. 38.

that an enemy having a powerful battle fleet was unlikely to undertake organized attacks on commerce or commercial ports until an attempt at least had been made against British naval power. Any attacks on commerce were likely to come, if at all, during a later phase of conflict, when the enemy's battle fleet had been reduced to inactivity, and his cruisers were then liberated for hit and run raids. Working on this hypothesis the C.D.C. felt that there was therefore no great need for large garrisons in naval bases, nor was there any need for defense against torpedo boat attacks.[41]

All of this assumed that any foe would fight a convenient war, run strictly according to the rule books. The unconventional was ruled out, and yet it was the unlikely and the unconventional that the Australians, in their strategic ignorance, were concerned about. So it was that to those cloaked with this armor of certitude, the proposals which came from Australia seemed childish and naïve.

Nor was the Colonial Defence Committee much more hospitable to the plans for the organization of the military forces of the Commonwealth which came from Australia. These were largely drawn up by Major General Hutton, now on his second tour of duty in the Antipodes, this time as General Officer Commanding the Australian military forces. Hutton was less inclined to go off the rails politically than he had been in Canada. He was learning, or had learned, that: "It would . . . be out of the question to suggest any control of the Dominion or of the Commonwealth military forces outside of Canada or Australia. Public opinion would never admit even a suggestion of outside interference with what they historically look upon as their Constitutional right. Co-operation in the defence of the Empire under the circumstances that exist must be solely a matter of sentiment, and in the present condition of public opinion it would be unwise to press anything more."[42] Nothing struck him so much upon his return to Australia in 1902 as the growth of this idea in public feeling, which he thought was brought about in large measure by the considerable number of troops who had served in South Africa.

In his efforts to organize the Commonwealth military forces, Hutton had not only to struggle against all of the forces of inertia, indifference, and hostility to military officers which were part of the Australian scene as much or more than most democratic governments, but also against the discouraging belittlement of such effort by the Colonial Defence Committee, because of the dominance of "Blue Water" thinking in that circle. Australia was feeling some of the effects of what the military correspondent of the *Times* in London referred to as the "extravagant claims" of

[41] Cab. 8/4/11, C.D.C. memo 348M.
[42] Royal United Service Institute, *Journal*, L (July–Dec., 1906), 887.

that school; for one of its main tendencies was to paralyze any efforts to create an effective army.[43]

With constitutional propriety, Hutton took his instructions upon arrival in Australia from Sir John Forrest, Minister of Defence. Forrest told him that he must make the most of the existing, partially-paid militia forces and the volunteer units, and Hutton based his plans on that consideration, while at the same time he tried to build up the organizations for logistical support of any armed force. He hoped to create a Field Force from the better militia units and the small permanent force allowed to him, and to have this force available for service outside Australia if crises arose. But if this were not possible, volunteers could still be called for at such times, as in the South African war.[44]

Unfortunately for Hutton, the C.D.C. thought rather poorly of his plans. They felt that his proposed organization involved too great a dispersal among a number of units of the small number of trained men that Australia had. A better defense system, it was suggested, would be provided by a greater concentration of true effectives, even if this meant a smaller number of men carried on the roster. Since there was no real possibility of any large invasion of Australia, this Field Force would be better organized for service in the western Pacific in early stages of a war with a European power.[45]

Governor General Lord Tennyson withheld the views of the C.D.C. from his Australian ministers. As he reported to the Colonial Office, he felt that since Hutton's scheme had already been worked out in detail and partly carried into operation, it would be unwise to interfere. Hutton's plans were designed to meet local needs and political considerations. It would be most impolitic to try to dictate the principles on which Australian military opinion should rest; if the memorandum of the committee were shown to the ministers of the government, it would do much harm to imperial interests.[46]

Colonial Office reaction to Tennyson's position was unfavorable, and the tendency was to regard Hutton as the real author of his action. Of Hutton's plans, Sir John Anderson minuted, "Knowing what we do of the discipline of the untrained Australian, the cohesion and efficiency of such a force, serving probably by itself without any stiffening of regulars, would be extremely doubtful."[47] Tennyson eventually showed the memorandum to Barton and Forrest. But he was not content with the situation and tried in a letter to Chamberlain to indicate the political

[43] John Leyland, "The 'Blue Water School'—Principles of Defence," *The Naval Annual, 1907*, ed. T. A. Brassey (Portsmouth, 1907), p. 179.
[44] C.O. 418/26, Hutton to Tennyson, March 9, 1903.
[45] Cab. 5/1, C.D.C. No. 301 R, Oct. 22, 1902.
[46] *Ibid.*, Tennyson to C.O., Feb. 7, 1903.   [47] *Ibid.*

realities of the matter. Any such communication from the Home Government as this C.D.C. memorandum, he pointed out, simply made the position of Hutton more difficult; the idea that Australia needed smaller forces would simply give the opposition an opportunity to call for further retrenchments in military expenditure.

Fundamental to the whole problem, Tennyson urged, was the fact that although Australia looked upon herself as an ally of Great Britain, as a self-governing community she would not bind herself. Britain must be content to trust to Australian loyalty and to her common sense in the organization of her own defense. Certainly thousands of volunteers would be available to assist Britain in any grave national crisis.[48]

But the C.D.C. stood behind its memorandum. Major Clauson, secretary of the C.D.C., commented that over the eighteen years during which the committee had operated, the presence of Colonial Office personnel on the committee had taught it to frame its memoranda in a manner agreeable to colonial sentiment. And Anderson thought it unfair to the Commonwealth government not to let them know what the experts in London felt about Hutton's plans before they committed themselves to them. Indeed, the C.D.C.'s interpretation was that the basic question seemed to be not one of Australian sentiment, but of Hutton's *amour propre*.[49]

Whatever the constitutional proprieties of the bickering, much of the tiff arose because of the strong "Blue Water" tincture to the C.D.C. views, with the consequent downgrading of any Australian military problems. This was an attitude which time and circumstances, especially the long concern of the Colonial Defence Committee with the problems of defense of a sea-linked empire, made natural as scratching. It was the same natural emphasis which the committee incorporated in its defense scheme for Australia which it formulated in response to a request from a later Australian government.[50]

The increasing strength of other naval powers, however, brought the mounting realization that in many areas of the globe Britain, at the outbreak of war, might temporarily have to relinquish command of the sea. The difficulties of maintaining British naval supremacy in home waters indicated that naval action in remote waters would have to be postponed until the clearing of the situation near Britain. "If it is decided that the temporary surrender of our local naval superiority in distant waters not only in time of peace, but also for a period at the beginning of a war, is a contingency that must in certain circumstances be contemplated, a material qualification of the guarantee that the Admiralty

[48] *Ibid.*, Tennyson to C.O., March 11, 1903.
[49] *Ibid.*   [50] C. of A., Parl. Pap., 1906, Vol. II, p. 62.

have hitherto given to protect British territory from organized invasion from the sea will be involved."[51]

While this C.D.C. memorandum was formulated in 1909, the situation on which it was based had been developing for several years. And significantly, the committee's statement not only acknowledged a possible temporary loss of local sea supremacy, but it also omitted the word "all" from the pledge given to protect British territory. That word had always been included in previous statements on general imperial defense, such as C.D.C. memo 57M issued in 1896, the statement which had been supported at that time in the Guildhall speech of the Duke of Devonshire. But in 1903, the Admiralty had acknowledged their inability to aid Canada against the United States because of the growing dimensions of American naval strength. That retreat from American waters was now being duplicated in other oceans. Of course, in the C.D.C. statement there was the qualifying condition that loss of sea supremacy would be only temporary, and would be re-established after the decisive battles for sea command had been fought. And for the British states in the Pacific, there was the assurance given by the Anglo-Japanese alliance. But this was cold comfort to a state that suffered from nightmares about the Japanese, and whose rudimentary military intelligence service was concerned only with the operation of Japanese luggers in northern Australian waters.

Admiral Fanshawe of the Australian Station was meanwhile continuing in his attempts to reconcile Australian opinion to the naval agreement. He sought to win the support of the officers of the old state naval forces for it by using them as recruiting officers and registrars in the recruitment of Australians and New Zealanders, who, under the terms of the agreement, could now enlist for service in the Royal Navy in Australia. Fanshawe also tried to instruct Lord Northcote, who succeeded Tennyson as Governor General, in some aspects of the problem of naval defense of Australia. He discounted in his letters the possibilities of any cruiser raids on Australian waters or coasts, doubtless in the hope that Northcote would pass these letters along to the ministers of the government. But Fanshawe had no success with these ministers in his efforts to secure the disbandment of the naval forces inherited by the Commonwealth from the states. Despite his argument that no money should be spent on their maintenance, and that, rather, all efforts should be bent toward making the agreement a success, the slight naval appropriations were continued.[52] For though the Admiral's efforts were well-regarded by his superiors, it would have required much greater diplomacy than he commanded to

[51] Cab. 8/4/3, C.D.C. 405M.
[52] Adm. 1/7670, Fanshawe to Admiralty, Nov. 30, 1903; Adm. 1/7730, Fanshawe to Admiralty, Feb. 20, 1904.

diminish Australian dislike of the agreement or prevent it from finding expression.

In the whirling uncertainties of the first decade of Commonwealth political life, it was left to the first—and most short-lived—Labor party government to make the opening move in the expression of this dissatisfaction. The first of the Labor prime ministers led a government which lasted from April to August, 1904. In June, this government requested the stationing of two or three torpedo boat destroyers in Australian waters. The Commonwealth would pay the interest on the cost of their construction; the vessels were to be manned and maintained locally. This was, of course, a repetition of the request for similar vessels which had come from the Barton Government as a sop to the opposition to the naval agreement; and the reaction of the Colonial Office was sternly unfavorable. Bertram Cox, the legal adviser of the time, termed the request ridiculous, and said that if Australians wanted to play the fool with such useless vessels, the whole of the capital cost should fall upon them. Sir Montagu Ommaney regarded the request as the first step toward the establishment of an Australian navy, tied to the Australian coast and therefore, according to the principles underlying Admiralty thinking, useless for the naval defense of the Commonwealth.[53]

Shifts in the Commonwealth Parliament soon ended the life of the Watson Government, however. It was followed by a ministry led by the leader of the free trade faction of the Parliament, George Reid. This government took the position that Australian defense efforts should be concentrated on military development. Reid felt that as long as the Royal Navy gave protection to Australia, she needed no seagoing force of her own. Captain Creswell, Commonwealth Naval Director, dissented strongly from this position. He asserted that the basic defense of Australia would have to be a sea-going defense. There was no question, he said, of the creation of an independent Australian naval force; rather, Australia must co-operate in imperial defense as an integral portion of the sea power of the Empire. Thus Creswell accepted fully the necessity of one control over all the naval forces in the Empire in time of war. While Australian vessels would normally operate in Australian waters, they should be available, Creswell felt, for service wherever the exigencies of war required them.[54]

The ministry which espoused the military-first policy of which Creswell so disapproved was soon followed by the second Deakin Government.

---

[53] C.O. 418/31, Northcote to C.O., June 22, 1904.
[54] Cab. 17/48, "Australia—Naval and Military Defence (1905–10)," Memo of J. W. McCay, Australian Minister of Defence, May 10, 1905.

This government had sufficient endurance to last out the life of the current Parliament, largely because of the collaboration given it by the Labor party. The Creswell view of Australian defense received substantial support from the Prime Minister. Deakin's first approach was to Sir George Clarke, former Governor of Victoria and now serving in the very highest echelons of British defense organization. The Balfour Government had recalled him from Australia to serve on the famous Esher Commission, and he had then become the first secretary for the Committee of Imperial Defence. Deakin wired that relying on Clarke's "sympathy with and knowledge of Australia," he was seeking aid in the formulation of a defense scheme for Australia. He followed this on the next day with a letter in which he said that only a rudimentary beginning on defense had been made in Australia; and that while the naval subsidy was unpopular, it could be made acceptable if it were directed toward the creation of something which would be obviously Australian in character, while imperial in value.[55] Clarke suggested in reply that Deakin submit a request for a defense scheme to the C.I.D. The Australian leader followed both the suggestion and, substantially, the wording of the request which Clarke had outlined for him.[56]

To some degree, Deakin was taking advantage of a speech made by Admiral Fanshawe. Fanshawe had complained of the meagerness of the Australian contribution under the terms of the agreement, and Deakin took the opportunity to interpret this as an expression of dissatisfaction with the agreement as a whole. Fanshawe protested that Deakin had no grounds for such a statement, and that there were large numbers of Australians who were favorable to the agreement; many Australians had a grasp of sound naval doctrine, and were anxious to spread it through the land.

At any rate, Deakin in his letter to Governor General Lord Northcote said that the naval agreement was not and never had been popular in Australia, and that this was because the funds appropriated were not applied to any specifically Australian purpose. Australians had no identification with the squadron maintained by the subsidy; there was nothing naval that could be called Australian or even Australasian. The agreement created no Commonwealth patriotism; it simply caused imperial patriotism to languish. Deakin suggested what he thought might be regarded as expedient substitutes for the agreement. Either, he wrote, the Commonwealth might create new coaling or general naval stations in Australia, or there might be a subsidy to increase commercial steamship

[55] Cab. 17/48, Deakin to Clarke, Oct. 2 and 3, 1905.
[56] *Ibid.*, Clarke to Deakin, Oct. 6, 1905; Deakin to C.O., Nov. 11, 1905.

connection between Australia and Britain, the ships supported being capable of conversion to armed commerce raiders in time of war.[57]

The Colonial Office remarks on Deakin's effort were, as could be anticipated, caustic. Bertram Cox rather welcomed the possibility that Deakin's initiative gave an excuse to get rid of the ridiculous situation with Australia and New Zealand over the subsidies. "Observe the Australians now want to convert their payment into a mail subsidy while calling it a contribution to the defence of the Empire. For the Empire as a whole they care little when it comes to paying for its expenses & the amount they contribute is but a drop in the ocean of our naval expenditure."[58] Cox suggested that the reply to Deakin should point out to Australians that they had been contributing to the defense of the Empire, that the naval defense of the Commonwealth would probably be conducted thousands of miles from its shores, and that to tie up ships where they were not needed was contrary to common sense and strategy. He further recommended that the British government should forego the small contributions and simply say that in the future as in the past, the naval power of Britain would be available for the defense of Australia, but that in this defense Britain would be guided by her own naval strategists. Let Australians go their own way, build their own ships, and man and operate them according to their own laws. In this, of course, the Colonial Office functionary was in accord with the more vehement of the Australian nationalists.

The Colonial Secretary was also inclined to write off the existing agreement. Lyttelton minuted that he personally did not believe in the policy of seeking money contributions from the reluctant Australians; some other arrangement was surely preferable.[59] But Ommaney pointed out that what Deakin was proposing was the abandonment of a policy which Britain had steadily pursued for some years, and which had bulked large in past colonial conferences.[60]

Adding to the irritation in the Colonial Office were the allegations from Australia that the Admiralty had not lived up to the terms of the 1903 agreement. Deakin complained that while Australia had been prompt in the payments outlined in the agreement, the Admiralty had in effect regarded the Australasian Station as a backwater portion of the globe, a nice retirement paddock in which to place weary ships before they went on their way to the shipbreakers.[61]

[57] C.O. 418/37, Deakin to Lord Northcote, Aug. 28, 1905.
[58] Ibid.
[59] C.O. 418/37, Northcote to C.O., Aug. 29, 1905.
[60] Ibid.
[61] C.O. 418/44, Deakin to Northcote, April 26, 1906, in Northcote to C.O., April 27, 1906.

Again the initial reaction of the Colonial Office came from Bertram Cox. As far as he was concerned, the sooner Britain gave up the dribble of money which it received from the Antipodes at the price of locking up vessels which would be more useful elsewhere, the better. Also, it would free Britain from the charges of bad faith which accompanied the driblets. Ommaney saw the comments of Deakin as simply paving the way for a local navy. Winston Churchill, the Parliamentary Under-secretary, agreed with Cox's remarks.[62]

This mood of mutual exasperation was not dissipated by the 1907 Colonial Conference. Atlee Hunt, the secretary of the Australian Department of External Affairs, who accompanied Deakin to London for the gathering, felt that the intention of the British government and the Colonial Office was to belittle the meeting's importance. According to Hunt, it was only the strong intervention of Deakin which changed the tenor of the remarks which Prime Minister Sir Henry Campbell-Bannerman had designed for the opening of the conference, and which thus helped change the meeting from a limited one, as was the original plan, to a true conference between governments.[63]

Hunt's irritation with the planning and organization of the conference, and with British officialdom in general, did not necessarily reflect the attitude of his chief, but his admiration for Deakin clearly suggests a substantial rapport between them. And Hunt's annoyance with Britain and the Colonial Office mounted steadily. He was particularly upset over the fact that as a subordinate member of the Australian delegation, he was excluded from the meeting, while his opposite members in Whitehall were admitted. In sum, "After our free life, our practical absence of snobbery, and our climate . . . existence here for me would be practically impossible."[64]

Naturally, not all the irritations were on one side. John Morley, the Secretary of State for India, found much of the Colonial Conference and the frequent meetings with colonial representatives greatly trying. "I am not at all without sympathy for your kindly views about our young colonial kinfolk," he wrote Lord Minto. "But say what you will, they are apt to be frightful bores, and if you had been condemned to eat . . . twenty meals day after day in their company and to hear Deakin yarn away by the hour, I believe you would be as heartily glad to see their backs as I am."[65]

[62] Ibid.
[63] Australian National Library, Canberra, Atlee Hunt papers, Hunt to Robert Garran, April 16, 1907.
[64] Ibid., Hunt to Garran, May 10, 1907.
[65] India Office Library, London, Morley Collection, Private correspondence, India, John Morley to Lord Minto, 1905–09, MSS Eur. D. 573, Vol. II, Morley to Minto, May 24, 1907.

Two years later, Hunt's irritation was still apparent in a memorandum which he prepared for C. P. Lucas of the Colonial Office. Hunt complained that to most Australians, the Colonial Office was simply Downing Street, and that meant a mixture of red tape, ignorance of and indifference to Australian conditions, disregard of Australian feelings and aspirations, and a certain lofty contempt for the Australian politicians to whom it once or twice threw a few titular distinctions to be scrambled for.[66]

Deakin's correspondence with Sir Charles Dilke suggests that he shared at least some of Hunt's irritation. While imperial relations had been better under Chamberlain, with the coming of Lyttelton things had drifted back to the old state of affairs and Australia was neglected as of old.[67] As for the Admiralty under Lord Tweedmouth, the First Lord under the Liberal Government, the answers which it had been giving to Australian suggestions for possible revisions of the agreement were "too much like those of the Delphic oracle to be really helpful to poor . . . laymen on this side of the world."[68] Deakin later complained that he got nothing but general statements from the Admiralty; "after all these months of waiting . . . we have been much embarrassed in our preparations."[69]

At the 1907 conference, Lord Tweedmouth did open the door slightly to a form of colonial participation in naval defense, though not going far beyond the limits of the Colonial Naval Defence Act of 1865. He told the assembled premiers and their entourages that while there was no abandonment of the one Empire, one Navy, and one Flag doctrine, the imperial government recognized the desire of the self-governing colonies to have a "more particular share" in providing naval defense of the Empire. As long as the principle of unity of command was preserved, His Majesty's Government was ready to consider the modification of the existing arrangements with the colonies. It would be useful if the colonies would provide and maintain some of the smaller vessels in the imperial squadrons which could be used against occasional raids. Britain would, of course, continue to provide the larger vessels of the squadrons, but since it was difficult to take such craft as torpedo boats and submarines across the oceans, it would be useful to find them locally provided, and manned by men trained to take part in the work of the fleet; submarines would be especially useful.[70]

Deakin did not respond with any degree of enthusiasm to the First Lord's overtures. The proposal was more an expression of the needs of

[66] Australian National Library, Canberra, Hunt papers, Memorandum to C. P. Lucas, Aug. 16, 1909.
[67] British Museum, Dilke Papers, Add. MSS, 43788, Deakin to Dilke, Jan. 22, 1906.
[68] Ibid., Deakin to Dilke, April 27, 1908.
[69] Ibid., Deakin to Dilke, July 27, 1908.
[70] Parl. Pap., 1907, Vol. LV, Cd. 3523, pp. 130–31.

the Admiralty than a recognition of the hopes of the Australians for a form of naval defense specifically Australian in character. Nor was the troublesome problem of control resolved in the First Lord's proposals.[71]

During the conference, Deakin had naturally presented his objections to the 1903 agreement to Admiralty officialdom personally. He had a discussion of the matter with the First Sea Lord, "Jackie" Fisher, and aired his views to a group which included Captain C. L. Ottley, Director of Naval Intelligence, the Assistant D.N.I. and Graham Greene, Assistant Secretary of the Board of Admiralty.

The Australian leader presented these officials with an argument that was essentially political in character. The payment under the existing agreement was in the nature of a "tribute"; it was desirable that Australia should find some way of co-operating in the naval defense of the Empire without offense to the constitutional principle that the government which levies taxes should be responsible for expenditure and management.

Deakin proposed the creation of local defense forces, under the control of the Commonwealth government as to finance, and allocated among the different ports of the nation. They would be subject to naval discipline and open to the inspection of the Commander of the Royal Navy's Australian Station. But the Australian government would retain control of these ships, even in time of war, for the Commander of the Australian Station might be thousands of miles away at the time of conflict.

Captain Ottley said that the proposal raised a variety of problems. Finance, discipline, international status of the force envisaged, would all have to be examined, though doubtless these matters could be settled amicably. But the basic question to be resolved was that of control. The Admiralty could not regard any such new force as part of the Navy except when it was placed under their control. Was the force to be colonial or imperial?[72]

Deakin renewed his contact with Fisher after he returned to Australia. In the hope of reaching a better mutual understanding, he summarized his recollections of the chief points the Admiral had made in their discussion. These were that the present subsidized squadron established by the agreement ought to be abolished, and its best ships removed from Australian waters and united with the China and East Indian squadrons to form a powerful Eastern Fleet. The remaining vessels of the force should stay in Australian waters, with the Eastern Fleet visiting the chief Australian ports each year or so. The Commonwealth should devote its efforts

[71] *Ibid.*, p. 132.
[72] Adm. 1/7949 contains a bulky binding of the memoranda and correspondence dealing with the problems created by the efforts of the Australian government to create a local naval force.

to the defense of its harbors and coasts—"You strongly urge submarines." These and the harbor vessels would represent the Australian contribution to imperial defense in place of the existing subsidy arrangements. These ships would remain under the control of the Australian government. Deakin added that in his opinion these vessels should in time of war be placed under the command of the Admiral in charge of the contemplated Eastern Fleet.

Fisher's marginal comments on this letter indicate only his utter distaste for the existing agreement. Never was there such an extravagant waste of money, ships, and men as the agreement entailed for the Admiralty. He detested it. But his reply to Deakin was that nothing could be done about his proposals until the Board of Admiralty had discussed them, and the Cabinet met in November.[73]

Upon his return to Australia after the 1907 Colonial Conference, Deakin had been somewhat more fertile in the creation of various devices and schemes to replace the agreement. He first called for the enlistment of 1,000 seamen in Australia to serve on two cruisers of the Royal Navy. These two ships were to be stationed permanently in Australian waters, both in peace and war. The Admiralty might also lend two ships for the training of the naval militia. Since the cost of the thousand seamen would not take all of the money Australia paid under the terms of the agreement, the remainder might well go to the support of submersibles, destroyers, or some other form of local naval defense.[74] He put these ideas forward, Deakin said, as a means of fostering mutual support between Britain and the Commonwealth. The sole aim was to unite with the mother country in securing better defense.

The Admiralty's reply to this suggestion gave no comfort to the Australian Prime Minister. The enlistment of a thousand seamen was in line with discussions between Deakin and Admiralty officials during the Colonial Conference, but the other suggestions he had put forward, the permanent stationing of the two cruisers in Australian waters, and the loan of two training ships, had not been contemplated in those meetings.[75]

While Deakin waited in Australia and continued to prod for some decision, the wheels of the Admiralty were beginning to grind. Greene and the new D.N.I., Captain Edmund J. W. Slade, (Captain Ottley had succeeded Sir George Clarke as secretary to the C.I.D.) drew up memoranda on Deakin's ideas. Greene said that when the 1907 conference dissolved it was understood that Deakin and Joseph Ward, the Prime Minister of New Zealand, would consult their respective legislatures

[73] *Ibid.*, Deakin to Fisher, Aug. 12, 1907.
[74] C.O. 418/52, Deakin to Lord Northcote, Oct. 16, 1907; Parl. Pap., 1908, Vol. LXXI, Cd. 4325, pp. 2–4.
[75] C.O. 418/52, C.O. to Northcote, Dec [*sic*] 1907.

about the merits of cancellation of the agreement. Deakin was also to put forward a scheme for local defense which would free the Royal Navy from some of its restrictions. It was recognized that it would take time to carry out any scheme agreed upon, and that during the process the Admiralty would carry on the duties of the station with such ships as it deemed necessary. There would be no obligation to keep all the existing ships on the station. Greene felt that Deakin's offer of 1,000 men did not help much; the Admiralty had no difficulty in recruitment. But the details of Deakin's proposals were too meager for effective discussion.[76]

Captain Slade said that the Admiralty had to hold to certain basic principles at all costs. There must be absolute control in time of war; any vessels provided by the Commonwealth must fly the White Ensign; and colonial vessels should have no right to cruise outside of colonial waters unless they came under the control of the Commander in Chief of the Station. If the Commonwealth ever wished to send any of its vessels among the Pacific islands, then they must hand them over to the Admiral of the Station for the time that they were away from Australian waters.[77]

Greene had a chance to discuss the Australian situation with Admiral Sir Wilmot Fawkes (Fanshawe's successor on the Australian Station), when Fawkes returned to London. The Admiral pointed out that neither Deakin, nor the Australian Minister of Defence, T. T. Ewing, nor any of their advisers, had the knowledge to work out any scheme of defense in detail. It would be useless to press them for more detailed statements; the Admiralty would have to clothe Deakin's general ideas with the necessary particulars.[78]

Deakin's capacity for troubling the Colonial Office and Admiralty was not exhausted by his efforts to revise the naval agreement. He may not have been able to come up with a substitute which would appeal to the Admiralty, but he was singularly effective in arousing Australian interest in naval matters. Perhaps the shrewdest of his moves was the invitation to the government of the United States to extend the round-the-world cruise of the American battle fleet in 1908 to Australian ports. To the profound annoyance of the Colonial and Foreign Offices, Deakin acted entirely on his own judgment in this, cabling the invitation to Washington through Whitelaw Reid, the American minister in London, and through the United States consul in Sydney. All of this caused no small distress in the Colonial Office. C. P. Lucas suggested that a dispatch should be sent to Deakin forthwith, pointing out the error of his ways, but Lord Elgin, to whom Campbell-Bannerman had given the Colonial Office,

[76] *Ibid.*, Oct. 30, 1907.
[77] *Ibid.*, Nov. 7, 1907.
[78] *Ibid.*, Memo, April 15, 1908.

wearily commented that "it is useless to explain to Mr. Deakin."[79] The Foreign Office also sought some rebuke for Deakin, but the Colonial Office again fell back on the difficulties of dealing with the incorrigible Australian leader.[80]

The visit of the American fleet to the Australian ports was, for Deakin, an unqualified success. There was a feeling of reassurance for Australians in this display of American sea might, for here was possible aid against a Japan whom most Australians distrusted. And for Deakin there was the political advantage of being able to point out that much of this sea power now in Australian harbors was a recent creation, and that while Australia had little of the mature strength of the United States, she could certainly emulate in a small way the American achievement in the development of sea power. Deakin saw in the American battleships one of the "greatest nation-making agencies which exist, and which we ourselves do not possess, but which we hope to possess by the sure and steady expansion of our marine and maritime effectiveness."[81] Lord Northcote, in a speech to the visitors, echoed the words of his Prime Minister. The American fleet, he said, "should be an object lesson to us in Australia as to what national defence should be . . . . We hope to profit by your example."[82]

By the time the American fleet had sailed away from Australian ports, Deakin's campaign against the naval agreement and in favor of defense arrangements more truly national in character was beginning to show results. The Commonwealth Prime Minister was beginning to command more attention in London than he may have been aware of. The squeaky wheel was beginning to be heard, no longer with annoyance alone, but also with a dawning sense that perhaps some grease needed to be applied.

[79] C.O. 418/60, April 4, 1908.
[80] F.O. 371/564, Adm. to F.O., Feb. 22, 1903.
[81] *The Age* (Melbourne), Aug. 21, 1908.
[82] *The Daily Telegraph* (Sydney), Aug. 21, 1908.

CHAPTER X

THE 1909 CRISIS,
CONFERENCE, AND
COLLABORATION

Alfred Deakin and others associated with Australian defense activities may have been winning no friends among the Colonial Office and Admiralty hierarchy, but their repeated expressions of antipathy toward the naval agreement and the principle of contribution which it exemplified were gradually being heard in Britain. More and more, the job of securing the collaboration of the dominions for the tasks of imperial defense was being acknowledged as a political problem rather than a purely strategic one. And consequently there was an increasing drift toward the views which Austen Chamberlain had presented to the Committee of Imperial Defence in its discussions of Canadian defense matters in 1905, when he said that he looked forward to the day when the major colonies would have fleets of their own to range alongside the squadrons of the Royal Navy in the defense of empire.[1]

Of course, the purely strategic arguments and the idea of colonial contributions still commanded much support. For example, the *Times* reported the appearance of a delegation before Balfour on December 10, 1904, lead by Sir Michael Hicks-Beach. The group included some forty or fifty peers and M.P.s, as well as other notable figures of Britain's naval and maritime world, and the burden of their remarks was that the Prime Minister should urge the colonies to assume a larger share of the defense costs of the Empire. Hicks-Beach said that it was impossible for the British taxpayer to bear the costs of naval defense alone any longer; and Sir John Colomb, still indefatigable in his concern for imperial defense, read Balfour a memorandum to the point that the Royal Navy represented a common effort, a fact not yet acknowledged by the colonies.[2]

[1] Cf. *supra.*   [2] *The Times* (London), Dec. 12, 1904.

To all of this, the *Times* gave its hearty support. It felt that the long years of peace that the colonies had enjoyed under the protection of the Royal Navy had made them unfamiliar with the problems of war and international relations, and that this was the basic cause of the colonial lack of understanding of the naval problems of the Empire. On the other hand, the *Times* was gracious enough to concede that even in Britain it was only in recent years that a true understanding of naval problems had prevailed; and the Forrest memorandum of the 1902 conference was cited as further evidence that the colonies were not totally without grace.[3]

A few years later, when the Gold Medal prize essay competition of the Royal United Service Institute posed the question of the ways in which the colonies could best contribute to the naval defense of the Empire, the first prize went to Captain Philip Game, R.H.A., who adhered strictly to the line of strategic orthodoxy. Rejecting the idea of colonial navies as unsound, he urged that the contribution of the dominions should be in the traditional form of maintenance of their own coastal defense, naval stations for the Royal Navy, and monetary subsidies.[4] In similar vein, Brassey's *Naval Annual* still waited for the time when the colonies would appreciate that Sir John Forrest's 1902 memorandum laid down the true and correct policy.[5]

But such specific indications of the prevailing strategic orthodoxy were of less significance than the total atmosphere created by the growing sense that "L'Allemagne, c'est l'Ennemi," and the growing conviction of the likelihood of a titanic struggle with that power, which pervaded so much of the British official and naval mind. Under the vigorous leadership of Fisher, the Admiralty was increasingly imbued with the belief that the Navy could do the whole job when it came to fighting Germany. Little or no interest existed in securing the collaboration of the French fleet; there was no naval parallel to the military conversations and certainly no equivalent among naval officers to the bicycle trips which Sir Henry Wilson was taking along the roads of northern France. Neither Fisher nor his successor as First Sea Lord were interested in any real French co-operation; it was not until after the latter's retirement that any such collaboration was sought. And if collaboration with France was not worthy of consideration to the Admiralty, then the minor assistance which might be available through concern for colonial susceptibilities in naval affairs was small potatoes indeed.

[3] *Ibid.*, Dec. 8, 1904.
[4] *Royal United Service Institute Journal*, LV (Jan.–June, 1911), 423–54. The author of the essay later became Governor of New South Wales. The second prize medalist was somewhat more favorable to the idea of colonial naval forces, saying that the "hen and chickens" concept of empire was outmoded. *Ibid.*, p. 549.
[5] T. A. Brassey (ed.), *The Naval Annual, 1907* (Portsmouth, 1907), pp. 15–16.

But even as the canons of strategic doctrine were apparently kept inviolate, and as the hierarchy of the Admiralty wrestled with the larger problems of the hour, in those areas of administrative structure where the concerns of the colonial world were sometimes dimly heard, there were discernable shifts of opinion away from the policy of seeking money contributions alone. An increasing recognition that it was futile to stand on the principles embodied in the Australasian naval agreement was certainly clearly suggested by the remarks of Lord Tweedmouth, shortly after he had accepted the seals of office as First Lord in the Liberal Campbell-Bannerman Government. The project of an Australian navy, said Lord Tweedmouth, was open to many objections. But the political aspects of the problem had to be considered, and if Australia decided to take steps toward the formation of a local naval force, the Board of Admiralty were firmly of the opinion that the most useful form which their work could take would be the construction and maintenance of ocean-going destroyers.[6]

By the time of the 1907 Colonial Conference, the adherence of imperial authority to the established doctrine was somewhat further diluted. Lord Tweedmouth conceded there that various dominions might construct coastal defense vessels if they so desired. This concession was somewhat grudging, and carried the colonial governments little beyond the position which had been allotted to them in the 1865 legislation. But it did acknowledge some right of action on their part, and in the face of the pressure being exerted by Deakin, it was a concession which promised even more yielding to come.

The opinion expressed by Admiral Fawkes on his return from Australia, that the Admiralty would have to provide whatever was necessary in the way of professional precision and interpretation to the proposals made by Deakin, persuaded Admiralty officials that it was no longer adequate simply to react, and negatively at that, to the sketchy conceptions coming from Australia. The question was no longer one of acceding or not to the ideas of Deakin, but rather, in the Admiralty view, of making those ideas as harmless as possible to the cherished necessities of unity of control of all naval vessels in time of war.

In May, 1908, the Admiralty offered to give some greater definition to Deakin's suggestions, though it said that consideration of the matter would require a good deal of time. Perhaps this offer, made in a letter to the Colonial Office, was prompted by complaints made by Deakin in the Commonwealth Parliament that his government's defense proposals

[6] Cab. 2/2/1, C.I.D. 88th Meeting, May 25, 1906.

were being delayed by the difficulty of getting the Admiralty's opinion on ideas submitted to it.[7]

The Admiralty's major effort to draw up a scheme which might in some approved manner give effect to Deakin's aspirations came in the form of a draft memorandum from the Director of Naval Intelligence. This memo began by restating the familiar objections to divided control of naval forces of the Empire. But it went on to concede that while theoretically the naval defense of Australia should remain in the hands of the imperial government, practically this was impossible after a time in a country with democratic parliamentary institutions. For money was voted year by year, in the expenditure of which the Commonwealth Parliament had no voice, and sooner or later a point would be reached when objections would be raised. This was a lesson which emerged clearly from the history of all democratic institutions. It was apparent in the British Parliament where the cry of taxation without representation and control always raised a storm. And it was therefore inevitable that a proposal like the one put forward by Deakin would be made.

The change in naval affairs in the Pacific, said the memorandum, was such that the Admiralty could no longer state that a force like the one suggested by Deakin would be useless. But while such vessels would serve a useful purpose in time of war, their control at that time would have to rest with the imperial government as represented by the senior naval officer on the spot, and all operations should be carried out under the White Ensign.

Some eighty-five officers would be needed for the effective manning of the projected nine submarines and six destroyers, but this raised certain difficulties. It was the experience of the Royal Navy that no officer over forty years of age was fit for service in either type of vessel. Thus if the service were to be purely Australian, it would be necessary to retire all Lieutenants who had not made the grade of Commander by the age of forty; a proper flow of promotion would not be possible unless the ships were officered from the Royal Navy. Yet even if junior officers of the Royal Navy were seconded to the service of the Australian force, it was doubtful whether they could keep to the level of efficiency prevailing in the Royal Navy because of the more limited nature of the service and the opportunities offered them. If the Royal Navy did lend the officers to the embryonic Australian force, the control of the careers of these men would have to rest with the Admiralty; the selection, promotion, and conditions of service would have to be set by the Navy, rather than by the Commonwealth government. It would be some ten years before any service could be purely Australian.

[7] Adm. 1/7949, Adm. to C.O., May 29, 1908.

Further, to provide such men for the projected Australian force would throw some aspects on the Navy's own table of organization awry. It would require an addition to the number of Lieutenant Commanders in proportion to other ranks, and would thus interfere with the proper promotion flow of the Navy. To create the necessary number of Lieutenants for the new Australian ships would require the creation of some five or six new Captaincies and a corresponding number of new posts for Commanders. The Australian government would certainly not want to have to pay for these new posts.

After considerable calculation, the final Admiralty estimate was that Deakin's proposals would involve some seventy-nine officers and 1,125 men, at an annual cost of £160,000. The capital cost of the suggested ships, the submarines and destroyers and necessary depot ships, would be about £1,275,000, with annual maintenance and depreciation charges of £186,000.[8]

This professional appraisal of the Australian suggestions at last brought these ideas into the realm of reality, though there were yet many difficulties in the way. And with the acceptance of the possibility that if the Deakin proposals were carried out they would add to British naval strength in the Pacific, the foundations of agreement were being laid.[9]

Lord Dudley, the new Governor General in Australia, urged strongly that the Deakin Government was in earnest on its defense proposals, even though it did not possess the technical skill to carry them out unaided. Dudley reported in October of 1908 that the all-absorbing topic in Australia was defense. While the defense program of the government was still vague and unsettled, and such proposals as it had made seemed to have been put forward from the editorial offices of the *Age*, Deakin, by the force of his personality and great eloquence, had undoubtedly won much support for the idea of compulsory military training and an Australian navy. Dudley, however, still doubted whether Australian public opinion was quite ready for either.[10]

By the end of 1908, a Labor party government had supplanted the Deakin Ministry. The accumulation of minor irritations in the relations between Labor and the Deakin Government, the basic need for a powerful party like Labor to take authority into its own hands instead of being simply the power behind the governmental bench, and the natural impatience of men for the prize of high office, all conspired to end the long-standing collaboration between the two activist groups in the Commonwealth Parliament.

---

[8] Adm. 1/7949, Aug. 24, 1908.
[9] C.O. 418/60, Greene to Colonial Office, May 4, 1908.
[10] C.O. 418/61, Dudley to C.O., Oct. 1, Dec. 22, 1908.

But the withdrawal of Labor support from Deakin did not come until after the introduction into the Commonwealth Parliament of legislation calling for the establishment of a system of compulsory military training for Australian youth. While the legislation actually called for little more than the instruction of the young men of the Commonwealth in the rudiments of military drill, and for some teaching of the use of the rifle, this legislation is notable as the first of its type—along with New Zealand—in the British Empire. Its whole approach was essentially in the democratic tradition, stemming from the *levée en masse* of the French Revolution, and the actual terms of the legislation were substantially modeled on the Swiss military organization. There was also a considerable residue of the South African experience in it, for the basic lesson drawn by many Australians from that conflict and from early British defeats was that the best soldier was a man who knew what he fought for, loved what he knew, and was a good shot. There was a strong predilection among many Australian politicians to speak well of rifle clubs, and to denigrate anything which gave much scope for an officer corps. The latter were too much in the category of what King O'Malley, the state of Vermont's rare gift to Australian Labor party leadership, called "gold-braided and epauletted cockerels."

The proposed legislation was not passed during the Deakin Government's last few weeks of power. It did, however, open a debate in which the problems of defense in its broader dimensions were discussed. The naval agreement was again the butt of much criticism, with Forrest once again defending the principles it incorporated.[11] But the most politically significant statements came from Deakin and from Andrew Fisher, the leader of the Labor party. Deakin said that the Commonwealth was still seeking some *modus vivendi* by which "in some rudimentary, and perhaps elementary way, we may match our political institutions with their necessary complement, a naval arm of defence, to be maintained and controlled by our people through their representatives in Parliament."[12] And Fisher extolled the long stand of the Labor party in favor of an Australian naval force. Had that policy been carried out, Australia would not have been placed in the humiliating position of having to meet the United States fleet without a single vessel of her own. Once the Commonwealth got some ships, he added, they would, in case of major emergency, find their place alongside the ships of the Royal Navy.[13]

It was Fisher who succeeded Deakin in what was a whirligig of shifting power in the Commonwealth Parliament. But this second Labor party

[11] C.P.D., XLVII, 1136–37.
[12] *Ibid.*, pp. 1320–21.
[13] *Ibid.*, p. 1459.

government had only a few months of power. It was supplanted in turn by another Deakin Government, this time one in which Deakin had reached an arrangement with his former foes of the free trade group against his erstwhile allies of Labor.

The storms which broke out in the ranks of the parliamentarians, and which swirled about the heads of Fisher and Deakin were, however, a small matter compared with the excitement which soon broke in the British Empire, both homeland and outpost, over the allegations that Germany would soon surpass Britain in the volume of battleship construction. As far as the Australian press was concerned, this was certainly the biggest item of news since the death of the old Queen.

The agitation first broke out in London in March, 1909, with the revelation of the fact—as it seemed to the Admiralty—that by 1913 Germany would come near to matching Britain in its number of dreadnoughts. It now became not a matter of maintaining the two-power standard, but simply of keeping abreast with what seemed to be the surging growth of German naval might. This new fear was based on the idea that the German capacity for heavy naval construction had vastly increased, and that the rate of naval construction would correspondingly accelerate. The disclosure of these causes of uneasiness led to violent repercussions, with the Conservatives in full attack against the Asquith Government, and a cry going out for an expanded program of naval building: "We want eight, and we won't wait!" Before this storm and hullabaloo, the Liberal party economizers bent and broke. As a leading member of the economizing bloc summarized it: "The Admiralty had demanded six ships; the economists offered four; and we finally compromised on eight." True, but not exhaustive, since the Board of Admiralty were not monolithic in their demands; it was the redoubtable Fisher and his powerful journalistic ally, J. L. Garvin of the *Observer*, who had worked for the enlargement of the program to eight.[14]

The naval crisis was a central feature of a by-election in which the Conservative candidate attacked the Liberal Government for neglect of naval strength. Great public excitement and interest was aroused: "The naval crisis was endlessly discussed in buses and railroad carriages, in West End clubs and country pubs, in theatre foyers and on factory floors, at football matches, trade union meetings and market ordinaries. . . ."[15] And the Conservatives doubled their majority over the previous election.

Part of the whole atmosphere of the period was the flood of invasion alarm literature which was pouring from British presses. One author of

[14] Alfred M. Gollin, *The Observer and J. L. Garvin* (London, 1960), ch. III.
[15] G. J. Marcus, "The Naval Crisis of 1909 and the Croydon By-election," *Royal United Service Institute Journal*, CIII (Nov., 1958), 505–11.

such material, LeQueux, wrote of a world which his imagination peopled liberally with German spies. Major Guy DuMaurier's play, *An Englishman's Home*, about the muddied oafs of the football field confronting the disciplined hordes of clearly Teutonic invaders, was attracting the multitudes to Wyndham's Theatre. And the American naval attaché in London took Erskine Childers' *Riddle of the Sands* seriously enough to send a copy home to his superiors in Washington.

Echoes of the debates and general alarm in Britain reverberated throughout the Empire, and nowhere more ominously than in the Antipodes. The naval crisis virtually drove all other news off the pages of the Australian press. Vast numbers attended the patriotic meetings summoned by various local authorities, meetings which naturally all closed with the hearty singing of "Rule Britannia" and "God Save the King." Some of the newspapers started popular subscription funds for the purchase of a ship of war for the Royal Navy. And in New Zealand, the Dominion government itself offered to pay the cost of construction of a battleship for the Royal Navy.

Lord Dudley reported on all of this to the Colonial Office. The news of the Commons debate on naval strength, he said, had produced a profound sensation throughout Australia, and had aroused a desire to give some assistance to the mother country. This, he said, was further stimulated by news of New Zealand's offer of a dreadnought; meetings urging some such national action were large, representative and enthusiastic, strong in the demand that the Commonwealth government should act.[16]

For the Fisher Ministry this storm was the source of embarrassment, a fact not altogether without interest to the anti-Labor groups in Australian life. The dreadnought scare, and the agitation to have Australia match the offer made by New Zealand, formed a convenient stick with which to beat the Fisher Government over the head. For the Labor Prime Minister showed a lamentable *sang froid* in the midst of the hullabaloo, and adhered rather stubbornly to the party line of seeking the establishment of an Australian naval force. But Fisher early assured Lord Dudley, the Governor General, that in any emergency the people and government of the Commonwealth would range themselves staunchly by Britain's side. "Re our conversations on subject Naval Crisis," he wrote, "I desire to formally convey to Your Excellency that the attitude of the present Government is that, whilst its policy is to provide for its own defence, still, in the event of any emergency, the resources of the Commonwealth would be cheerfully placed at the disposal of the Mother Country."[17]

[16] C.O. 418/70, Dudley to C.O., April 12, 1909.
[17] C. of A., Parl. Pap., 1909, Vol. II, p. 147, Fisher to Dudley, March 22, 1909.

In the midst of all the turbulence, Prime Minister Fisher defined the policy of his government in matters of naval defense. The naval agreement would be maintained for the term specified, but also the Commonwealth would begin the creation of its own naval force. The sphere of action of such a force would be the coasts of Australia and Australian-administered territories. The control of the vessels would rest with the Commonwealth government, with naval discipline administered as in the Royal Navy. When these ships went beyond Australian waters, they would come under the command of the senior officer of the Royal Navy on the naval station involved. In time of war or other emergency, all vessels would come under the control of the Admiralty. But in such circumstances, vessels were not to be moved from Australian waters without the assent of the Commonwealth government.[18] To implement this program, the Fisher Government placed orders in British shipyards for two destroyers; a third was to be assembled in an Australian dockyard from materials largely secured from Britain. This order was to be followed by others until the Commonwealth controlled a force of over twenty such vessels.[19]

The Fisher program fell under a fusillade of criticism from Australia's conservative press and politicians, bent on having Australia follow New Zealand in the offer of a battleship. The Premiers of the two states of New South Wales and Victoria sought to place the phylacteries of imperial loyalty conspicuously on their own brows by jointly offering a battleship on behalf of their two states if the Commonwealth did not act.[20] "Had New South Wales been in the position she was before Federation, the action of the Government would have been prompt and emphatic," said the leader of the government in New South Wales. And with regard to Fisher's destroyers, George Reid said that they would give no more protection to Australian commerce than would the man in the moon.[21]

Lord Dudley greatly regretted that the matter of assistance to Britain was becoming embroiled in party politics in Australia. The more that projects of imperial aid were made part of the program of Australian Tory groups, he said, the more the Australian working class, "thoroughly loyal and perfectly willing to take a share in Imperial burdens," was pushed into accepting the views of the more selfish and narrow-minded in its midst. Dudley reported that the idea of an Australian naval force was generally popular, but there was much uncertainty as to how to proceed. Lord Tweedmouth's attitude at the 1907 conference seemed to point to small vessels and submarines. "If Australian opinion in this

[18] *Ibid.*, Fisher to Dudley, April 15, 1909.
[19] C.O. 418/70, Dudley to C.O., April 12, 1909.
[20] *The Daily Telegraph* (Sydney), April 3, 1909.
[21] *Ibid.*, April 9, 1909.

regard is mistaken and if the Admiralty would prefer to see Australia building some type of war vessels other than torpedo boats or submarines, then I would suggest . . . that the sooner a frank communication is made on the point the better."[22]

Even the *Age* was somewhat intimidated by the circumstances and the uproar, and momentarily bent before the vociferous professions of imperial loyalty. It was apparent, said the *Age*, that Germany had outgeneraled and stolen a march on Britain, and that she was very near to being Britain's naval equal. The British Empire faced a crisis without parallel since the time of the Armada, and in the conflict which might come, a single dreadnought might decide the issue. Australia was rich enough and loyal enough to make the gift of such a vessel. And since such action would be a gift, it would not qualify attitudes on the matter of naval subsidy. In such vein, the *Age* hammered away on the issue for the better part of a month.[23]

In taking this stand, the *Age* parted company from the *Bulletin*. The whole issue was wonderful grist for the mill of the latter paper, which regarded the agitation for the gift of an Australian dreadnought as a form of garishness, a mental drunkenness. "Dreadnoughtism," it said, was another manifestation of imperial hysteria akin to Mafeking.[24] The *Bulletin* argued that even from the British viewpoint, such offers might be unwelcome, for the offers contained no promise of maintenance, and in effect meant saddling the British taxpayer with yet further burdens. "Prime Minister Asquith rages inwardly at the blatant Dominion which won't prepare to defend either itself or all the millions that Britain has lent it, and which instead presents an embarrassing ironclad, and thus draws a bill on J. Bull's gratitude which will quite probably have to be dishonored."[25] The *Bulletin* naturally took considerable satisfaction in the lagging contributions to the "Dreadnought Fund" which had been started by a Sydney daily.[26]

During this period when the Fisher Government continued to be under fire for its rejection of the dreadnought offer idea, and for its initiation of the construction of destroyers, the various anti-Labor forces on the Australian political scene were moving toward a joining of their forces.

[22] C.O. 418/70, Dudley to C.O., April 18, 1909.
[23] Lord Dudley was greatly puzzled by the policy of the *Age*. He said it was the *Age* which started the dreadnought gift agitation, and he found this odd for a paper which was usually run on anything but imperialistic lines. To Dudley, the *Age's* suggestion was so incomprehensible that he sought some motive behind the apparent shift. He felt that the purpose of the *Age* was to create a public willingness to spend a great deal of money for naval defense, and then divert this willingness to support the creation of an Australian naval force. C.O. 418/70, Dudley to C.O., April 18, 1909.
[24] *The Bulletin* (Sydney), April 1, 1909.
[25] *Ibid.*
[26] *Ibid.*, May 6, 1909.

For Deakin, this meant abandoning his general alliance with the Labor party as an activist-nationalist element of the Australian political scene, and casting his lot with the inheritors of the conservative free trade elements, against whom most of his political battles had been waged. Deakin's general position in political life was gradually being eroded by the growing power of Labor, and the weakening of those who held the middle ground, as he did. Taking advantage of the dreadnought agitation, among other causes, he formed a Fusion group with the new leader of the free trade faction, Joseph Cook. When Parliament reassembled, this new group unhorsed the Fisher Ministry from the seats of power amid some of the stormiest scenes in the short history of the Commonwealth Parliament. Deakin was damned as a Judas, and William M. Hughes, the brightest star in the Labor party's constellation of talent and its foremost orator, turned on Deakin with a vehement and bitter summary of the latter's political life. "What a career his has been! In his hands, at various times, have rested the banners of every party in the country. He has proclaimed them all, he has held them all, he has betrayed them all."[27]

One of the first fruits of the change was the cabling to the British government of the offer of a "dreadnought or its equivalent." For Deakin, the phrasing left an out against the charges of having betrayed the cause for which he had so long spoken, that of Australian control of its own defenses. Dudley wired the Colonial Office his opinion that although the attitude of the Australian government toward Admiralty suggestions was one of good will and open-mindedness, some uneasiness prevailed over the dreadnought offer. There was, he said, the old fear that the sacrifice of the sums involved would not bring any result visible in Australian waters. Dudley suggested that if the money could be spent on vessels useful in South Pacific waters, the Australian government would be relieved of considerable difficulties and would be able to reconcile its patriotic offers with local prejudices.[28]

Australia was not the only outpost of empire stirred by Great Britain's apparently sudden awakening to the growth of German naval power in 1909. Before the speeches of First Lord Reginald McKenna in the House of Commons in which the first intimations of alarm had appeared, various Canadians had been discussing the possibility that the Dominion might well start on the road toward the establishment of a naval force of its own. This discussion, however, had never gone beyond a most casual consideration of the question, for there was no Canadian party or political leader who gave it any force. The issue seemed to have about it a rather remote and nebulous quality, until this remoteness was ended abruptly by the disclosures in the British Commons.

[27] C.P.D., XLIX, 114ff.
[28] C.O. 418/71, Dudley to C.O., July 22, 1909.

Canada suffered little from the feeling of isolation which afflicted Australia and made that country so much more sensitive to naval matters. Comfortably close to the center of British naval strength, the mental radar of the Canadians was centered on the republic to the south. The sea frontiers of the Dominion had historically been much more secure than those of land, a factor which was naturally important in shaping Canadian thought. Little consideration had been given to a Canadian navy or to Canada's place in imperial naval defense until the new revelations of the fears of accelerated German naval construction.

Of course, for some Canadians the United States stood not as a threat, but as the true and natural ally of Canada. These felt that the security of the Dominion was grounded in the Monroe Doctrine. Thus that long-time exponent of continentalism and foe of imperialism, Goldwin Smith, pooh-poohed the possibility of any menance to Britain, and certainly to Canada, arising from Germany's actions, and lashed out against those "jingoists" who expressed such alarms. Smith found support for this attitude among substantial elements of the farm population of the prairie provinces.[29] And there were many others who were repelled by an imperial loyalty which meant greater involvement of Canada in the "vortex of militarism." Naturally, this number was enlarged, and the problems of Canadian political leadership, complicated by the French Canadians, increasingly inclined at this juncture to take their political leadership from Henri Bourassa.

But despite all these dissidents of both English and French inheritance, the bulk of Canadian press and parliamentarians were for some form of aid to Britain in the naval crisis. In the final analysis, both major political parties pledged themselves to the support of the United Kingdom; the real issue, as in Australia, was the form that support should take. J. S. Willison of the Toronto *News* wrote Richard Jebb that the naval situation had excited Canada greatly, and that "at last the indifference of our people has been penetrated."[30]

As in Australia, the government ran behind the clamor for action which swept through large sections of the press. The initiative rested with those who wanted Canada to do something, and to do it quickly. The Montreal *Star* sounded the note typical of most of the Conservative cries for action, when it said that the situation revealed in the debate in London "presses home to Canada still more grimly [the question] as to what it intends to do by way of help." In the *Star's* view, the construction of a supplementary

[29] *The Canadian Annual Review of Public Affairs*, ed. J. Castell Hopkins (Toronto, 1910), p. 109.
[30] Institute of Commonwealth Studies, London, Jebb Papers, Willison to Jebb, March 23, 1909.

naval force would require the maximum of effort with the minimum of result.[31]

Out in the prairie areas, the *Manitoba Free Press* of Winnipeg, which was the voice of prairie Liberalism, applauded in a front page editorial the many spontaneous offers of naval aid from the colonies to Great Britain. They gave the world, it said, "due notice that the British Empire is one and indivisible; and that on the sea, as on the land in the past, the sons of the race will be found in the battle line, if the need arises." Yet despite this extolling of the unity of the Empire and its defenses, the *Free Press* did not adopt the "One Flag and One Fleet" approach, for it urged that the work of creating a Canadian navy should go forward without delay.[32]

In the midst of all the storm and outcry, Prime Minister Laurier was in the advantageous position of having an established policy and tradition to refer to in the confronting of these new problems. His views on the naval crisis were essentially those with which he had met the efforts of Chamberlain in 1902. He had been prepared at that time, as he had written J. S. Willison, to relieve England of any military expenditures she had in Canada, and in line with that the Canadian government had assumed the charges of the garrisons of Halifax and Esquimalt.[33] Faced now with the demand for action in naval matters, it was predictable that Laurier would respond to the crisis in a way consistent with all that he had done in the past to defend Canadian freedom of decision and action and to enlarge Canadian autonomy. A Canadian navy controlled by a Canadian government was consonant with all that Laurier had worked for. On the other hand, a contribution to the imperial treasury for battleships to be controlled by the British government involved all the constitutional dilemmas and denials of nationalism which on the other side of the globe had led Deakin to reject the principle of contribution.

The Conservatives had no such established body of faith and doctrine. Admittedly more imperialistic in their attitude than the Liberals, they were far from united on the desirability of aiding Britain by a simple contribution for the construction of battleships. Laurier's policies in naval affairs provoked resistance among some of his followers, especially among the *Canadiens*, but the Conservative ranks were even more divided.[34] Most of the Parliamentary leadership of the party were initially in favor of the creation of a Canadian naval force, while the bulk of the Conservative press and leadership out of Parliament were

---

[31] *The Star* (Montreal), March 19, 1909.

[32] *The Manitoba Free Press* (Winnepeg), March 27 and 31, 1909.

[33] P.A.C., Laurier MSS, Vol. CCXXXV, p. 65767, Laurier to Willison, June 12, 1902.

[34] Gilbert N. Tucker, *The Naval Service of Canada* (Ottawa, 1952), I, 138.

strongly in favor of an immediate contribution of battleships to the Royal Navy. [35]

The Conservatives had the good fortune to have already on the order paper of the Commons in Ottawa a resolution stating the opinion of the House that Canada ought "no longer delay in assuming her proper share of the responsibility and financial burden incident to the suitable protection of her exposed coastline and great seaports." This resolution had been sponsored by the ardent imperialist and Conservative, George E. Foster. It might well have lain dormant had the events in London not put all matters of naval defense in the spotlight. But with the exciting flow of news from London, the members of the Opposition caucused and unanimously agreed to support the passage of the Foster resolution. [36]

The Liberals were not without their own resolutions befitting the hour. The staunch Canadian nationalist J. S. Ewart offered Laurier one whose wording he felt was suitable to the occasion, but the Prime Minister replied: "We are prepared to offer a resolution which, I think, will be satisfactory to all except mad imperialists." [37]

In the debate of March 29, 1909, Foster, urging the passage of his resolution, drew on the lessons of history, which he said indicated that only the nation forewarned and forearmed was secure. Much of the peace and security which Canadians enjoyed would, he said, vanish were even a third class cruiser of a hostile power to appear in Canadian ports. Canadians had safe embarkation and safe convoy across the oceans of the world, but this safety was furnished to Canadians by Britain rather than Canada. Canada had done nothing in naval defense; in comparison with other dependencies and overseas British territories, Canada stood silent and ashamed. Nor could the traditional argument of the costs of internal development be regarded as making any contribution to defense. Indeed, such development might actually be a weakness, for riches weakly held were a temptation to the aggressor. And Canada, said Foster, could not rely on the Monroe Doctrine. Such dependence would exact a price "of continual demand, continual concession, until at last absorption finished the craven course. . . ."

Foster parted company, however, with much of the Conservative clamor outside of Parliament for an immediate contribution to the Royal Navy. This, he felt, was an approach lacking in self-respect and one which would create nothing in the way of a tradition of defense and a maritime sense. The better course for the Dominion was to assume the task of defending her own ports and coasts, and in time Canada would have a

---

[35] *Canadian Annual Review*, 1909, pp. 91–97.
[36] *The Globe* (Toronto), March 24, 1909.
[37] P.A.C., Laurier MSS, Ewart to Laurier, March 27, 1909; Laurier to Ewart, March 29, 1909, Vol. DLXVIII, pp. 154082–154085.

force which would be an adjunct to the Royal Navy, would defend Canada, and would be an aid to the defense of the Empire. Further, Canada would be placing her own brains, bones, and sinew in such a force.

But having thus marshaled and arrayed some of the better arguments for making a start on creating a Canadian naval force, Foster proceeded to back water vigorously. The policy he had outlined, he said, was one for normal times. If in the existing emergency the Laurier Government wished to propose a gift of a dreadnought or of money, his side of the House would stand beside it!

Sir Wilfrid Laurier said in reply that he was not conscious that Canada had in any sense been remiss in her duty to the Empire. But the present situation should be examined calmly. One of the difficulties, he pointed out, was to ascertain the beginning of the business. In 1902, the talk was all of training ships; in 1907, of ships for local and harbor defense. And at the moment, if one were to listen to much of the press, and give attention to the wave of passing excitement, Canada should send a dreadnought to Britain. Laurier felt that Canada should consult with the British authorities, as it had done about the militia, and after having organized a plan in such consultation, Canada should carry out the plan with her own resources and money.

As for the dreadnought gift, Laurier did not feel that the menace was as great as had been suggested. Germany, he felt, could not have brought her navy, in the few years she had had at her disposal, up to the British standard of naval power. Britons were not unduly alarmed; the government there had postponed the acceptance of the dreadnought offered by New Zealand. And so the Prime Minister urged the passage of his resolution, which asked the House to approve expenditures designed to promote the organization of a Canadian navy along the lines suggested by the Admiralty at the Imperial Conference of 1907.

The Leader of the Opposition, Robert L. Borden, felt that too much of the defense effort and expenditure of the Dominion went for the militia, to the detriment of naval defense. There were many Canadian towns which were open to raids or attacks from second or third class cruisers of a hostile state. Even while the Admiralty was carrying out its program of concentration of British sea might, it was also giving approval to Australian efforts for greater protection against such raids in Australian waters. Borden felt that Canada should move in the direction of having a naval force of her own, and cited the Australian experience with subsidy as failing because Australians "felt that the contribution which they had been making for some years past was not really being used to give that protection to Australia which her interests demanded." Borden agreed with Laurier both on the wisdom of creating a Canadian naval force, and on the desirability of securing the advice of the Admiralty. After that, Canada should "lend itself to such cooperation and coordination as will be best for the whole empire." But the Conservative party leader did feel that it might be wise to delete the paragraph in the Laurier resolution condemning the principle of contribution, for the day might come when such contribution would be the only available manner in which Canada could assist in imperial defense.

In the end, the Commons passed the Prime Minister's resolution unanimously. It was somewhat amended, but not in the manner hoped for by Borden. Before the close of the debate, however, some seven or eight members of the House other than the party leaders had raised questions which revealed that many deeply rooted residual attitudes still remained despite all the sense of alarm. Canada should make sacrifices for a navy only if it remained under Canadian control; Canada needed all the funds it had for peaceful development; Canada was in no danger from any foreign aggressor; the Monroe Doctrine gave Canada what security she needed. But the final outcome of the debate was that by the passage of the Prime Minister's resolution the Laurier Government had clear support from both parties to undertake the building of a Canadian navy. Canada was to be a late starter but apparently a swift runner along the course over which the Australians had had heavy going for so many years.[38]

But there was no unanimity outside the House; there the policy of the creation of a separate navy was rejected by many. The Conservative *Mail and Empire* of Toronto parodied Tennyson in condemning the whole idea:

> Britain's myriad voices call
> Sons to be welded each and all,
> Into one Imperial whole,
> One with Britain heart and soul!
> One life, two flags, several fleets, one throne,
> Britons, hold your own.[39]

Yet for the nonce, despite objections, the Laurier program seemed to have relatively clear sailing weather ahead.

Few of the difficulties confronted by his opposite numbers in Australia and Canada had been encountered by Prime Minister Joseph Ward in New Zealand. Ward was the political heir of Seddon, whose ardent imperialism had been so much a feature of the Colonial Conference of

[38] Canada, Parliamentary Debates, 1st Sess., 11th Parl., XC, 3486–3562.
[39] *The Mail and Empire* (Toronto), Sept. 1, 1909.

1902. It was no accident that men of such convictions gained ascendancy in New Zealand, nor that what was left of the imperial federation movement had the greatest degree of life in that dominion. A sense of the general weakness of the small dominion, rather than any lack of appreciation of their own virtues, led its leaders to feel that they could gain more security and more influence for New Zealand by effective participation in imperial affairs than by trying out their own legs in matters like naval forces.[40]

Certainly to the conservative (conservative in its New Zealand context) government, which Ward led, the disclosures in London of the apparent naval weakness of Britain presented an opportunity for a demonstration of imperial loyalty which might enhance the voice of New Zealand in imperial affairs. It was an approach quite in the tradition carried forward by Seddon in his support of the policy of creating imperial military reserves in the colonies. Thus it was that Ward proposed to his Cabinet in March that New Zealand should "offer one, and, if necessary, two first-class battleships of the Dreadnought or latest types and that the offer should be on behalf of New Zealand at our own cost; the battleships to be controlled both in peace and war by the British Admiralty. . . ."[41]

The Governor of New Zealand, Lord Plunket, reported to the Colonial Office that the idea of the battleship had originated with Ward, and that the Cabinet was unanimous in its approval of his suggestion. Despite the fact that the Cabinet contained two members who a few years before had been regarded as pro-Boer, and two others who had been active in various peace movements, Ward's proposal had been criticized only as not being generous enough. The idea had been enthusiastically approved by the press of the Dominion, though there were some who maintained that Parliament should have been consulted in the matter.[42]

Ward was not able to derive full political advantage from his initiative, however, for he somewhat overplayed his hand by suggesting in public speeches that his government had secret information on the general naval situation which it could not disclose. With the publication of the correspondence between Britain and Australia on naval matters, it was soon apparent that there was no such information, much to the discomfiture of Ward and the delight of his opponents. Ward was further embarrassed by the fact that he would apparently be unable to go to London to confer with Admiralty authorities about the battleship gift. The time conflicted with the date of an impending meeting of the Parliament, and since a recent election had conferred on him the dubious blessing of a slim ma-

[40] Sinclair, *A History of New Zealand*, p. 217.
[41] New Zealand, Parl. Pap., 1909, A 4.
[42] C.O. 209/270, Plunket to C.O., May 1, 1909.

jority, he had to feel his way cautiously. To go to England under these circumstances would be a dangerous political venture, though the Governor suggested that perhaps in view of his battleship initiative, Ward might receive a special invitation for London consultations, to get him off the hook.[43]

When the New Zealand Parliament met, it was almost unanimously with Ward in authorization of the battleship gift, despite one or two voices raised in support of the idea of a local naval force which Ward strongly opposed. The legislators apparently felt, with Ward, that contributing something tangible to the Royal Navy and to imperial defense was better than a money gift. Subsidies were mistaken; a greater generosity and sense of identification was evoked by an H.M.S. Something than by merely paying so much per year in ignorance as to how it was spent.[44] In general, there was certainly less carping over imperial affairs in New Zealand than in any of the other self-governing colonies. On his retirement from the post of Governor there, Lord Plunket said it "would be difficult to conceive of a people more devoted to the Crown, more proud of their British origin, or more deeply interested in the Empire."[45]

The impulses of imperial loyalty which prompted so many leaders of government and opinion to urge support for the imperial government might have been somewhat tempered had these same people had a better inside knowledge of the crisis in London. Despite the general inadequacy of the overseas news in the Australasian press—about a column and a half each day, largely clippings from the London press—Antipodeans knew well enough the general developments which had been building to a greater tension between Britain and Germany in naval affairs. The growth of German naval power, the Tweedmouth letter, the *Daily Telegraph* interview, were all known and had their impact on colonial thought. Australians shared the invasion fears which were so all-pervasive "at home." *An Englishman's Home* played in Australian cities, and the *Age* carried a serial story of a German commerce raid and attack on Australian shores.

What was not known, however, was the political pushing and shoving which was going on in the inner circles of British political life. There were no representatives of Australia, for example, to transmit the gossip of the lobby or of Fleet Street to their home government.[46] Nothing was known of the dextrous use Lord Fisher was making of the press in order

[43] *Ibid.*, Plunket to C.O., May 7, 1909.
[44] *Ibid.*, Plunket to C.O., June 14, 1909.
[45] C.O. 209/271, Plunket to C.O., May 18, 1909.
[46] George Reid, who was appointed first Australian High Commissioner to London as a part of the bargaining which brought the Deakin-Cook Fusion government into office, did not actually take up his post until 1910.

to rouse the sense of alarm, or of the fact that though the clamor was for
eight battleships, Fisher would have been satisfied with six, and that he
looked upon the whole agitation of the "We want eight and we won't
wait" variety as a "heavenly panic now proceeding for 8 Dreadnoughts
a year!"[47] Only the slightest reverberations of this, and other disputes
within the Admiralty such as the Fisher-Beresford struggle, reached the
eyes or ears of the colonial leaders of either government or public opinion.
Of course, the responses in the colonies to the news from London were so
strong that it is unimaginable that even had the full story of the contention
in London been known, it would have changed the desire to support
Britain. But it certainly would have furnished more ammunition to those
critical of such co-operation.

In view of the apprehension which had spread so rapidly throughout
the Empire, it was natural that a desire should arise among colonial
leaders for consultation with the imperial authorities. The Fisher Government in Australia suggested such a conference; and in the debate in the
Canadian Parliament, Laurier had said that Canada should consult with
the imperial government and carry out whatever plan should be devised
through such consultation. In New Zealand, too, Ward was anxious for
such a meeting; he chafed at the parliamentary situation which seem-
ingly prevented him from journeying to England. And so the imperial
authorities invited representatives of the colonial governments to London
for a supplementary Imperial Conference on the problems of defense.

The conference on the role which the dominions might play in imperial
defense, and especially in imperial naval defense, was essentially a by-
product of the naval crisis of 1909. It was considerably less than the
customary full-scale gathering of colonial prime ministers, and it received
only peripheral attention from leaders of the British government. But in
terms of actual accomplishment, this subsidiary conference far out-
stripped many of the more regular and imposing gatherings, and it was
particularly significant for the recognition which it accorded to the idea
that the dominions might play a real and effective part in the system of
imperial defense.

The air of crisis naturally contributed to this. In all previous conferences discussions of defense matters had displayed a certain feeling of
remoteness. The cause of collaboration had received lip-service, but for
nearly all colonial leaders there had been other and more important
considerations. All of that was changed now. With the sense of approaching conflict, with the fear that the protective power of the Royal Navy,

[47] Gollin, *The Observer and J. L. Garvin*, p. 73; Fisher to Garvin, March 21, 1909.
Cf. ch. III for the Fisher-Garvin relations and activity in promoting the enlarged construction program.

under which the colonies had grown to a measure of strength, might be endangered, there was a single-mindedness that had been lacking before. The degree of concentration which Dr. Johnson discerned in the mind of a man about to be hanged would be too strenuous a conception, but it was incontestable that the sense of comfortable assurance drawn from repeated singing of "Rule Britannia" was shattered. It was no longer possible for colonists to regard aid to Britain in defense of empire as simply a move to relieve the British taxpayer of part of his burden. Now it was a matter of self-defense.

The conference was the result not alone of the battleship crisis, however, but also of the pushing nationalism of some of the dominions and particularly of Australia. It was no longer in keeping with the status and dignity to which such governments aspired to play a totally insignificant part in their own defense, and in the defense of the Empire to which they adhered. Canada had accepted the responsibility of maintaining and defending the naval bases, which seemed to most Canadians an indispensable element of sea power. Australia had long pushed for an enlarged participation in naval defense. And New Zealand, limited as it was by its small population, was nevertheless willing to contribute funds on a scale never before indicated. From such roots there would inevitably have developed a new concept of colonial activity in defense; the naval race with Germany simply hastened the growth.

And within the British government there had been a change of attitude toward colonial participation. The recognition of the unworthiness and limitations of the contributive principle, the understanding now that the problem was no longer one to be approached on strategic considerations alone, had penetrated into official consciousness. Grudging and limited acceptance of this had been apparent in the 1907 Imperial Conference, but in the intervening months even further concessions to these facts had been made in the minds of officials, a change to which Deakin's agitation had contributed as much as anything.

Symptomatic of the change was the attitude of the *Times*, which had abandoned its former somewhat nagging emphasis on the need of the colonies to contribute to the Royal Navy in favor of an approach giving greater understanding to colonial aspirations. A. W. Jose, the Australian correspondent of the *Times*, summarized in a lengthy dispatch the long resistance of much of Australian opinion to the 1903 pact. It was the weakness of Barton which had led Australia to the blunder of that pact; and it was only the loyalty of his colleagues in the Cabinet, plus the hangover of imperial enthusiasm after the South African war, which had enabled him to get it ratified by the Parliament. The ratification was politically manipulated, and was at odds with public opinion. The agreement, said Jose, had never been popular, for it ran contrary to Australian national aspirations, and public opinion had never been reconciled to it. Further, Australian feelings had been hurt by the peremptory dismissal by imperial authorities of the Australian suggestions concerning defense. While there was little anti-imperial feeling in Australia, substantial distrust of the Admiralty did exist.[48] On the eve of the opening of the conference, the *Times* said that it thought it important that the vessels offered to the Royal Navy should not be placed in European waters. If that were done, "we shall be committed to dependence upon the Empire for the discharge of a duty which would confront us equally if no Empire existed. . . ."[49] Even the *Bulletin* of Sydney could not have said it more forthrightly.

For this conference, then, the Admiralty and the War Office were much better prepared, having made the fundamental change in their approach to bring themselves in line with the thinking of the major colonies. That in the midst of what was essentially a war scare these political concessions were made, that this understanding of political reality was revealed, and that the old "One Empire, One Flag, One Fleet" approach was abandoned, constituted something of a minor miracle.

The preoccupation with dreadnoughts dominated the technical approach of Admiralty officials to the conference. For the crisis of 1909 was not one of general naval strength, but simply of the new great massive embodiments of sea power which had come to the fore in the last few years. The pre-dreadnought battleship did not enter into any realistic measurement of sea strength. Britain had enough of these and to spare; the D.N.I. in 1909 told the Committee of Imperial Defence that Britain, even in the midst of war with Germany, could spare twenty battleships for Far Eastern waters.[50] But these were of the pre-dreadnought era.

Yet the dreadnought could not fight alone; there had to be supporting vessels to create an effective fighting unit. To be considered also were the problems of manning and promotion which, among other factors, had caused the Admiralty to look askance at some of the early suggestions of Deakin. A force of destroyers and/or submarines furnished no answer to such problems. But all of these issues had to be met if there was to be, with all the colonial aspiration and eagerness, some real addition to the naval strength of the Empire.

Some of the approaches to the problems of harnessing this co-operative attitude of the colonial governments still smacked of the old, contributory system. Admiral Sir Arthur K. Wilson, recently Commander in Chief

[48] *The Times* (London), July 31, 1909.
[49] *Ibid.*, July 30, 1909.
[50] Cab. 2/2/1, 102 Meeting, C.I.D., June 29, 1909.

of the Channel Fleet, then a member of the C.I.D. and later to be Fisher's successor as First Sea Lord, drew up an elaborate table by which member states of the Empire might each equitably contribute to the support of the Royal Navy according to the value of their sea-borne trade. In all, the self-governing colonies plus India should contribute about 25 per cent of the costs, with the assessment to be paid in either money or ships. Australia would have been assessed at a far higher rate than Canada under this scheme, since much of Canada's produce moved into international trade over land frontiers, while there was no such overland trade in sea-surrounded Australia.[51] This, however, was certainly an exercise in trying to breathe life into the dead.

The proposals which the government of the United Kingdom intended to submit to the colonial representatives upon their assembly in London were formulated by the Admiralty and War Office. Prime Minister Asquith appointed a subcommittee of the C.I.D. to give the final gloss to the suggestions, with Lord Crewe, who had succeeded Lord Elgin at the Colonial Office, as chairman. The group included Viscount Esher, John Morley, Haldane, McKenna, who was the new First Lord of the Admiralty, and Sir Charles Hardinge of the Foreign Office. Also included, as naval and military representatives, were Admiral Wilson, Rear Admiral A. E. Bethell, who was the current D.N.I., General Sir John French, and General W. G. Nicholson, the current Chief of the General Staff. The points which the committee were to consider included the functions which could be allotted to the forces of the dominions in a scheme of general imperial defense; the means of reconciling the local control of their forces desired by the colonial governments with the principle of unity of command in time of war; the manner in which the interchange of ships of war and of naval and military personnel could best be handled; the advice which could be given to colonial governments about measures that could be taken to maintain efficiency in their military and naval forces; and the legislation, if any, required to give to naval forces of the dominions, acting under the orders of their own governments, international status as ships of war.

The most significant of the submissions to this subcommittee was the Admiralty memorandum of July 13, 1909. In this, a broad program of naval collaboration was laid out. But the heart of the Admiralty argument was based on the long and generally unhappy experience with Australian discontent over the subsidy principle. The Admiralty assumed that a simple contribution to the Royal Navy would not satisfy public opinion in that Commonwealth (there was no mention of the other self-governing

[51] Cab. 17/78. This file contains much of the documentation relating to the 1909 Imperial Defence Conference.

states). The Commonwealth should therefore seek the creation of a distinct fleet unit, one which would be manageable in time of peace and would have the component elements to be of effective use in time of war.

The force of destroyers which the Commonwealth government had suggested in past years would possess only limited usefulness. It would be circumscribed in its operations and would present problems in manning and efficient operation.

> To give practical effect to the suggestion of a fleet unit, the system followed by the Admiralty in the distribution of the fleet in stations according to the interest to be protected, might be adopted as the basis of a scheme of Colonial Co-operation, and each of the Dominions or group of Dominions might be made responsible for the maintenance of a certain naval strength in its own sphere of interest, thus relieving the Imperial fleet of direct responsibility in distant seas. There would then be, in lieu of the Imperial Australian, Cape, and North Atlantic or Pacific Squadrons, in future an Australian and New Zealand Squadron, and a Canadian Squadron (in the Atlantic and Pacific) capable of action not only in defence of coasts, but also of the trade routes, and sufficiently powerful to deal with small hostile squadrons should such ever attempt to act in those waters.[52]

The fleet unit which the Admiralty suggested would be led by a battle cruiser of the *Indomitable* class, with supporting cruiser, destroyer, and submarine elements.

The whole idea was substantially tailored to meet the needs of the Australasian areas. If carried out as planned, the Commonwealth government would have under its control a viable and effective force, capable of being of very considerable assistance to the imperial government in time of war. It was disputable, however, whether the idea met the needs of other colonial governments equally well. Canada with her two coasts had unique problems which a single integrated naval unit certainly did not meet.

The tone of the Admiralty memorandum marked a considerable retreat from the former *hauteur* with which their pronouncements on colonial participation in naval activity had been marked. The raids by single cruisers on colonial shorelines, which had once been all they had envisaged as possible, were now enlarged to possible raids by small hostile squadrons; and there was some measure of return to the discredited idea of localization in the emphasis which was placed on station interests to be protected, and on responsibility in distant seas which might be better met by forces in those waters.

The delegates came to London for the conference armed with little

[52] *Ibid.*

more than hope. Joseph Ward managed to shake off the parliamentary difficulties which had beset him and attended the conference. As the first and foremost of those who had brought offerings to the altar of imperial faith, he was to some degree the hero of the imperialists. But Ward was the only Prime Minister of a senior dominion state to attend. Canada and Australia sent delegates of Cabinet rank; the political heads stayed home. Sir Frederick Borden, the long-time Canadian Militia minister, was surely senior in conference experience. He brought with him a Cabinet colleague, Louis Brodeur, Minister of Marine and Fisheries, and also the heads of the military services of the Dominion, General Lake and Admiral Kingsmill.

Though the conference opened the door wide to the creation of the Australian naval force for which he had worked so long, Deakin did not attend. The Australian representative was Minister without Portfolio Colonel J. F. G. Foxton. Colonel Foxton seemed to many an odd choice from a government led by Deakin, for he had been identified as an advocate of a dreadnought gift. Nor was he in any sense a prominent figure in Australian political life. He was accompanied by Captain Creswell, and on the military side by Colonel W. T. Bridges, the brightest luminary in the developing Australian military organization.

Foxton's first business was easily disposed of, for it was to find out whether the Commonwealth should present Britain with a dreadnought or whether some other form of assistance was preferred, and the Admiralty memo made it clear that the latter was the case. Foxton reported that Admiral Fisher was very explicit in his rejection of the Labor Ministry's program of a covey of destroyers. On the other hand, he was equally forthright in his urging that the Commonwealth create a fleet unit led by a battle cruiser of the improved *Indomitable* class, which Admiral Fisher said could catch anything and sink anything. A strong feature of the Admiralty's recommendation was that the proposed fleet unit should provide every class of training from battleship to submarine service, and should be large enough to open a life career for officers and men who entered the naval service of the Commonwealth.[53]

The Admiralty's proposals were certainly acceptable to the Australian delegates. As Foxton cabled Deakin, they were closer to the Australian views than those of any of the other dominions.[54] The Admiralty envisioned the establishment of a much greater naval force than anyone in Australia had expected or dreamed of even a few months before. And for the Australians there was the ironic surprise that in the Admiralty's

[53] J. F. G. Foxton, "The Evolution and Development of an Australian Naval Policy," *Commonwealth Military Journal*, I (1911), 654.

[54] Foxton to Deakin, Aug. 5, 1909, Prime Minister's File, 12/975, Australian National Archives, Canberra.

proposals the boot of subsidy was to be on the other foot. For the Admiralty suggested that in order to assist the Commonwealth in the early years of creating its new naval unit, the British government should make an annual payment of £250,000. The chief dissenter to all of this was Creswell, who felt that the whole fleet unit approach was too schematic, and allowed no place for natural growth and development. But Creswell admitted that the plan, however faulty, did have the saving grace of conceding the major point that Australia had the right to share in her own naval defense. [55]

For the Canadians, however, the Admiralty program of dominion fleet units offered no easy solution to their problems, and they were quick to point this out to Reginald McKenna and other Admiralty people. The basic difficulty, of course, arose because Canada had two coasts. It would be politically impossible to concentrate all naval defense on one, to the neglect of the other. And yet the proposed fleet unit would have to operate substantially as a unit in order to be an effective force.

The Admiralty's hope was, according to McKenna, that Canada would create the unit and place it in the Pacific. He did not see any necessity for a Canadian unit in the Atlantic, since the British fleet controlled the whole sweep of the waters there. But there was grave British weakness in the Pacific, and McKenna told the Canadians that he would prefer to see all the fleet units which might be undertaken by the various dominions stationed there.

Borden and Brodeur both told McKenna that this was totally unacceptable. Further, they felt some concern over the emphasis which the Admiralty placed on the need for battle cruisers as opposed to vessels of lesser size. Brodeur wondered whether this approach reflected a desire of Asquith and his associates to be able to proclaim a political triumph by dominion offerings of such additions to British naval strength. "This would perhaps be for them an excellent election cry, but I don't think it would be as popular with us," he wrote Laurier. [56]

The Canadian delegates found McKenna in a most agreeable frame of mind, however, willing both to listen and to act on the basis of their difficulties. Brodeur reported to his Prime Minister that the First Lord said that he understood the entire Canadian situation, and that he would see to the preparation of a scheme for Canadian naval activity which he would first show to the Canadian delegates before formally submitting it to them. McKenna was not only conciliatory in dealing with the Canadians

---

[55] Institute of Commonwealth Studies, London, Jebb Papers, Creswell to Jebb, Sept. 29, 1909.

[56] P.A.C., Laurier MSS, Vol. 586, Brodeur to Laurier, Aug. 10, 1909.

themselves; in the course of a general meeting of the delegates, after listening to some remarks about the uselessness of local navies by Ward of New Zealand,[57] McKenna replied with the gist of the argument which the Canadians had put forth. Dominion naval organizations, he said, would be of considerable service, and would have considerable impact on the countries close to the various dominions.[58]

McKenna's conciliatory attitude was not shared by Fisher. While McKenna was willing to forego the battle cruiser, Fisher seemed adamant, at least in his first meeting with the Canadians, on the necessity for its construction. It must be the central feature of their program, he said; no naval unit for Canada unless it began with a dreadnought, and unless it was placed in the Pacific. In subsequent meetings, however, while Fisher adhered to the essential priority of the dreadnought, McKenna overruled him and said that this was not a realistic program for the Canadians.

The whole approach of the Admiralty under McKenna was essentially to allow the fullest measure of discretion to the Canadians. They were willing to take the maximum and minimum figures of possible Canadian expenditures, and to devise a program of naval development for either amount. In this mood of general conciliation, the naval aspects of the conference went along as if greased. The Admiralty program for Canada when submitted called for a force of armored cruisers which could be divided between Canada's east and west coasts.

Thus, everything developed in most satisfactory fashion for the Canadians. Sir Frederick Borden reported to Laurier that the conference had gone well. The press on both sides of the Atlantic had been fair and favorable; and the Canadian position had been appreciated by both government and public in England.[59]

Of course, to some degree the Canadian stand had broken the essential symmetry of the original proposition. This had called for the creation and establishment in Pacific area waters of four fleet units, each in itself a formidable fighting unit, and of major weight in battle when combined. The China unit was to have as its flagship the dreadnought contributed by New Zealand; the British government was to create a similar unit for the East Indian Station; and to these forces were to be added a Canadian and an Australian unit. In combination, the four battle cruisers with their supporting vessels would have been the most modern and powerful vessels in the Pacific. Even with the Canadian rejection of the Admiralty

[57] Actually, Ward had told Brodeur privately that he would have preferred the Australian and Canadian course of a local naval force, except that he was limited by lack of means. *Ibid.*, Brodeur to Laurier, Aug. 10, 1909.

[58] *Ibid.*

[59] P.A.C., Laurier MSS, Borden to Laurier, Sept. 1, 1909.

program, however, there would still be a formidable re-establishment of British naval power in the Pacific if the other aspects of the program were carried out. And undergirding the whole conception was the appreciation of the larger role which the dominions would now play in their own naval defense as well as the defense of the Empire. Perhaps nothing so suggests the new approach as the fact that the long-established centralizing Imperial Federation (Defence) Committee changed its name to Imperial Co-operation League.[60] The judgment of the *Times*, that the conference "brings us definitely in view of a practicable and effective system of co-operation on . . . naval . . . defence"[61] seemed eminently sound.

[60] *The Times* (London), Aug. 3, 1909.
[61] *Ibid.*, Aug. 27, 1909.

CHAPTER XI

BORDEN, CHURCHILL, AND COLLABORATION

Australians heard the news of the work of the Imperial Defence Conference with almost universal satisfaction. The sense of gratification at its results extended through nearly the whole of the nation's political spectrum, embracing the supporters of the dreadnought gift idea and the long-time advocates of an Australian navy as well. Melbourne's conservative daily, the *Argus*, a leading supporter of the gift idea, said that the dreadnought offer had borne great fruit.[1] The *Age*, sobered somewhat after its heady binge of dreadnought imperialism, had returned to its traditional support of Australian handling of Australian defense, but it flattered itself that the results of the conference justified its own long advocacy of a local naval effort. The arrangements which had been reached between the Admiralty and the Commonwealth government, said the *Age*, were a "triumph for Australia." The features of the new agreement were excellently wise and acceptable. But the best feature of all, to the *Age*, was that the Commonwealth government was to retain control of the new force in time of peace, and that even in war the force would not come under the control of the Admiralty without the assent of the Australian authorities, (an assent, said the paper, which would be immediately forthcoming).[2]

The *Call*, journal of the New South Wales branch of the Australian Defence League, which spearheaded much of the agitation for universal military training of Australian youth, also regarded the efforts of the conference as outstanding and epoch-making. It felt that the results had been richer than anyone might have anticipated, and that the projected

[1] *The Argus* (Melbourne), Aug. 18, 1909.
[2] *The Age* (Melbourne), Aug. 19, 1909.

fleet unit would be infinitely more effective than the small force of destroyers planned by the Fisher Government.[3]

For the supporters of the latter, the encouragement now being given to the creation of an Australian naval element by the imperial authorities was a chance to score on old foes, and a chance too good to be ignored. The leading journal of the trade unions, the *Worker* of Sydney, demanded to know whether the ardent supporters of the dreadnought gift idea were now going to attack the imperial authorities as "disloyalists" and as incapable madmen for their acceptance and support of the idea that Australians were capable of running a naval force of their own.[4]

There were dissenting voices, of course. Perhaps the liveliest was heard in the island state of Tasmania, where the *Mercury* of Hobart entertained an abiding distrust of all Australian efforts to inject themselves into what the journal regarded as the proper imperial sphere of power. The *Mercury* regarded the tendency of the imperial government to pay increasing attention to colonial wishes and aspirations as generally savoring of imbecility. It wished for nothing so much as some vigorous language from the imperial government, bluntly telling the dominions what the situation in naval matters was, and what they should do about it. Instead, the leading statesmen in Britain were carrying to ludicrous length the policy of not saying anything unpleasant to the colonies. And as the results of the conference became known, the ire of the *Mercury* mounted. It held that the imperial government had been pusillanimous in yielding to nothing more than colonial vanity and conceit.[5]

The first opportunity for the Commonwealth Parliament to discuss the new agreement came with the introduction of a defense bill by the Deakin Cabinet. The bulk of the bill dealt more with compulsory military training than with naval matters, but the Minister of Defence, Joseph Cook, made considerable allusion to the results of the recent conference, which he presented to the House of Representatives. Australia, he said, was to create a fleet unit with one battle cruiser, three smaller cruisers, six destroyers, and three submarines. This, said Cook in rather a flight of fancy, was an alternative to the dreadnought offered by the government; a statement properly provoking a snort of dissent from the leader of the opposition, former Prime Minister Fisher. The construction cost of the flotilla would be £3,750,000 and the annual cost of its maintenance and operation £750,000, to which the imperial government would make an annual contribution of £250,000 for an unspecified period. This new force would be the main naval element on what had been the Australian

[3] *The Call* (Sydney), Sept., 1909.
[4] *The Worker* (Sydney), Aug. 26, 1909.
[5] *The Mercury* (Hobart), July 20, 30, 31, Aug. 19, Sept. 23, 1909.

Station, and it was not yet clear whether any vessels of the Royal Navy would remain in Australian waters once the new ships had taken up their duties.

The new Australian unit was to be one of the three major divisions of a new Eastern fleet. With this, Australia had been assigned a definite role in the support of British interests in the Pacific, along with other states of the Empire. As for the more immediate areas, Australia was to share these with the New Zealand section of the Royal Navy's China Station forces.[6]

The Labor party was not willing to accept all aspects of the new arrangements without some expression of dissent on a variety of points. Its principal spokesman on defense matters, W. M. Hughes, said that there were a number of issues yet to be resolved, including the financial arrangements, the location and sphere of operation of the new unit, its basic control, and its liability to be transferred to parts of the globe remote from Australia. To take an Australian ship and to transfer it simply to serve a need of the Royal Navy was, he felt, but a form of increased subsidy.[7]

Andrew Fisher was also concerned with the matter of control. He wondered if the possibility of the Australian vessels coming under the command of the Royal Navy in time of war would not require re-swearing in of the officers and men of the ships, to bring them under the British Naval Discipline Act;[8] and he felt that the ships should not be transferred to what he called "remote seas" without the express consent of the Commonwealth authorities.[9]

There were other Labor expressions of concern over the degree to which the new unit was to form an integral part of the Imperial Navy. One indication of this cited by Labor spokesmen was the inclusion of submarines in the naval unit. Australia, it was argued, had no need for any such vessels, and their inclusion suggested all too strongly that what was being planned was simply another unit of the Imperial Navy.[10]

The introduction of the legislation giving effect to the agreement came later in the session, and consideration and passage of it were unfortunately impeded by one of the strident outbreaks of personal abuse which occasionally marred the relative legislative calm of the Commonwealth Parliament. Joseph Cook was in the midst of his presentation of some of the details of the new arrangements when an opposition member arose and moved that the speaker no longer be heard. The honorable member

[6] Commonwealth of Australia, *Parliamentary Debates* (C.P.D.), LI, 3615–3624.
[7] C.P.D., LII, 4463.
[8] C.P.D., LI, 3624.
[9] C.P.D., LII, 4460.
[10] C.P.D., LII, 4483, 4492.

who so moved was not one who stood high in the appreciation of most members, and he found few supporters. But when the parliamentary wrangle had died down and Cook was on his feet once again, the gentleman swung into action once more by repeating his motion. Cook was so annoyed at the total collapse of any decent parliamentary atmosphere that he refused to continue; he abruptly moved the passage of the second reading with only a portion of the details disclosed in parliamentary fashion.

In what he was permitted to discuss, Cook spoke in a somewhat grandiloquent manner of Australia's assignment to what he called the "wardenship of the Pacific." While the program of naval construction undertaken by Australia was designed primarily for the security of Australian shores and floating trade, it would also enable the Commonwealth to participate in the defense of the Empire, largely by relieving Britain of the burden of defending Australia and thus facilitating the greater concentration of British naval might at the points of greatest danger. Again, Cook stressed the Australian understanding that the Australian unit would be part of a larger whole, the Eastern fleet of the Empire, which would restore the diminished strength of Britain and the Empire in the Pacific. Despite the truncated nature of Cook's exposition, the enabling legislation which put much of the agreement into force passed its second reading in the House with little difficulty, by a majority of 39 to 9.[11]

The debate so abruptly terminated was resumed a few days later with the introduction of a bill authorizing the government to finance the construction of the Australian vessels. Where there had been substantial support from all corners of the House for the general policy of the construction of the unit, there was considerable Labor opposition to the government's proposal that the necessary funds be raised by securing a loan of £3,500,000, to be retired in sixteen years. Fisher attacked the loan program as lacking in pride and national self-respect. In seeking this loan, he declared, the government was making a declaration of Australian impotence. Further, what would be the value of the ships in sixteen years? They might well be worthless before the loan was taken care of. And how could the strength of the squadron be maintained by new construction when the old vessels were still to be paid for? He also protested against the receipt of subsidy by the Commonwealth. A "more robust, Australian-minded Government" would have rejected the £250,000 a year proffered by the imperial authorities.

In defense of the loan program, Deakin commented that the advance in British attitude concerning the possibilities of Australian participation in naval defense had been remarkable. Australia was no longer thinking

[11] C.P.D., LIV, 6251–6259.

and talking about mosquito fleets, but of a naval unit which would be one-third of "the great fleet which will protect the imperial flag, Australia, and other British possessions in the eastern Pacific." As for the borrowing, Deakin said that the reason for it was that it would hasten the construction of the vessels by six months. The imposition of the taxation necessary if borrowing was to be avoided would mean lengthy delays; their imposition at that time—an election was approaching—was just not practical politics.

The taxation issue cited by the Prime Minister certainly clouded the question of paying for the fleet unit. Had the wishes of the Labor party prevailed, the raising of some of the needed funds would have been by the imposition of a tax on the value of lands worth over £5,000. Such a tax program had been part of the Labor program since the 1906 election and was to be a prominent plank in its platform for the next election.

The government majority in both houses of the Parliament was sufficient to carry the loan bill through, though the lower house limited the rate of interest to be paid to three per cent. But this policy of financing the development of the naval force did not stand, for the Labor party, which had opposed this method, won a substantial victory in the Commonwealth election of 1910.

The internal difficulties of finance did not indicate any wavering in the intentions of either of the major political groups in Australia to go forward as briskly as possible in the implementing of the 1909 agreement. Contracts for the construction of the vessels of the proposed force were placed in British shipyards, and while the ships were being built, negotiations went forward also on the legal status of the new ships of war, and for the better co-operation of the emergent Australian unit with the Royal Navy. The new Labor government also approached Sir John Fisher with the idea of obtaining his advice and services in getting the new fleet unit effectively manned and underway. Fisher at first agreed to help, saying that it was so momentous that the Navy of the Pacific, as he called it, should be started on the right basis, that like the Emperor Diocletian he was prepared to leave his cabbages to be of service in the matter. But the assent which he gave one day he withdrew the next, for what he called "private considerations" which prevented his acceptance.[12]

Instead of Fisher, the Australian government secured the services of Admiral Reginald Henderson, an officer who had commanded the British coast guard and the naval reserves during the five years previous to his Australian mission. Henderson drew up an elaborate plan for the expansion of the Australian naval forces, centering upon eight dreadnoughts, and with all the necessary supporting ships for such a force.

[12] Australian National War Museum Library, Pearce Papers, Fisher to Sir George Reid, May 25, 26, 1910.

But his plans called for the expenditure of something like £23,000,000, a figure apparently well beyond the financial capacity of the Commonwealth at that time. The recommendations aroused a good deal of criticism in Australia on this account, though the proposed amount loomed larger in the headlines than the fact that they were to be spread over a more than twenty-year span.[13] But although some Australians were not pleased, Fisher, who had been largely responsible for guiding the Australians in their selection of Henderson, told the latter that he had done a splendid piece of work in Australia.[14]

Henderson discussed with Australian authorities the matter of control of the vessels expected soon in Australian waters. Problems arose from the fact that Australia was not yet a sovereign state, and that the flag of the Commonwealth flown over ships of war would therefore have no international status or recognition. The Colonial Defence Act of 1865 had granted to colonial governments the rights to raise and maintain naval forces, and to provide and maintain ships of war. In the case of Australia, there had been further powers granted in the act establishing the Commonwealth government. These included the naval and military defense of the Commonwealth, but this was merely a shift of such powers from the previous state governments to the new federal authority. In matters tinged with extraterritoriality, the new Commonwealth was empowered to deal with external affairs, fisheries beyond Australian territorial limits, and relations with islands in the Pacific. Nor could it be overlooked that the Commonwealth became the administering authority of the British portion of New Guinea. But for all this, it was only by inference that the Commonwealth government could be regarded as possessing rights to control war vessels in international waters. The 1865 legislation was designed for a time when naval possibilities were severely limited; an Australia on the verge of possessing mammoth naval vessels of great cruising range could not then have been imagined. But the growth of colonial naval aspirations had made the old act totally inadequate.

The Minister of Defence in the second Fisher Government in Australia was Senator George F. Pearce of Western Australia. Among Labor party members, Pearce had shared with Hughes leadership in defense matters, and he became an able administrator in this field. Of course, he did have the advantage of taking office when basic policies had apparently been settled with the adoption of compulsory military service and the creation of a naval force. It was under Pearce, however, that these matters of policy took form and substance.

[13] George F. Pearce, *Carpenter to Cabinet* (London, 1951), p. 101.
[14] Marder, *Fear God and Dread Nought*, II, 387.

Pearce was aware of the necessity in point of law to give the warships of the Commonwealth the status of ships of a sovereign state. In time of war, he said, the Australian vessels would in almost every conceivable case be placed at the disposal of the Admiralty. But in peacetime, when the Commonwealth government would be in direct control, there were questions of relationships with foreign countries, status, flag, etc. with which existing imperial or colonial legislation did not effectively deal. It seemed to Pearce that such difficulties could be overcome only by the passage of imperial legislation.[15]

While the Minister of Defence in Australia was occupied with these legal issues, the work of the construction of the ships of the Australian squadron went on, though with minor irritations. For example, one of the representatives of the Australian Defence Department in Britain complained of the secrecy with which one of the shipyards surrounded its construction of an Australian ship. His methods of getting information about the construction, he said, would have led to his expulsion if they had been found out, though whether from the yard or from Britain he did not make clear. And he further reported that British shipbuilders were annoyed at the possibility of Canada building some of her own ships, and that the Australian and New Zealand contributions during the dreadnought crisis had simply been jeered at.[16]

The 1909 conference, which brought settlement of the political conflicts centering about defense problems in Australia, had quite opposite results in Canada. There it brought not peace but the sword. The Laurier Government encountered intense political storms over its proposals for the establishment of a Canadian navy, storms which eventually contributed to the overthrow of the Liberal party after many years in office. For while Australians regarded a navy as a token of their developing nationalism, many Canadians felt that a naval force was a symbol of a resurgent imperialism, a revived Chamberlainism.

The political and, to some degree, racial conflict which raged in Canada over the Laurier program of naval development has been amply dealt with elsewhere.[17] The basic reason why the program which Australia embraced with such general enthusiasm lit the fires of controversy in Canada lay naturally in the dualistic character of the population of the Dominion, though not in that alone. The Canadian nationalism which Laurier exemplified, and which he had done so much to encourage,

---

[15] Pearce Papers, Pearce to Henderson, Sept. 29, 1910.

[16] *Ibid.*, W. G. Robertson to Pearce, Oct. 10, 1909.

[17] *The Canadian Annual Review of Public Affairs* (Toronto, 1909–12) gives full summaries of the public activities and comments dealing with naval issues. Tucker, *The Naval Service of Canada*, pp. 119–210 and Mason Wade, *The French Canadians* (New York, 1955), pp. 562–642 emphasize the French-Canadian reactions to the naval dispute.

had been founded on the possibility of the growth of friendship and understanding between English and French Canadians. The most promising approach to this objective had lain in efforts to find for both peoples a common center of allegiance in Canada: not in English Canada nor in French Canada, but in the wide sweep of the great land from the Maritimes to the Pacific, and in the riches which the two cultures could contribute to the national life. Nor was there to be any repudiation of the imperial connection, but rather a transformation of the status of Canada from subordination to alliance with Britain. This was a course of the utmost delicacy, and the safest way to pursue it was to avoid action, decision, and excitement as much as possible, to shun responsibilities and reject all the enticements of imperial action. For in a country "resting on paradoxes and anomalies, governed only by compromise and kept strong by moderation,"[18] the enlargement of responsibilities and duties could easily exacerbate the racial tensions in the national community, and should be assumed only under the most demanding circumstances.

At the time of the Boer War, Laurier had referred to the dispatch of the contingents as an instance of Canada acting in the full independence of her sovereign power. But with the exception of the contingents and the assumption of garrison duty at the two naval bases, Canada had done little in the exercise of such sovereign power. Laurier had spoken in 1902 and on other occasions of the possibility of creating a Canadian navy, and he was thus able to claim that Australians were only following the lead of the Dominion. But nothing had actually been done toward this end, neither the acquisition of ships, nor the preparation of the public mind for such a course. Canada lacked a maritime tradition, and most especially a naval tradition. Had there been some small vessels acquired under the authority of the 1865 Colonial Naval Defence Act which had flown the Canadian ensign, the possibility of developing a Canadian naval unit would not have been such a disturbing novelty. Such a unit, when created, would have seemed to have a more Canadian character; it would have seemed less ominously imperial.

Further, the nature of the Laurier naval program affected the character of the debate. The Canadian government may well have carried the virtue of moderation too far, and in so doing robbed their naval program of any emotional appeal. Laurier rejected in parliamentary debate the idea that the government's course was a neutral and colorless compromise. But the studied *via media* which was so characteristic of Laurier's career had faults as well as virtues. A naval program that was to start with the purchase of two over-age cruisers, and to continue with the construction of newer vessels over a period of six years, surely did not comport with

[18] W. L. Morton, *The Canadian Identity* (Madison, Wis., 1961), p. 51.

the atmosphere of emergency and crisis which had triggered the whole enterprise. There was much too much of a piecemeal and casual air about it.

Nor did the Laurier program show any recognition that the crisis was, after all, a dreadnought crisis. It was this behemoth of the sea that had thrown the Empire into convulsion in 1909. The tendency in the popular mind was to think of sea power in terms of the dreadnought. And the Laurier program, unlike the Australian, included no such vessels. However useful the cruisers and destroyers of that program might be, they did not have the primitive power appeal of the dreadnought; it was difficult to feel that the smaller vessels would really affect the balance of power or the destinies of men and nations. Lacking a dreadnought, it was easier for Laurier's political foes to damn the government's program as creating a "tin pot" navy, a token force of little usefulness, a toy for politicians to parade, and with which to flatter the Canadian ego while at the same time appeasing the appetites of imperialists anxious to do something for the Empire.

The essential moderation of the government's program did nothing, of course, to arouse the Canadian people to any awareness of dangers threatening their general security. As one historian pointed out, "The foreign offices and war staffs of Europe were not of much interest to Canadians, and competition in armament, though it was described in the newspapers, remained largely unreal to a people most of whom had never seen a battery or a warship."[19] The government's approach to the problem was unlikely to dispel this sense of unreality. There was the natural reluctance of any people to believe that the fixed points of their national life were endangered. Canadians had enjoyed the security furnished by British sea power in the Atlantic for so long that it was difficult to conceive it might be successfully challenged, and even more difficult to feel that if it were, Canada could do anything about it. Here, of course, the nature of the naval program of the government entered the picture, but the traditional security was more fundamental. Certainly the defense discussions in Australia suggested that there existed in the Antipodes a greater sense of awareness of the extent to which the shift of power might affect the destinies of Australians. Lord Roberts' dictum about the world shift of power to the Pacific was widely quoted, and while the sense of change may have been superficial, it contrasted strongly with the comparative indifference displayed toward such possibilities in Canada. That the comfortable world in which Canada had grown to its existing stature was in any real manner threatened, and that there might come a situation in which Canada should move, not for the defense

[19] Tucker, *The Naval Service of Canada*, p. 209.

of Britain, but for the prolongation of that power structure in the Atlantic which had permitted Canada the luxury of its growth, was never stressed to the extent that such matters were in Australia.

This difference between the two dominions was to a great extent the creation of geography. Holding the vast Australian land mass for a white, European-derived civilization in a Pacific world in which the slumbering millions of Asian peoples were apparently awakening, created much of the sensitivity in the Australian mind. Further, the efforts of Australians to get Britain to establish a form of British Monroe Doctrine over the areas of the southwest Pacific had been ignored in Britain, and Australians had been irritated at what many of them regarded as the intrusion of France and Germany into the Australian corner of the world. In addition, a nation without land frontiers, and with the overwhelming bulk of its population clustered in great seaport towns, was likely to be more concerned with maritime power than a nation to whom the land frontier with a great power had always been of paramount importance. Moreover, the centers of strength from which aid might be dispatched to Australia were not only on the other side of the globe, but were themselves increasingly beleaguered. (Hence the welcome given to the American fleet in 1908.)

Few such considerations existed in the Canadian mind. The security of that land rested on two foundations: the Monroe Doctrine, reflecting the reasoned necessity for the United States to protect Canada if she were to have her own borders secure, and the predominance of British sea-power in the Atlantic, which had made the Western Hemisphere so safe during the nineteenth century. If this security was apparently threatened by the growth of German naval might, it was perhaps more than corres-pondingly increased by the compensating concentration of British naval forces. This change, which increased the Australian sense of insecurity, had the opposite effect in Canada. Thus for many in Canada, the only eventuality by which the Dominion might be endangered was an Anglo-American rift, and the possibility of that seemed to grow more remote with each passing year.

It was not, however, such considerations as these that gave the naval controversy which developed in Canada the measure of bitterness and acrimony it ultimately engendered. Of course, many opposed any action on the ground that Canada had no need to take action, and indeed could not afford such action. But the vehemence of the controversy came from different assertions—from the charges that Canada, by taking any naval action at all, was becoming embroiled in the intrigues of imperialists, warmongers and militarists, and that she was being maneuvered into acting not for her own interests but for those of Britain alone. The leader in this challenge to the Laurier program was the great French Canadian Henri Bourassa.

In true Cobdenesque vein, Bourassa prophesied that doing anything in the naval arena involved a greater danger of war for Canada. Canada, he said, could get involved in whatever notions occurred "to a Chamberlain, a Rhodes, a Beers, to gold-seekers or opium merchants . . . ." If they started a conflict "in South Africa or India, in the Mediterranean or Persian Gulf, on the shores of the Baltic or the banks of the Black Sea, on the coasts of Japan or in the China seas, we are involved, always and regardless, with our money and blood . . . ." [20]

The opposition roused and spearheaded by Bourassa created Laurier's major political difficulties. Bourassa's genuine concern for a Canadian nationalism which embraced both of the great streams of Canadian life in substantial equality had great kinship to the ideas of Laurier; both sought a Canadian and not a French Canadian nationalism. But though both men had seen in the imperialism of the Chamberlain stripe a threat to the growth of Canadian autonomy and nationalism, Bourassa felt that the naval program was little more than a prolongation of Chamberlainism, while Laurier decidedly disagreed. While Bourassa was not, either in his advocacy of Canadianism as opposed to imperialism, or in his championing of the place of the French Canadians in the Canadian confederation, an Anglophobe, his position inevitably attracted the extremists of the French Canadian groups. It brought into his ranks the simplistic approach and the narrow zeal of those who could see in Laurier and his associates nothing more than the agents of the wily Britons who had for so long denied French Canadians their rights.

This opposition among the French Canadians broke the long dominance which Laurier and the Liberals had held over the voters of Quebec. And the opposition to the naval program in that province was bipartisan, for the dissident Liberals of the Bourassa group formed an alliance with the Quebec Conservatives. Both the power and the tactics of the new combination were spectacularly revealed in the Drummond-Arthabaska by-election. In this contest a political unknown defeated the Liberal party candidate largely on the basis of his opposition to the naval program, but also by the device of having men in spurious uniforms going from household to household apparently making a manpower census of the district, thus raising the specter of conscription and scaring a part of the voters into voting against the Liberal candidate.

Lord Grey was sufficiently concerned over the drift of affairs to embark upon a confidential personal intervention. He asked the leaders of the Conservative party in Quebec to meet with him, and pointed out to them

[20] *Le Devoir* (Montreal), Jan. 17, 1910, quoted in Wade, *The French Canadians*, p. 568.

what an opportunity they had for further consolidating the Dominion and amalgamating in closer mutual sympathy and appreciation Canadians of French and British descent. He urged that if the Conservatives would lend their support to the founding of branches of a Canadian Navy League in Quebec, the English-speaking Canadians would be compelled to admit that they had wronged the French Canadians in attributing to them a lukewarmness in their loyalty.

This argument had no effect upon Quebec Conservative leader F. D. Monk. He replied that it would be impossible for him to join in any such movement. The naval policy of the Liberal Government presented the Conservatives with an opportunity to weaken the hold of Laurier upon the affections of the people of Quebec, something which the Conservatives had long sought. He had been in opposition for thirteen years, Monk said, and he was tired of it; to ask him to abstain from any course which might be the means of bringing about the downfall of Laurier and the return of the Conservatives to power was just asking too much. Lord Grey commented that he would be personally humiliated if he were obliged to report to the King that there was any political party in the Dominion so determined to subordinate the interests of the Crown to its own fancied interests, and so animated by such disloyal principles. But Monk simply shrugged his shoulders and said that however shameful it might be in the eyes of the Governor General, this would be the true position to lay before the King.[21]

This somewhat clumsy effort at viceregal intervention did nothing to help the Laurier Government or its program. That program continued under attack from many French Canadians, and from those who saw in its timidity, and in the delays involved in the construction of the vessels planned for, no addition to the naval strength of empire. The Conservative Montreal *Star* lambasted the Canadian naval scheme of the Liberal Government as little more than an "uproarious farce" which would cost the Canadian taxpayer a great deal of money and create a naval force ripe only for destruction, as Admiral Cervera's (sic) at Manila Bay. And the Toronto *Telegram* characterized the Government's plan as one of "scuttle, shirk and skulk."[22] That this sort of thing made difficult the task of deciding what was Canada's proper duty in the defense of the Empire was surely not remarkable. And the distinctions so finely drawn by Laurier were too complex to be understood by all the voters; indeed, his confreres at the 1911 Imperial Conference had considerable difficulty in following his efforts to arrive at a suitable definition of just what

[21] C.O. 42/939, Grey to H. M. George V, Nov. 4, 1910.
[22] *The Canadian Annual Review*, 1910, pp. 176–77.

circumstances would have to prevail before Canada would join whole-heartedly with Britain in any war.[23]

Laurier accepted the fact that when Britain was at war, Canada was also; the legal status of the Dominion allowed no other course. But he also stressed that while Canada might be legally *at* war, she did not necessarily have to be *in* the war. She would be legally bound by virtue of the British declaration of war, but not actively engaged in hostilities. There might, he averred, be wars so remote from Canada and of such a character that Canada would have no interest in them. But Laurier specifically told the Committee of Imperial Defence and the other colonial leaders who met with that body in 1911 that war with Germany did not fall into the latter category. "If war were declared with Germany probably our duty would be to go to war at once, but I can conceive there are many smaller nations who might be at war with Great Britain in which war we should take no part whatever . . . ."[24] The final judgment in such matters as the measure of commitment, Laurier felt, should be left in the hands of the government, Parliament, and people of Canada.

The situation which dominated the headlines was not, however, the possibility of conflict on the borders of Afghanistan, nor the renewal of the struggle in the African veldt, but the naval rivalry with Germany and the threat which it contained to the long-established British naval supremacy in the North Atlantic. Laurier might commit himself to a "probably" in discussing this matter with the C.I.D., although this was being more explicit than he customarily liked to be. But Laurier's political foes in the Conservative ranks naturally zeroed in on this issue, and extracted from the Canadian leader the admission that if the naval supremacy of Britain were seriously challenged, any naval force that Canada might possess, and all the resources Canada could command, would be placed at British disposal. On the other hand, the isolationists and Nationalists in Quebec were convinced that the mere possession of any Canadian naval force would enhance Canada's possibility of becoming involved in any war in which Britain might be engaged. It would, they claimed, enlarge the commitment which Canada had to the defense of empire, implicitly if not explicitly, and they held that such commitment should be limited to the defense of Canadian soil only. Thus Bourassa and his followers would have Canada neutral in all save direct attacks on Canadian soil; Laurier would have Canada neutral in wars remote from Canadian interests but not in a struggle for naval power with Germany. And the bulk of the Conservatives were perhaps less con-

---

[23] See Cab. 5/2/1, Minutes of 112th Meeting of C.I.D., May 29, 1911, pp. 12–17.
[24] *Ibid.*, p. 15.

cerned with such legalistic issues than with the extension of some form of immediate aid to Britain.

The Canadian Naval Service Act, as presented by the Laurier Government, called for the creation of a Department of Naval Service under the older Department of Marine and Fisheries. There was to be a new Deputy Minister in the older department to care for naval matters; the professional head of the new service was naturally to be a naval officer, hopefully one with the rank of Rear Admiral or better. For the discipline of the new force, the Naval Service Act made the King's Regulations and Admiralty Instructions applicable when they did not conflict with Canadian law. Section 23 of the Act said that in time of emergency, the Naval Service of Canada, whether in whole or in part, would be placed at the disposal of His Majesty for service with the Royal Navy.[25]

Leading the Liberal party with a substantial majority in the Commons, Laurier secured the eventual passage of the bill with little difficulty; but the debate was not without its embarrassment. The Prime Minister was caught in the bind that the words he used to hold Liberal dissidents in line, words which reminded them of the benefits which Canada derived from its membership in the British Empire, could be quoted against him by those who felt that the Government's naval program was far too limited, and involved too many delays, to give any effective aid to the empire which Laurier extolled.[26]

Laurier also encountered some difficulties in trying to define the conditions under which the ships of the Canadian force might be brought into action in war. Borden argued for standing instructions which would have them act on conditions identical with those of the Royal Navy.[27] But the Laurier position was that the Canadian ships should not engage in warlike activities, save in cases of pure self-defense, without instructions from the Canadian government. Canada would judge for herself whether it was in her national interest to join in any war in which Britain might be engaged.[28]

The fact that the Laurier program was not identical with the fleet unit being constructed by Australia, that it contained no battleships, and that it was not in line with the first recommendations made by the Admiralty to the 1909 conference, also brought criticism. Borden charged that the Laurier program was not along the lines suggested by the Admiralty, but marked a rejection of Admiralty suggestions.[29]

[25] Tucker, *The Naval Service of Canada*, p. 140.
[26] Canada, *Parliamentary Debates* (Can., P.D.), XCIII, 1749–1750, remarks of R. L. Borden.
[27] *Ibid.*, XCVII, 7466.   [28] *Ibid.*, p. 7472.   [29] *Ibid.*, p. 7531.

During the course of the debate, Borden's position gradually shifted away from his earlier support of the project of a Canadian navy and toward the idea of giving a dreadnought gift to the United Kingdom. In 1909, Borden had said that the "proper line" on which to proceed was for Canada to have a naval force of her own.[30] And in the Address-in-Reply debate of the session of 1909-10, Laurier congratulated Borden on having stood by the idea of a Canadian navy against the murmurings within his own party.[31] Certainly the position of the Conservative leader seemed substantially in accord with that of the Liberals. Borden stated his opposition to "annual contributions" even though he acknowledged their strategic wisdom. He further said that "permanent co-operation in defence, in my opinion, can only be accomplished by the use of our own material, the employment of our own people, the development and utilization of our own skill and resourcefulness and above all by impressing upon the people a sense of responsibility for their share in international affairs."[32] And Earl Grey dispatched to the Colonial Office a clipping from the Ottawa *Citizen* giving a speech of Borden's in which he said that a Canadian unit of the Imperial Navy could be made powerful and effective.[33]

But a note of reservation was also to be heard; perhaps, indeed, it was implicit in the emphasis placed on the possibility of a Canadian unit being made powerful. As the national debate wore along, Borden charged that there was too much that was untried and experimental in the Canadian navy project, and that it promised little effective and immediate aid to Britain.[34] This, increasingly, was the Borden line. In February, during the second reading of the bill, he proposed that Canada appropriate the funds that would allow Britain to build two dreadnoughts;[35] and during some of the later stages of the debate, he said that at all times he had tried to keep the question of aid to Britain in the immediate crisis, and that of a permanent Canadian contribution to imperial defense, absolutely distinct. Ever since the debate on the resolution of March 29, he had favored granting a sum of money to the Admiralty, to be disposed of as the latter pleased.[36]

Although the Laurier program got through the Parliament with ease, with its passage and the purchase of two cruisers, the *Niobe* and the *Rainbow*, from the Royal Navy, the whole enterprise of establishing a Canadian navy fell under the baleful spell of mounting political bitter-

[30] *Ibid.*, XC, 3517.
[31] *Ibid.*, XCIII, 44.
[32] *Ibid.*, pp. 1746–47.
[33] C.O. 42/931, Grey to Colonial Office, Nov. 8, 1909.
[34] Can., P.D., XCIII, 1749.
[35] *Ibid.*, XCIV, 2990–91.
[36] *Ibid.*, XCVII, 7528–29.

ness. The unnatural Conservative-Nationalist alliance in Quebec and its success in the Drummond-Arthabaska by-election, stunned the government, and little real satisfaction was to be found in Laurier's comment that some defeats were more creditable than victories. The mounting opposition of the Conservatives, and the lack of an emotional appeal in the program itself, all tended to diminish the prospects of the new service and to discourage enlistments, even in the maritime regions. Canadians were apparently more willing to enlist in the United States Navy than to trust their future to the uncertain fate of the embryonic Canadian navy.[37] The two cruisers drew the bulk of their officers and men from the Royal Navy. Certainly the whole project seemed to have become becalmed.

This was a situation from which the Conservatives drew some embarrassment as well as satisfaction. They were delighted with the discomfiture of their political enemies, and gratified over the apparent weakening of Laurier's influence over the voters of Quebec. But there was also a sense that many of those attacking the Liberal Government were doing it from the wrong motives, and were, moreover, most dubious characters for Conservatives to associate with.

Nevertheless the Conservatives got their chance to deal with the naval problem, for the election of 1911 ended the long period of Liberal Government and put Laurier out of office for the first time since 1896. The main issue of the contest was the proposed reciprocity treaty with the United States; Borden and the other Conservative leaders made comparatively little reference to naval matters. This was chiefly due to the fact that the Conservatives had as yet no program of their own to present to the voters; they also desired to garner the votes of those opposed to all naval action whatsoever, and to maintain the support of that alliance which had been so successful in the Drummond-Arthabaska by-election of the preceding year. Since the Liberals had little chance to point with pride, and the Conservatives the most to gain by being mute on the whole issue, little was said.

The silence of the election campaign had to be supplanted by the formulation of policy once Borden and his associates had taken office. But it was not an easy task. The alliance with the Quebec Nationalists, and the inclusion of their leader, F. D. Monk, and two likeminded gentlemen in the Cabinet, only emphasized the division within the ranks of Borden's supporters. But most of the support for the Conservatives came from the advocates of swift action to aid Britain in the battleship emergency.

[37] Approximately 1,300 Canadians enlisted in the United States Navy from 1908 to 1912. *Ibid.*, CIX, 5433.

As for Borden himself, he had managed to work both sides of the street with considerable success. But a clear indication of the thinking of many of his followers was given in a series of editorials in the Montreal *Daily Star*. These were written by its proprietor, Sir Hugh Graham, and the gist of his proposals was that Canada should build two or three dreadnoughts, or "naval units," or whatever the Admiralty might desire. These ships would be constructed in British yards, under the eye of the Admiralty, and would bear the names of Canadian provinces. They would be an integral part of the Royal Navy. Any such program, urged the *Star*, would accomplish several desirable ends. It would rid Canada of a navy which she did not need, and it would provide effective help to Britain because it would fit in with the well-considered Admiralty policy of the concentration of forces. Graham produced these ideas after consultation with Borden and other ministers, and they seemed to represent, as the new Governor General of Canada, the Duke of Connaught, suggested, a "ballon d'essai" of the new government.[38]

But such editorials did not constitute a government program. The only item that was clear was the condemnation of the Laurier naval policy. And as it became clear that the Dominion government had no real program, an opportunity for the Admiralty to influence developments emerged. As A. B. Keith of the Colonial Office commented, the Admiralty needed to make up their minds definitely on the lines of policy they wished to adopt. In the circumstances, he believed, the Admiralty were free to reach their decisions, "having regard only to strategic considerations and no longer to considerations of what will best please Canada."[39]

Others in the official hierarchy of the Colonial Office were not so sure that Borden's position left the Admiralty free to formulate a policy on strategy alone. Henry C. M. Lambert, the Principal Clerk of the Colonial Office and a man of substantial experience, felt that Borden's statements about the need for the dominions to know where they stood within the Empire, and to have a greater voice in its councils, meant that discussion of naval matters would take second place to larger issues in which Canada would claim a part in formulating the foreign policy of the Empire. And to Hartmann Just, the Assistant Undersecretary, Borden seemed to be seeking pressure from Britain: expressions of British anxiety for dominion co-operation, and reassurances as to the value Britain attached to such co-operation. Just felt that while the Government of the United Kingdom could not properly propose any policy, the Admiralty would certainly

[38] C.O. 42/939, Duke of Connaught to C.O., Oct. 24, 1911.
[39] Keith's comments were appended to C.O. 42/958, Duke of Connaught to C.O., March 20, 1912.

be able to make suitable proposals when invited to advise. He did think, however, that Borden would have a difficult task, both in justifying the abandonment of the Laurier policies and in substituting a contributory arrangement. This would be especially hard to justify in Quebec, where Bourassa's influence was strong.[40]

While British officialdom speculated on Borden's intentions, the latter seemed far from impatient to bring the issues involved to a resolution. The backbone of much of the Conservative and some of the non-partisan opposition to the project of a Canadian naval force was that it would be no support to Britain in its current difficulties. Yet for all of this Conservative emphasis on emergency, the new government was in no hurry to act. There was no mention of the naval problem in the Speech from the Throne in the middle of November.[41] And while the Minister of Marine and Naval Affairs of the Borden Government announced the intention of the Cabinet to seek the repeal of the Naval Service Act, some aspects of the new service were maintained by the appropriation of a million and a half dollars.[42]

More than three years after the passage of the Foster resolution, and nine months after his electoral victory, Borden sailed for London, accompanied by a gaggle of ministers, to confer with the Admiralty and other officialdom. He left Canada still claiming to have an open mind on the naval problem, and he further remarked that he had not discussed the issue with his Cabinet colleagues,[43] surely an extraordinary statement if the assertions of an emergency, on which the Conservatives based their case, were sincerely made. Nevertheless, at the time of his departure it was abundantly clear that the Laurier program, if not dead, was at least moribund.

The Admiralty with which Borden went to consult had experienced a change in leadership since the Imperial Conference of 1911. Reginald McKenna, by no means welcoming the shift, had been transferred to the Home Office, and Winston Churchill had been named First Lord in his stead. This exchange of posts stemmed from several factors, but most substantial were the disclosure at the meeting of the Committee of Imperial Defence of August 23, 1911, of the almost total lack of co-ordination between the war plans of the military and naval commands of the nation, and the insistence of Haldane that the Admiralty must have a naval war staff comparable to the General Staff at the War Office.[44]

[40] *Ibid.*, All minutes appended to Connaught to C.O.
[41] Can., P.D., CIII, 8–9.   [42] *Ibid.*, CV, 4242.
[43] Henry Borden (ed.), *Sir Robert Laird Borden: His Memoirs* (2 vols.; Toronto, 1389), I, 355.
[44] Marder, *From Dreadnought to Scapa Flow*, pp. 239–51.

Among the various concerns of the new First Lord, the problems of the dominion governments, and the role they might play in the naval defense of the Empire, did not bulk large. Despite his experiences in various areas of the imperial domain and his term at the Colonial Office as Undersecretary, Churchill had never demonstrated much interest in problems of imperial relations. In the Colonial Office he had been scornful of the various naval ideas which had come from Deakin, and his famous "banged, bolted, and barred" dismissal of the possibility of imperial preference had earned him the contempt of that perceptive student of empire, Richard Jebb.[45]

The principal public statement of the First Lord had been one of apparent approval of the program of dominion naval construction as sketched by the 1909 conference. In mid-May of 1912, Churchill had addressed the Shipwright's Guild in London, and had spoken in approving terms of dominion naval development:

> If the main developments of the last ten years have been the concentration of the British Fleet in decisive theatres, it seems to me . . . not unlikely that the main naval developments of the next ten years will be the growth of the effective naval forces in the great Dominions overseas. Then I think we shall be able to make what I think will be found to be the true division of labour between the Mother country and her daughter States—that we shall maintain a sea supremacy against all comers at the decisive point and that they should guard and control all the rest of the British Empire.[46]

But any such polycentric conception of the naval defense of the Empire had apparently been dispelled from Churchill's mind by the time of Borden's arrival from Canada. By that time, the problems holding the mind of the First Lord in their grip were the changed situation in the North Sea arising from the adoption of the 1912 Naval Law in Germany, and the weakening position of Britain in the Mediterranean. The need for yet further concentration of British naval power in northern waters was emphasized by the new German naval law, whose effect was to raise the proportion of German ships and crews prepared for instant action, and ready to strike at the selected moment of the attacker as opposed to the average moment of the defense. And the Italian and Austro-Hungarian programs of battleship construction in the Mediterranean caused alarm in some British circles. Though a realistic view of the power alignments of Europe at the time suggested strongly that these two members of the Triple Alliance were arming more against each other than against the Entente powers, the effect nevertheless was to place in

[45] Richard Jebb, *The Imperial Conference* (London, 1911), I, ch. 13.
[46] *The Times* (London), May 16, 1912.

jeopardy the British and French position in the inland sea. That they might confront the Entente powers with a conjunction of battleship power of formidable dimension was not a possibility which could be ignored.

The whole movement of events served to increase Britain's dependence on France for the security of her communications through the Mediterranean. But this was a dependence which many leaders in Britain refused to accept. The more pacific group of the Liberal party opposed it as adding to the British commitments to French policy and power on the Continent. And those of sturdier nationalist strain felt that such dependence upon another state for the support of Britain's vital interest was a matter of national humiliation.[47] Lord Esher, for example, said that calling in the foreigner to help was too suggestive of Rome in decline.[48] And Sir Arthur Nicolson lamented of the Mediterranean to Austen Chamberlain: "We have abandoned it! And Italy and Austria are going on building Dreadnoughts and we haven't an alliance. I think it very dangerous . . . . It isn't safe! It would only be safe if we had a firm alliance. We have abandoned the Pacific, we have abandoned the Far East, we have abandoned the Mediterranean. I don't call it safe."[49]

The dilemmas arising from the need to spread British naval power so thinly between the North Sea and the Mediterranean could most effectively be met by the addition of yet more ships to the battle squadrons. But this would also provoke an outcry because of the larger costs and the greater tightening of the naval race. Churchill had an opportunity to become even better acquainted with the Mediterranean problem when he and other leaders met in Malta for an appraisal of these matters. And following these consultations, on July 4, Churchill pleaded with the C.I.D. for the maintenance of two or three battle cruisers there. Such vessels, in conjunction with the French fleet, would assure a safe margin of strength over the powers of the Triple Alliance. In addition, the forces maintained at Gibraltar, the fourth Battle Squadron, could on occasion be sent into the Mediterranean. There was, said Churchill, no need to make public the fact that this force was maintained primarily for use in home waters.[50]

This concern for the measure of British power in the Mediterranean preceded by one week the discussions with Borden and his colleagues. The First Lord had a chance to inform them of the matters troubling his

---

[47] Marder, *From Dreadnought to Scapa Flow*, pp. 287–98.

[48] *Ibid.*, p. 290.

[49] Austen Chamberlain, *Politics from Inside* (London, 1936), p. 485. The weakened position of Britain in the Mediterranean was nothing new, however; it dated from the creation of the Franco-Russian alliance. G. W. Monger, *The End of Isolation* (London, 1963), pp. 1–3.

[50] Marder, *From Dreadnought to Scapa Flow*, pp. 293–95.

mind at the 118th meeting of the C.I.D. on July 11, 1912. In a masterly survey of the naval problems confronting the Admiralty given to the C.I.D. with Borden and the other Canadians present, Churchill said that despite the enormous sacrifices which had been made in recent years by British taxpayers, and the likelihood that yet more would be required within the next few years:

> It comes to this, that really we ought to lay down now three more ships over and above the four we are building. . . . But it is a difficult thing for us to lay down three new ships now. Financially it is inconvenient, but that can be got over. Beyond that, it is a difficult thing for us to do, because here are our numbers—four, five, four, four, four, which we have collated and which we have made correspond to the German construction. If we come forward now all of a sudden and add three new ships, that may have the effect of stimulating the naval competition, and they would ask us what new factor had occurred which justified or which required this increase of building on our part. If we could say that the new factor was that Canada had decided to take part in the defence of the British Empire, that would be an answer which would involve no invidious comparisons, and which would absolve us from going into detailed calculations as to the number of Austrian or German vessels available at any particular moment. It would be an answer absolutely inoffensive to any of the Great Powers of Europe, and no answer could possibly contribute more effectively to the prestige and security of the British Empire. The need, I say, is a serious one, and it is an immediate need. I hope during the visit of the Canadian Ministers to this country we shall have long consultations upon the details of a permanent naval policy, but it has not been to a permanent naval policy that I have directed the remarks which I have offered to the Committee this morning.[51]

Here was a naval program for Borden, presented by one of the master expositors of the age, and with the ingenuous angle that all this could be done without adding to the naval competition of Europe. The mark of the salesman is clearly apparent in the suggestion that the Germans would not notice three additional battleships flying the White Ensign because they were paid for by the Canadian rather than the British taxpayer.

Several meetings between Churchill and Borden followed the meeting of the C.I.D. Borden wrote the Governor General that a great deal of discussion had gone on about the matter of Canadian representation in the higher councils of imperial defense and foreign policy. "It may be," he reported, "one of our Ministers without portfolio will become a member of the Imperial Defence Committee and will live in London part of the year in close touch with the Foreign Office and with the Colonial

[51] Cab. 2/2/3, 118th Meeting of the C.I.D., pp. 13–14.

Secretary." He further stated that his government had made a sharp distinction between temporary assistance for the existing emergency, and a permanent policy. In the formulation of the former program, he had been promised an "unanswerable case" from the Admiralty for aid from Canada.[52]

The "unanswerable case" which the Admiralty were preparing for Borden to equip him for debate on his return to Ottawa eventually took the form of two memoranda, one for the instruction of the Canadian Cabinet, and the other for public consumption. Churchill sent the draft of the secret statement to Borden toward the close of August, with the request that it be returned. He wished to submit it to Asquith and Sir Edward Grey, and to the Board of Admiralty, so that it might be in the highest degree authoritative. He further told Borden that if he could be of any use in coming to Canada, "you have only to send for me and, if it rests with me, I'll come at once."[53]

Borden received from the Admiralty not only the "unanswerable case" which he was seeking, but also a strong intimation that the Admiralty really had little desire to co-operate with Canada should it pursue a course leading to the creation of a Canadian navy. An undated memorandum in the Borden "Naval Notes" said that the Admiralty would try to assist in any practicable naval program which might commend itself to Canada, but that the prospect of the Admiralty being able to co-operate in manning any units was much dimmer in 1912 than it had been in 1909. Construction of any Canadian naval units would be a much greater matter than the estimates of 1909 had suggested. Indeed, the whole idea of a Canadian naval force as projected earlier would "lock up a large number of very efficient officers and men which would have to be lent by the Admiralty for a policy and strategy for which it would be practically impossible to obtain expert support . . . ." The establishment of two such fleet units, one for the Atlantic and the second for the Pacific, the memorandum went on, would place a strain on the resources of the Admiralty which that body could not undertake to meet.[54]

The Borden naval program, conceived by emergency out of imperial loyalty, with Winston Churchill acting as midwife, was presented to the Canadian Parliament on December 5, 1912. The floor and gallery of the House were crowded, with the Duchess of Connaught and Princess Patricia gracing the occasion. The Government's program called for the appropriation of $35,000,000, to be given to the British government for the construction of three battleships. And the Prime Minister's speech was

[52] P.A.C., Borden MSS, Borden to Duke of Connaught, July 30, 1912, O'C 656, 67292–67293.
[53] P.A.C., Borden MSS, Churchill to Borden, Aug. 26, 1912, O'C 656, 67366.
[54] P.A.C., Borden MSS, "Naval Notes," pp. 460–62.

accompanied by the introduction into the record of the public memorandum which had been prepared for the Canadian leader.[55]

The subsequent debate dragged along for many wearying weeks and hauled out arguments which by now had become completely threadbare from excessive use. Little emerged that was novel, either in matters of strategy, imperial relations, or the handling of Canada's defenses.

To the Borden resolution calling for the appropriation of funds for the battleships, Laurier opposed his own amendment. This condemned the Borden program as neither expressing the aspirations of the Canadian people, nor representing any assumption by Canada of her fair share of the responsibility for the defense of the Empire. It called for the construction of two fleet units of unspecified strength, one for the Atlantic and one for the Pacific. (It was apparently the introduction of this resolution which led to the Admiralty's statement of their inability to assist effectively in manning such units.) In commenting upon the public memorandum which Borden presented to the House, Laurier said that whenever it was necessary for Britain to withdraw naval forces from distant seas, such forces should be replaced by ships built, equipped, maintained, and manned by the dominions.[56]

Laurier's espousal of fleet units as a suitable Canadian contribution was not without irony, for it represented a belated conversion to the program which his government had modified to the point of rejection in 1909. That modification had opened the way to a rather piecemeal and dispirited naval development under the Laurier Government, certainly the source of much of the dissatisfaction which built up support for the Borden program.

After the statements of the government and Opposition leaders, the tedious debate dragged on. It became increasingly apparent that the Liberals were resorting to stonewalling tactics, filling up the pages of Hansard with lengthy speeches all designed to bring the government to the abandonment of its naval program. Anxious to give no co-operation to the Liberals' obstructionist tactics, Cabinet members usually sat in tight-lipped silence as the Opposition droned on. But eventually the government moved to stem the flow of words, and brought the legislature back to legislation by the imposition of closure for the first time in the Dominion Parliament's history.[57] Armed with this control over debate, the Government finally, in mid-May of 1913, obtained passage of its resolution through the lower House.[58] Conservative elation over this

[55] Can., P.D., CVII, 679–84.
[56] Ibid., p. 1028.
[57] W. F. Dawson, *Procedure in the Canadian House of Commons* (Toronto, 1962), pp. 121–23.
[58] Can., P.D., CX 10061–10062.

victory was short-lived, however, for the Borden program was defeated
by the Canadian Senate, most of whose members were Laurier appointees.
To paraphrase Stephen Leacock, the Senate came out of the cupboard like
a bad old witch and laid a curse on all the pretty gifts of imperial unity
sponsored by the Conservatives.

In addition to the adoption of closure, the Commons debate—if it
can truly be called that with one side of the House silent most of the time—
had been notable for the tone of asperity with which some of the Liberal
members discussed the activity of the First Lord of the Admiralty.
Churchill's manifest eagerness for the proposed Canadian dreadnoughts
naturally provoked charges that he was intervening in Canadian affairs.
A member of the former Liberal Government, H. R. Emmerson, charged
that Churchill had offered "gratuitous political advice" to Canadians.
Enlarging on this theme, he said that when Churchill offered such advice
to the people of Canada on their capacity, aspirations, and what he seemed
to regard as their limitations, "I can say it is the veriest insult to the people
of Canada . . . ."[59] One of his colleagues "defended" the First Lord,
saying that Churchill was only reflecting the requests made of him by the
Canadian Conservatives and was therefore not really to be blamed.[60]

Despite the collaboration between Churchill and the Conservative
Government, the prospect of the First Lord matching his offer with his
deeds and coming to Canada in support of the dreadnought program
aroused substantial Conservative fears. George Perley, "the right hand
man of the Prime Minister," and Acting Prime Minister during Borden's
occasional absences from the country, wrote in some alarm over newspapers reports in August, 1912, that Churchill might pay a visit to the
Dominion after crossing the Atlantic on a dreadnought. Perley said that
the idea had not found much favor; it smacked too much of pressure on
Canada. The Premier of Ontario, Sir James Whitney, expressed similar
alarm. He was afraid that Churchill might mount a pedestal and try to
instruct Canadians in their duties.[61]

In spite of Churchill's efforts to establish clearly that his views were
solicited by the Canadian Prime Minister rather than offered volun-
tarily,[62] there was considerable resentment, no doubt much of it politically inspired, over his comments about the practicality of building warships in Canada. Reflecting in a letter to Borden upon the costs and the
special skills and facilities that would be needed, he had concluded that
"it would be wholly unwise for Canada to attempt to undertake the

[59] *Ibid.*, CIX, 5336.
[60] *Ibid.*, p. 5223.
[61] P.A.C., Borden MSS, O'C 656, Perley to Borden, Aug. 9, 1912; Whitney to
Borden, Aug. 15, 1912.
[62] C.O. 42/976, Churchill to Borden, draft telegram, March 5, 1913.

building of battleships at the present moment." And in a second letter he had estimated that the cost of a fleet unit of the sort proposed by the Admiralty in 1909, and currently being constructed by Australia, would cost a great deal more than the estimates given to the conference in 1909. In this same letter he also expressed his doubts about the ability of the Admiralty to assist in manning of the craft of any such unit.[63]

The pressures upon the First Lord make much of this understandable. The lack of assurance of the Canadian contribution certainly complicated the Admiralty's plans in the years just prior to the outbreak of war.[64] But the tone of these letters to Borden nevertheless aroused much resentment, and gave opportunity to the opponents of the dreadnought contribution to indulge in much patriotic hyperbole in which the changes were rung upon the industrial capacity of the Dominion and the skill of its workers. As for the reluctance of the Admiralty to aid in the manning of fleet units, if built, and the estimates of the greater costs of such units, the Liberals seized upon these as flagrant in their intent to direct Canadian affairs. Churchill seemed to many the personification of the revival of the old colonial system. The Liberal *Free Press* of Ottawa, for example, reacted in staunch manner: "If Winston Churchill's special pleading does not have the effect of awakening Canadians to the tremendous assault which the Borden Naval policy is making upon Canada's most cherished possessions—freedom, liberty, absolute autonomy within the Empire—then we do not know our Canada."[65]

The Conservative press commented in an equally partisan tone. The Toronto *News* regarded the Liberal opposition as humiliating to Canada. "It is to the discredit of Canadians that they lag behind the people of New Zealand and Australia in co-operation with the Mother Country in defence of the common Empire."[66] As long as the debate dragged on, according to this view, Canada stood indicted before the world as willing to sponge her defense out of the taxpayers of Great Britain.

Perhaps the most notable feature of the entire debate as it moved drearily on through the winter and spring of 1913, was the testimony which it afforded of the extent to which Germany had supplanted the United States as the enemy in view. Truly Canadian defense planning, such as it was, had moved into a new era when the "manifest destiny" of the colossus to the south was no longer uppermost in the minds of Canadians.

[63] P.A.C., Borden MSS, O'C 658, Churchill to Borden, Jan. 23, 24, 1913.
[64] Marder, *From Dreadnought to Scapa Flow*, p. 298.
[65] *The Free Press* (Ottawa), March 11, 1913, quoted in *Canadian Annual Review*, 1913, p. 135.
[66] *The News* (Toronto), March 6, 1913.

Very striking also was the failure of the efforts made by the First Lord to secure the passage of the Borden naval program. But as a matter of fact, despite the large role which he had played, Churchill revealed to at least one prominent Canadian a degree of disquiet over the course he was following. On January 18, 1913, when the hopes of the Conservatives were still high, and before the final outcome of the debate had become apparent, the First Lord had a long conversation with Laurier's old political associate, W. S. Fielding. Fielding reported on the discussion to his former chief: "Mr. Winston Churchill sent for me yesterday and I had a long interview with him, necessarily of the most confidential character. Of course I understood that I was free to let you know all about it. But even to your closest friends do not make use of his name in any way that could possibly be known. He is much troubled about the naval question in Canada. He begins to see he made a grave mistake in overlooking the fact that the Liberal party of Canada had a declared naval policy which Mr. Borden assails."[67] Fielding went on to say that Churchill was hoping for some compromise in Canada. But "he now sees that the wrong course has been taken."[68]

Surely Churchill's vision must have been remarkably concentrated on the problems of the North Sea and the Mediterranean for him to have "overlooked" what had been decided and what had been done by the Liberal party in Canada. But part of the seeming intransigence of Laurier, and because of him, the Liberals as a whole, may perhaps be explained by the knowledge that the First Lord, upon whom the Prime Minister was relying so heavily for guidance in naval matters, was indirectly sustaining the Opposition in their resistance to the government. There is this to be said for Churchill's intervention in Canadian naval matters, if intervention it was: it was certainly bipartisan!

[67] P.A.C., Laurier MSS, Vol. 694, Fielding to Laurier, Jan. 19, 1913.
[68] *Ibid.*

CHAPTER XII

AUSTRALASIAN CONCERNS AND RECRIMINATIONS; EPILOGUE

While the Borden naval program had gone down in political defeat, and other troubles arose in carrying out the naval program accepted at the 1909 conference, the years both before and after 1909 saw an appreciable growth of co-operation among the military forces of the Empire.

This new co-operation was a far cry from the old idea of colonial military forces guaranteed for imperial service. A variety of factors, not the least of which was dominion nationalism, had barred the adoption of any such scheme. This nationalism had certainly not abated since the time when such plans were considered. It still placed substantial limitations on any contemplated military commitments; nothing like a comprehensive plan for the utilization of the military resources of the Empire ever emerged. But for all the nationalism, and for all the associated suspicions of European involvement and British imperialism which lingered in dominion minds, political leaders of the various dominions more and more came to accept the necessity of paying greater attention to defense organization and planning.

In all of this there was the melancholy fact of new societies, still retaining some of the utopianism of their early years, becoming involved in the "blood drenched glory of the power state." But such order and security as these developing societies had known had come from the power of the Empire, and that they should wish to support that power and prolong that security seemed but common sense to most. Few cried out against the implications of the actions and decisions which brought the peoples of the various dominions closer to the "vortex of militarism" which Laurier had discerned and feared.

Among the men holding political power in Great Britain few were aware of the "dark secret tide" of events and decisions which later carried hundreds of thousands of men from Britain and the dominions to their deaths in France and Flanders. Few men had an inkling, either in Britain or the dominions, of the degree to which British military planning was becoming subordinated to French needs and concepts of strategy through the staff conversations, and of the lack of any British war plans with which to counter the French conceptions.[1]

But while there may have been only a few who knew of Britain's increasing commitments, hardly any observer could have escaped knowledge of the degree to which military and naval considerations pre-occupied the minds of the British government. "It is a remarkable historical irony that the Liberal Administration, despite the deep veins of Radicalism and pacificism that ran through the party, the absolute aversion to militarism in all forms that possessed so many of its members, should have been the one to have prepared for war more logically and more thoroughly than any other at any time."[2]

That the dominions, who largely took their political lead from Britain, should have shared such preoccupations was surely natural. Diplomats might surmount various political crises in northern Africa or the Balkans, and seem to dispose of contentious issues like the Berlin-to-Baghdad railway, but the prevailing atmosphere of competitive militarism still remained. The air was heavy with thunderclouds discernible even in the western hemisphere and in the remote southern Pacific. Under such pressures, defense considerations mounted in importance both in domestic policy and in imperial collaboration.

In the southern hemisphere, both Australia and New Zealand adopted a system of compulsory military training for their young men. Both communities were affected by two major considerations: their loyalty to Britain, and their fear of Japan. Perhaps there was more emphasis on the latter in Australia, and more on the former in New Zealand, but both were operative factors. In both communities the systems of training adopted were essentially more pre-military than truly military in character, but from them came at least some knowledge of the rudiments of military discipline and rifle fire. Adoption of the measures for compulsory training came without any violent political controversy. Most Australians and New Zealanders would have agreed with the words of Senator George Pearce of Australia that in a democracy having no standing army and no military class, there was no alternative to the compulsory training of every citizen for military service.[3]

[1] John Terraine, *Ordeal of Victory* (Philadelphia, 1963), pp. 61–62; John Terraine, "Armistice: Nov. 11th, 1918," *History Today*, Vol. VIII (Nov., 1958).
[2] Terraine, *Ordeal of Victory*, p. 55.   [3] C.P.D., LIII, 5395–96.

Such training did not mean, however, that the manpower of the southern dominions was pledged to anything other than the defense of their homeland. Compulsion did not extend to overseas service. William "Billy" Hughes, the leading Australian advocate of compulsory military training, said that while "it is right to compel a man to fit himself to defend his country, it is not proper to compel him to fight beyond it."[4]

Canada, of course, did not adopt the compulsory training system. But there the existing militia system was increasingly being licked into shape. The political storms of the Hutton and Dundonald era were a thing of the past, and the new system of command through the Militia Council worked at least more effectively than that which it replaced. The Royal Military College continued to turn out trained junior officers, and a number of British officers and N.C.O.'s accepted service with the permanent Canadian forces. All of these were steps in the direction of an effective military organization rather than its realization; there remained much to be done. But General Percy Lake, who had done so much to help restore amicable relations between the Canadian military and their political superiors, asserted in 1909 that Canada could put and maintain 60,000 men in the field.[5] Perhaps there was a pardonable degree of exaggeration in this, but the Canadian military establishment showed increasing signs of professional competence.

Also under the pressures of the time, steps were being taken to improve the collaboration between the military systems of the United Kingdom and the leading dominions. In this, the Committee of Imperial Defence took a leading role, tending to supplant the Imperial Conference as the forum in which the major imperial problems were discussed. The preoccupations of foreign policy and defense could be better presented to the select group invited to attend the meetings of the C.I.D., than to the old conference type of meeting. Thus the committee became, in the words of one student, "the key forum of imperial consultation upon those policies which determined the external security of the Empire."[6]

Not all observers of the imperial relationship were happy over this trend toward discussion of the major current problems in the secrecy of the C.I.D., for there was a lively interest in defense problems in the various dominion parliaments. But dominion parliamentarians were not, after all, the only ones uninformed of decisions which would mold the pattern of their lives in the years immediately at hand.

One prescient commentator on imperial matters regarded the whole trend of elevating the C.I.D. to the derogation of the Imperial Confer-

---

[4] *Ibid.*, LII, 4473.

[5] C.O. 42/929, Lake to Colonel Aston, Oct. 20, 1908, enclosed with Grey to C.O., Jan. 15, 1909.

[6] Johnson, *Defence by Committee*, p. 113.

ence as dangerous. To Richard Jebb, convinced advocate of dominion autonomy, the whole C.I.D. was unconstitutional, and was created largely to safeguard British ascendancy within the Empire.[7]

But Jebb's fears, even though conveyed to the world through the columns of the *Times*,[8] found little echo in the dominions, perhaps an indication of the waning colonial sensitivity to British "imperialistic" leadership. George Pearce, one of the most effective of the pre-war Australian ministers of defense, and a prominent member of the Labor party of the Commonwealth, felt that one should not worry too greatly about the origin or constitution of any agency through which imperial co-operation was achieved. No doubt the Imperial Conference was more consistent with democratic government than the C.I.D. But from a practical viewpoint, greater results were achieved by the sittings of the C.I.D. That had been his experience during the 1911 conference, when he had felt that the opportunities for consultations with the naval and military advisors in the C.I.D. meetings made that body more useful than the conference itself.[9]

But the occasions for such consultations of dominion representatives with the C.I.D. were relatively rare. For the C.I.D. was, of course, an agency of the government of the United Kingdom, and there were ample duties connected with the defense tasks of the imperial government to occupy all of its energies. Despite frequent suggestions and some discussion of the possibility of having permanent dominion representation on the C.I.D., nothing was done until 1914. In that year, the Canadian government appointed Sir George Perley as a permanent representative, though the appointment had not become fully operative before the outbreak of the war in 1914.[10] But Australia took no such action. Prime Minister Fisher was reluctant to allow the High Commissioner for the Commonwealth government in London the authority to speak for that government in such matters. Only a "live member" of the Ministry, he felt, should express the Australian government's views.[11] Nor did the short-lived Cook Government, which succeeded the Fisher Government, reverse this decision.

This failure to turn the C.I.D. into a truly imperial agency should not, however, obscure the fact of the growth of collaboration among the

---

[7] Institute of Commonwealth Studies, Jebb Papers, Jebb to Geoffrey Robinson, Sept. 27, 1912.

[8] *The Times* (London), Oct. 23, 1912.

[9] Australian National War Museum, Canberra, Pearce MSS, Pearce to R. M. Collins, Dec. 3, 1912. Collins was the representative of the Australian Defence Department in London.

[10] Johnson, *Defence by Committee*, p. 124.

[11] Cab. 5/3/1, Minutes of 112th meeting of C.I.D., May 30, 1911; *The Times* (London), Sept. 20, 1912.

military forces of the Empire. The effective starting date of this collaboration was the Imperial Conference of 1907, with the Liberal Government of Henry Campbell-Bannerman reflecting the old Liberal traditions of voluntarism and respect for colonial self-government.

The recognition that there was no effective basis for military collaboration other than trust in the imperial loyalty of the people of the various dominions pervaded the proposals made by the Army Council to the Imperial Conference of 1907. The principal submission of the council, "Strategical Conditions of the Empire," acknowledged at the outset the difficulties which barred self-governing colonies from guaranteeing to furnish Britain with any contingents in time of war; hence, reliance on the loyalty of the dominions was the only course possible. The council saw a strong possibility that the colonial governments would take an increasing role in future wars in which the welfare of the Empire was at stake. Unfortunately, the South African war experience had included not only indications of imperial loyalty, but also evidences that military training was somewhat scorned by colonials. Yet there was greater need than ever for training, and for greater compliance of the war organization and military forces of the Empire with the standards and forms of the United Kingdom. There was need for uniformity in organization, nomenclature, and small arms among the military forces of the Empire overseas.

This shift from the seeking of binding commitments from dominion governments to the relatively modest proposals for collaboration, did not secure universal approval. Sir George Clarke, for instance, favored the presentation to the coming conference of a resolution which would refer to the "obligation" of the self-governing states of the Empire to afford such military assistance as their circumstances permit and their governments may decide. But Secretary of State for War Haldane felt that only one resolution dealing with military co-operation should be presented to the conference, and that priority should be given to the formation of a General Staff for the Empire.[12]

There was general acceptance of the War Office's proposals by the colonial delegates to the 1907 conference. Possibly seeking to restore a measure of colonial confidence in Britain's military leadership, shaken by the events of the Boer War, Haldane outlined the reforms which he and his associates had carried out in Britain's armed forces. He pointed out that Britain's military structure divided into two parts: part existed for the defense of Britain alone, with no obligation to go overseas, and part was for overseas service for the defense of the Empire as a whole.[13]

[12] Cab. 17/77, "Strategical Conditions of the Empire," March 14, 1907; G. C. Ellison to Clarke, April 19, 1907.
[13] Parl. Pap., 1907, Vol. LV, Cd. 3523, p. 95.

Haldane sought the acceptance of a "common conception" behind Britain's new Territorial Army and the various dominion militia forces. It would be helpful, he suggested, to have staff officers of the various forces trained in a common school, and educated in military science according to common principles. The civil and military authorities should work in concert against the time of the possible outbreak of war.

Sir Frederick Borden of Canada accepted the principle of uniformity for the organization of the forces and the education of staff officers. He also agreed to the exchange of officers between Britain and Canada, and with other forces of the Empire. And Deakin welcomed the prospects of closer association among the military forces of the Empire offered through exchange of officers, and of collaboration with a general staff for the Empire, though there had been some criticism in Australia of too slavish imitation of European examples in the formation of military forces.

Amid the general chorus of approval and acceptance of Haldane's suggestions, Dr. Thomas Smartt of Cape Colony alone sounded something like the older call for closer military connections through guaranteed forces. He suggested the creation of special forces in each of the colonies. These were to be raised and maintained for the defense of the Empire, and would thus provide the nucleus of a really imperial army. The members of this force would accept the obligation of overseas and imperial service with their enlistment.[14]

Haldane joined in the general rejection of any such scheme. It would entail, he urged, far too many difficulties. One problem which such a force would create was the question of control and command. To whom would it be responsible?[15] Sir Frederick Borden returned to the position which he said he had held in the 1902 conference in regard to similar proposals then. Any such force would constitute an elite corps whose existence would damage the basic militia force. It was far better, he felt, to have an effective militia force for home defense, and rely on the voluntary principle when imperial issues were at stake. Even Sir Joseph Ward, the most ardent of imperialist voices in the councils of empire, dissented from Smartt's suggestion, and stuck staunchly by the voluntary principle.[16]

With the gentle yielding to Australian pressure, indicated in Lord Tweedmouth's statement that other than purely strategical considerations were involved in the organization of the naval defense of the Empire, and the clear lead for military co-operation based on a full acceptance of dominion self-government and imperial loyalty, the conference of 1907 marked a clear advance in the development of defense collaboration. As one student has indicated: "The restriction of this programme [of the

---

[14] *Ibid.*, pp. 112–14.   [15] *Ibid.*, p. 114.   [16] *Ibid.*, pp. 114–15.

imperial government] to guidance and co-ordination, the fact that
Britain did not ask for forces from the Dominions . . . and that she did
not claim control in any respect, commended the design to their different
Governments; and they at once accepted it, and the recommendation,
which it contained, for a General Staff to advise them all."[17]

The conference members had, as indicated, given their approval to
the idea of a General Staff, selected from the forces of the Empire as a
whole. The duties of this group were "to undertake the preparation of
schemes of defence on a common principle, and (without in the least
interfering in questions connected with command and administration)
at the request of the respective governments, to advise as to the training,
education, and war organization of the forces of the Crown in every part
of the Empire."[18]

The manner in which this was to be done was outlined by General
Sir W. G. Nicholson, Chief of the British General Staff, in a paper dispatched to the self-governing dominions in January, 1909. Among the
assumptions of this paper, "The Imperial General Staff," was that there
would be no adequate military planning which did not contemplate
offensive action. And General Nicholson felt that the actions taken at the
Imperial Conference clearly indicated acceptance of the possible need for
the concentration of all imperial forces for the defense of the Empire.
It was thus clearly necessary for the forces to have similar training, and
for the whole training enterprise throughout the Empire to be directed
by one brain, that of the General Staff.

In order to do this, General Nicholson suggested that there be a central
body working in London under the control of the Chief of the Imperial
General Staff, and that a number of local sections, replicas of the I.G.S.,
be established in the United Kingdom, in India, in each of the self-
governing dominions, and in the regular garrisons abroad. Each of the
local sections should have its own chief; it should be charged with the
responsibilities of planning for local defense and with the training of
troops on lines similar to those followed by the War Office in Great
Britain. In the self-governing dominions, the chief of the local general
staff would also be the principal military adviser of his own government.
While such heads of local sections would be in close contact with the
I.G.S., and receive advice and guidance from it, they would be responsible to, and would receive orders from, the local governments only.

To get such an Imperial General Staff under way effectively, it would
be necessary to act swiftly, before too many divergencies developed among
the growing military systems of the Empire, and before the dominions

[17] Ehrman, *Cabinet Government and War, 1890–1940*, p. 44.
[18] W.O. 32/452/33, Gen. No. 354, "The Imperial General Staff."

pushed ahead with the formation of their own staff colleges. General Nicholson urged that the dominions send officers to the British staff college at Camberley for training, to help insure that such training when carried on in the dominions would be imbued with the British influence and example. In addition, frequent close and personal contacts between the center of imperial strategic planning in London and the various local general staffs would be needed to prevent the growth of disparities.[19]

General Nicholson's paper strongly emphasized the need of uniformity in strategic conceptions and military training among the forces of the Empire. This was all natural enough, but the implications are clear. With the military forces of the dominions being increasingly assimilated to the training standards and techniques of the British army, and with that army being increasingly trained for continental warfare, the idea that the military forces of these dominions were primarily for home defense was increasingly obscured. For one example, Australia's militia forces were to be trained, even though indirectly, for a European war, despite the fact that her military law did not allow her military forces to be sent outside the Australian Commonwealth's area, and even though the thrust of her policy in naval matters was toward the establishment of a local force.

In spite of the contrast between the purport of General Nicholson's proposals and the sensitive nationalism of at least some of the dominions, there was general acceptance of the proposals. The Canadian government, which considered them in a Cabinet meeting in February, 1910, accepted them without demur. Sir Frederick Borden noted that the basic principle of complete local control was fully safeguarded in the memorandum, unlike some of the previous proposals of the same nature which had been made in earlier years. But he felt that it should be established at the outset that all communications from the chief of the Imperial General Staff to the head of the Canadian section, other than those of a purely routine character, should be submitted to the Minister of Militia for concurrence.[20]

The Canadian government proposed for the moment that it make no efforts to establish a staff college of its own; that it send four officers to Camberley for study; that it beef up the quality of the work at its own Royal Military College by importing some staff college instructors from Britain; and that it require candidates for selection to the Camberley posting to pass through special study at the Military College so that they would be fully equipped to take advantage of the work at Camberley.

The memorandum of the Canadian Militia Department establishing the Canadian General Staff was, however, strongly Canadian and

[19] *Ibid.*   [20] *Ibid.*, Borden to Gov. Gen. Lord Grey, Feb. 9, 1909.

nationalist in its emphasis. It was more a Canadian staff than a Canadian section of an imperial staff which it authorized. The duties of the new chief of staff were substantially those which had devolved upon the old G.O.C. Militia before that post was abolished in the re-organization of 1904. These duties were purely Canadian in character and had no imperial implications. It was all rather as if the Canadians had read only that portion of General Nicholson's memorandum which spoke of the local responsibilities of the new staff. There was some reference to the evolution of the new Canadian staff into a section of the Imperial General Staff, but this was subordinated to its work in purely local defense, and no tangible indications of its imperial collaboration were suggested.[21]

But this purely Canadian emphasis in the establishment of its general staff was balanced by the establishment of a mobilization committee. The creation of this committee followed upon the recommendation of Sir John French, who had visited Canada in 1910 to inspect and report upon the quality of Canada's military system. Under the orders of the Canadian General Staff, an imperial officer seconded from the Imperial General Staff in London developed mobilization plans that included the creation of an overseas force in case the Canadian government should decide to direct such a movement. It would consist of a division and a mounted brigade, organized as nearly as possible along lines laid down for the British Expeditionary Force.[22]

Work on the plans commenced in July of 1911, and went forward briskly. The main elements of the plan were ready by October, when they were dispatched under great secrecy to appropriate officers in Canada. This was the last major act in the career of Sir Frederick Borden, who had been the civilian head of the Canadian military forces for the fifteen years in which the Liberals had held power.

Perhaps nothing in his entire career in office is more surprising than this last business. Borden had stood shoulder to shoulder with Sir Wilfrid Laurier over the years in championing Canadian control of its military establishment against intruding imperialist forces. His acceptance of the need for planning against contingencies in which Canadian forces might have to be sent overseas in substantial numbers is strongly evidential of the degree to which the pressures of the hour, the atmosphere of rivalry with Germany, and the more tactful approaches of imperial authority toward dominion opinion were bringing results beyond the hopes of the most strident imperialism of a few years before.

In all of this, there was a distinct derogation of a specifically Canadian content to defense preparations. The closer alignment of Canadian defense

---

[21] W.O. 32/452/33, Gen. No. 354, Memo. of Militia Dept. of Canada, May 28, 1909.
[22] Canada, Dept. of National Defence, General Staff, *Official History of the Canadian Forces in the Great War, 1914–18* (Ottawa, 1938), Vol. I, App. 1.

planning with that of the government of the United Kingdom, and the acceptance of the principles of co-ordination and of uniformity, all tended to make the Canadian militia man, as one authority has noted, into a replica of the British Tommy.[23] And so the Canadian militia was preparing to fight a European war at a time when Canadian opinion and political parties were debating vehemently the circumstances under which Canadian naval vessels, as yet unbuilt or unacquired, might come to the aid of British vessels. The controversy over naval issues helped greatly to obscure the degree to which the military authorities were bringing the Canadian forces into line with those of Great Britain and the rest of the Empire, and thus preparing them for services on the European continent. The defeat of the Borden naval bill may have been a defeat for the more ardent imperialists, and Henri Bourassa could boast that after four years of agitation, the nationalists whom he led had succeeded in defeating all imperialist proposals for contributions, for dreadnoughts, or for a Canadian navy.[24] But for all the nationalist efforts, and for all the natural reluctance of a peaceful people to be pulled into the "vortex of militarism," the alarms and perturbations of the time were working inexorably in that direction. With the informed intelligence which made him the most effective Secretary of War Britain ever had, Haldane was working to create an army which would stand by the French against German aggression. And with tact and skill, armed with cogent arguments for better professional training and for uniformity, the British General Staff was gradually transforming itself into the "brains of an army" which would embrace not Britons alone, but additions to British strength from Canada and the Antipodes.

At the time of the next Imperial Conference, that of 1911, the British General Staff was able to report considerable progress in its transmogrification into an imperial agency. A Canadian General Staff was in the process of formation. In Australia, the Australian Section of the General Staff had been organized in August, 1909, and in New Zealand, comparable action had been taken in December of 1910. In South Africa, then in the midst of the creation of the Union of South Africa, the papers concerning the creation of a South African section of the Imperial General Staff had been received by the governments of the various self-governing colonies there, but any action was delayed by the tasks of political unification.

By the time this report was made to the conference, the first dominion soldier had been appointed as a dominion representative to the Imperial General Staff. The officer was Colonel William Bridges of Australia.

[23] Stanley, *Canada's Soldiers, 1604–1954*, p. 304.
[24] Wade, *The French Canadians*, p. 633.

Colonel Bridges had been most influential in the establishment of the Australian system of military training. He was also representative of the web of closer connection and identification developing between the military forces of the Empire. Between 1905 and 1910, over forty British officers had been seconded to Canada for various types of staff and training duties. British officers were also serving in similar duties with Australian and New Zealand forces, though not in the same numbers. In addition, there had been an interchange of officers between various dominion forces and those of India, and an increasing number of dominion officers were taking staff courses at either Camberley or Quetta, the staff college in India.[25]

In this growth of closer association among the officers and leaders of the military forces of the various states of the Empire, the Imperial General Staff was emerging as a most effective agency of imperial co-operation. No such success prevailed in the naval field. The course pursued by the Admiralty was leading not to greater co-operation, but rather to an exacerbation of imperial relations. The difficulties of the Borden Government in pursuing a naval program which was substantially of Admiralty creation have been labored sufficiently. There were neither an effective Canadian naval service as envisaged by the Laurier program, nor the battleships of the Borden program, at the outbreak of the war. The exact measure of Admiralty responsibility for this may be measured only with difficulty, but it was not small, for it involved the abandonment of a program which it had once supported, and which had, in its widest aspects, the largest measure of support which any program of naval collaboration had ever received from the dominions.

The Admiralty's implied abandonment of the program agreed to in 1909 was clear enough in the Canadian imbroglio. It was also revealed in the casual disregard of some of its obligations in the Pacific. The conception of a Far Eastern Fleet of the Empire which had been advanced in 1909, and which called for the creation of three fleet units, Canadian, Australian, and a combined British and New Zealand unit on the China Station, had gradually frittered away. The Canadians had not accepted the original proposal; and the British government made no effort to live up to it. New Zealand's dreadnought gift, the *New Zealand*, which was allocated to the Pacific as the flag ship of the China Station unit in the 1909 agreement, never saw such service, but instead was dispatched by the Admiralty on a series of "hurrah trips" about the Empire, as if to spur other colonial peoples to follow New Zealand's example. When war came in August of 1914, there was no Eastern Fleet of the Empire. The

[25] Cab. 5/2/2, "The Progress of the Imperial General Staff and the Development of its Functions."

most powerful British vessel on the China Station was of the pre-dread-nought era, and the most powerful form of British sea power in the Pacific was the Australian unit, which had alone been carried to completion along the lines of the 1909 understanding.

In extenuation of this wayward course of action was the fact that Britain was relying substantially on the Anglo-Japanese Alliance for the security of British interests in the Pacific. This was not a fact which all Australians and New Zealanders could accept happily. There was fear of Japanese naval and military power among the people of these dominions; and there was the irritant of the Australian immigration policy which troubled the relations between the Japanese government and the Australian Commonwealth. Under these circumstances, it was not surprising that Sir Edward Grey, British Foreign Secretary, felt that the Australians needed educating on the value of the alliance.[26]

This educating must have been effectively carried out, for at the 1911 conference the Australian government agreed to the extension of the alliance beyond its existing expiration date of 1915. These educational sessions, like so much of the other important work at the conference, were carried on, not in the formal meetings, but rather under the cloak of secrecy of the C.I.D. meeting. Perhaps there was some gain for Australian feelings in the fact that their opinion on the issue was sought, and the formalities of consultation observed. But it was clearly the intention of the imperial authorities to renew the alliance, regardless of Antipodean opinion, and thus to continue to rely upon Japan for the basic protection of British interests in the Pacific. The pressures of the North Sea front permitted no other course.[27]

Once again, however, strategic correctness was insufficient to control a situation essentially political in character. The Admiralty might continue to deplore the fact that "time will be required before the true principles of naval policy are comprehended in the Dominions," and to insist that the situation in the Pacific would be "absolutely regulated by events in the North Sea."[28] But this was quite unsatisfactory to the political leaders of the Pacific dominions. Even that most imperially loyal of all dominions, New Zealand, was growing restive about the British defense posture in the Pacific.

There that paladin of imperialism, Sir Joseph Ward, had fallen from power in the election of 1911. After some twenty or more years in office, the Liberal party, which Sir Joseph led, had been supplanted by the Reform party led by William Massey. The differences in the degree of

[26] G. M. Trevelyan, *Grey of Fallodon* (London, 1937), pp. 203–4.
[27] I. H. Nish, "Australia and the Anglo-Japanese Alliance, 1901–1911," *The Australian Journal of Politics and History*, Vol. IX (Nov., 1963).
[28] Cab. 5/3/2 "Imperial Naval Policy." Memorandum, 123rd Meeting of C.I.D.

imperial loyalty between Ward and Massey were perhaps measurable only in micromillimeters, but while not all of the members of the Reform party were dissatisfied or anxious about the Admiralty's Pacific policy, all who were worried, and who wished that New Zealand might follow the example set by Australia, were members of the Reform party.[29]

Among the most active and powerfully placed of those so concerned was Colonel James Allen. Allen had long experience and interest in the defense affairs of the dominion, and it was natural that he should receive the Defence portfolio in the Massey Government.[30] (Allen wore other hats in addition to that of defense, for he was also Minister of Finance and Minister of Education.)

In a speech to a conference of the Navy League branch in New Zealand, Allen said that no defense arrangement could be satisfactory to those living in the Pacific unless the British fleet commanded the Pacific as it commanded the Atlantic. "As a New Zealander, I cannot take my mind away from the responsibilities in the Pacific Ocean. With these always in view, centralization in European waters is not all that a New Zealander can desire, and I personally look forward with some alarm and fear to such an isolation in the Pacific."[31] Allen went on to speak favorably of the possibility of greater co-operation between Australia and New Zealand in defense of the Pacific.

Colonel Allen, as was perhaps inevitable, joined the parade of dominion ministers who had to make the pilgrimage to London soon after installation in office. While the chief purpose of his trip was financial, it afforded him a chance to consult with defense officers and to state his views to British officialdom, including the First Lord of the Admiralty. On February 10, Allen had a meeting with Churchill, and then carried on the exchange of views by correspondence. He also met with the Committee of Imperial Defence.

To Churchill, the New Zealand minister expressed disquiet over the defense position in the Pacific, and over the disposition of the battle cruiser H.M.S. *New Zealand*, the gift of the dominion during the crisis atmosphere of 1909. Churchill took the line of strategic rectitude in his efforts to reassure the New Zealander. New Zealand and Australia, he said, were both safe from any external attack, protected as they were by the naval power of Britain and the alliances based on that power. Since there was nothing these dominions could do, either together or apart, which would fit them to cope with the naval might of Japan, the correct course for them was that which New Zealand had followed so far: con-

---

[29] Institute of Commonwealth Studies, London, Jebb Papers, John Allen to Jebb, Oct. 27, 1912.
[30] *Round Table*, #8, Sept., 1912, p. 761.
[31] *Round Table*, #10, March, 1913, pp. 390–91.

tribution to the general strength of the British navy. The Admiralty had done what it could to make the Australian fleet unit a success, but it could not conceal its preference for the contribution method adhered to by New Zealand. As for the Admiralty's use of the *New Zealand*, it would be a waste of the might of this vessel to place it in the Pacific. From the strategic point of view, it was not necessary to place that vessel on the China Station (as had been provided by the 1909 agreement), for she would not find there any vessel of corresponding strength belonging to any of the European powers. As for other parts of the 1909 agreement, while it was true that the Admiralty had then agreed to place two *Bristol* type cruisers in New Zealand waters, great changes had taken place since then in the naval situation. The need for such cruisers in home waters was serious; there was no military reason which required them in New Zealand. So far as those waters were concerned, the Admiralty was eager to encourage naval sentiment and interest in the dominion, but it was reluctant to take any steps which might encourage the principle of local navies against that of one imperial fleet.[32]

Allen replied that he did not think that local naval units and imperial fleet were necessarily antagonistic. Separate fleet units could be directed and handled in a manner that would allow for concentration and unified command whenever necessary. As for the "great changes" which had occurred in the naval situation since 1909, Allen realized, he said, that this might be so, but New Zealand had been told that the situation was also serious in 1909, and gave material expression of her desire to aid Britain then. In the light of what the First Lord had told him, he could not now demand that the 1909 agreement be carried out, but he felt that New Zealand had the right to know whether any policy agreed upon would have any permanence. Australia, he pointed out, had utilized local sentiment and patriotism in the creation of its fleet unit, and had thereby achieved a permanent policy, had created in that unit a force superior to that of the old Australasian force of the Royal Navy, and had, in doing this, given substantial relief to the mother country.[33]

That Allen was not content with the First Lord's expression of naval doctrine, nor silenced by the hostility of the Admiralty to the idea of local naval forces, was apparent in the request which he made of Churchill on the eve of his return to New Zealand. He requested the advice of the Admiralty as to the manner in which the dominion might best carry out a decision to maintain a naval force of its own. The First Lord replied that New Zealand could do no better than follow the Australian example.

[32] Cab. 5/3/2, "Correspondence with Regard to New Zealand Naval Policy," Churchill to Allen, Feb. 14, 1913.
[33] *Ibid.*, Allen to Churchill, March 18, 1913.

New Zealand would have to apply the Naval Discipline Act and the Admiralty Instructions to any naval service it might create. But in the advice extended to New Zealand, the Admiralty returned to the position taken in 1909: if there were to be local naval forces, it would be necessary to maintain forces sufficient to furnish an active career for officers and men. Churchill assumed that New Zealand would act along the general lines followed by Australia, that there would be close understanding with any force created by New Zealand, and that in time of war, that force would come under the Admiralty's control. [34]

In the midst of this intermittent exchange of views with Colonel Allen, Churchill presented to the Commons the Admiralty estimates for 1913–14. The speech of the First Lord included a suggestion that Britain and Germany halt any new construction of capital ships for twelve months. His other major proposal called for the establishment of an Imperial Squadron, formed largely from vessels contributed from the colonies and dominions. The main striking power of this force was to be five mighty ships: the *New Zealand* and the *Malaya*, and the three hypothetical vessels which were being debated in the Canadian Parliament. This force, with supporting vessels, was to be based on Gibraltar, and from there it would patrol the outer sea-frontiers of the Empire. It would be in a position to hasten to the defense of any threatened part of the Empire. Vancouver would be but twenty-three days steam away, Sydney twenty-eight, and New Zealand thirty-two. "And the Channel a very much shorter time." [35]

In substance, this was a scheme designed more to support the weakening British position in the Mediterranean, and to further strengthen the Royal Navy in northern waters, than to hasten to the succor of any beleaguered outpost of the Empire. The whole strategic doctrine of the Admiralty, with its emphasis on the concentration of strength in a crucial area, was far too well known to the governments and peoples of the various dominions for them not to penetrate easily the verbiage of the First Lord and discern in the proposed Squadron yet another implementation of that doctrine. For all of Sydney's being only twenty-eight or so days away, the Channel could be reached in much shorter time. This was not the sort of approach that was going to ease the anxieties of Colonel Allen, for instance.

Indeed, it might well have added to them. For despite Allen's presence in London, and his exchange of views with Churchill, the First Lord did not either inform him or seek his advice on the proposed Imperial Squadron, a main component of which would be H.M.S. *New Zealand*.

---

[34] *Ibid.* Allen to Churchill, April 18, 1913.
[35] *Hansard*, 5th Series, L, 1762, March 26, 1913.

Allen wrote Jebb that he had not been consulted in any way about what he called the Gibraltar Squadron scheme.[36] For a government which was seeking some assurance of permanence in British naval policy, this sudden conjuring up of an imperial force, without warning or consultation, could only have been evidence that there was little hope of permanence save for the concentration of force in the waters adjacent to Britain, and even less hope that the wishes of the dominion would ever be effectively consulted. Further, the allocation of the *New Zealand* to the newly proposed squadron indicated in a manner beyond hope that there was no chance of it being the chief unit of a revitalized British naval force on either the China Station or the Pacific generally.

Small wonder then, that on his return to New Zealand, Allen sought to bring about the creation of a New Zealand naval force. A year or so before, his son, John Allen, had written Jebb that the "fleet unit" party was but a small group as opposed to the subsidizers. But by the close of August, 1913, Colonel Allen informed Jebb that the Cabinet had accepted in principle his proposal for the commencement of a New Zealand naval service.[37]

In December, 1913, the New Zealand government introduced in the Parliament at Wellington a bill authorizing the government to spend the £100,000 currently being paid to the imperial government as a naval subsidy, in any way which it thought best for the defense of New Zealand. The bill also authorized the government to acquire a cruiser of the *Bristol* class, which was not to be under the control of the Admiralty, but retained under the authority of the dominion government. In introducing this bill, Allen referred to the agreement of 1909. Pointing out that the arrangements made under that agreement for the China Station and New Zealand were to have been completed by the close of 1912, he said, "We are now at the end of 1913, and the only portion of the China unit that is complete is the battleship *New Zealand*, and not one other item."[38] The two promised *Bristol* type cruisers had not come to New Zealand waters. He concluded, "The chief partner of the 1909 agreement—namely, the Mother Country—has failed to carry out her obligation."

There was no dissent from this statement during the debate, nor indeed could there have been. As far as New Zealand was concerned, the program and the promises accepted at the 1909 conference had been either ignored or forgotten by the imperial government. There was no strengthened force on the China Station, and the prospect of there ever being an Eastern Fleet of the Empire, maintained by Britain and the

[36] Institute of Commonwealth Studies, London, Jebb Papers, Allen to Jebb, April 16, 1913.
[37] *Ibid.*, Allen to Jebb, Oct. 27, 1912; Allen to Jebb, Aug. 27, 1913.
[38] New Zealand, *Parliamentary Debates*, CLXVII, 463.

dominions bordering on the Pacific, had faded away completely. Of course, the creation of the Gibraltar squadron as proposed by Churchill, designed, according to his words, to look out for the world-wide needs of the Empire, should certainly have been a matter of general consultation among the major dominions. After all, the force was to take its main striking power from vessels either contributed or, hopefully, about to be contributed by two of those dominions. But the First Lord made no such effort at consultation. Aside from a hasty cable to Borden in Canada[39] suggesting such a possible use for the vessels to be built when his program was adopted, no such consultations occurred. The Australasian dominions, as Allen indicated, were confronted with a scheme entirely of Admiralty creation, involving the rejection of plans which they were currently attempting to carry out.

Further, in the presentation of the scheme there was no suggestion by the First Lord that the dominions were to have any voice in the control of the squadron's movements. He did indicate that these movements would be governed by other than military considerations, implying that the force would from time to time show the flag to impressed colonials, as the *New Zealand* was then engaged in doing. But of course the aspirations of dominion governments were not likely to be satisfied by the creation of any such squadron, however imperially titled.

Certainly the proposal failed to affect the course of the debate on the Borden program which was currently occupying the Canadian Parliament. There the lines of party conflict had hardened too severely. The Laurier resistance had undoubtedly been reinforced by the doubts of the First Lord as to the wisdom of the program which had been passed along by W. S. Fielding, and the Parliament stood on the verge of the adjunct quarrel over closure. Under these circumstances, it is little wonder that the Churchillian venture in *fin de siècle* imperialism fell flat on its face. Overriden by such other considerations, the proposal of the First Lord was virtually ignored.

In Australia, the proposal encountered essentially the same fate, though there was also uneasiness over the Admiralty's general disregard of the agreement of 1909 under which the Australian Commonwealth was acquiring its naval unit. But as to the wisdom of the course followed by the Commonwealth, there was little publicly expressed doubt. The support given to the idea of a naval force under Commonwealth control, and to the limited degree of compulsory military training, are the clearest example of the growth of Australian national consciousness; these were essential elements of the nation-welding process. The Australian insistence upon having a responsible role in its own defense was also working toward

[39] P.A.C., Borden "Naval Notes," pp. 483–84, 494.

the transformation of the Empire into the polycentric structure—the empire of equals—which was rapidly developing.

But as Australians generally rejoiced at the assembling in their ports of the vessels of their naval squadron, political leaders in both Australia and London faced the problems of giving the new force a status in international law. Some means had to be devised to give the new vessels the status of ships-of-war of a sovereign state. The Commonwealth of Australia was not a sovereign state, and yet it was acquiring warships which would range the high seas, and which would be under the control of the Australian government. But the liability for any international complications or legal actions arising from the conduct of these vessels or their crews would rest with the imperial government, not with Australia. To reconcile the Australian control of the force with the legal fact of the responsibility of the imperial government was but one of the dilemmas created by the naval policy pursued by Australia and, for a while, by Canada. There were other dilemmas, such as the debatable legal capacity of the various dominion parliaments to legislate extra-territorially for the discipline of their forces outside of their territorial waters, and the very practical matters of securing uniformity of training and discipline between the dominion forces and the Royal Navy, and of assuring unity of command in time of war.

These problems had all emerged with the decisions of the 1909 conference, and were the subject of discussion between imperial and dominion representatives in subsequent months. The Canadians were involved equally with the Australians in the earlier phases of these discussions, but with the reversal of the Laurier naval program by the Borden Government, they had less interest in the matter, and the burden of the problem was largely to be shared by the representatives of the United Kingdom and Australia.

While some of the legal issues were complicated and difficult, they were approached generally with good will by both sides. Once it had been conceded that the dominions might acquire their own naval forces, any bitterness had been drained away from the debate. Senator Pearce, the able Australian Minister of Defence, recognized that there was a serious problem in giving the men-of-war of the Australian Commonwealth international status.[40] He also indicated that some of the claims of more ardent Australian nationalists would have to be held in check when he told a delegation from a patriotic society that since the Australian flag had no standing or recognition on the high seas, the vessels of the new naval force would have to fly the White Ensign of the Royal Navy.[41] And

[40] Australian National War Memorial Library, Pearce Papers, Bundle 5, Pearce to Adm. W. H. Henderson, Sept. 29, 1910.
[41] *The West Australian* (Perth), April 15, 1913.

among most British officialdom was complementary recognition that the degree of British control over the Australian squadron would have to be confined to the narrowest possible limits.

That was the note sounded in the first submissions made by the imperial officials to the Canadian and Australian governments. The recommendations in that paper were largely based on the study of the problem made by an interdepartmental committee formed by representatives of the Admiralty and the Colonial and Foreign Offices. This committee, formed at the initiative of the Admiralty in January, 1910, adopted the relatively novel view that in the light of the general success with which the dominions of the Empire ran their own affairs, it would be best to limit imperial intervention or control as severely as possible. But the matter of imperial liability for the acts of the men-of-war of the dominions remained. And there was also the need for some disciplinary control over the officers and crew. The jurisdiction of the Commonwealth of Australia, for instance, extended beyond the three-mile limit, both by terms of Part V of the act of the imperial Parliament creating the Commonwealth, and also by implication of the Territorial Waters Jurisdiction Act (1878) of the imperial Parliament. The latter extended the jurisdiction of governments under the Crown to the high seas adjacent to their coasts as far as was necessary for their safety and security. But there were no powers of the Australian government nor of any dominion, to regulate the conduct of their officers and men on shore in other parts of the Empire or in foreign countries. There would be, for example, no way of punishing the offense of incitement to desertion, were the offense committed in a foreign port.[42]

The formal memorandum of the Admiralty, arising from the work of the interdepartmental committee, was forwarded to the Australian and Canadian governments in August, 1910. It stressed the need of some sanction which the imperial government might have over the dominion naval forces, in view of its ultimate legal liability, and also the desirability of the Royal Navy and the dominion naval forces being under the same disciplinary code if they were not to be anything more than quasi-foreigners to one another when they met. The Imperial Naval Discipline Act of 1866 should apply to all the naval forces of the Crown. The assent of the dominion governments should be obtained to the proposition that their officers and men were "persons in or belonging to His Majesty's Navy and borne on the books of one of His Majesty's ships in Commission" within the meaning of section 87 of the Naval Discipline Act.

In addition, the Admiralty memo urged the creation of agreements with the Australian and Canadian governments respectively, outlining the conditions under which the naval forces of these dominions might

[42] Cab. 17/48.

come under the authority of the senior imperial naval officer. The agreement suggested covered a variety of contingencies, arising both within and without Canadian and Australian "waters."[43]

Based on this document, representatives of Canada and Australia carried on negotiations with the Admiralty during the months prior to the 1911 Imperial Conference, and by the time that body convened, simplicity had prevailed over the elaboration of detail in the Admiralty submission.

In the discussions with the C.I.D. in 1911 covering the arrangements for fleet co-operation, the tenor of the comment was that it was unwise to adopt words or phrases which in any manner impinged upon the complete local autonomy of the dominion governments, and further, that there was no justification for assuming a lack of co-operation because there was no elaborate definition of the terms under which it was to be given.[44]

The final agreement for the control of the dominion naval forces was more generous than had been suggested in the original Admiralty memorandum. The Royal Navy and the forces of Canada and Australia were to be "sister members" of the King's Navy, each vessel flying the White Ensign, and in addition, its own distinctive flag. Each fleet was to be under the administrative control of its own government. The training and discipline of the dominion fleets was to be "generally" uniform with that of the Royal Navy, and by arrangement, officers and men were to be generally interchangeable between the three forces.

As to measures for imperial control, in time of peace, the dominion governments were to have complete control of the movements of their vessels within their own naval stations. Outside of these stations, the dominions were also to control the movements of their vessels. But since it was essential that the imperial government, carrying the ultimate responsibility for foreign affairs and for the conduct of war should it occur, should at all times be informed as to the disposition of naval forces, the Admiralty was to be kept informed of the movement of dominion vessels outside their own stations. In visits of dominion vessels to a foreign port, prior consent of the imperial government was to be secured, and a report of the proceedings of the visit forwarded to the Admiralty. The officer in command of the dominion vessel was also to obey any orders of the imperial government as to the conduct of international affairs while on such a visit. When ships of different fleets met, it was only in certain rather limited circumstances that the senior officer took command of the combined forces, unless there had been some prior agreement between the governments.

[43] Cab. 5/2/2, "The Status of Dominions' Ships of War," No. 83–C, Aug., 1910.
[44] Cab. 5/2/1, Minutes, 112th Meeting, C.I.D., May 29, 1911.

In time of war, when the dominion fleets, either in whole or in part, had been placed at the disposal of the imperial government, the ships involved were to form an integral part of the Royal Navy, and to remain under the command of the Admiralty. They were liable for service then anywhere in the globe.[45]

The measure of dominion control written into the agreement was large and generous. Indeed, the whole discussion of the problem in the 1911 conference was pervaded with a spirit based on the realization, in Prime Minister Asquith's words, that "the only way of carrying on in such an Empire as ours this task of Imperial Defence is by hearty and spontaneous co-operation in every quarter."[46] As for the larger issue of the constitutional powers of the various dominions, British acceptance of the idea that those governments should have the power to bind their citizens beyond their territorial limits when serving in naval vessels marked an important step in the establishment of extraterritorial powers of these governments. The prevailing view of the British government had been clearly reflected in the Colonial Naval Defence Act of 1865, which conferred no extra-territorial powers upon colonies that might construct and operate naval vessels. Outside their territorial limits, discipline could be enforced only under the enactments and regulations governing the Royal Navy.[47] And Senator Pearce had been fearful lest the definition of Australian waters, and the attempt to draw a distinction between the powers of Australia within those waters and those that it might exercise outside, imputed some weakness in the constitutional position of Australia. It seemed to suggest that Australian law could not go wherever her ships went. He was grateful that the imperial government had given way on that point, and had recognized the need to accept the principle that Australian law bound its subjects serving on its naval vessels throughout the globe.[48]

But the authority for such extra-territorial rights could not simply be an agreement made at the Imperial Conference. The British authorities felt that it required an amendment to the Naval Discipline Act. Brodeur, the second ranking Canadian, was reluctant to accept the need for such imperial legislation, feeling that the 1865 Act sufficed. But in this he was overborne by the assurances of McKenna, supported by Pearce, that some amending legislation was needed.[49]

[45] Cab. 5/2/2, "Co-operation between the Naval Forces of the United Kingdom and Dominions," No. 82–C; and Cab. 5/2/1, Minutes, 113th Meeting, C.I.D., May 30th, 1911.

[46] Ibid., p. 5.

[47] B. A. Knox, "Colonial Influence on Imperial Policy, 1858–1866: Victoria and the Colonial Naval Defence Act, 1865," Historical Studies, Australia and New Zealand, XI (Nov., 1963), 71.

[48] Cab. 5/2/1, Minutes, 112th Meeting, C.I.D., May 29th, 1911, p. 19.

[49] Cab. 5/2/1, Minutes, 113th Meeting of C.I.D., May 30th, 1911, p. 14.

The arrangements thus agreed upon at the 1911 conference were adopted without demur by the parliaments of the states involved. The required amendments to the Naval Discipline Act of the United Kingdom passed through the Commons without debate, so little concern was shown about the measure.[50]

With the adoption of this legislation comes the sense that the high tide mark of co-operation for the naval defense of the Empire had been reached; the tide then began to ebb. Much of this decline has been indicated in the Borden abandonment of the Laurier naval program, and the ambiguous stand of the Admiralty under Churchill toward the 1909 agreement. The failure of the imperial government to stand by that agreement caused increasing disquiet in the Australasian dominions. This was reflected in the decision of the New Zealand Massey Government to abandon the contributory principle to which New Zealand had adhered since 1887, and in the increasing fear and irritation in Australia that the burden of defending the British naval position in the Pacific was falling solely on Australian shoulders. And as mentioned before, the proposal of the Imperial Squadron by the First Lord in the naval estimates of 1912 had encountered a chilly reception in the Antipodes. Nor was there any improvement in matters during subsequent months.

Co-operation at the actual service level was effective. The Royal Navy lent the developing Australian naval force the necessary officers and men to get the latter off to an effective beginning.[51] But on the political level, there was increasing strain and annoyance felt by Australian officials over Admiralty policy and the secrecy which accompanied it. It was repeatedly claimed that during 1912–14 Australians were left completely ignorant of Admiralty policy.[52]

Despite the mounting distrust of at least some aspects of imperial policy, and a mounting sense that the Admiralty was abandoning the 1909 agreement without either consulting or informing the other governments concerned, the Australians adhered staunchly to the principles they had adopted for defense. In the election campaign of 1913, Prime Minister Andrew Fisher, so far from expressing any regrets over the course adopted, outlined a program of further naval construction. The Commonwealth government, he stated in his policy speech, should enlarge the Australian fleet unit by the addition of another battle cruiser, three more destroyers and more submarines.[53] Joseph Cook, the leader

---

[50] *Hansard*, 5th Series, XXXII, 2447, Dec. 13, 1911.

[51] A. W. Jose, *The Royal Australian Navy, 1914–18*, Vol. IX of *The Official History of Australia in the War of 1914–18* (Sydney, 1928), p. xxxix. Of the initial complement of men for the Australian force, approximately one-third were seconded by the Royal Navy.

[52] *Ibid.*, p. xxxvii.

[53] *The Argus* (Melbourne), April 1, 1913.

of the opposition Liberals, urged no such expansion, but he made much of the Liberals' part in the establishment of the system of compulsory military training and in the establishment of the naval unit.[54]

But while there was this adherence to the course adopted, the irritation simmered under the surface. Fisher made no reference to the apparent junking of the 1909 agreement in his policy statement, but his principal coadjutor, Senator Pearce, felt that the failure to carry out the 1909 arrangements was the "greatest blow yet dealt to Imperial co-operation." It surely would have been better had the members of the 1911 conference been told frankly by the British representatives that the agreement would not be honored.[55]

Churchill, who had already exacerbated Australian feelings by his eager embrace of Borden's plans and by the Gibraltar Squadron scheme, was to add yet further to Australian irritation by his estimates statements to the Commons in March 1914. These estimates, the fruit of such intense debate and conflict among Cabinet members that at times they seemed likely to split the Cabinet, aroused little genuine satisfaction in Britain.[56] But they aroused more than dissatisfaction in Australia, for in them Churchill announced what seemed to be the end of the 1909 agreement. That which had seemed dying, but not beyond hope of resuscitation, was now pronounced, though not in so many words, dead. For the First Lord stated that "a battle cruiser is not a necessary part of a fleet unit provided by the Dominions," and that "the presence of such vessels in the Pacific is not necessary to British interest." Of the naval agreement and British vessels in the Pacific, Churchill said:

> The Naval Agreement of 1909 with the Dominions had as its central principle the idea that we should keep in the Pacific and Indian Oceans double the force of the Australian Fleet unit. We are doing more than that. We are not doing it with the same types. We are keeping the new battle cruisers at Home, where alone they will meet their equals, and we have placed on the China station and on the Indian station the two battleships, "Swiftsure" and "Triumph", and other armoured cruisers which are quite sufficient for the work they will have to do, and which are not only an equivalent, but are an improvement upon the mere duplication of the Australian Fleet unit.[57]

Once again the contributory principle received the endorsement of the First Lord, when he stated that the Dominion of New Zealand had provided in the most effective way for its own and the common security, in its gift of the battle cruiser. As for the Australian course of action,

[54] *Ibid.*, April 4, 1913.
[55] Australian National War Museum, Canberra, Pearce Papers, Bundle 7, Pearce to Collins, Dec. 3, 1912.
[56] Marder, *From Dreadnought to Scapa Flow*, pp. 319–27.
[57] *Hansard*, 5th Series, LIX, 1932, March 17, 1914.

he said that two or three dreadnoughts in the decisive theater of action might turn the tide of battle; in Australian waters they would be useless if the British navy were defeated.[58]

This return by the Admiralty and its leader to the priority of strategic doctrines over political considerations, and the praise of the contributory principle, was obviously not likely to be accepted gratefully by the Australians. The replies and comments were not slow in coming. The *Bulletin* may have lost some of its bite since the days when it was attacking the "H'empah" and all imperialists with such vigor, but it still had some of the old fire when it remarked that for a government which had been usually futile, the First Lord had spoken with unwonted clarity about the Pacific. The imperial eagles had left for home, just as the Roman eagles had in their day. The Pacific had become a Japanese sea. But in their flight the eagles had taken something they didn't own: the *New Zealand*.[59] Australia's senior daily, the *Sydney Morning Herald*, a journal which had not joined in the campaign against the naval subsidy which Australians had so long paid, had come to another view by 1914. The Admiralty view had been made quite plain—there was no need for a British fleet in the Pacific. "With all respects we do not believe it . . . ." And the lesson drawn by the *Herald*: "The Empire will help the Pacific if the Pacific helps itself. That is the object towards which New Zealand and Australia are working."[60]

The Age, closest to Deakin in his long efforts for the creation of an Australian naval force, at first took Churchill's implied renunciation of the 1909 agreement with considerable aplomb. After a week or so, however, it managed to work up high indignation. If the Admiralty had been in earnest five years ago, and imperial naval circumstances had so radically changed since then, naval policy must be as fleeting and evanescent as feminine fashion. Churchill's policy "leaves the Australian navy completely isolated from any association with the British fleet. An agreement solemnly entered into, on the basis of which Australia has already spent several millions of money, has been deliberately renounced . . . ."[61]

Such editorial pronouncements received official support in a formal statement by the current Minister of Defence in the Australian Government. The 1913 election brought a victory of slim margin to the Liberal party led by Joseph Cook, and Senator Pearce had been succeeded in the Defence Ministry by Senator E. D. Millen. Once a member of the free trade faction of the Australian Parliament, Millen had been a supporter

---

[58] *Ibid.*, p. 1933.
[59] *The Bulletin* (Sydney), April 2, 1914.
[60] *Sydney Morning Herald*, March 19, 1914, quoted in H. C. Grimshaw, *Some Aspects of Australian Attitudes to the Imperial Connection, 1900-19*, Unpublished thesis, University of Queensland, n. d., p. 158.
[61] *The Age* (Melbourne), April 14, 1914.

of fiscal policy which ardent nationalists tended to regard as anti-Australian. But there was nothing lacking in the vigor with which he defended the Australian position and rejected the recent twists in Admiralty policy. Millen prepared a memorandum on the subject, dated April 13, 1914, which he released to the press. In it, he said that the agreement on which Australia based its policy had been accepted by the Admiralty in 1909. And the Admiralty had further indicated its support when it had dispatched Admiral Reginald Henderson to Australia to give further guidance to the Commonwealth government. Admiral Henderson not only had accepted the complete fleet unit idea, but had urged the construction of several other such units. Nor had anything been said at the Imperial Conference of 1911 to suggest that the Admiralty was wavering in its support of such ideas.

But now under Churchill, Millen went on, the Admiralty seemed to discard the ideas of 1909, and to regard the battle cruiser as unnecessary, either as a component of the fleet unit, or as an adjunct of British naval strength in the Pacific. In the Pacific, the defense of British interests was entrusted to the alliance with Japan. But that alliance had been in existence in 1909 and in 1911. It was as much a factor then as now. Australians would join in the hope that the good understanding with Japan would continue. But it was difficult to accept the existence of the alliance as reason for departure from Australia's current naval policy. "The Alliance covers the next few years. Australia's efforts to create a Fleet are the outcome of a very natural desire to be possessed of the means of protecting herself and assisting in the protection of Imperial interests in the Southern seas for all time."

There was another aspect of the problem, Millen asserted: the failure of the Admiralty to live up to the agreement. That agreement had been departed from in two important respects: the *New Zealand* had been placed in the North Sea rather than in the Pacific, where its service had been pledged in 1909; and Britain had failed to furnish a third vessel, similar to the *New Zealand* and the *Australia*, in Pacific waters. All this had been done without consultation and presented to Australia as a *fait accompli*.

As for the possibility that in time of crisis Britain might be able to hasten with naval aid to the Pacific, certainly that would be effective only if there were a nucleus of naval power already there, with the necessary support facilities to make naval power operative.

In summary, the Australian Minister said that the Churchill statement meant the non-fulfillment of pledges undertaken in the 1909 agreement, and the destruction of the basis on which the Australian navy had been formed. It meant the abandonment of that feature of the Australian naval program which the Admiralty had stressed as most essential, namely the creation of a unit headed by a battle cruiser. And it meant the replacement of a definite scheme of imperial co-operation with an unco-ordinated and ephemeral approach that had neither permanence nor clear aim and function; all of this done without any Admiralty consultation with the other parties to the agreement.[62]

This formidable indictment of Admiralty policy was perhaps the most significant in the history of the emergence of the dominions from imperial tutelage since A. T. Galt's defense of the Canadian right to protective tariffs. And it was backed by practically all Australian opinion. Certainly its arguments were supported and given greater depth by the views of the Australian members of the *Round Table*. These added to Millen's statement a criticism of the degree of British dependence on the Anglo-Japanese alliance by suggesting that it was an alliance in which Britain, without real naval strength in the Pacific, was unable to offer Japan any *quid pro quo*. "Great Britain has no fleet in the Pacific, and, therefore, can do no service to Japan there. Japan has no interests in the Atlantic, and therefore, Great Britain cannot render any services to Japan there."[63]

And from New Zealand, Colonel Allen weighed in with the statement that the 1909 agreement had been abandoned, and most improperly so, by the Mother Country, without having taken the matter to both Australia and New Zealand before acting.[64] Colonel Allen suggested that the way out of the situation was the summons for yet another imperial conference on defense. The idea of such a gathering had been bruited about since the early indications that the Admiralty was turning hostile to the 1909 understanding. Both Andrew Fisher and Joseph Cook, successive Prime Ministers in Australia, had sought the convocation of a conference to discuss British defenses in the Pacific.[65] But these approaches had been in vain. While Pearce, at least, received the impression that Churchill was not hostile to such a gathering,[66] there was certainly no haste in summoning it, and Lewis Harcourt, the Colonial Secretary, told the Canadian High Commissioner in London, Sir George Perley, that while the Australians were pressing for such a conference, he had, without actually rejecting the idea, been postponing it from time to time without giving the Australians any reasons for delay. The Colonial Secretary told Perley that he thought any such conference would be "premature," and he hoped the Canadians would feel the same way. Borden agreed, for he did not wish to have the naval issue brought to the fore again until

[62] Commonwealth of Australia, *Parliamentary Papers*, 1914, II, 205.
[63] *The Round Table*, June, 1914, pp. 394–403.
[64] *The Daily Telegraph* (Sydney), April 23, 1914.
[65] Parl. Pap., 1914, Vol. LX, Cd. 7347.
[66] Australian National War Museum, Canberra, Pearce Papers, Bundle 7, #113.

death and resignations had given him a chance to get a majority in the Canadian Senate.[67]

A few days after Harcourt's discussion with the Canadian representative, the action of Gavrilo Princip in Sarajevo gave the signal for the descent of the curtain not only on such considerations and issues, but on the age to which they belonged. The discussion of British naval strength in the Pacific was no longer a matter of hypothetical considerations but part of the harsh realities of war.

With the opening of conflict, the British political position in the Pacific turned out to be better than Australians had anticipated. Despite some initial Australian fears that the Japanese might take advantage of the opportunities presented by the war, the latter responded to it by the speedy offer of aid to Britain, and within a few months much of the Australian fear had subsided. But the British naval position in the Pacific was certainly weaker than Churchill had argued it would be. The chief British naval vessels were predreadnought battle cruisers, of a range, armament, and manning totally ineffectual for the demands of war. They were certainly markedly inferior to the projected British naval strength planned at the 1909 defense conference. Of those planned forces, only the Australian unit was actually in existence and in any sense battle-ready.[68]

The operations of that force, both in the Pacific in the earlier phases of the war, and elsewhere after the dangers in the Pacific had passed, lie beyond the scope of this study. But two comments may perhaps be offered. The first comes from a British naval officer, Admiral William Hannam Henderson, writing admittedly after the shock of the battle of Coronel: "There is no doubt that had the arrangement of 1909 been stuck to, we should from the first have controlled the waters of the Pacific and Indian Oceans. As it is—it is the Australian Squadron that has saved the situation—its existence with the "Australia" at its head had prevented the German ships from molesting the shores or the commerce of Australasia . . . ."[69] It could of course be argued that the Admiralty dispositions had taken account of the presence of the Australian vessels in the Pacific. Had they not been there, the Royal Navy would have been present with greater force than it actually did command there. But in view of the general fear in British circles that the British margin of superiority in the North Sea and Mediterranean was already razor-thin, and in the light of Churchill's reiterated statements that the more powerful vessels,

[67] P.A.C. Ottawa, Perley Papers, Perley to Borden, June 24, 1914; Borden to Perley, July 13, 1914.

[68] Julian Corbett, Naval Operations (London, 1920), I, 145.

[69] Institute of Commonwealth Studies, London, Jebb Papers, Henderson to Jebb, Nov. 11, 1914.

such as the *New Zealand*, would be held where they could counter the modern German ships, the possibility that any vessels of striking power comparable to the *Australia* would have been detached for duty in the Pacific seems remote.

The other comment is that the Admiralty's rather uncritical acceptance of the doctrines of Mahan, the deprecation of commerce raiding, the belief that the *guerre de course* must fail, did tend to leave the sea frontiers of empire overexposed. Admiral Sir Herbert Richmond has remarked that Admiralty policy had left British commerce exposed to cruiser forays at the beginning of the war, and later in the struggle, to the enemy's submarines[70]—to which one might add that the peril existed for other movements than those of commerce. The convoys which carried Australian and New Zealand forces to the seizures of German Pacific outposts in New Guinea and the Samoan group risked the German cruisers *Scharnhorst* and *Gneisenau* in the Pacific. The New Zealand Samoan force reached New Caledonia under the protection of two British cruisers of such antediluvian qualities as to make them the easiest of prey had they been intercepted by almost any German vessel in the Pacific.[71] According to Churchill, the principle of first things first and of concentrating in the decisive theater had governed everything. "The inconvenience in other parts of the globe had to be faced. It was serious."[72] That it was only serious, and not disastrous, was perhaps due mostly to the stubborn Antipodean resolve also to put first things first, and to the fact that for them, the Pacific came first.

The shrinking dimensions of the *Pax Britannica*, the degree to which Britain had retreated from world-wide commitments from the time when the vessels were summoned home from the outer reaches of empire by the Fisher re-organization, was perhaps somewhat disguised from British understanding by the commanding place that "Blue Water" school doctrines held in the naval mind. To be strong in the vital places, in the threatened areas, was to be strong everywhere. Win the great impending battles in the North Sea, and all else will be open to you. The essential truth of this doctrine blinded many to the possibility that it was not the whole truth. It commanded such regard that all other possibilities of naval warfare were essentially excluded, and those who suggested them stood outside the inner circle, condemned by their ignorance to outer darkness. This applied even to naval men themselves, such as Lord Charles Beresford, as well as to all civilians who rejected the faith revealed to Fisher and those of the Fish Pond.

[70] Herbert Richmond, *Naval Policy and Naval Strength* (London, 1927), pp. 226–27.
[71] H. T. B. Drew, *The War Efforts of New Zealand*, Vol. IV, *Official History of New Zealand's Effort in the Great War* (Wellington, 1923), p. 27.
[72] Winston Churchill, *The World Crisis* (New York, 1949, abridged ed.), p. 181.

But the prepossessing hold of this doctrine upon the mind of the Admiralty naturally tended to reduce to relative insignificance the complaints coming from the outer fringes of empire. These complaints came from those who had never been instructed in the essential truths of naval warfare; they came from amateurs, denied, through no fault of their own, the understanding which came from tradition and the professional gloss of the Royal Navy and the Board of Admiralty. To the end, and perhaps most staunchly at the end, the Admiralty clung to the strategic truth of the need to concentrate all effort in the North Sea, with the complementary idea that the best policy that the dominions could follow was to give the Admiralty all the tools they could to help finish the job there.

The policy of the 1909 conference, accepted by the McKenna Board of Admiralty, that in the direction of the naval policy of a polycentric empire political considerations ranked with strategic, was the one notable deviation from the path of strategic rectitude. And from it came the most vigorous efforts of the part of the junior states of the Empire to make their additions to the naval strength of the Crown. The recognition of their new maturity, the acceptance of their capacity to manage at least some portion of the business of naval defense, the effective combination of national aspiration and imperial loyalty which the scheme combined, opened the way to the most effective period of imperial collaboration in defense before 1914.

But only one-third, the Australian third, of the 1909 plans came to fruition. It was perhaps more fate than anyone's fault that this was so. The preoccupations of the Admiralty were such that there could be little time for such extraneous matters as hurt feelings in Melbourne or Wellington. The pressures of the North Sea and the Mediterranean made Little Englanders of most of those charged in London with the defense of Britain.

In the field of imperial relations, however, such preoccupations were dangerous. And even more disturbing was the manner in which major decisions affecting the 1909 plans were made without consultation. The British government's eager acceptance of the idea of an imperial conference in 1909, when the satellite states were anxious to make their offerings on the altar of imperial unity, contrasts oddly with the reluctance to engage in further such consultations when the purpose of any such meeting was likely to be a call for an accounting of the use which the British government had made of the offerings. From such embarrassment, however, the imperial authorities were saved by the gun: the gun that fired in Sarajevo, and the other guns that did not cease from their firing until the names of Gallipoli, Hamel, and Vimy Ridge had become part of the mingled story of British and imperial heroism.

BIBLIOGRAPHY

PUBLIC RECORD OFFICE

Official Correspondence and Records

    Adm. 1/6705–8050: Correspondence from Commander of Australian Station to Admiralty.

    Adm. 116/68–69: Correspondence concerning the 1887 agreement.

    Adm.116/942: Fisher comments and memoranda on naval reorganization.

    Adm. 116/993: Transfer of Halifax and Esquimalt to Canada.

    C.O. 808/59–91: Confidential Prints, Australia.

    C.O. 418/9–75: Original Correspondence, Australia.

    C.O. 209/245–272: Original Correspondence, New Zealand.

    C.O. 42/868–976: Original Correspondence, Canada.

    W.O. 32, 33, 106: Largely devoted to colonial and imperial defense.

    Cab. 2: Minutes of Committee of Imperial Defence.

    Cab. 5: Memoranda on colonial defense.

    Cab. 7: Minutes of Colonial Defence Committee.

    Cab. 8: Memoranda of Colonial Defence Committee.

    Cab. 9: Remarks on defense schemes prepared by the colonies.

    Cab.11: Defense schemes of colonies.

    Cab.16: *Ad hoc* committees of inquiry of Committee of Imperial Defence.

    Cab.17: Correspondence and miscellaneous papers of Committee of Imperial Defence.

    Cab. 18: Miscellaneous volumes.

Private Papers

    P.R.O. 30/40: Sir John Ardagh

    P.R.O. 30/6: Carnarvon

    P.R.O. 30/29: Granville

    P.R.O. 30/57: Kitchener

BRITISH MUSEUM

    Add. MSS. 43517–43560: Ripon

    Add. MSS. 41213, 41231: Campbell-Bannerman

    Add. MSS. 49698–49732: Balfour

    Add. MSS. 43877: Dilke

PUBLIC ARCHIVES OF CANADA

Borden Papers
Laurier Papers
Perley Papers
Governor-Generals' File

AUSTRALIAN NATIONAL LIBRARY

Barton Papers
Deakin-Jebb Correspondence
Atlee Hunt Papers

AUSTRALIAN NATIONAL WAR MUSEUM LIBRARY

George Pearce Papers

INSTITUTE OF COMMONWEALTH STUDIES LIBRARY, LONDON

Jebb Papers

UNPUBLISHED THESES

Chappell, Marjorie G. "The Select Committee of 1861 on Colonial Military Expenditures and its Antecedents." London University, 1933.

Grimshaw, H. C. "Some Aspects of Australian Attitudes to the Imperial Connection, 1900-1919." University of Queensland, n.d.

Pidgeon, A. L. "The Development of Canadian Naval Bases." Oxford University, 1947.

Sissons, D. C. S. "Attitudes to Japan and Defence, 1890-1923." University of Melbourne, 1956.

OTHER UNPUBLISHED MATERIAL

Richmond, Sir Herbert. Preliminary draft of an article on imperial naval defense in the possession of Professor Gerald Graham, London University.

PUBLISHED OFFICIAL SOURCES

Commonwealth of Australia. *Parliamentary Debates.*
——. *Parliamentary Papers.*
Dominion of Canada. *Parliamentary Debates.*
——. *Sessional Papers.*
Dominion of New Zealand. *Parliamentary Debates.*
Great Britain. *Parliamentary Debates (3d and 4th series).*
Great Britain. *Parliamentary Papers.* Especially the following:
    1861 Vol. XIII, "Report from the Select Committee on Colonial Military Expenditure."
    1887 C.5091: Proceedings of the Colonial Conference.
    1897 C.8596: Proceedings of a Conference between the Secertary of State for the Colonies and the Premiers of the Self-Governing Colonies.

1902 Cd. 1299: Papers Relating to a Conference between the Secretary of State for the Colonies and the Prime Ministers of the Self-Governing Colonies.

1907 Cd. 3404: Published Proceedings and Précis of the Colonial Conference.

Cd. 3523: Minutes of the Proceedings of the Colonial Conference.

Cd. 3524: Papers Laid before the Colonial Conference.

1908 Cd. 4325: Correspondence Relating to the Naval Defence of Australia and New Zealand.

1909 Cd. 4475: Correspondence Relating to the Proposed Formation of an Imperial General Staff.

Cd. 4948: Correspondence and Papers Relating to a Conference with Representatives of the Self-Governing Dominions on the Naval and Military Defence of the Empire.

1911 Cd. 5745: Minutes of the Proceedings of the Imperial Conference, 1911.

Cd. 5746-2: Papers Laid before the Imperial Conference, Naval and Military Defence.

1912 Cd. 6513: Memorandum on Naval Defence Requirements, Prepared by the Admiralty for the Government of Canada.

1913 Cd. 6689: Correspondence Between the First Lord of the Admiralty and the Prime Minister of the Dominion of Canada.

1914 Cd. 7347: Correspondence Relating to the Representation of the Self-Governing Dominions on the Committee of Imperial Defence and a Proposed Naval Conference.

New South Wales. *Parliamentary Debates.*

Queensland. *Parliamentary Debates.*

Victoria. *Parliamentary Debates.*

——. *Votes and Proceedings.*

NEWSPAPERS

The Age (Melbourne)

The Argus (Melbourne)

The Bulletin (Sydney)

The Call (Sydney)

The Citizen (Ottawa)

The Colonist (Victoria, B.C.)

The Courier (Brisbane)

The Daily Telegraph (Sydney)

Le Devoir (Montreal)

The Economist (London)

The Free Press (Ottawa)

The Globe (Toronto)

The Mail and Empire (Toronto)

The Manitoba Free Press (Winnipeg)

The Mercury (Hobart)

The Morning Post (London)

The News (Toronto)

The Star (Montreal)

The Sydney Morning Herald

The Times (London)

The West Australian (Perth)

The Worker (Sydney)

PERIODICALS

Australian Journal of Politics and History

Blackwood's Edinburgh Magazine

Canadian Defence Quarterly

Canadian Historical Review
Canadian Journal of Economics and Political Science
Commonwealth Military Journal
English Historical Review
Foreign Affairs
Historical Journal
Historical Studies, Australia and New Zealand
History Today
Nineteenth Century
Round Table
Royal Colonial Institute, London. Proceedings.
Royal Historical Society. Transactions.
Royal United Service Institution. Journal.
Society for Army Historical Research. Journal.
United Services Magazine (New series)
Victorian Studies

BOOKS AND ARTICLES

BARTLETT, C. J. *Great Britain and Sea Power, 1815-1853.* Oxford, 1963.

BEAN, C. E. W. *Two Men I Knew.* Sydney, 1957.

BENNETT, GEORGE (ed.). *The Concept of Empire.* London, 1953.

BLACKTON, CHARLES S. "Australian Nationalism and Nationality: the Imperial Federationist Interlude, 1885-1901," *Historical Studies, Australia and New Zealand,* VII (November, 1955).

BODELSON, C. A. *Studies in Mid-Victorian Imperialism.* New York, 1925.

BOND, BRIAN. "Recruiting the Victorian Army," *Victorian Studies,* V (June, 1962).

BORDEN, HENRY (ed.). *Sir Robert Laird Borden: His Memoirs.* 2 vols. Toronto, 1938.

BOWEN, GEORGE. *Thirty Years of Colonial Government.* London, 1889.

BRASSEY, T. A. (ed.). *The Naval Annual, 1907.* Portsmouth, 1907.

——. "Imperial Federation for Naval Defence," *The Nineteenth Century,* XXXI (January, 1892).

BREBNER, J. BARTLET. *Canada: A Modern History.* Ann Arbor, 1960.

BRIGGS, JOHN HENRY. *Naval Administrations, 1827-1892.* London, 1892.

BRODIE, BERNARD. *Sea Power in the Machine Age.* Princeton, 1941.

BROWN, R. CRAIG. "Goldwin Smith and Anti-Imperialism," *Canadian Historical Review,* XLIII (June, 1962).

BUCHAN, JOHN. *Lord Minto: A Memoir.* London, 1924.

Cambridge History of the British Empire.

CANADA, DEPT. OF NATIONAL DEFENSE, GENERAL STAFF. *Official History of the Canadian Forces in the Great War, 1914-18.* Ottawa, 1938.

Canadian Annual Review, 1909.

CHAMBERLAIN, AUSTEN. *Politics from Inside.* London, 1936.

CHESNEY, GEORGE. "Memoirs of a Volunteer" (The Battle of Dorking), *Blackwood's Edinburgh Magazine,* May, 1871.

CHILDE-PEMBERTON, WILLIAM S. *Life of Lord Norton.* London, 1909.

CHURCHILL, WINSTON S. *The River War.* London, 1899.

——. *The World Crisis.* Abridged Ed. New York, 1949.

CLARKE, GEORGE S. *Fortification.* London, 1890.

——. *Imperial Defence*. London, 1897.

CLOWES, WILLIAM. *The Royal Navy: A History from the Earliest Times to the Present*. 7 vols. London, 1897-1903.

COBBETT's *Parliamentary History*. Vol. XVIII.

COLOMB, JOHN. *Colonial Defence* (a paper read before the Royal Colonial Institute, 1873) . . . and *Colonial Opinion*. Dublin; London, 1877.

——. *The Defence of Great and Greater Britain*. London, 1880.

——. *The Protection of our Commerce and Distribution of our Naval Forces*. London, 1867.

——. "Wanted, an Imperial Conference," *The Nineteenth Century*, XXXVI (December, 1894).

COLOMB, PHILIP. *Essays on Naval Defence*. London, 1896.

—— (ed.). *Memoirs of Admiral the Right Honble. Sir Astley Cooper Key*. London, 1898.

CORBETT, JULIAN. *Naval Operations*. (*Official History of the War*, Vol. I), London, 1920.

CREASY, EDWARD. *Fifteen Decisive Battles of the World*. Edited by Robert H. Murray. Revised edition. Harrisburg, Pa., 1943.

CREIGHTON, DONALD. "The Victorians and the Empire" *in* Schuyler, R. L. and Ausubel, Herman (eds.), *The Making of English History*, New York, 1952.

——. *John Macdonald*. Vol. II. Boston, 1956.

DAWSON, R. MACGREGOR. "The Cabinet Minister and Administration: Winston S. Churchill at the Admiralty," *The Canadian Journal of Economics and Political Science* (August, 1940).

DAWSON, W. F. *Procedure in the Canadian House of Commons*. Toronto, 1962.

D'EGVILLE, HOWARD. *Imperial Defence and Closer Union*. London, 1913.

DEWAR, K. C. B. *The Navy from Within*. London, 1939.

DILKE, CHARLES. *The British Army*. London, 1888.

——. *Greater Britain*. 2 vols. London, 1868.

—— and WILKINSON, SPENSER. *Imperial Defence*. London, 1892.

——. *Problems of Greater Britain*. 2 vols. London, 1890.

DREW, H. T. B. *The War Efforts of New Zealand*. Vol. IV of *Official History of New Zealand's Effort in the Great War*. Wellington, 1923.

DRUS, ETHEL. "The Colonial Office and the Annexation of Fiji," *Transactions of the Royal Historical Society*, Fourth Series, XXXII, London, 1950.

DUNDONALD, EARL OF. *My Army Life*. London, 1926.

DUNLOP, J. K. *The Development of the British Army*. London, 1938.

EGERTON, H. E. (ed.). *Selected Speeches of Sir William Molesworth*. London, 1903.

EHRMAN, JOHN. *Cabinet Government and War, 1890-1940*. Cambridge, 1958.

ELLIOT, ARTHUR D. *The Life of George Joachim Goschen, First Viscount Goschen*. 2 vols. London, 1911.

ENSOR, R. C. K. *England: 1870-1914*. Oxford, 1936.

FIELDHOUSE, D. K. "New Zealand, Fiji and the Colonial Office, 1900-1902," *Historical Studies, Australia and New Zealand*, VIII (May, 1958).

FOXTON, J. F. G. "The Evolution and Development of an Australian Naval Policy," *Commonwealth Military Journal*, I (1911).

GARVIN, J. L. and AMERY, JULIAN. *The Life of Joseph Chamberlain*. 4 vols. London, 1934-51.

GOLLIN, ALFRED M. *The Observer and J. L. Garvin*. London, 1960.

GORDON, DONALD C. *The Australian Frontier in New Guinea, 1870-1885.* New York, 1951.

GRAHAM, GERALD. *Empire of the North Atlantic.* Toronto, 1950.

GREEN, H. M. (ed.). *Modern Australian Poetry.* 2d ed. Melbourne, 1952.

GRENFELL, RUSSELL. *Sea Power.* London, 1941.

HALE, ORON J. *Publicity and Diplomacy.* New York, 1940.

HALL, D. O. W. *The New Zealanders in South Africa, 1899-1902.* Wellington, 1949.

HALL, HENRY L. *Australia and England.* London, 1934.

HAMILTON, LORD GEORGE. *Parliamentary Reminiscences and Reflections.* 2 vols. London, 1916-22.

HARDINGE, ARTHUR. *The Life of Henry Howard Molyneux Herbert, Fourth Earl of Carnarvon.* 3 vols. London, 1925.

HOPKINS, J. CASTELL (ed.). *The Canadian Annual Review of Public Affairs.* Toronto, 1910.

HOUGH, RICHARD. *Admirals in Collision.* New York, 1959.

HUNTINGTON, SAMUEL P. *The Soldier and the State.* Cambridge, Mass., 1957.

HUTCHINSON, FRANK and MYERS, FRANCIS. *The Australian Contingent.* Sydney, 1885.

JACOBS, MARJORIE J. "The Colonial Office and New Guinea, 1874-1884," *Historical Studies, Australia and New Zealand,* V (May, 1952).

JEBB, RICHARD. *The Imperial Conference.* 2 vols. London, 1911.

———. *Studies in Colonial Nationalism.* London, 1905.

JOHNSON, F. A. *Defence by Committee: The British Committee of Imperial Defence, 1885-1959.* London, 1960.

JOSE, A. W. *The Royal Australian Navy, 1914-18.* Vol. IX of *The Official History of Australia in the War of 1914-18.* Sydney, 1928.

KEMP, P. K. (ed.). *The Papers of Admiral Sir John Fisher.* Vol. I. London, 1960.

KERR, D. G. G. *Sir Edmund Head.* Toronto, 1954.

KNAPLUND, PAUL. *Gladstone and Britain's Imperial Policy.* New York, 1927.

———. *The Gladstone-Gordon Correspondence, 1851-1896.* Philadelphia, 1961.

———. "Great Britain and the British Empire," in *The New Cambridge Modern History,* XI, Cambridge, 1962.

KNOX, B. A. "Colonial Influence on Imperial Policy, 1858–1866: Victoria and the Colonial Naval Defence Act, 1865," *Historical Studies, Australia and New Zealand,* XI (November, 1963).

KOEBNER, R. and SCHMIDT, H. D. *Imperialism.* Cambridge, 1964.

LA NAUZE, J. A. "Alfred Deakin and the *Morning Post*," *Historical Studies, Australia and New Zealand,* VI (May, 1955).

LANG, ANDREW. *Life, Letters and Diaries of Sir Stafford Northcote.* 2 vols. Edinburgh, 1891.

LANGER, WILLIAM L. *The Diplomacy of Imperialism.* 2d ed. New York, 1960.

———. "Farewell to Empire," *Foreign Affairs,* XLI (October, 1962).

LEYLAND, JOHN. "The 'Blue Water School'—Principles of Defence," *in The Naval Annual,* 1907. Edited by T. A. Brassey. Portsmouth, 1907.

LLOYD, CHRISTOPHER. *The Nation and the Navy.* London, 1954.

LUCAS, C. P. *The Empire at War.* Vol. I, 1921.

LUCY, HENRY. *A Diary of Two Parliaments.* 2 vols. London, 1885-86.

LUVAAS, J. *The Military Legacy of the Civil War.* Chicago, 1959.

MACANDIE, G. L. *The Genesis of the Royal Australian Navy.* Sydney, 1949.

MAHAN, ALFRED T. *Naval Strategy*. Boston, 1911.

MARCUS, G. J. "The Naval Crisis of 1909 and the Croydon By-election," *Journal of the Royal United Service Institute*, CIII (November, 1958).

MARDER, ARTHUR J. *The Anatomy of British Sea Power*. New York, 1940.

———. *Fear God and Dread Nought*. 2 vols. London, 1952, 1956.

———. *From the Dreadnought to Scapa Flow*. London, 1961.

———. "The Origin of Popular Interest in the Royal Navy," *Journal of the Royal United Service Institution*, LXXXII (November, 1937).

MONGER, G. W. *The End of Isolation*. London, 1963.

MORTON, W. L. *The Canadian Identity*. Madison, Wisc., 1961.

MURDOCH, WALTER. *Alfred Deakin*. London, 1923.

NISH, I. H. "Australia and the Anglo-Japanese Alliance, 1901-1911," *The Australian Journal of Politics and History*, IX (November, 1963).

OMOND, J. S. *Parliament and the Army*. Cambridge, 1933.

OUTIS (pseud.). *Mr. Churchill, the Admiralty and the Self-Governing Dominions*. London, n.d.

PARKES, HENRY. *Fifty Years in the Making of Australian History*. 2 vols. London, 1892.

PEARCE, GEORGE F. *Carpenter to Cabinet*. London, 1951.

QUICK, JOHN and GARRAN, ROBERT. *The Annotated Constitution of the Commonwealth of Australia*. Sydney, 1901.

RAMM, AGATHA. "Great Britain and the Planting of Italian Power in the Red Sea, 1868-1885," *English Historical Review*, LIX (May, 1944).

RICHMOND, HERBERT. *Naval Policy and Naval Strength*. London, 1927.

———. *Statesmen and Sea Power*. Oxford, 1947.

ROBINSON, RONALD, GALLAGHER, JOHN and DENNY, ALICE. *Africa and the Victorians*. New York, 1961.

ROPP, THEODORE. "Continental Doctrines of Sea Power," *in* Edward Mead Earle (ed.) *Makers of Modern Strategy*, Princeton, 1948.

RUMILLY, ROBERT. *Henri Bourassa: La Vie Publique d'un Grand Canadien*. Montreal, 1953.

SCHUYLER, ROBERT L. *The Fall of the Old Colonial System*. New York, 1945.

SEELEY, JOHN. *The Expansion of England*. New York, 1931.

SHANNON, R. T. "The Liberal Succession Crisis in New Zealand, 1893," *Historical Studies, Australia and New Zealand*, VIII (May, 1958).

SINCLAIR, KEITH. *A History of New Zealand*. London, 1959.

SKELTON, O. D. *Life and Letters of Sir Wilfrid Laurier*. 2 vols. New York, 1922.

SMITH, HUMPHREY H. *A Yellow Admiral Remembers*. London, 1932.

SPENCER, HERBERT. *Facts and Comments*. New York, 1902.

STACEY, C. P. *Canada and the British Army, 1846-1871*. London, 1936.

STANLEY, GEORGE F. G. "The Army Origin of the Royal Canadian Navy," *Journal of the Society for Army Historical Research*, XXXII (Summer, 1954).

———. *Canada's Soldiers, 1604-1954*. Toronto, 1954.

STOKES, ERIC. "Milnerism," *Historical Journal*, V, No. 1, 1962.

STRAUSS, ERIC. *Irish Nationalism and British Democracy*. New York, 1951.

SYDENHAM, LORD. *My Working Life*. London, 1927.

TAYLOR, A. J. P. *The Trouble Makers*. London, 1957.

TEMPERLEY, HAROLD. "Disraeli and Cyprus," *English Historical Review*, XLVI (April, 1931 and July, 1931).

TERRAINE, JOHN. "Armistice: November 11, 1918," *History Today*, VIII (November, 1958).

——. *Ordeal of Victory*. Philadelphia, 1963.

THORNTON, A. P. *The Imperial Idea and Its Enemies*. London, 1959.

TREVELYAN, G. M. *Grey of Fallodon*. London, 1937.

TUCKER, Gilbert N. *The Naval Service of Canada*. 2 vols. Ottawa, 1952.

TURNER, E. S. *Gallant Gentlemen: A Portrait of the British Officer, 1600-1956*. London, 1956.

TYLER, J. E. *The British Army and the Continent, 1904-1914*. London, 1938.

——. *The Struggle for Imperial Unity*. London, 1938.

UNDERHILL, FRANK H. "Lord Minto on his Governor-Generalship," *Canadian Historical Review*, LX (June, 1959).

WADE, MASON. *The French Canadians*. New York, 1955.

WARD, JOHN M. *Earl Grey and the Australian Colonies, 1846-57*. Melbourne, 1958.

——. "The Colonial Policy of Lord John Russell's Administration," *Historical Studies, Australia and New Zealand*, IX (November, 1960).

WILKINSON, SPENCER. *Thirty-five Years*. London, 1933.

YOUNG, G. M. *Victorian England, Portrait of an Age*. London, 1936.

Index

THE DOMINION PARTNERSHIP
IN IMPERIAL DEFENSE, 1870-1914

BY DONALD C. GORDON

designer	:	Edward D. King
typesetter	:	Baltimore Type and Composition Corporation
typefaces	:	Baskerville Text, Goudy Gimbel
printer	:	The John D. Lucas Printing Company
paper	:	Perkins and Squire GM
binder	:	Moore and Company
cover material	:	Columbia Riverside Linen